Vernacular Literacy

OXFORD STUDIES IN ANTHROPOLOGICAL LINGUISTICS

William Bright, *General Editor*

Vernacular Literacy

A Re-Evaluation

by members of
The International Group for the Study of Language
Standardization and the Vernacularization of Literacy
(IGLSVL)

edited by

Andrée Tabouret-Keller, R. B. Le Page,

Penelope Gardner-Chloros, and Gabrielle Varro

CLARENDON PRESS · OXFORD
1997

Oxford University Press, Great Clarendon Street, Oxford OX2 6DP
Oxford New York
Athens Auckland Bangkok Bogota Bombay
Buenos Aires Calcutta Cape Town Dar es Salaam
Delhi Florence Hong Kong Istanbul Karachi
Kuala Lumpur Madras Madrid Melbourne
Mexico City Nairobi Paris Singapore
Taipei Tokyo Toronto Warsaw
and associated companies in
Berlin Ibadan

Oxford is a trade mark of Oxford University Press

Published in the United States
by Oxford University Press Inc., New York

British Library Cataloguing in Publication Data
Data available

Library of Congress Cataloging in Publication Data
Data available

ISBN 0–19–823713–8 (pbk)
ISBN 0–19–823635–2 (hbk)

10   9   8   7   6   5   4   3   2   1

Typeset by Graphicraft Typesetters Ltd., Hong Kong
Printed in Great Britain on acid-free paper by
Biddles Ltd., Guildford and King's Lynn

Preface and Acknowledgements

Since 1968 the Department of Language and Linguistic Science of the University of York, England, and the Institut de Psychologie of the Université Louis Pasteur of Strasbourg, France, have been linked in an ongoing programme of research into the language problems of multilingual communities, with particular but by no means exclusive reference to the former colonies of Britain and France. The International Group for the Study of Language Standardization and the Vernacularization of Literacy (IGLSVL) grew out of this link. The original invitation, which was sent out by R. B. Le Page, A. Tabouret-Keller, P. Christie, and L. Carrington, brought a number of scholars, all with first-hand experience of the problems and coming from many universities world wide, to a series of workshops—in 1986, 1988, 1990 at the University of York and in 1992 at Sèvres, Paris. The present book has grown out of this link and these workshops. For each of the first three workshops Le Page edited and circulated a mimeographed volume of the participants' *Abstracts* and his transcription of the recorded discussions. At the end of the Sèvres meeting, however, it was decided that, as forty years had elapsed since the meeting in Paris which gave rise to the Unesco monograph *The Use of Vernacular Languages in Education*, it would be appropriate to publish a volume in which we would re-evaluate the questions and attitudes and recommendations of that earlier volume in the light of the very considerable and varied experience of the contributors to IGLSVL.

We would like to acknowledge the generous help we have received during the whole programme from the following:

The Department of Language and Linguistic Science, University of York
L'Institut de Psychologie, Université Louis Pasteur, Strasbourg
CNRS, Laboratoire LADISIS URA 668, Strasbourg
The Social Science Research Council and its successor the Economic and Social
    Research Council, London
The Nuffield Foundation, London
The British Academy
The Cultural Attaché to the French Embassy, London
UNICEF, France

Maison des Sciences de l'Homme, Paris
Maison des Sciences de l'Homme, Strasbourg
Centre d'Études Pédagogiques, Sèvres, France
Mr Tony Hayes, a Jamaican businessman in London, via the High Commissioner for Jamaica

Contents

List of Tables

List of Abbreviations

ACCT	Agence de Coopération Culturelle et Technique
ACPO	Accion Cultural Popular
AIDS	Acquired Immune Deficiency Syndrome
BAC	Basque Autonomous Community
BGVS	Bharat Gyan Vigyan Jatha
C	consonant
CAR	Central African Republic
CIIL	Central Institute of Indian Languages
CLAP	Liaison Committee for Literacy
CLE	Compter, Lire, Écrire
CNRS	Centre National de la Recherche Scientifique
CP	Cameroon Pidgin
ESF	European Science Foundation
ETA	*Euskadi ta Askatasuna* (Basqueland and Freedom)
EEC	European Economic Community
ELCO	Enseignement des Langues et Cultures d'Origine
ESL	English as a Second Language
ESRC	Economic and Social Research Council, London
EU	European Union
EWLP	Experimental World Literacy Project
FAS	Fonds d'action sociale
HIV	human immunodeficiency virus
IAS	Indian Administrative Service
IDRC	International Development Research Centre
IGLSVL	International Group for the Study of Language Standardization and the Vernacularization of Literacy
IIEP	International Institute for Educational Planning
INSEE	Institut National de la Statistique et des Études Économiques
IPA	International Phonetic Alphabet
ITA	Initial Teaching Alphabet
JAMAL	[Jamaican campaign]
KEJAR	[Indonesian campaign]
KSSP	Kerala Shastra Sahitya Parishad
LAD	language acquisition device

LINC	Language Information Network Coordination
LMP	Linguistic Minorities Project
LO	official language
L1	first language
L2	second language
MOBRAL	[Brazilian campaign]
MOTET	Mother Tongue and English Teaching
MSC	Modern Standard Chinese
NCNA	New China News Agency
NGO	non-governmental organizaton
NLC	National Literacy Mission
p.c.	personal communication
PEIP	Primary Education Improvement Project
PRC	People's Republic of China
PROPELCA	Projet de Recherche Opérationnelle pour l'Enseignement des Langues Camerounaises
SCE	Singapore Colloquial English
SEMRY	rice production society
SIDA	Swedish International Development Agency
SYYP	Six Year Yoruba Project
UCWI	University College of the West Indies
UN	United Nations
UNDP	United Nations Development Programme
Unesco	United Nations Educational, Scientific and Cultural Oganization
UNFPA	United Nations Population Fund
UNICEF	United Nations Children's Fund
UNO	United Nicaraguan Opposition
USA	United States of America
USSR	Union of Soviet Socialist Republics
V	vowel
WHO	World Health Organization

Introduction

R. B. LE PAGE

This book addresses a crisis in human affairs, not by prescribing remedies but by attempting to increase understanding of its nature and some of its underlying causes. Our scope is limited in time and covers the second half of our century. We start from the 1953 Unesco statement which aimed at the promotion of vernacular literacy and we try to assess what has happened during the forty years since. We may begin by contrasting the climate of opinion in the 1950s with that in the 1990s.

I. FROM THE 1950S TO THE 1990S

1.1. *The 1990s*

The year 1990 was declared by Unesco to be International Literacy Year. No fewer than twenty-two organizations, led by Unesco, The World Bank, UNICEF, and UNDP, came together at Jomtien, Thailand, in March 1990 at a World Conference on Education for All. As Andrée Tabouret-Keller reported to our group (*Abstracts* 1990: 117–24), one urgency above all was stressed: nearly one-third of the adult population of the world (nearly 1,000 million people) is illiterate; and literacy is inaccessible to more than 100 million children. 'If the present trends go on, by the year 2000 the actual numbers will have doubled; even the more industrialized countries will see an increase in their rate of illiteracy that amounts already to 10 per cent' (ibid. 117).

These 'present trends' have a number of interacting factors built into them, including:

(*a*) population increase and consequent social, political, and economic pressures;
(*b*) ignorance about and/or inability to practise birth control—today discussed under the heading of 'population education';
(*c*) the contribution of inadequate provision for literacy and education to that ignorance and/or inability, and to associated political, economic, and social problems;
(*d*) the nature and effectiveness or ineffectiveness of a political will to limit

population increase and to make adequate provision for literacy and education;

(*e*) the possible role of non-standard vernaculars—that is, of the first languages of the vast majority of the world's population—in political, ethnic, nationalist, and economic processes which might be affected by literacy;

(*f*) the competing or complementary roles of written text *vis-à-vis* film and the broadcast media in propaganda and education;

(*g*) the role of literate élites within the body politic;

(*h*) the role of the international agencies themselves in creating the conditions (for example, of Third World poverty) which contribute to illiteracy today.

Some Conclusions drawn from the Jomtien Conference

The conference stressed the high drop-out rate in primary schools; the alarming rise in the number of illiterates worldwide; the fact that past and current efforts are inadequate even to maintain present literacy levels. Above all, it dealt with economic problems, from the high costs ascribable to lack of literacy in advanced industrialized countries (work accidents, loss of productivity, increases in unemployment, etc.) to the drag of external debt on 'development' in the poorest countries; in the thirty-seven poorest, the amount spent per enrolled pupil has gone down by 25 per cent since 1989. The 'austerity measures' taken to deal with that debt are cutting the budgets for health, for education, and for food. In Kenya, before the loan for 'development', from 1964 to 1973 the per capita budget for education increased every year by 10–15 per cent; but from 1973 to 1984 the interest on the external debt increased by 13.7 per cent and during the same period the education budget dropped each year by 3 per cent, while the annual population increase was 4.1 per cent. In Jamaica external debt increased from $813 million in 1976 to $1,700 million in 1980; as a consequence, 11,000 public-service officers were sacked, including 2,500 teachers at all levels. Overall, two out of three teachers in the developing countries earn less now than in 1980. In 1990 the sum spent per enrolled pupil on education was $29, whereas in the developed countries it was $1,987. In the discussion which followed Tabouret-Keller's 1990 presentation, David Barton maintained that the reduction of social funding in the developing countries was the outcome of deliberate policies by the World Bank, to stop the public supply of funds for social purposes so that the need would be supplied by the private sector; but the private sector has failed to fund basic education. He felt that Unesco today was less interested in basic education than in international communication systems and new technologies. Lawrence Carrington reinforced this view; the concentration by the agencies on so-called 'post-literacy' activities was intended to draw people into the use of international communication networks so that there will be less need to bother with the troublesome questions of a multiplicity of vernaculars.

The 1994 Cairo Conference on World Population Problems

The 1994 international conference on world population problems in Cairo (see *Populi* 1994) once again highlighted—often dramatically—the reciprocal fears of the 'developed' and the 'developing' worlds about poverty and exploitation; the perceived threats to the vested interests of the rich, the economically power-ful, the politically powerful, the religions; and the impotence of vast masses of the desperately poor, often also the desperately sick. At bottom, the conference concluded, there still lay problems of education, and one of the main beacons along the road ahead was that of education for women, who then could educate their children. (*Africa: Make or Break* (Oxfam 1993), to which we return later, makes the same point.) This in turn has been seen, stereotypically, as involving literacy—and the question immediately arises: in what language?

Facts for Life

In 1993 the agencies UNICEF, WHO, Unesco, and UNFPA produced a new edition of their book, *Facts for Life*, addressed to:

- heads of state and political leaders
- educational systems and the teaching profession
- the medical profession and the health services
- media professionals in television and radio, newspapers, and magazines
- religious and spiritual leaders
- employers and the business community
- trade union and cooperative leaders

- community health workers, nurses, and midwives
- development workers and voluntary agencies
- women's organizations
- youth movements
- community organizations and traditional leaders
- all departments of national and local governments
- artists, writers, entertainers, sportsmen and -women

The book, full of information about how to plan and achieve safer childbirth and to protect children from disease, has been translated into 176 languages and has involved 160 international children's agencies in its preparation. The languages range widely, from the international to the national standard to the lingua franca to the pidgin; this number, of course, constitutes only a tiny fraction of the world's languages. It is addressed to 'communicators'. Clearly its effectiveness at present depends upon educated people translating it, orally, for those who most need its information. Would it be more effective to have it translated into 500 languages —or 5,000? As we shall see later, Nigeria alone uses an estimated 400 vernacu-lars; only the 'big three', Yoruba, Hausa, and Igbo, together with the lingua franca Pidgin English and the international languages Arabic and English, so far carry the book there. Do we concentrate resources on a comparatively functional education for a minority in those languages, or try to reach out more directly to all the teenagers of Nigeria (a country with a very high birth rate)? Unless the Nigerian policy-makers aim for the latter, they may be depriving the mass of their population of the dignity and possible fulfilment of education in their own language; if they do aim for the latter, they may be spreading their human and economic resources so thinly that they achieve very little for anybody, and may feel that they are sacrificing national unity and economic and employment opportunities.

1.2. *The 1950s*

In the early 1950s the climate of opinion was more hopeful, at least among linguist-educationists.

Unesco was set up to be the flag-bearer of the brave new post-war post-colonial world from which both economic and cultural poverty were to be eradicated along with illiteracy. The Monograph on Fundamental Education VIII, *The Use of Vernacular Languages in Education* (1953), was the outcome of a conference of specialists in Paris in November 1951. The Preface sets out some of their basic beliefs:

To say that a world language problem exists is . . . to make an enormous understatement. The exact number of languages spoken in the world is not known but the figure runs into many hundreds . . . Most of them either have no literature—because no written form of the language exists—or have only an incipient literature or a literature based on classical forms of the language now divorced from the contemporary spoken mode. Because of this lack of literature—and for other social, political, and economic reasons—there still exists an immense number of illiterate people, most of whom are found among under-privileged groups.   (Unesco 1953: 5)

We take it as axiomatic that every child of school age should attend school and that every illiterate should be made literate. We take it as axiomatic, too, that the best medium for teaching is the mother tongue of the pupil . . . all languages . . . are capable of becoming media of school teaching; some perhaps merely as a bridge to a second language, while others may be used at all levels of education. But while this is true linguistically, there are many other factors—social, political, economic and practical—which impede . . . the employment of certain languages already well suited to be used in education. Some of these difficulties may be promptly overcome (e.g. orthography); others (social or political), at best, may take much longer.   (ibid. 6)

The sense in which we ourselves are using 'vernacular language' is set out below (see Section 2.2); in the monograph it is defined as follows: 'A language which is the mother tongue of a group which is socially or politically dominated by another group speaking a different language. We do not consider the language of a minority in one country as a vernacular if it is an official language in another country' (ibid. 46).

The monograph certainly introduced many of the constraints already acknowledged to govern the ideal of 'mother-tongue education'. However, forty years later, much of that hopeful, purposeful opening stance would have to be challenged. Counting the number of languages in the world itself depends upon what many today would regard as an outmoded concept of inherently discrete language systems rather than linguistic continua focused from place to place and generation to generation around social group nodes, and labelled accordingly. (How many 'languages', for example, make up the Hindi continuum of northern India and Pakistan, or the Bantu continuum of southern Africa, or the Romance/Iberian continuum? The count has always had to be rationalized in ideological and political terms; it would in any case today be expressed in thousands, rather than hundreds.) Then, the concepts behind such terms as 'mother tongue', *Muttersprache*, and *langue maternelle* were the subject of a conference at the University of Graz in 1985 which concluded that the meanings attached to these terms were so various as to make them incapable of any precise definition and, in many mixed multilingual communities, misleading (Denison *et al.* 1986).

In the 1950s, under the impact of structural linguistics, our problems and questions though daunting at least seemed susceptible of being resolved. We thought we knew how to describe 'a language'. Kenneth Pike had produced his *Phonemics: A Technique for Reducing Languages to Writing*, and Eugene Nida his companion volume *Morphology*. H. A. Gleason's development of Pike's *tagmemics* seemed to offer a parallel approach to syntax. We all knew, under F. G. Cassidy's direction, how to produce a dictionary. Similar initiatives were emerging from the School of Oriental and African Studies in London under J. R. Firth; they were still busy at that time training colonial civil servants and studying and teaching the African and Asian vernaculars they would encounter.

By way of a practical exemplum of the 'problems and questions' I would instance those which arose when we began our study of West Indian creole dialects at the new University College of the West Indies in 1952; similar questions arose for Andrée Tabouret-Keller in her study of Alsatian dialects, and for workers in many other parts of the world. They included:

(*a*) Ontological questions: what is a language? were we wasting our time studying 'patois' or 'broken talk' or 'jargon'?

(*b*) Questions as to social functions: could such vernaculars possibly be written? or considered as 'correct'? or used for education? Were we not undermining established social order by studying them?

(*c*) Within what kind of linguistic theory could we describe them so as to write them? What sort of orthography would make them readable and writable? Phonetic transcriptions and phonemic orthographies are clear to the linguist, but the lay reader and writer generally find it easier to adapt or read some adaptation of an already standard orthography.

(*d*) Could they be used for any sort of literature so that there would be something for the newly literate to read?

All of these questions are still relevant, and are among our concerns in this book.

2. VERNACULAR LANGUAGES IN EDUCATION

2.1. *The IGLSVL Workshops*

The International Group for the Study of Language Standardization and the Vernacularization of Literacy (IGLSVL) has been an informal group of linguists of various persuasions confronted with similar problems in different parts of the world: particularly in the former colonies of Britain and France, but also in Europe, the Americas, East, South, and South-East Asia and in Oceanic Australasia. The group has met biennially since 1986 to discuss these problems, our transcribed discussions being published each time in mimeo within a few months of the meeting (*Abstracts* 1986, 1988, 1990). In preparation for our 1992 meeting at Sèvres (France) we agreed to produce out of our work a book-length study of vernacular literacy, to try to assess what had happened in the forty years since the publication of the 1953 Unesco monograph.

The chapters of this book all reflect the involvement in those discussions, over the years and as recorded in our *Abstracts*, of the members of our group, whose names are listed at the end of this book. We have collectively contributed to each chapter and have a collective responsibility for the book as a whole, although the final collation of each chapter has been the responsibility of the chapter editor; and that of the book, of the four main editors who have overseen the book's production.

2.2. *The Meanings of 'Vernacular', and Some Preliminary Theoretical Considerations*

The use of the term 'vernacular' is certainly not for us synonymous with 'minority' or 'dominated' language. We use it in this book to mean 'the everyday spoken language or languages of a community, as contrasted with a standard or official language'—generally, a 'Low' as opposed to a 'High' variety in Ferguson's (1959) terms. But in addition, bound up with stereotypes about the possibility of 'reducing a language to writing' and of literacy in a language, are stereotypes about the discreteness and homogeneity of 'languages', to which literacy itself helps give effect. Indeed, it might often be preferable if we spoke of 'vernacular behaviour' rather than of 'vernacular languages'; the diffuseness of vernacular behaviour has been the subject of much sociolinguistic work since the 1950s, highlighted by work on multilingual and contact situations, and on pidgins and creoles—most recently and outstandingly in work on Papua New Guinea by, for example, Romaine (1992) and Mühlhäusler (1986a); the problems raised as to the viability of conventional stereotypes about linguistic systems have been shown to be universal—they are part of our observable data, but inadequate as a basis for scientific theories about language (see e.g. Grace 1992).

As to Unesco's 1953 'axioms', quoted above, each must be questioned. It is no longer very meaningful to say that languages are capable of doing things, such as being used for education; people do things—languages are abstractions from what people do, and language is in a symbiotic relationship with other social processes. Perhaps above all the tone of the passage quoted is, in spite of its liberal stance, very ethnocentric. There have after all been many non-literate societies in which oral literature and oral culture have formed the basis of education and it is far from 'axiomatic' that these have been less satisfactory than our own. As for the axiom itself, although there is some impressive evidence to support its validity, under ideal conditions there can be, as the monograph itself suggests later, so many countervailing variables that it can lose much of its force. In an immigrant home in Britain, for example, the 'mother tongue' or vernacular ordinarily used by the children may be a very diffuse contact variety which no teacher would know or could be persuaded to teach in, or it may be quite impossible to make available the resources to make such teaching practicable; whereas in Singapore, where the government is lavish with resources, it is also the government which defines what each child's mother tongue is to be for the purposes of education—rarely what is actually spoken in the home, but standard Mandarin, Bahasa Malaysia, Tamil, or English.

The European Science Foundation's Network on Written Language and Literacy held a workshop, Orality versus Literacy, in September 1992 (see ESF 1993); the *Proceedings* highlight with historical examples from Judaism and from Western Europe aspects of the relationship between spoken and written language, speech and literacy, oral and written literature often overlooked by those concerned with literacy programmes. In particular, Colette Sirat offered a long and detailed examination of 'Orality/literacy, languages and alphabets. (The) example of the Jewish people'. Her Introduction draws attention both to the antiquity and pervasiveness of writing in the records of the Jewish people from the 'tablets of stone' onwards and, at the same time, to the long-continuing strength of *oral* literature. This strength is illustrated incidentally in David Daiches's (1975) autobiographical account of a Jewish boyhood in Edinburgh, *Was*. He was the son of a rabbi, and his head was full of spoken and sung Hebrew texts from the liturgy, in addition to his familiarity with written texts. Having myself grown up in a church-going Anglican environment, singing in church choirs, with school chapel every day and twice on Sundays and frequent choir practice, I can testify that my own head was full of spoken and sung liturgical texts. In the West Indies in the 1950s we found that many children had their heads full of traditional stories, and in addition the formal rhetoric of many adults had a distinctly liturgical cadence. More recently it seems that entertainments such as film and radio and television have displaced oral literature. Nevertheless, in many parts of the world the recitation of oral folklore epics still forms an important ingredient in the education of the people and in the inculcation of a sense of national identity. The people of Kyrgyzstan, whose language was only alphabetized in the nineteenth century, have just (August 1995) concluded a year of celebration of their independence of the former USSR and the thousandth anniversary of the events related in their immensely long national epic, the Manas, by re-enacting those events. From various sources we see radical attempts being made to bypass conventional education with education in the critical use of these visual and oral alternatives.

3. EDUCATION AND DEVELOPMENT

3.1. *Literacy and 'Development'*

Ayo Bamgbose (1991) repeats the often-cited argument that, since the most literate nations are the most developed nations, literacy must be a factor leading to development. Another frequently repeated argument in favour of vernacular literacy, as also of literacy in general, is that it aids the full 'development' of the individual. There have been a great many conferences and books on these two themes since 1953, as also on the general prospects for 'underdeveloped' nations. At our workshops, attempts have been made from time to time to relate the concept of development in individuals to development in nations. The concept of helping individuals to reach a full and confident maturity within their own society is as relevant in relation to Western countries as it is in relation to developing countries; but we must beware of false analogies. The cases of the Welsh-speaking child growing up in a comparatively rich society which depends economically on the use of English, or of a Basque child in a Spanish-using milieu, or of an Alsatian-speaking child in France, are not necessarily exemplars for the Creole-speaking child of the Caribbean. Each case needs careful inspection. The relevant variables are ethnic, demographic, social, political, economic, geographic, linguistic. We have attempted to examine these in the chapters of this book.

A major problem facing most 'developing' nations, particularly in Africa, is that they are *not* developing by Western economic criteria. A recent report (Oxfam 1993) suggests a fresh and urgent approach: 'That approach must start from a recognition that Africa is suffering not from a temporary problem of liquidity, but from bankruptcy . . . African governments must not be put in a position where "creditworthiness" can be achieved only by deepening the poverty of their citizens, and by jeopardising prospects for recovery'. This deeply pessimistic report should become required reading for us all. In Appendix I we print some sections of great relevance to us, on the role of women, on health and education, and on prospects for the future. Tables A1 and A2 illustrate very dramatically the lack of growth to date and the projected further increase in relative poverty in sub-Saharan Africa.

Thus, when we add to the economic burdens those caused by overpopulation, disease, drought, famine, and warfare, we can understand, on the one hand, the powerful motivation that must exist for revolutionary solutions and, on the other, the missionary instinct that tries to bring about change through education whether in the Islamic or Christian or any other faith; radical change in social development and in individual development. Each road is liable to involve a more-than-basic degree of literacy to be effective; but in order for that to be achieved as widely and as quickly as possible it would at first sight seem probable that the literacy should be in a vernacular.

Anti-revolutionary forces may well, as in India, resist any move towards literacy for their workforce. On the other hand, as we illustrate from the case of Scotland in Chapter 1, Section 3.3, the ability to read in the vernacular may be seen, as it was all over Calvinist northern Europe, as an aid to securing a docile and well-indoctrinated population. Seeing literacy as a necessary precondition for development is, in the terms of Bamgbose's argument, based on false analogy. In Britain it was industrial development which *preceded* and led on to mass literacy; the mass literacy was then needed as a means to subduing the new urban industrial populations, and also to enable the new labour unions to communicate effectively among their membership (see, for example, the papers in Resnick 1983). Oral instruction sufficed for the majority of shop-floor workers in the early days of the industrial revolution—as indeed it sufficed for very large numbers of workers recruited from the subcontinent of India to work in British factories after the Second World War.

Today, as Oxfam (1993) mentions, there is one comparatively new ingredient in the socio-political mix for 'development' of so-far incalculable importance: the women's movement leads to the establishment of self-help groups, usually involving education and literacy classes. These are to be found almost worldwide, frequently sponsored by such international agencies as Oxfam or Associated Countrywomen of the World. Another comparatively new ingredient, which we have already mentioned, is the use of radio and television either directly to aid in the acquisition of literacy, as in Britain, or to bypass the need for literacy in a variety of ways, including their use for propaganda, and, on the other hand, training people to 'read' the broadcast message critically so as to be less at the mercy of propaganda and advertising.

3.2. *Population Education*

We have already referred to the 1994 Cairo conference. It came after three earlier international conferences had already, in the 1990s, underlined the urgency of population problems. It is a tragic irony that two sets of political crises face us in many parts of the world today: those caused by excessive population growth, and those bringing about the mass slaughter of populations.

The hope and in many states the avowed intention is that mass education and propaganda will lead to a reduction in the rate of population growth, partly through greater prosperity and partly through a greater awareness and use of contraception. The subject of birth-control education is politically sensitive, partly because of the opposition of the Roman Catholic Church. The term 'birth control' was replaced by the more benign 'family planning', and that in turn is nowadays being subsumed within 'population education'. The First International Congress on Population Education and Development was held in Istanbul in April 1993. It had been preceded in 1990 by a World Conference on Education for All and a World Summit on Children; it was followed, in December 1993, by the Delhi Declaration, in which the leaders of the nine high-population developing nations of the world—Bangladesh, Brazil, China, Egypt, India, Indonesia, Mexico, Nigeria, and Pakistan, countries which together contain more than half the world's population—pledged themselves to achieve basic education for all in their countries by the end of the millennium or at the earliest possible moment and, among other pledges, to 'eliminate disparities of access to basic education arising from gender, age, income, family, cultural, ethnic and linguistic differences, and geographic remoteness'. The declaration contains many other pious pledges. The second paragraph of the 'Summary of the Plenary Discussions' of the Istanbul Congress runs as follows:

31. The message that came through loud and clear from all the presentations and reports was that population education was real, that it could not be brushed aside, and that the very survival of humankind and our environment in the twenty-first century depended upon a pragmatic short-term and long-term far-sighted plan of action. All the participants, irrespective of the size, form of government or religious orientation of their countries, realized that uncontrolled population increase was a global phenomenon for which macro-level solutions could be evolved. However, each country had its unique problems, and national abilities to deal with these would need to be strengthened.

32. . . . population education must be viewed as perhaps the most important part of a nation's strategy to contain the growth of population. Population education should be integrated appropriately, at all levels of education, with the objective of inculcating in youth and adults an awareness of the problem and the need for responsible parenthood. (Unesco/Unfpa 1993: 8)

In his opening address to the Istanbul Congress the Director-General of Unesco claimed that 'The fundamental problem that has to be addressed if escalating population growth is to be mastered is that of improving access to basic education, of providing learning opportunities to the 100 million or so out-of-school children and the one billion illiterate adults, three-quarters of them women' (ibid.: annex III, p. 2).

It is clear that the messages of population education need to have reached each individual member of each society by the time they reach their teens, either directly or via their parents; that these messages are parts of general education and at the same time highly specific to birth control and to health; and that getting them across, even if governments and politicians and landowners and entrepreneurs and bankers are prepared to divert resources from armaments and from their own enterprises to education for all and to implement their brave pledges to that end, is a very daunting task. It can only be carried out in a language which everybody can understand, but the preparation of teachers and materials for every vernacular seems impossible.

3.3. *Literacy and Ethnic Rivalries; Rival Orthographies*

A recent paper by Coulmas (1993–4) documents the increasing claims to recognition for their vernaculars of fissiparous pressure groups within Europe and in other parts of the world—for example, the claim of Valencian speakers to be distinct from Catalan speakers, and hence to have their own 'state'. States once preoccupied with enforcing national unity are under great pressure to accept 'multiculturalism' as a way of life. Any attempt at a universally valid sociolinguistic model for vernacular literacy must face the complexities not only of the variation in political and economic circumstances from country to country, from region to region within the same country, from ethnic group to ethnic group within a region, and from caste to caste within each ethnic group, but also those of linguistic variation, and the degree of standardization needed. When all these problems are solved we are left with the question: what access to education has an 11-year-old girl earning subsistence by breaking up old bricks with a hammer by the roadside in Dakka?

Coulmas also draws attention to the political symbolism attached to rival orthographies, with the result that, for example, Serbo-Croatian may increasingly become two languages because of the use of the Cyrillic alphabet by the Serbs and the Roman alphabet by the Croats. Questions of orthography cannot be separated from social questions. Both orthographies and social hierarchies may be related to religion—either that of the state, or that of various missionary sects—the fact that the Baptist missionaries who christianized the Karen in the nineteenth century chose to use a Burmese script to write Karen had many consequences, as had Atatürk's decision to switch Turkish from an Arabic to a Roman script (Falla 1991). The difficulties created for children in multilingual societies where they have to cope with more than one orthography were dealt with at some length in the 1953 monograph. In some societies so much time may have to be devoted to learning how to write different languages in different scripts that there is little time for anything else in the curriculum.

When studying the ethnology of literacy today we need to be aware not only of the relationship between speech and writing but also of the networks of social relationships between the literate and the non-literate, and the assignment of tasks between them; and, within this framework, between adult and child literacy, male and female roles, the roles of various social ranks, passive and active users of writing, and writing and non-writing societies. All varieties of language use are socially marked; there can be no such thing as a purely linguistic description. The 1953 monograph complained of the difficulties caused by the great multiplicity of languages in Africa and South America, and resistance in Africa to the idea of creating 'unified dialects' as vehicles for writing, but the reasons for the multiplicity, and for the resistance, stem to some extent from social focusing around leaders and identities, sometimes also from the missionary activities of rival sects.

4. LITERACY AND BEING LITERATE

4.1. *Teaching Literacy in the Vernacular: The Linguists, the Educationists, and the Social Anthropologists*

The introduction to the 1953 monograph cited and quoted from Bloomfield (1933), still in 1953 the bible of structuralists, as follows:

The scientific study of language is the task of linguistics. Linguistics is a new science, still in its infancy, which has not yet reached the schools. Bloomfield says: 'It is only within the last century or so that language has been studied in a scientific way, by careful and comprehensive observation . . . *Linguistics*, the study of language, is only in its beginnings. The knowledge it has gained has not yet become part of our traditional education; the "grammars" and other linguistic instruction in our schools confine themselves to handing on the traditional notions. Many people have difficulty at the beginning of language study, not in grasping the methods or results (which are simple enough) but in stripping off the preconceptions which are forced on us by our popular scholastic doctrine'.   (Unesco 1953: 11)

By 1953, the Unesco introduction continues:

It is an interesting fact that the study and teaching of many vernacular non-official languages now being used as vehicles of education, and of some vernaculars which recently became official . . . are ahead of the study and teaching of some of the most important old literary official tongues; scientific linguistic methods being applied for both purposes and social anthropologists and educators as well as linguists being engaged in the task. (Unesco 1953: 11)

   That was written in the full flush of the then-new structuralist language-teaching drills, the audio-lingual methods, the language laboratories, the behaviourist theories sponsored by Bloomfield as to language acquisition, the primacy of speech, and its consequent 'reduction to writing' via alphabetization, and so on. Since then, successive revolutions have overtaken linguistic theory, learning theory, and pedagogical theory, as well as the ideas of social anthropologists and sociologists as to the role of literacy and of literates in societies. Not only has linguistic theory changed in a way that implied a considerable revision of language-learning theory and a rejection of behaviourism, but the development of the comparatively still-newer disciplines of sociolinguistics, psycholinguistics, ethnography, ethnolinguistics, and the sociology of language has led some of us to question in turn the validity of the claims made for some of the new linguistics: in particular, to see some aspects of Chomskyan theory as being not only ethnocentric but fundamentally flawed, as being inside out in seeing the language user as the imperfect user of the system rather than 'the system' as an imperfect and idealized specification of a stereotyped abstraction from the behaviour of language users, while at the same time being in symbiotic relationship with ideological and political concepts about language.

4.2. *What is Involved in being 'Literate'?*

In our discussions we have constantly encountered (*a*) questions of definition as to what constitutes literacy, and (*b*) questions about the validity of claims and statistics concerning literacy.

Research which has been cited (e.g. in Resnick 1983) concerning literacy rates over the centuries in Britain has used the criterion of whether a man and/ or a woman were able to sign their names in the marriage register. Recent adult literacy campaigns in, for example, India or Tanzania have been assessed on the ability of the learners to answer and perform at the end of the campaign simple questions and tasks drawn from the primer they had been using, as if they were then being tested on what they had learnt in the campaign rather than in their everyday life. The assessment of literacy in some communities has rested on the ability of the children to read and answer the questions asked in their church catechism, texts which in any case they could have memorized. In Unesco-led campaigns a good deal has been heard about 'functional literacy'—an ability to read and write (and possibly also to do some arithmetic) at a level which enables the users to perform some particular functions in their society. In China and in other character-writing societies the ability to *read* characters is likely to develop more widely and earlier than the ability to write them, even though the two skills may be taught together from kindergarten; child and adult are, at least in towns and villages, daily surrounded by street and shop signs whose meanings will come to be recognized, and people may well have a much larger passive vocabulary of recognition of the meanings of characters than active command of the spoken vocabulary and how to write it. At the other extreme, languages written with an alphabet which is reasonably phonemic, such as Spanish, may be quite easily 'read' aloud in a literacy test without much comprehension of the meaning. Carrington has described for us the tests he devised for Caribbean schoolchildren while noting that the various governments in their returns often assumed that children and adults who had passed through a number of grades in school were able to read and write.

As to the assessment of literacy rates and populations, we have certainly learned to treat governmental claims in both censuses and in official reports with a great deal of scepticism. There are often good reasons for this in the way the information has been collected. There are other less creditable reasons in the political motivation either to play up literacy rates or to play them down. Both from Tanzania and from India we learn of government employees feeling compelled to make favourable returns about the effects of literacy campaigns when close subsequent evaluation shows the campaigns to have been very largely a waste of time and money. From Nigeria we learn from at least one observer of the gulf which separates the claims made in official slogans from what is actually happening on the ground. Such a gulf is by no means unique to Nigeria. Nor do many evaluations of literacy campaigns pay attention to what happens to the skills of the newly literate when there is nothing for them to read and no motivation to read. It has recently been claimed that as many as 99 million people in the USA are 'barely literate' and never exercise any literacy skills they may once have possessed.

4.3. *Creating a Favourable Environment*

The 1953 monograph included a worldwide survey of the state of knowledge at that time about the 'named languages' spoken in each continent, and the extent to which they were written and used in education. As we have said, not only has a good deal of the information since been shown to be inaccurate, but a great deal of sociolinguistic and ethnolinguistic research has shown more clearly what it means to make such generalizations about a nation, a country, or a community as that 'they speak Language X' or 'they are bilingual in X and Y', ranging from Charles Ferguson's well-known characterization of some communities as 'diglossic' to more recent studies of all kinds of contact situation.

In the past a number of factors have contributed to the development of vernacular literacy. We have mentioned religion, which has continued to be important, as have grass-roots political movements. The contributions of writers who have chosen to use the vernacular—King Alfred, Dante, Chaucer, and a host of others—continue today in countries where we may see vernacular literature preceding mass literacy, as with the Krio drama and poetry of Sierra Leone, and the vernacular literature of the Caribbean. The case of Wolof in Senegal illustrates the importance of the economic climate; the conflicts between political and economic motivation are the general subject of Chapter 1. The importance of a genuine political will to move towards vernacular literacy is clear when we contrast Malaysia with Nigeria. The continuance of older colonial social hierarchies and attitudes has been important in shaping attitudes towards vernacular speakers and their languages; so also have older prejudices about bilingualism and the bad effects it was supposed to have on children. There has been a good deal of experience since the Second World War in many parts of the world of large-scale immigration and of programmes to cope with the language problems of immigrant children. We need to know something about the relative values for the education of these children (and those of the host communities) of overtly integrationist policies, of covertly integrationist policies which pay lip-service to multiculturalism, and of convincing multicultural education with no hidden agenda for integration. All of these questions have been discussed in our workshops and are discussed in the following pages. We have tried in this volume to pay special attention to questions of motivation, both at the communal and at the personal level, discussing also the motivation of those intellectual leaders who have often been the driving force behind movements for vernacular literacy.

5. PRESENTATION OF VERNACULAR LITERACY

5.1. *The Role of 'Academics'*

One topic which has not been comprehensively covered in our book but which is certainly of some importance is the role of groups of intellectuals in promoting vernacular literacy, whether as informal pressure groups with an interest in mass education, or as formally instituted academies, such as the Institute for Swahili Research in Dar es Salaam or the Dewan Bahasa dan Pustaka (Language and Literature Agency) in Kuala Lumpur. To some extent we ourselves, the members of IGLSVL, constitute such an informal agency; Unesco and its various agencies constitute more formal agencies. It may be that we need at some time to turn a critical eye upon ourselves and our fellows to evaluate the effectiveness with which money is spent on our activities. We do in this book illustrate how literacy campaigns which appear quite well in plans and reports have in fact failed miserably on the ground; we will be guilty of *la trahison des clercs* if we fail to confront the gulf which often appears between academies, and academic avowals and intellectual pressures, and what is actually happening in the real world. This said, it is also often up to us to spot underground as well as above-ground movements. Movements towards the recognition of local as opposed to standard metropolitan varieties of English or French, for example, have usually been led by, as well as vehemently opposed by, academics. Our task also is to educate the politicians and the governmental agencies, and in this we have often failed or at best achieved only lip-service from them.

5.2. *Presentation of this Book*

One of this book's chief characteristics is that it is the outcome of observations on literacy made by a large number of people all of whom have, at some period of their careers, been plunged into fieldwork where vernacular-literacy questions came to the fore. Even more important is the fact that most of them testify about communities of which they themselves have been members. The whole book is thus filled with exemplification from both the so-called 'developed' world and from countries worldwide in various stages of 'development'.

Its two main parts are distinguished not primarily in the density of the observations made but in the relative weight given, in Part One to general issues of universal application and, in Part Two, to case studies.

The general issues dealt with in Part One begin with social considerations (Chapters 1 and 2) and then proceed to technical matters (Chapters 3 and 4), all felt to have some universal applications. They concern, in turn: political and economic aspects of vernacular literacy (Chapter 1); social aspects of the vernacularization of literacy (Chapter 2); problems of writing vernacular languages (Chapter 3); and pedagogical aspects of vernacular literacy (Chapter 4).

The case studies which predominate in Part Two deal with four sets of contrasting case histories which may be thought of as 'special cases' each illuminating different facets of the considerations explored in Part One: those of immigrant communities in Europe (Chapter 5); of some post-colonial pidgin-using communities (Chapter 6); of motivation and attitudes in three post-colonial African countries (Chapter 7) and, in considerable contrast, in four East and South-East Asian countries, three of them post-colonial (Chapter 8).

The general conclusion tries to give an overview of the main results of our enterprise.

5.3. *Summary of the Chapters*

Part One. General Issues: Political, Economic, Social, Orthographic, Pedagogical

Chapter 1, edited by Le Page, draws attention to factors which are often in conflict in their effect on mass literacy and the choice of a language for education: political and economic; demands of nationalism, or national unity, or identity, sometimes working in harmony with, but more often in opposition to, economic survival at the personal, or interest group, or state level. Initially, the case of Britain is examined, with special reference to Scotland and the mass vernacular literacy encouraged by Calvinism. We follow with the case of the Spanish Basques, where a very considerable political will has been exerted to try to ensure the success of policies favouring the use of the Basque language in every domain alongside Spanish, and where the financial resources have not been lacking to implement those policies, although success is now threatened by current high levels of unemployment. The case may be contrasted with that of some of the countries of la Francophonie—for example, Senegal, where high unemployment among white-collar workers educated in French has led to greatly increased use of the vernaculars such as Wolof for business purposes. Cases from India, Africa, and Latin America are then scrutinized. Frequently a wide gulf separates the pieties in support of mass education expressed by politicians at the international conferences mentioned at the outset of this introduction with

what actually happens on the ground because of poverty and conflicts of political will—or simply lack of political will.

Chapter 2, edited by Carrington, examines the assumptions which have been
implicit in the transfer of literacy and education from the colonizers to the colonized, making the case that vernacular literacy ought to transcend the limitations
of such assumptions. Where the colonizers and the colonized have not shared a
language, the perception should be nourished that vernacular literacy is not only
of importance in limited spheres, but of general importance. Giving the vernacular
official status may be helpful, as for Swahili, but it may have a negative effect
as a form of tokenism. Carrington states three broad principles for creating a
favourable environment, and sets out his own arguments, contrasting with those
of Devonish, as to whether it is most effective to work within, or outside, the
domains of officialdom.

Chapter 3, edited by Baker, gives a careful and detailed diachronic and syn-
chronic account of the world's writing systems, with a discussion in each case
of their systematic linguistic significance, of the social processes which brought
them into use, and the technology needed or available to sustain that use. Illustrative of his eye for significant detail is the fact that, since at the end of 1990
the Indigenous Languages Unit of the Ministry of Education in Sierra Leone had
only one typewriter equipped with the characters ε and ɔ, needed for phonemes
common in important languages of the country, it might greatly help the teaching of vernacular literacy if the digraphs <eh> and <oh>, already in use for Krio,
could be more generally adopted. After his detailed worldwide survey Baker
discusses the relative merits of different systems—logographs, syllabaries, semi-
syllabic systems, alphabets—and their 'learnability'. His conclusions draw attention to some important general lessons that may guide future decisions in the
new technological age.

Chapter 4, edited by Gerbault, examines in historical perspective the theory
and practice of the pedagogical means that have been advocated and tried out
to give effect to vernacular literacy, placing each in an ecological setting and
relating it to the relevant teacher guidance and training. She examines the gulfs
between theory and practice; she relates, and explains the need to relate, the means
adopted to the aims which it is sought to achieve. Throughout, the importance
is stressed of motivation in teachers and learners, as of pre-literacy and post-
literacy measures to help supply motivation. She discusses very many aspects of
campaigns which have failed as well as some which have succeeded: the provision of resources and training, the provision of materials, the care needed (and
often lacking) in the design of materials in relation to particular circumstances,
and the possible uses of the broadcasting media and the press. The question of
evaluating progress is discussed, and the need for research here stressed. Case
histories from Cameroon and from India are set out in some detail, and some
conclusions reached as to the need for great adaptability in literacy pedagogy

today, the importance of women's groups, and the need to enable innovative but small-scale approaches to be reconciled with and to inspire mass programmes.

Part Two. Cases from Migrant Settings in Europe; East, Central, and West Africa; East, South, and South-East Asia; Pidgin- and Creole-Speaking Communities

Chapter 5, edited by Gardner-Chloros, studies the particular problems of vernacular literacy for immigrant populations, with special reference to those making up the 'new minorities' in European countries; the dominant myth of 'monolingualism' in education systems; the needs of first-generation immigrants in contrast with those of subsequent generations; the political and ideological re-education needed for host communities to make the best use of and give the most just treatment to these groups from other cultures. The legal provisions of the European Union in relation to equality of opportunity for all members of the population in Europe are dealt with, particularly in relation to what actually happens in France, Germany, the UK, and Scandinavia.

Chapter 6, edited by Charpentier, concentrates particularly on literacy problems in the pidgin-using countries of Melanesia and West Africa and the extreme complexity of the sociolinguistic situations of which they form part. Charpentier draws on his seven years' residence in the New Hebrides/Vanuatu, and his experience there as teacher, fieldworker, and researcher, and as first Curator of the Cultural Centre; also, on reports to our workshops from other pidgin- and creole-using communities. There was resistance to writing down traditional oral literature in any Melanesian vernacular because of the sacred and reserved nature of ancestral knowledge; but in general pidgins were not attached to any particular culture and so could be used as a vehicle for preserving recorded oral literature by transcribing it. There had been experiments in teaching in Bislama in Vanuatu, most successfully at the Agricultural School. As in Papua New Guinea and elsewhere, the pidgins had the advantage of being mutually intelligible over wide areas otherwise occupied by a variety of not always mutually intelligible indigenous languages. Nevertheless, extensive missionary use and, subsequently, the nationalist feelings which had given an impetus to the use of pidgin for writing in Melanesia seem on the whole to have given way to the greater certainties of writing in English. 'Literacy in pidgin vernaculars encounters too much prejudice and too many linguistic and technical problems to really develop' in spite of the use that has already been made of pidgins by some established writers (as, for example, by Chinua Achebe in Nigeria). Moreover, the Melanesian urban pidgin varieties are being constantly Anglicized, leading to the use of a 'post-pidgin continuum' no longer understood by rural speakers. Overall the need to differentiate, in both form and meaning, between two closely related codes, pidgin and English, is seen as a major source of difficulty for learners (as it is also in the Creole-speaking Caribbean).

Chapter 7, edited by Fasold, collates particular contributions to the IGLSVL discussions. They concern *East Africa* (by Carr-Hill, who carried out an extensive and intensive evaluation of the results of literacy campaigns in Kenya and Tanzania); the *Central African Republic* (by Gerbault, who contrasts it with Cameroon); and *Nigeria* (by Ndukwe, who knows intimately the politics and educational practices of his home country, and introduces the concept of 'disassociation' between the vernacular languages and literacy, instanced in various guises from other parts of the world also—for example, the Caribbean). In Fasold's conclusions he re-examines the notion of 'mother tongue'; the general importance of cultural and economic motivation for literacy and of successful demonstration as a means of persuasion; some problems of standardization; and some 'hopeful signs' for the future.

Chapter 8, edited by Kwan-Terry and Luke, natives of and university teachers in Singapore and Hong Kong respectively, brings together contributions from themselves and other native and expatriate but domiciled teachers to compare and contrast the role of 'vernacular' education *vis-à-vis* that in the various standard languages in China, Hong Kong, Malaysia, and Singapore. In each of these countries 'vernacular' usage has to compete for recognition with very strong conventions of education in Chinese, in English, and in the more-recently standardized Putonghua and Bahasa Malaysia. Moreover, the concepts of 'mother tongue' and 'vernacular' have also to be re-examined in the light of the official policies of each country, of contrasts between these, and between declared policy and what actually happens in the classrooms. In the case of Malaysia particular attention is paid to the contrasts in school achievement between urban and rural populations, especially to the plight of the rural Tamils. Comparing and contrasting the four countries, the achievements and failures in their education systems, and the differences between the outcome for various groups, leads to certain conclusions in the Discussion section. 'The notion of vernacular education turns out to be far harder in practice than it seemed in 1953 . . . people in some societies may acquire in early years not one but many languages. Indeed, it may be the norm in some societies for bilingualism to begin very early . . . most children in Singapore are now growing up speaking two (or more) languages'. Definitions are culturally relative; the idea of vernacular education in Malaysia ignores the aboriginal languages completely; in China, provincial standards may be regarded as vernaculars in relation to Putonghua, but standard in relation to numerous local dialects. Singapore and Malaysia present (on the surface at least) radical contrasts in relation to the colonial legacy of English; Hong Kong may steer a cautious middle course, even while the political situation there is in the process of changing dramatically.

PART ONE

General Issues: Political, Economic, Social, Orthographic, Pedagogical

1

Political and Economic Aspects of Vernacular Literacy

R. B. LE PAGE

with contributions from R. K. Agnihotri, R. A. Carr-Hill, A. Choudry, M. Diki-Kidiri, J. Gerbault, M.-A. Hintze, Shail Jha, C. Juillard, A. L. Khanna, R. B. Le Page, A. Mendikoetxea, K. G. Mkanganwi, H. Mwansoko, P. Ndukwe, A. E. Odumuh, C. Pyle, J. Russell, W. J. Samarin, S. Saxena, N. Shrimpton, M. Verma, and K. Williamson

I. INTRODUCTION

We begin this chapter with a consideration of the problems of nationism and nationalism—that is, of the acts of identity and collective self-protection which have drawn together groups of people feeling they had a collective interest in combining, whether for genealogical or geographical or cultural or social reasons. These acts have frequently been exploited by providing a power base for political leaders, and linguistic identity, either indigenous to the group or imposed upon them, has become a political issue and weapon, so that the question of which language to employ for literacy in turn becomes an issue. It will be seen from the case histories then examined that such acts of identity sometimes run in harmony with, but frequently are in conflict with, questions of economic self-interest.

There are many other cases of fissiparous nationalism in Europe with the language banner flying from the masthead accompanied by a call from idealistic (or power-hungry) nationalist intellectuals for 'their language' to be acknowledged as the badge of their identity and the medium for literacy. Corsica, Catalonia, Valencia, Brittany, and Wales are among them. Finland has already won this long battle, separated now from Sweden, released from the shadow of Russia. Each case is different, unique in some respect: demographically, politically, economically, geographically, historically, linguistically. It has been easier for Basque and the Celtic languages and Finnish to be recognized as distinct from the languages around them, the Romance and Germanic majority languages, than it has been for Romansh or Swiss German or Corsican—the latter usually denigrated as either a patois or an Italian dialect (the puzzle then being to know what Italian it is a dialect of). Being an island helps the linguistic focusing process, as in the case of Maltese. On the other hand, Corsica is politically and economically interdependent with 'France', as is Brittany, and Catalonia and Valencia with 'Spain', and as Wales and Ireland and Scotland are with 'Great Britain', so that no intellectual élite will ever risk the impotence of being literate only, or even mainly, in Corsican or Catalan or Valencian or Welsh or Irish or Gaelic; and, as long as the political-economic pull is powerfully in favour of the majority language, so that fewer and fewer, with their coming to literacy, are content to remain within the identity of the minority language, so the minority leaders will feel frustration with their impotence and the radical among them tend to turn to violence to achieve public notice. Jan Morris, a Welsh writer, has recently written a utopian fantasy about the Republic of Wales in the twenty-first century which is reminiscent of present-day (late 1994) Quebec:

> The legislation . . . decrees that those who declare themselves Welsh, and who are prepared to honour the Welsh language and culture, *are* Welsh. It has not, however, made for mass immigration. The language proviso is so demandingly enforced, by repeated examination, and the standard of living in Wales is relatively so simple, that the flow of settlers has long since dried up.   (Morris 1993: 36)

If one sets on one side the possibilities of success, or limited success, or failure of nationalist movements to achieve or define their targets in linguistic terms, one is left with the drive provided by the proposition that it is in the interests of the children themselves to be introduced to literacy first of all in their 'mother tongue'.[1] In support of this we have, for example, Tove Bull's evidence from Norway (see *Abstracts* 1990: 45–50). It is very persuasive evidence, from a country in which the political will was clearly present and the resources made available to make a success of the experiment. When we look, however, at some Indian cases, we find a different story, as also in those cases examined by Charpentier in Chapter 6.

We begin, therefore, with a discussion of general questions of nationalism, of 'democracy', and of 'human rights'. We then consider in turn a number of case histories which illustrate the tensions between political and cultural loyalties, on the one hand, and economic considerations, on the other, tensions which have affected, or are affecting, or can be expected to affect, the outcome of language choice.

We lead with an account of what might seem to be an almost wholly successful vernacular-literacy campaign, that of Scotland, whose success has been a

---

[1] A good deal of powerful evidence that children's education is best advanced by teaching them first in their home language or 'mother tongue' was presented to a conference on bilingualism held as an appendage to the Imperial Education Conference in London in 1911, born out of the practical experience over many years of education officers in India, Canada, Malta, and Wales. Interestingly the South African representative treated 'bilingualism' as a matter of the two languages being English and 'Dutch' (i.e. Afrikaans), and made no mention of education in any indigenous African language. Apart from that, most of the opinions expressed at the conference were very much in support of mother-tongue teaching at least for the first few years of school. (See *BPP* 1911.)

model for export particularly in its religious context. We then consider the case of the Basque region of Spain, where it might have seemed that there was an excellent chance, at least since Franco's death, of political and cultural and genealogical loyalties converging to enable vernacular literacy and education to become accepted as the norm in the now-autonomous region, with the support of considerable financial resources. We see, however, that Spanish retains its pull as the language of economic advancement.

Next, four cases from India are compared in order to draw out some of the reasons for success or failure in government initiatives to try to stem the ever-rising tide of illiteracy: they are those of Narsinghpur and of Bihar and of the so-called 'JJ' ghettos of Delhi in the north, and of Kerala in the south; a high literacy rate exists in Kerala while the National Literacy Mission flounders in the other cases, and we see that there has been a failure of the political will to make adequate resources available to overcome inertia. Agnihotri (p.c.) comments: 'The dismal condition of primary education in India is a major factor in defeating all efforts towards literacy. Over 75 per cent of children abandon school after Class V for educational and economic reasons. There are schools without teachers, drinking water, toilets, blackboards, etc., and no serious efforts are being made to improve these conditions, Operation Blackboard notwithstanding.'

We then refer to the former colonial territories of France and Britain in Africa south of the Sahara, some of which are dealt with in more detail by Fasold and his contributors in Chapter 7, and see how, particularly in the case of la Francophonie, neocolonial aid and economic policies tied to the maintenance of the colonial language have militated against mass vernacular literacy and have contributed to the impoverishment of the mass of the indigenous population. A number of cases are reported briefly from Latin America, especially where attempts have been made to use vernacular television to circumvent the lack of vernacular literacy and teach indigenous American Indian people to 'read' the television screen critically and so improve their participation in democratic politics; in each case the political will to implement education programmes in the vernacular, and to see that resources are allocated and put to proper use, is examined.

The urgent political and humanitarian importance of vernacular education to help limit population increase and control the spread of AIDS and other diseases is relevant throughout.

While in many parts of Africa one might well lament that a higher level of literacy was not achieved in time to combine with vigorous campaigns to limit the spread of AIDS (we learn that in the worst-affected part of Uganda 70 per cent of the population is HIV positive and 50 per cent of children are being born HIV positive) and to limit the population increase (Kenya has one of the highest rates of increase in the world), across much of the continent drought, endemic famine, and endemic warfare seem for the moment to make discussions about literacy academic, whether in the vernacular or in any other language. At the same time we realize that the technology which makes us all immediately aware of these horrors might perhaps enable us at some time to sidestep literacy in propaganda campaigns to educate: we will discuss the potential and the limitations of the alternative media further in this chapter, with particular illustration from Latin America; they are illustrated also by Jean-Michel Charpentier in Chapter 6.

2. NATIONALISM, DEMOCRACY, AND DEVELOPMENT

2.1. *Nationalism*

Anybody who tries to write about the political and economic aspects of literacy at this time is confronted in many parts of the world with seeming chaos. Eric Hobsbawm, in his 1985 Wiles Lectures (updated for publication to 1989 and published in 1990 as *Nations and Nationalism since 1780*) wrote:

Hence, as we can now see in melancholy retrospect, it was the great achievement of the communist regimes in multinational countries to limit the disastrous effects of nationalism within them. The Yugoslav revolution succeeded in preventing the nationalities within its state frontiers from massacring each other almost certainly for longer than ever before in their history, and though this achievement is now unfortunately crumbling, by the end of 1988 national tensions had not yet led to a single fatality.   (Hobsbawm 1990: 173)

As we write (1995), the miseries of Bosnia-Herzegovina are daily recorded, millions of refugees are on the move, the UN and the EU seem almost impotent to stop the slaughter and maiming which the ethnic and religious communities are inflicting upon each other. Vernacular literacy does not seem to be a salient issue here; linguistic nationalism has certainly added to the separatism inherent in the structure of the former republic of Yugoslavia, and literate schooling in the different languages of the republic has no doubt focused ethnic identities as well as the language norms, but clearly literacy has not done much for peaceful development in the present dissipation of the legacy of communism and control. The hopes and fears expressed below for the Basque Autonomous Community of Spain present a contrast here.

Ethnic nationalism, often accompanied by linguistic nationalism, poses salient problems also in the new states emerging from the break-up of the former USSR. In many cases it is too early to say, or to discover on what grounds one could say, what the outcome of present struggles is likely to be.

Hobsbawm, in his chapter 'Nationalism in the Late 20th Century', contrasts the zealotry (our term) of nationalism with that of religious fundamentalism. The latter, he says, can by definition appeal to universal truths, and provide practical and moral guidance on all subjects, whereas 'The call of ethnicity or language provides no guidance to the future at all. It is merely a protest against the *status quo*, or, more precisely, against "the others" who threaten the ethnically defined group . . . Yet ethnicity *can* mobilize the vast majority of its community

—provided its appeal remains sufficiently vague or irrelevant' (Hobsbawm 1990: 168–9).

The claims made by Unesco in 1953 for mother-tongue literacy were not vague or irrelevant; they were very definite, and seemed highly relevant to the development of countries in the throes of decolonization, becoming new states, trying to establish their identities as 'nations' out of the frequently arbitrary and multilingual boundaries of colonies held together only by the accidents of colonial administration and a colonial language. Even if we consider only the relatively weak form of the claims made for mother-tongue literacy, that it should at least be every child's introduction to education, the claims made for the benefits accruing to the children in their subsequent education and development were strong, with considerable economic implications. The claims made by the idealists among us for vernacular literacy are even stronger in their political implications, and are thrown into relief when we have to consider in careful detail what the terms 'vernacular' and 'mother tongue' might mean, as we do elsewhere in this book.

2.2. *Democracy*

Today 'democracy' and 'human rights' are constantly linked as export commodities by the Western powers, and sent out for fostering. Among the arguments used are:

(*a*) that 'democracy' is a form of government (its *modus operandi* is often assumed to be transparent and self-evident although in fact it differs greatly from one country to another, and some 'democracies' may on examination be asserted to be more 'democratic' than others) towards which all states should be moving, and which is the best guarantor of individual human rights, lack of regard for which is liable to incur economic and political sanctions;

(*b*) that 'democracy' means universal adult suffrage;

(*c*) that 'democratic' proceedings must be carried on, and recorded, in an open way which everybody can understand (a condition far more breached than observed);

(*d*) that a fully informed electorate means a literate electorate;

(*e*) that successful economic, cultural, political, social, and personal cognitive development are more likely if the above conditions are met.

Of course, they are met hardly anywhere in the world, but represent an idealized target, a return perhaps to an idealized Athenian democracy, extremely difficult to realize in any multilingual state. Indicative of the ideal was a recent approach to one of us from the chairman of one of the London Borough Councils, a borough with a considerable ethnic mix in its population. It had been agreed in the interests of good government, he explained, that the Minutes of Council proceedings should be made available translated into all the languages spoken in the borough. This was already being done for several of the languages of the Indian subcontinent, for the Greek Cypriots, and others. Could we advise whether it was practicable for the patois of the West Indian immigrant population, who were claiming that theirs was a recognized language and that it should be done to put their treatment on a par with the others? We had to point out that a reading ability in one of the ways of writing Jamaican Creole would involve a fairly high degree of linguistic sophistication, and to translate the minutes into this an even higher degree. Not even *The Dictionary of Jamaican English* would provide the necessary lexicon; and, in any case, anybody able to read and understand the minutes in patois would certainly be able to read them more easily in the standard English version. It was not possible to say that the expense would be justified, nor were we able to think of a possible translator. This small incident illustrates in a microcosmic way a great many of the difficulties in the way of ideal democratic practices with regard to language. It illustrates also some legitimate aspirations of a minority-language group in our society, however far they may be from being realizable.

The assumptions listed above are much more easily justified in established democracies such as the USA or Britain or France or Australia than in much of the rest of the world where considerations of national unity or economic or political power far outweigh what the West regards as basic human rights. Many governments are obsessed with resisting revolutionary change; and many have had the long-standing support of the USA in doing so, whatever their record on human rights. The idealism that has motivated some left-wing governments has been a powerful stimulus in favour of achieving universal literacy; Castro's Cuba is a case in point, Sandinista Nicaragua another. The Indian state of Kerala has been claimed as another.

2.3. *Development*

The claims made by Unesco and other agencies for the economic and 'development' gains which were thought to depend upon and likely to flow from the extension of literacy in Third World countries have been surveyed in Foster (1971) for sub-Saharan Africa. The claim is made in its most general form by Bamgbose (1991: 7): 'Since literacy liberates untapped human potential and leads to increased productivity and better living conditions, it is not surprising that countries with the highest rates of literacy are also the most economically advanced.'

Foster and others point out, as we ourselves observe in relation to India and to Britain, that the logic here is circular. Thomas W. Laqueur (1983: 46, 51) points out that 'Evidence from other societies suggests that quite complicated economic transactions are possible without the use of the written word. Moreover, until quite recently, only a tiny proportion of the work-force needed, in some absolute sense, to be literate . . . Our problem is understanding the formation of a literate culture, the making of a world in which it means something to be able to read and write.' It may well be true that literacy, at a certain level, 'liberates untapped human potential', but the example of the collapsed USSR makes us doubt that this of itself 'leads to increased productivity'. David Cressy (in the same 1983 volume), deals critically with the 'high claims made for literacy by a succession of writers from the sixteenth century onward' (1983: 23), while finding from the evidence that husbandmen, small farmers, had small incentive to learn to read and write. However, as one moved from husbandman to production for the market, the ability to read and to write became a commercially valuable skill. Carr-Hill's (1991) Unesco report on Tanzania (see Chapter 7) suggests a similar conclusion—the small subsistence farmers learning what they needed about cultivation practices by word of mouth and by observing their more prosperous neighbours; the bigger farmers gaining in their farming practice and commercially from being able to read and write. For the English husbandman, his schooling in religion came from the pulpit, his limited literacy needs were met by the scrivener. It was the yeomen and shopkeepers who sent their children to school. Certainly today in an industrial and urban society to be illiterate is to be barred from upward social mobility, but, as we see from the case of India, the illiterate population is frequently superfluous to industry and commerce anyway, and productivity is much more likely to be affected by our ability to read and write in a language of wider communication rather than only in one's mother tongue. However, Bamgbose's claim (1991: 7) that information flow in the indigenous languages is a necessary requirement for mass involvement is on sounder ground. One question today is the extent to which radio and television can replace writing in this respect, as we discuss below in connection with Chile.

3. BRITAIN

3.1. *Vernacular Literacy in Britain, with Special Reference to Scotland; Religion and Nationism*

In all of the cases we examine here religion has been a factor, sometimes a major component, in determining the role of literacy in nation-building, whether through clerics acting as civil servants or through a mass religion-led movement. Such movements may well be seen as a threat to the Establishment, as the Baptists were to the slave-owning West Indian plantocracy and to the Church of England on eighteenth-century plantations when they taught slaves to read and write, and as Wyclif's Lollards and vernacular translations of the Bible were seen by Chaucer's Shipman when the Parson reproved the Host for swearing and the Host invited him to preach to the pilgrims:

> This Lollere heer will prechen us somwhat.

The Shipman broke in

'Nay, by my fader soule, that schal he nat . . .
He wolde sowen som difficulte,
Or springen cokkel in our clene corn . . .'
(Robinson, n.d.: B1173, 1178–83)

Missionaries have seen it as their duty to transmit the word of God either orally or by transmitting the ability to read it, and so open the road to civilization and salvation. Rulers have found it expedient to have a literate clerisy for the administration of government, and a population made dutiful and law-abiding through scripture. The élite and the rich have often resisted mass literacy for the reasons adduced (see 5.1 and 5.6 below) by the landlords in the case of India or because, as the Shipman says, if the masses can read the scripture for themselves their interpretation may not be pure, there may be weeds in the corn. The major concern here is that the masses should not learn to *read*, whereas for rulers the concern has been that civil servants should be able to *both read and write* the language of government. Democratic government has been far from the concerns of either group. The 'benefit of clergy' which the playwright Ben Jonson was able to plead in order to avoid execution for killing a fellow-actor in 1598 was a measure designed to conserve a precious commodity, clerks.

In many countries and religions there has been a progression from what were originally vernacular scriptures to their status as 'mysteries' only to be read and understood by initiates, as in the case of St Jerome's translation of the Bible into fifth-century vulgar Latin—the Vulgate. It is only in recent years (since the 1960s) that the Roman Catholic Church has sanctioned celebration of the Mass in the vernacular—a move which led to schism within the Church.

3.2. *Religion and Vernacular Literacy in Anglo-Saxon Britain*

Despite the strength of Romano-British culture in such centres as Colchester, Chester, and York, the country as a whole was never Romanized to anything like the same extent as Gaul. The languages of some of the pre-Anglo-Saxon tribes survive today in Scots and Irish Gaelic and in Welsh. Only a century after St Augustine arrived to convert Kent in 597, the Northumbrian monasteries— Christianized under the influence of both Augustinian and of Irish/Scots missionaries—produced a remarkable culture in which vernacular literacy and writing flourished alongside Latin scholarship with the earliest extant Anglo-Saxon translations of the Gospels being made in the Northumbrian dialect and vernacular poetry being written down. After the Viking destruction of much of this culture the centre shifted to Mercia and then to Wessex, where the monastic scriptoria and the cathedral schools continued their parallel activities in Latin and English.

The Norman Conquest saw the replacement of English by French abbots and scribes but never caused a complete break in vernacular writing. The progressive loss of French possessions was accompanied by 'English' nationalism, a reverting to the use of English in parliament, and a remarkable renaissance of vernacular poetry in the second half of the fourteenth century. The tradition of Bible translation was continued in the fourteenth century by Wyclif and his followers and in the fifteenth and sixteenth centuries by Tyndale, whose version was the basis for the 1611 Authorized Version. By the sixteenth century the emphasis in the 'grammar schools' had shifted from Latin to English, so that Ben Jonson could sneer at Shakespeare's 'little Latin and less Greek'. From 1476 the advent of printing led to a tremendous supply-led expansion of the market for vernacular reading matter, and the revolutionary activities of the seventeenth century, once again marrying the political and the religious, provided a strong fillip in the number of tracts and broadsides published.

3.3. *Scotland*

Houston (1987: 94, 50) asserts that

The literacy campaign that was initiated in Scotland at the time of the Reformation and carried through by legislation in the seventeenth century was the first truly national literacy campaign. Some principalities and city states of Protestant Europe had tried to encourage literacy from the beginning of the sixteenth century. However, these initiatives were small in scale and enjoyed little success compared with the Scottish aim to organize education at a national level . . . Working side by side, church and state sought to create a national, universal, and religiously oriented educational system centered on a school in every parish. Legislation between 1616 and 1696 set up the parochial school system, administered by the church in rural areas and by the secular authorities in the towns . . .

The perceived results of the drive for literacy, and the values it supposedly embodied, have formed an important focus of identity for the Scots as a people.

These 'perceived results' were a distortion of reality but provided a myth about what could be done in and through education in an economically and socially primitive country. Partly its origins lay in the need of the Scottish Calvinist reformers to mould mass support for Calvinism and against the pro-French pro-Roman Catholic monarchy. The Church needed to transmit an approved body of doctrine, the State to have a biddable and employable population. There was no thought of democracy in either Church or State.

As to the success of the programme: one must look at the linguistic divide between Highlands and Lowlands; at the rural/urban divide; at the lowly status of women in the male-dominated Scottish society; and at the migrations of population into the rapidly growing industrial towns and abroad to the colonies. The Highlanders spoke Gaelic, the Lowlanders Lowland Scots or English—modern Lallans. The agents of education, whether the State, the Church, or the Scottish Society for the Propagation of Christian Knowledge, or the private schools (which though made illegal played an essential role) insisted on teaching in English. The 1616 Scottish Education Act was enacted in part so that 'the

Irish language' (i.e. Gaelic) 'which is one of the chief, principal causes of barbarity and incivility . . . may be abolished and removed' (Houston 1987: 61). The presumption was that Gaelic, Roman Catholicism, and disorder were linked. As a result the literacy campaign made comparatively little progress in the Highlands until the Gaelic language was given more recognition in the nineteenth century. (Today the number of its speakers has dwindled to around 40,000.)

The campaign made better progress in the Lowlands especially in the urban areas and among boys and men. Girls were taught little beyond domestic skills, particularly in the Highlands, other than among the urban professional and merchant and landowning classes: 'Gentry and professionals were all literate in the 1750s and 1760s and had been since the early 17th century. Craftsmen and traders were only 20 per cent illiterate, farmers around one third, but nearly 70 per cent of the working classes could not sign their names in full' (Houston 1987: 59).

Although their education systems were quite different, by the mid-eighteenth century the Lowlands of Scotland shared with northern England a popular appreciation of literacy as a valuable asset, despite the sacrifices entailed in perhaps having to give up the labour on farms of children who went to school (as in most countries, school and university holidays were timed to coincide as far as possible with planting and harvest). Literacy was both a boon to and a product of the rapid expansion of the industrial towns of the Lowlands in the eighteenth century; a boon also to those who wished to emigrate. Jamaica seemed, to its eighteenth-century historian Edward Long, to be full of Scottish overseers who became plantation managers and finally owners, giving Scottish place-names to their properties (see Le Page 1960: ch. V); James Boswell referred to a 'rage for emigration', and it affected the Highlands even more than the Lowlands. In the early stages of industrialization the vast majority of the workforce does not need to be literate, but the foremen need to be (see Cressy 1980; Vincent 1989).

3.4. *The Myth Exported*

One success of the Scottish literacy campaign, aimed as it was at every social class including the poorest, was in producing a stereotype of what could be achieved in a Protestant country through vernacular education in religion and civic duties and basic skills in literacy and numeracy, and in exporting this stereotype—particularly to the colonies, but also to other parts of Europe. The stereotype was exemplified by the eighteenth-century English novelist Tobias Smollett, who justified making his hero Roderick Random a Scot on the grounds of the general availability of cheap education in Scotland (1748: Preface): 'learning was so cheap in my country, that every peasant was a scholar.' The stereotype about the inherent superiority and egalitarian quality of Scottish education survives to this day, and many institutions in the USA, in Canada, and in New Zealand have been modelled upon it. It was seen as egalitarian and democratic in contrast to that of England, felt to be dominated by the private fee-paying model tailored for the wealthy—although this in turn was a stereotype. A great deal of schooling in England had always been provided for the children of the poor by endowed charities and by the Church.

4. THE BASQUES

4.1. *Nationalism, Literacy, and the Basques*

The Basques of south-western France and north-western Spain are among a number of communities on the Atlantic coasts of Europe and North Africa apparently pushed to these western extremities by later waves of immigration and conquest, and struggling in historical times to reassert their identity partly by reviving their language and making it one symbol of that identity. In their case, as in the cases of the Celtic peoples of Brittany, Wales, Scotland, and Ireland, their language is clearly distinct from the Romance or Germanic languages of the majority around them. But they share their struggle also with people the discreteness of whose languages is far more difficult to establish—the Romance speakers of Galicia, of Catalonia, of Valencia, of different parts of Italy, of Corsica and Sardinia and so on, and also 'Lallans' speakers in Scotland. We return later to the general question of small-nation identity in Europe, only observing here that it is the emergence in each case of a written variety of these languages that has focused them as discrete languages. It was Dante who observed that the Sardinians had no language, they just spoke very bad Latin; Zuanelli Sonino (*Abstracts* 1986) pointed out that at the time of the unification of Italy in 1861 'Italian', which became the national language, was used for written purposes; the dominant groups who wrote it spoke dialects of Italy or France or Spain or of the Italian cities. We will return to this point of the function of literacy in helping to focus nationalism when we have examined the case of the Spanish Basques.

In what follows[2] we will be concerned with the part played by sponsorship of vernacular literacy in focusing and standardizing a spoken language (or dialect) and the concomitant inculcation of nationalism and a sense of racial discreteness, aided and abetted by what Hobsbawm has called a pseudo-science of race. We will also be concerned with economic factors both in the background to this nationalist movement and in the fall-out from it.

4.2. *The Genetic Argument Undermined*

We will start with the genetic work of Bertranpetit and Cavalli-Sforza, not without relevance to the racist rhetoric of one of the founding fathers of modern

---

[2] Reference will be made to Urla (1987*b*), Congreso (1988), Hobsbawm (1990), Bertranpetit and Cavalli-Sforza (1991), Cavalli-Sforza (1991), Garmendia Lasa (1991, 1992, 1994, and p.c.), and Mendikoetxea (p.c.), and to papers given at the 1989 Basque Language Congress in San Sebastian (see Congreso 1988).

Basque nationalism, Sabino Arana; consider Hobsbawm's comments on the role of language awareness in modern nationalism; then consider the results of Urla's 1982–3 fieldwork (in Urla 1987*b*), quite narrowly focused on one town of Usurbil and its immediate environs, and relate them to the much wider context of the 1986, 1987, and 1991 sociolinguistic studies, sponsored by the Basque government, of the whole Basque country in Spain.

J. Bertranpetit and L. L. Cavalli-Sforza are distinguished geneticists who have become obsessed with the possibility of tracing the entire migration history of the human species from the distribution of genes today, and have buttressed their hypotheses with appeals to other disciplines, in particular to historical linguistics. They have mapped the incidence of certain genes—in all, fifty-four alleles of blood groups, proteins, and enzymes—in 635 sample populations in the Iberian peninsula. Applying principal component analysis to the distribution of variation in the genetic make-up of these populations, the authors claim:

The first principal component shows the difference between the Basque population and the rest of the Iberian peninsula, with a clear gradation in all directions . . . The first isopleth (isogenic curve) coincides fairly well with what is now called the Basque Country and the Basque-speaking region. Although the area of distribution of the Basque language has been narrowing in historic times . . . the area remaining today clearly shows the coincidence of cultural and genetic preservation of very ancient characteristics.

The genetic difference of the Basques has been well known since the classical studies on the Rh blood groups in the 40s [1940s] showed the highest frequency of Rh– in the world, with marked differences from surrounding populations. Mourant (1947) proposed a first interpretation in terms of the history of the population, in the sense that, by isolation, modern Basques would maintain the genetic characteristics of a 'proto-European' population, mostly or entirely Rh–, as opposed to later Rh+ migration waves.

When more genetic information was gathered, differences were also detected in other polymorphisms . . . *but they did not show parallel clines to the Rh gene. Nevertheless, the genetic differentiation of the Basques was accepted* and they are considered as a genetic isolate in gene frequency compilations . . . Within this context a pre-Neolithic (Paleolithic or Mesolithic) hypothesis of the origin of the Basque population, which would have survived the impact of genetic admixture with later comers to a greater extent than other old European populations, seemed adequate.

In the present study, the Basque identity has been ascertained in a geographical perspective and with a large number of genes, allowing us to undertake an interpretation of its meaning on a detailed spatial basis. The Basque phenomenon can now be studied in the light of the evidence related to the history of populations: archaeology, historical linguistics, population history and physical anthropology . . . there are many signs of an identity in the Basque area since Upper Paleolithic times, of a delay in absorbing most cultural innovations, and of the maintenance of special cultural aspects, mainly the languages, of unquestionable antiquity.   (Bertranpetit and Cavalli-Sforza 1991: 56–7; emphasis added)

Cavalli-Sforza (1991) followed similar arguments to find that his hypothetical 'family tree' for mankind, starting with a dispersal from Africa perhaps 100,000 years ago, can be matched by the family trees of the historical linguists for the world's languages. He neglects the gross disparity in the period of time covered by the two trees, and also the considerable modifications which have had to be made by linguists to the concept of linguistic 'relatedness' in the light of the findings of sociolinguistics and creole language studies.

Quite apart from these points, however, both the genetic and the linguistic arguments have been effectively undermined by, among others, Jacques Guy (1992), who has shown that Cavalli-Sforza's neat family trees are to some considerable extent the product of his statistical method and the unwarrantable assumption of a constant rate of genetic drift built into it. We do not need to pursue the matter further here except to underline the point (argued at some length in Le Page and Tabouret-Keller 1985: ch. 6) that the stereotypical view of the relationship between 'a people' and 'their language' rests on fallacious use of the genetic metaphor. This is nevertheless part of the base on which much proud nationalism is built.

4.3. *The Language Component in 'Nationalism'*

Hobsbawm has examined at length the part played by linguistic consciousness in modern nationalism and nationism. Still today 'the German nation' tends to be defined in terms of those who speak German as their home language, although sociolinguists and sociologists of language have provided us with many examples of the lack of isomorphism between language and social boundaries, and also of whole communities who have changed their language in the course of three generations. Many Basques themselves exemplify this. One can refer to the linguistic history of Alsace, of Ireland and Scotland, of Dravidian Indian groups who have adopted an Indo-Aryan language, of immigrant groups and indigenous groups in the Americas and in the Malay Archipelago and in many parts of Africa. In the building of modern 'nations', compulsory education for all, and hence literacy for all, in whatever has been decreed to be 'the national language', has been a frequent ingredient, as in post-Napoleonic France, although, as we shall see when we come to consider various African cases, it is a desideratum which has had to be abandoned in many polyglot states (see also Le Page 1964*a*).

Hobsbawm (1990: 162–5) traces changes in the concept of 'a nation' since 1780. His conclusion as he reaches the 1950s is that by then:

ethnic and linguistic nationalism may be on divergent routes, and both may now be losing their dependence on national state power.

At first sight there has been a triumphant world-wide advance of 'the principle of nationality'. All states of the globe are today officially 'nations', all liberation movements tend to be 'national' liberation movements, 'national' agitations disrupt the oldest nation-states in Europe—Spain, France, the United Kingdom, even, in a modest way, Switzerland —the socialist regimes of the east, the new Third World states liberated from colonialism, even the federations of the New World, where Canada remains torn and in the USA pressure is growing to make English the only language for public official purposes, in response to the mass immigration of Spanish Americans, the first wave of immigrants not to feel the attractions of linguistic assimilation. Above all, where ideologies are in conflict, the appeal to the imagined community of the nation appears to have defeated all challengers . . .

Yet . . . The characteristic nationalist movements of the late twentieth century are essentially negative, or rather divisive. Hence the insistence on 'ethnicity' and linguistic differences . . . Time and again they seem to be reactions of weakness and fear, attempts to erect barricades to keep at bay the forces of the modern world . . . a combination of international population movements with the ultra-rapid, fundamental and unprecedented socio-economic transformations so characteristic of the third quarter of our century. French Canada may illustrate this combination of an intensified petty-bourgeois linguistic nationalism with mass future shock.

States, he says, by contrast, are now having to accept multiethnicity and multi-lingualism as the norm.

4.4. *'Being Basque', Speaking 'Basque'—and Writing 'Basque'*

According to Urla (1987*a*), whose very sympathetic study is based on eighteen months' fieldwork and residence in the Basque country in 1982–3, Basque nationalist ideology has followed a developmental pattern rather similar to that of Quebec (though of course with the important difference of the hostility of France and 'French' in the Basque case as contrasted with the support given by France in Quebec—'Vive le Quebec Libre', as De Gaulle cried). It began as a reaction against industrialization and urbanization, and the influx of 'foreign' (i.e. Spanish) workers at the end of the nineteenth century:

Basque nationalist ideology, first formulated in the 1890s by Sabino Arana, the son of a Bizkaian industrialist, was highly conservative and religious. It proclaimed the Basques to be a separate race plagued by contamination from foreign workers and abandoned by its hispanicized capitalist oligarchy. Nineteenth century nationalism condemned the cities and industries as the breeding ground for the corruption of authentic Basque values and idealized the rural life of Basque farmers.   (Urla 1987*a*: 31)

(By way of contrast, whereas Sabino Arana was not himself a native speaker of Basque, Catalan *was* the language of the pioneers of industrialization in Catalonia, and remained therefore a prestige urban variety.) In the Basque country, as in Quebec, ethnic identity and solidarity came to be taken over and asserted by urban intellectuals as a reaction to the inflow of aliens brought by, and bringing, the very industrial prosperity on which the nationalist movement was to draw to achieve its aims. It was an anti-hispanicization movement whose sentiments were in due course strongly reinforced by Franco's attempts to hispanicize and so 'unify' the whole of Spain, outlawing the use of both the Basque and the Catalan languages. But anti-hispanicization was the obverse of a strong assertion of Basque 'racial' identity, Basque language, social organization, and cultural traditions. The first Congress of Basque Studies was held in 1918. Arana had written: 'We will raise up a healthy nation, a religious nation, and an educated, prosperous and happy people . . . supported by the pillars of our language, our culture, our traditions, the ideals of our race, our sensibilities and social freedoms, and with the protection of the Virgin of Arantzazu and Saint Ignatius of Loyola' (quoted in Urla 1987a: 31). (Those of us who are old enough can hardly help hearing Hitler's voice; according to Mendikoetxea, the same strain runs strongly all through Sabino Arana's writings.)

Almost from the outset a great deal of attention was paid to the possibility of creating a standard Basque language out of the dialects spoken in the Basque country. This could then be used as a medium of education in 'Basque' schools and as a vehicle for literature other than the religious literature which made up the bulk of what written Basque was available. The Roman Catholic Church has played an important role in the maintenance of Basque; prayers and hymns may be sung in Basque by non-Basque-speakers even when the rest of the Mass is in Spanish; but, with the exception of the priests, Basque intellectuals have generally studied and written in Spanish. It has been felt that this lack of a literature made the Basque language 'incomplete'—Urla (1987a: 78) refers to 'the widespread and ethnocentric assumption in the West that languages are those which have a literature while the rest are "vernaculars" or "tongues" . . .'. (We would refer also to the criteria used by the French speakers in Mauritius to establish that French was 'a language' whereas Creole was not—see Baker, in *Abstracts* 1988: 39–42.)

The projects for schools and for language reform were halted by Franco's *españolismo*, 'a holy war for the glory of God and the glory of Spain, understood as a monolithic entity' (Urla 1987a: 102). Basque was proscribed as 'exotic', to be eliminated. Thus to speak and to write in Basque was to signal one's opposition to Franco's regime. With the death of Franco and the reinstatement of a more liberal regime and the monarchy, Spain was left with the complex political problems, including the growth of the militant separatist movement *ETA* (*Euskadi ta Askatasuna*, 'Basqueland and Freedom'), which Franco's policies had exacerbated. At the same time, there came the granting of autonomy to a Basque government within the Spanish state, and the freedom which that has brought to introduce new education programmes and the use of Basque as a medium of education in Basque schools and the teaching of Basque as a subject in Spanish-medium schools. Urla's fieldwork as a social anthropologist was concerned to a large extent to study 'the Basque country as a linguistic battleground', centring her work on the town of Usurbil and the surrounding countryside.

What emerged from her various accounts is the extent to which Spanish remained for the older generation of Basque-speakers and became (with early adolescence) for the younger generation (at least in Usurbil—but for the more general picture see below) the prestige language. By 1983, when she did her fieldwork, the formerly clandestine Basque-medium schools had become official 'ikastolas' receiving substantial subsidies from the Basque government, parallel with, but not replacing, the Spanish-medium public school system. Because of the large number of non-Basque immigrants, 'creating a single Basque public school system was symbolically very appealing to Basques' (Urla 1987*a*: 268), yet fraught with the danger that if all the schools then had to make substantial concessions to the Spanish speakers, the completely-Basque schools would disappear.

She illustrated the 1983 situation in Usurbil with a vignette of one Basque family. The grandparents almost always used their Basque dialect to each other and to family and friends and neighbours and felt most comfortable in it, but the grandmother said it was easier for her to read and write in Spanish; she read the Spanish parts of the newspaper thoroughly each day but skipped the occasional articles in Basque, not feeling at home with the 'new Basque'—that is, the standardized Batua. She code-switched frequently when needing the Spanish vocabulary, and switched to Spanish when spoken to in Spanish. Basque had been the first language of both her son and his wife, but they spoke to each other almost exclusively in Spanish, having been sent away to school, and having grown up in the Franco era. They had the status-consciousness about Spanish from that earlier period, but spoke only Basque to their children. Their children would belong to the first generation to be literate in Basque when they reached adulthood, and to know the standard Basque, Batua, as well as the local dialect:

There are already in Usurbil young people who have been able to carry out all of their schooling up to university in Basque and this trend will continue as more children come out of the Model D classrooms in Udarregi . . . The problem for ikastola teachers today, is that some of their euskaldun children speak Spanish, not Basque, when they play. This is a change which . . . has many language planners very worried . . . As a result of the language movement, especially the Basque language schools and the new awareness of the need to take active measures to preserve Basque, many parents are sending their children to ikastolas. This is resulting in the acquisition of literacy and standard Basque, skills which were lacking in the linguistic competency of prior generations of euskaldunes. (Urla 1987*a*: 277–80)

Nevertheless, the prestige attaching to Spanish remained and also, with increasing urbanization, the stigma attaching to rural dialects of Basque. There have been frequent campaigns to promote the regular use of Basque in all spheres. In 1982 there was a major campaign for literacy at all levels, trying to change language habits by propagating new images of Basque speakers, reconstituting Basque as a modern urban and intellectual language, the language of the whole Basque country, which the people of that country would use for all purposes as a matter of course. Through constant propaganda the older unselfconscious use of the local dialect for domestic purposes and Spanish for public formal purposes became highly politicized into a self-conscious public use of Batua. It is this which is the language of examinations for teaching certificates and education; it is the sole language of one of the two television channels, the language taught in the schools, the language most used in official documents; 'it is the language of the translator . . . most of the people learning Batua and using it are educated people from the cities, not rural farmers (who have been the traditional euskaldun) nor working class immigrants . . . Batua is losing some of its radical connotations and emerging as a formal register, associated with a new social category of speakers, that is, a Basque speaking intelligentsia and administrative bureaucracy' (Urla 1987*a*: 314).

In spite of the evident consciousness-raising role of language use in relation to demonstrating and having pride in Basque identity, Urla did not believe that language use had been uniformly accepted as the defining feature of Basque ethnic identity as Catalan had among Catalans; 'given the low number of Basque speakers, there are many people who consider themselves Basque by ancestry (race), though they do not speak *euskera*. Language has gained in importance, but it has not replaced genealogical or racial understandings of Basque identity' (Urla 1987*a*: 334). (Mendikoetxea (p.c.) feels that many who are very keen on their Basque ancestry are hypocritical in the lip-service they pay to the importance of preserving the language while not attempting to speak it.)

Urla shows 'language planning' serving ideological ends. We can see the 1953 idealistic view of literacy in 'the mother tongue' as being what is best for the child's development being turned into a major tool of a nationalistic political movement which has some of its roots in opposition to another political movement of which again language policy was a major ideological weapon.

4.5. *Later Surveys and Studies*

A much wider perspective on Basque and Spanish is given by studies based on two large-scale sociolinguistic surveys commissioned by the Basque government. In the first (see Ayestaran *et al.* 1986) 3,010 teenagers (14–18 years) were interviewed; in the second, 2,030 respondents aged 25–29 (see *Juventud Vasca* 1986 in Ornstein-Galicia 1988: 447). Clearly, taking the Basque country as a whole, there is considerable variation in the use made of each language, some of the variables being:

(*a*) the kind of Basque used:
  - one or other regional dialect
  - standard Batua
  - code-switching to varying degrees
(*b*) the extent of use over domains and modes:
  - public/domestic
  - oral only/oral and written only
(*c*) attitudes towards it, and prestige or stigma attached to it.

These variables can be correlated to a certain extent with parentage, age, level of education, sex, geographical location, religion, political allegiance, occupation, socio-economic status, etc.—the usual sociolinguistic variables.

In the survey of the older group only 27.3 per cent of the sample claimed to be able to write in Basque, while 99.4 per cent claimed literacy in Spanish. This group were at school during the last years of the Franco regime. The highest proportion claiming literacy in Basque (64 per cent) was in the small towns of fewer than 2,000 people, even though these were furthest from Basque educational facilities (which may of course make the claim itself suspect). In towns of more than 50,000 and in the provincial capitals Gasteiz, Donostia, and Bilbo, only between 16.3 per cent and 17.7 per cent claimed Basque literacy (Ornstein-Galicia 1988: 446). Nevertheless, it appears that many who felt themselves to be Basque accorded the language high prestige as a symbol of that identity but did not need to use it. Only 15.9 per cent of the younger age group thought that speaking Basque was an essential component of that identity. Attitudes towards Basque expressed in these surveys are generally very positive even among those who could not speak it; and it is, of course, far easier in general for a Catalan-speaker to use the closely related Castilian than for a Castilian-speaker to learn and use Basque. Mendikoetxea (p.c.) comments that Basque is a prestige and 'glamorous' language among the younger age group, especially among university students, and 'Batua' has lost any connotations of rural backwardness. 'There are many non-Basque-speakers who want their children to be educated in Basque; people who were educated in Spanish in post-war Spain and thus cannot speak Basque but feel Basque and have pride in being Basque. I know of cases where the parents have started learning Basque along with the children to be able to help them with their school work and not feel somehow inferior to the child' (Mendikoetxea, p.c.).

Young people of mixed parentage (as also of Basque parentage) can thus choose how much they wish to identify with 'the Basques'. The economic and international pull of Spanish remains powerful, projected in the media and in advertising. The Basque regime, trying in the 1980s to 'regulate and centralize control over the administration of Basque schools and cultural organization' and to enhance and entrench the legal status of the standard language, had, like the Quebec government, become involved in legal battles over where one person's legal rights ended and another's began. Some non-Basque-speakers did not wish to be forced to have their children educated in Basque, any more than non-French-speakers wish to have French-medium education forced on their children in Quebec where previously there was choice. The non-Basque-speakers sought legal protection, just as the Basque-speakers had. Thus the debate about vernacular literacy, politicized from the outset, assumed new forms. Urla (1987*a*: 337) concluded: 'In this new discursive terrain, the Basque speaker, the *euskaldun*, has become reconstituted as social victim to be protected under the wings of the welfare state. It is difficult, as yet, to determine exactly the political consequences of this shift, yet it seems clear that the incorporation of language into the logic of welfare state rationality will bear directly on the future experience of Basque language and identity.'

Today people can choose between three models for educating their children: A, B, and D; the first is wholly in Spanish, the second teaches Basque as a second language, and D is wholly in Basque.

4.6. *The Submissions of the Secretary-General for Language Policy*

We can bring this account of the progress of literacy and education in Basque even more up to date and at the same time present a rather different and more optimistic view of that progress from various submissions made to the Institutions and Home Affairs Commissions of the Basque Parliament by the Secretary-General for Language Policy (M. Carmen Garmendia Lasa) in 1991, 1992, and 1994 (we are indebted to her for the English translations we quote from) and from the results of a further sociolinguistic survey carried out by her secretariat in 1991. (Our view of her optimism must be tempered by the fact that the survey, like the earlier ones, was carried out by recording opinions expressed in response to a questionnaire testing attitudes towards Basque and government policies—the answers liable, as Mendikoetxea (p.c.) has pointed out, to be rather hypocritical and loaded; the submissions also place weight on census data, which, as we have noted, are notoriously unreliable in relation to language loyalty and use.) The questions asked related mostly to *learning* and *speaking* Basque rather than to *reading* and *writing*. The Secretary-General herself notes (p.c.: 38) that 'there are "grey" areas which cause contrary opinions on the present and future of the Basque language . . . Many people are worried about the demolinguistic situation, linguistic transmission in families and the "gap" between knowledge and use of Basque. However, we should not underestimate the positive indicators which exist.' By 1994 she expressed herself as convinced that they were on the threshold of a new era.

After noting positive achievements she sets out a résumé of what still remains to be done. Among the achievements were the fact that, thanks in particular to the use of the education system for the propagation of Basque, there were according to the 1991 census 95,000 more bilinguals than had claimed this status in 1981; also, that

cultural life in Basque has increased tremendously in recent years. No longer is Basque used just in oral literature and liturgy, as it was only a few years ago, but there are now films, books, songs and even research projects in Basque . . . the social use of Basque has increased dramatically over the past ten years . . . the basquization programmes and adult literacy programmes and the educational system have caused a radical change in the linguistic situation of the Basque country in the last decade. The effort which the Civil Service has made to ensure the presence of the Basque language in the media, especially in radio and television . . . has meant that it has obtained access to areas fundamental for modern life . . . the language policy which has been carried out during the last decade has produced the geographic, demographic and functional expansion of the Basque language. (Garmendia Lasa, p.c.: 38–9)

Nevertheless there are worries that the transmission of the language to new generations at family level is inadequate.

There were in 1991 virtually no monolingual Basque speakers any longer. The proportion of monolingual Spanish speakers has declined from 64 per cent in 1981 to 54 per cent in 1991. The government's policy is bilingualism, and, within that, the 'normalization' of Basque, its use in all walks of life. These ends are to be achieved within a framework of peaceful coexistence and mutual respect between the Basque-using and the Spanish-using and the code-switching members of the community; but 'promoting the Basque language is a duty which is derived from the Statute of Autonomy and . . . based upon a social and political consensus' (Garmendia Lasa 1992: 18). The policy is a means to an end —the depoliticizing of the language issue, the peaceful unification of a bilingual community not as two language communities living side by side but as one bilingual community. Thus Arana's Basque nationalism and Franco's Spanish nationalism are to be replaced by pride in citizenship of a civilized, tolerant society within which the Basques can feel secure.

As to what remains to be done: whereas the schools have advanced a long way in the teaching and use of Basque in the classroom, still in tertiary education, in the civil service, in the labour market, and in business far more is needed. 'It would seem that the business world, because of its economic interdependence and the present international dynamics is an area which it is difficult to tackle . . . As far as the service sector goes, what we are attempting to do is to break the inertia which in the end is what causes Spanish to be the only language used' (Garmendia Lasa, p.c.: 40). Moreover, although most people surveyed thought that more Basque is spoken today than ten years ago, less progress has been made in using the language than in knowing it.

When one examines the statistics presented with these reports, one is struck by the fact that the total population of the Basque Autonomous Community (BAC) declined by 29,000 (1.4 per cent) between 1981 and 1991, and the nursery-school population by about 27,000 in the same period, within which there has been a marked shift from Spanish-only to bilingual or to Basque-medium-only schools, the percentage in Spanish-only schools being halved. The censuses give a doubling of the percentage of Basque-speaking children in the 5–9 age group, a halving of Spanish-only speakers, between 1981 and 1991—these figures must be interpreted against the overall drop in the population. The population of the district of Alava, the most Spanish-speaking region, actually increased during that period by 14,500, and within that region Spanish monolinguals still in 1991 made up 71.3 per cent of the population.

Thus the strands which must be woven into an appreciation of the degree of success for vernacular literacy in the BAC are many and complex: demographic, economic, political, social. Spain today has one of the highest rates of unemployment in the EU; just how this will affect (*a*) a drive for more literacy and (*b*) a drive for literacy in Basque rather than only in Spanish is itself a complex question. One individual solution to unemployment is through migration, possibly into a world in which literacy in Basque is of no further use. Even within the BAC, however, the number of jobs *requiring* literacy in Basque must be rather small. The civil service is an area in which bilingual literacy is obviously desirable. In Gipuzkoa, the most-Basque region, a command of Basque is required of one in two regional civil servants, in Bizkaia of one in four, in Alava of one in six. In the 1991 entrance examination for the Basque government service, for which 700 jobs were on offer, a pass in Basque was required for 11 per cent. There were 4,378 people who passed the exam, but a smaller proportion of these in relation to the population of the region came from Gipuzkoa than from Alava. Can it be that non-Basques are better at passing examinations in the school-learned Batua than Basques, just as in Malaysia the non-Malays have proved better at passing examinations in school-learned Bahasa Malaysia than the Malays? Perhaps there is some other explanation.

It is clear that the propaganda and practical efforts in favour of the policy of peaceful bilingual coexistence and mutual respect in the BAC have borne good fruit. It is not yet clear that the processes engendered so far will be self-sustaining in the face of economic problems. It is a sad irony that, whereas both the Basque region of Spain and the Tyneside region of England have been devastated in employment by the decline in each case of the shipbuilding industries, two recent very large Japanese industrial investments have gone to Tyneside in preference to Spain, partly because of the international language of the workforce.

5. INDIA

5.1. *Some Cases from India*

Any observations about political and economic aspects of literacy in India must be seasoned throughout with reminders of the immensely hierarchical pigeon-hole characteristics of Indian society.[3] The caste system, social class, religious, sex and race divisions compartmentalize it to a degree difficult for members of

---

[3] Arnove and Graff (1987: 5) state: 'The wealth and resources of a country have not been the critical factor in shaping the scope and intensity of a war on ignorance. Rather, the political will of national leaders to effect dramatic changes in personal beliefs, individual and group behaviours, and major institutions emerges as the key factor. Cases in which a strong political will has been lacking include India, with approximately one half of the world's more than 800 million illiterate adults, and the advanced industrialized countries of the USA, the UK, and France, which, according to Limage, have profound illiteracy problems.' (Limage contributes ch. 13 of the same book.)

what they imagine to be more homogeneous societies to appreciate (although perhaps any homogeneity may be in the gaze of the beholder). Among the difficulties noted by Choudhry (Agnihotri *et al.* 1991) in making a 'total literacy' programme in West Bengal effective, especially in rural and semi-urban areas, were the facts that married women would not attend classes after dark for fear of physical punishment by their husbands, as it is taboo for married women to stay away from their homes after dusk; and that, during the forty days of fasting before Ramadan, classes in Muslim areas had to be discontinued. Even in Kerala the low-caste Hindus, today's scheduled castes, and the poor generally were in the past denied access to literacy. Caste today remains an immensely powerful principle of categorization controlling social mobility, marriage, and economic opportunity, even though mitigated to a certain extent by the reservation of jobs guaranteed to the scheduled castes by the Indian Constitution and by internal migration to another state or to the city. Most of the members of the scheduled castes are poor, backward in education, poorly politicized, and generally disadvantaged. Their self-image is such that they seem to accept these disadvantages as part of the natural order. In rural areas the village élite or feudal lords do not in any way help them to have access to education, some even reminding them of the dire consequences in terms of further economic deprivation if they encourage their children's education.

An extended report in the London *Independent* (10 January 1995) speaks of 'a caste war blighting India's poorest state' and tells how a guerrilla movement is arming and training rural labourers, men and women, to defend themselves against the rapacity and abuses of the landlords.

As an example of the difficulties confronting governments revolutionary enough to try to break down these barriers, we may cite from Lieten (1992: 103–4):

The Left Front government [in West Bengal] has made at least two attempts in its endeavour to change the class bias in education: the abolition of English at the primary level and the introduction of new textbooks. Both measures have unleashed a storm of protest with a range of arguments with one imposing message: the communist-led government was portrayed as destroying the educational system and as attempting to regiment and remould the minds of the children into a communist strait-jacket. The sharp reaction, comparable with the efficacious movement against the Kerala Education Bill of the first communist government in Kerala which ultimately led to its downfall (Lieten 1982), may have served as a sign to the Left Front government that too much tampering with the organization and contents of the educational system would be suicidal.

India is supposed to be the world's largest democracy in population terms. Writing from an Indian perspective, Agnihotri and Khanna (1992*a*) make the following salient opening points:

There are two significantly divergent approaches to the relationship between literacy and social change. The first views acquisition of literacy as an inevitable consequence of revolutionary movements for social change. In the second, literacy is considered to be a necessary prerequisite for initiating any social change. Whatever be the approach, the history of literacy work shows that literacy itself cannot solve social problems. It is also wrong to club illiteracy with poverty and disease and to assume that oral societies are by definition culturally and cognitively impoverished. Oral societies possess their own stock of valuable knowledge and have efficient systems of communication to transmit that knowledge from one generation to another. The significance of literacy lies in its potential as a tool for change . . . [In India] Literacy has spelt power for the select few who have had access to it; acquisition of literacy by the underprivileged may become an important input into participatory democracy.

In relation, however, to the question of *vernacular* literacy, Agnihotri and Khanna conclude that it has become suspect because of the greater economic attraction of standard-language or lingua-franca literacy, questions of national integration, difficulty of defining the mother tongue, and lack of teaching resources. Such difficulties have led many to conclude that literacy is best imparted in the regional language of the area where the learner lives.

5.2. *Constitutional Provisions*

Questions of national integration versus state and regional identity have bedevilled India, and have assumed a linguistic aspect at least since independence. Some states within the Union have been established along linguistic boundaries to try to resolve some of the problems of identity. Hindi and English are the two official languages for federal government use, so that literacy in these two (with of course two different scripts, Hindi being prescribed in the constitution 'in the Devanagari script') is a requirement for all Government of India civil servants. Within each state, State government civil servants will need literacy in the State language, in the non-Hindi areas involving yet another script. In the tribal areas the tribal languages, the 'vernaculars', may add yet another set of complications in the interaction of economic and political motivation *vis-à-vis* 'identity'.

Since the 1968 National Policy on Education a Three Language Formula has been in use in various forms in most of the states. Its true implementation could amount to children studying the two official languages, Hindi and English, in two scripts and the official language of their state in a third script (see also Chapter 3). This approach has been criticized in that it not only perpetuates both the classical and modern diglossia but also fails to take into consideration the minority mother-tongue languages or dialects for literacy.

After a discussion of some general Indian Government perspectives we will turn to consider four cases, from Narsinghpur, Bihar, Delhi, and, in the south, Kerala.

5.3. *General Indian Considerations and the National Literacy Mission*

Agnihotri, Khanna *et al.* (1991) point out that, although the Indian education budget has improved slightly since 1989, the government has spent eight times as much on defence as on education since 1980. The relatively high defence expenditure has been justified in terms of frontier wars with China and Pakistan, and persistent internal unrest in, for example, Telengana, Jharkhand, Nagaland, Assam, Jammu and Kashmir, and The Punjab. In a society which is hierarchically organized and in which the officer corps of the army and of the Indian Administrative Service (IAS) have always been near the top of the hierarchy, and where access to literacy and knowledge has traditionally been restricted to an élite, these events have helped to relegate issues of literacy and health and hygiene to the background. Traditionally, Indian society has transmitted knowledge, whether philosophical or practical, orally. It was only with the growth of trading activities that the importance of literacy surfaced.

The Indian government, looking at rising illiteracy caused by a number of factors including the fact that population increase outstripped any increase in the number of literates, launched the National Literacy Mission (NLM) in 1988. The aim was to gain 80 million more literates in the 15–35 age group by 1995, with a functional literacy defined as self-reliance in literacy and numeracy. According to Indian census figures (and all such figures must for a variety of reasons be treated with extreme caution and scepticism), the literate population rose from 61 million in 1951 to 247 million in 1981; but during the same period the non-literate population rose from 300 to 437 million. Apart from population growth the ministry has blamed inadequate school and adult education programmes and inadequate work done in them, but also the relapse into illiteracy of those with no incentive or opportunity to maintain their literacy. In 1989 there were reported to be 278,000 adult education centres in the country, with an enrolment of 9 million people, but of these it was reported that only 5 million became functionally literate.

The NLM programme involved a new strategy, for which the first two years of the seven are spent in preparation of mass campaigns, instead of working through existing schools and institutions. A limited period of time is set within which there has to be large-scale mobilization of educated youth—students and volunteers from the community—in an environment of enthusiasm within which they can take upon themselves the responsibility of improving literacy levels.

5.4. *Aims and Methods of the NLM*

The Director-General of the National Literacy Mission, Lakshmidar Mishra, described the *raison d'être*, aims and methods in an article, 'Literacy—Now or Never' in 1990:

Today, we are confronted with . . . 450 million illiterates in all age groups . . . Of this, about 100 million illiterates are in the 15–35 age group which is considered to be the most productive age group crucial to the task of national reconstruction. This number is constantly on the increase and by the turn of the century, [India] will have the single largest number of illiterates in the whole world.

Evidently, no nation can put up with such an ignominious situation. This, therefore, becomes a matter of national conscience . . . The need for and the rationale of mobilising student volunteers . . . arises out of the following considerations.

The students . . . are full of patriotism and have a genuine . . . urge for community service. They are unsullied by the corrupting forces around them . . .   (Mishra 1990: 4–5)

There follows a rather vague explication of the 'each one teach some' methods to be used and the illiterate populations to be targeted; of the cooperation desired between the volunteers, the government agencies, the banks, and the business sponsors; of the disadvantaged rural workers, especially the women, who make up the majority of illiterate adults; of the social and economic benefits which will accrue to them when they can demand the legal minimum wage and freedom from purdah practices and so on. The tone of the article becomes that of a crusade, truly a 'mission'. The volunteers will need

empathy and sensitivity . . . patience, tolerance and fortitude . . . Training must equip the volunteers with life-skills and communication skills . . . with the tools and techniques of establishing a total identification or rapport with the learners . . . the end being individual and social transformation. This cannot be brought about by any single . . . agency and far less by the Government. This will have to be a collective effort of those who believe in the . . . relevance of literacy and . . . view literacy as a tool or weapon for social change. (Mishra 1990: 21)

Nowhere in the article is the question of the vehicular languages for literacy addressed, but there are rather mystical references to 'language':

each member of the target group is important for the mission. We need to approach them, talk to them in the language of their soul which is intelligible to them, talk to them in the language of predicament and try to identify ourselves with their laughter and tears, it is only when we succeed in doing this, some rapport may be established and they may treat us as part of their being and not as outsiders . . . when such understanding . . . is generated, they will feel naturally and spontaneously drawn towards the teacher-learning process. And the interest generated can be sustained only this way.   (Mishra 1990: 21)

There is no recognition here of the fact, well authenticated elsewhere, that very many of the potential 'learners' are far too exhausted after long hours of menial work for starvation wages to have time or energy to spare for what seems to them the irrelevant luxury of literacy classes. (Britons may be reminded of the tones in which Mrs Thatcher once appointed the successful entrepreneur Richard Branson to mobilize the residents of British cities to pick up the rubbish in their streets. It was a very short-lived initiative, an attempt at political kudos on the cheap.) Of the NLM Choudhry (p.c.) wrote:

VTs, or Voluntary Teachers, no longer show the same enthusiasm as when the NLM programme first got underway, as was shown in surveys in July 1992. They had joined with the hope of economic incentives or of state recognition; a majority were disillusioned as neither incentive nor recognition was forthcoming. A majority of them are unemployed educated youth. In West Bengal the exceptions were those VTs who belonged to the SFI

(Student Federation of India), the youth wing of the Left Front government in power. They did not express any dissatisfaction, either in hope of government recognition or from fear of what the government might do.

5.5. *Narsinghpur*

Narsinghpur is a rich agricultural region lying between the cities of Jabalpur and Sagar. The remnants of a feudal system are still dominant. Sadhna Saxena, who today works with the National Institute of Adult Education in Delhi, in 1977 had organized literacy classes for adults and children in a few villages of a neighbouring block of land. These classes met with fierce opposition from the landed élite, who physically terrorized those who tried to attend, and abused the organizers, claiming that literacy would rob the landlords of their workforce. Since then, the landless labourers and the small farmers have begun to organize themselves.

When recently the Chief Minister of Madhya Pradesh declared Narsinghpur to be totally literate, Saxena took the opportunity to go with an evaluation team as an observer. Volunteers had been recruited at village level to run one class each, and schoolteachers released from their normal duties for a year to supervise the classes and train the volunteers in five or six villages each. At the end of the year there had been a good deal of media hype about the achievements.

Saxena found instead that the volunteers had mostly withdrawn from the campaign; they had not been paid the promised stipend, and the hoped-for follow-up jobs in government had not materialized. The teachers themselves had had to bear the brunt of the campaign, and had not been consulted before the Chief Minister made his claim—it was a wholly political act without any of the scientific evaluation ostensibly required by the NLM.

The evaluation team and the observers were taken to a showpiece village where adults and children who had learned the answers by rote were asked prepared questions by the head teacher. All visitors were taken to the same village and given the same performance. The teachers were demoralized by the falsity of the promises made and the shams imposed upon them, with which they had to fall in or risk losing their jobs. They felt constrained to observe caste barriers in their classes. The observer was in one village discouraged from visiting the houses of low-caste people who had claimed that no literacy classes had been held; the project officer dismissed this claim on the grounds that these were 'loose women'.

In this village most of the beedi factory workers had come out from the nearby town in search of work, and were in fact already literate and interested in and agitated about getting education. They were nevertheless being exploited by the factory owners, being paid less than they were entitled to. They could no longer see the point of being literate if they were still to be so cruelly exploited, contrary to what the publicity slogans proclaimed. The teachers had to battle with all the adverse social influences, and teach classes of reluctant and tired workers in the evenings. In Muslim areas there was the added problem of purdah keeping the women away.

Saxena concluded that the district was nowhere near total literacy, and that even if the NLM pumped in more money and ran a more vigorous campaign it would not become so. The false claims were felt to belittle the workers who had tried so hard to achieve something. 'The constraints of the socio-political and economic structure of our rural society reduce the concept of total literacy to a myth' (Saxena 1992: 13). Traditional oral literature thrives, but owes nothing to book learning. Studying such cases might lead to a better understanding of why literacy programmes do not make much headway in the Hindi belt: 'In this kind of fragmented, feudal and caste-ridden society, where main economic activity is agriculture . . . the kind of commitment, outlook, sensitivity and political under-standing needed to deal with such situations cannot be generated overnight by official fiats . . . The poor and the backward caste people are not accessible easily and at the village level there are forces working against them all the time' (Saxena 1992: 11).

5.6. *Bihar*

The report from Bihar (Verma, in *Abstracts* 1988) presents a very similar situ-ation. As elsewhere, education through the schools is free and compulsory, but the schools and institutions have had a monopoly of education, and literacy is seen as inalienably part of the school process and not as a skill which can be independent of education. The language of education is Hindi, although the mother tongues of most of the people are actually Maithili, Bhojpuri, and Magahi —government agencies treating these as identical with Hindi.

Bihar society is very traditionally and hierarchically structured, with the old caste system modified to some extent by the hierarchy of government appoint-ments available to those who are literate and educated to the required level.

Many adult literacy programmes in Bihar have had no sustained success, because, among other things, of the lack of motivation that adults feel to become literate themselves; rather, they would concentrate on the importance of their children getting the appropriate certificate of education to open up the possibility of a non-menial job.

In addition, bureaucratic apathy pervades the whole system. Perhaps plans made in Delhi or in the state capital cannot be implemented for some reason in the target rural areas—in which case the plans may simply be shelved by the lower bureaucracy, or a report sent back to the planning authority through slow bureaucratic channels. Materials for literacy—books, paper, pens, etc.—are not readily available; if they are made available, they may be misappropriated. The language of the books supplied is not really the language of the people.

The agricultural landlords who dominate the rural areas can see no need for literacy among their workforce, and may see the programme as a possible political or caste threat. The piecemeal attitude towards societal literacy by the planners, which ignores the other social needs of the society, generates corruption and keeps the people unmotivated. In these respects the situation is similar to that noted in rural West Bengal.

5.7. *Kerala*

A high literacy rate in Kerala is actually not a new phenomenon. We list below some of the reasons such as maritime trade connections. In addition to a centuries-old tradition of Brahminical scholarship in Sanskrit, both oral and written, the ruling family made Malayalam versions of the ancient Indian epics which circulated from the sixteenth century; the merchant classes and state administrators kept records in Malayalam; they had extensive contacts with Arab and other Muslim, Jewish, Syrian Christian, and Portuguese traders; and, according to Gough (1968), almost all the men of the merchant classes and a high proportion of Jewish and Christian women appear to have been educated in at least simple Malayalam, arithmetic, and the rudiments of religious knowledge. In the early nineteenth century the benevolent rulers of the two smaller states which later formed Kerala enacted a series of important landownership reforms. The lack of beggars and the high rate of literacy go back a long way. Sun Shuyun (1992) drew attention to the importance of the matrilineal social influence: 'As early as 1896, the progressive maharajas of Travancore introduced free primary education for girls and children from all lower castes . . . But the real explanation lies deeper—in the power of Kerala's women . . . As the Keralans say: "if you teach a man you teach one person; if you teach a woman you teach a whole family."'

Today it is noticeable in southern India that a wide range of attractive reading material is available, and is read. Kerala contrasts with Bihar in a number of ways. Until mid-1991 it had a very left-wing government; a Dravidian vernacular—Malayalam—used as the official language of the state and the medium of education; and a claimed literacy rate of 100 per cent. In this last respect it has been linked with other left-wing countries where egalitarian enthusiasm and the political will to achieve high rates of literacy have led to a claimed high success rate. Castro's Cuba, Sandinista Nicaragua, China, the former USSR: in each of these states a historical period of great left-wing proselytizing during which universal education has been seen both as an egalitarian good and also as a route to releasing the dormant creativity of a large but poor population has led to high claims being made for literacy. The case of China is discussed elsewhere in this book (Chapter 8), and for detailed study of the proselytizing atmosphere and its effects on the claims made for achievement we cannot do better than refer to Jung Chang's (1991) extraordinary autobiographical account *Wild Swans*. For the moment we may just note one of the limitations of the Chinese achievement, the conflicts of interest created in that country in the new atmosphere of encouraging capitalist enterprise within a communist state: the peasant now farming for his own profit preferring to keep his children at home to help on the farm rather than letting them go to school; the vast migrations of peasant population to the cities and the new economic zones in search of work and needing some of their literacy in Chinese to help them survive in environments where the spoken language may not be their own.

Agnihotri *et al.* (1991) have suggested that among other factors that have contributed to a high level of literacy in Kerala have been the following:

(*a*) the physical location of the state—its long ocean shoreline, its long-standing maritime links overseas; fertility, favourable rainfall, etc. (although at present an area of high unemployment);
(*b*) a matrilineal social structure assuring women of their economic security;
(*c*) early Christian mission activity in schooling;
(*d*) the activities of present-day voluntary organizations such as the KSSP.

KSSP—Kerala Shastra Sahitya Parishad, or the Association for the Preservation of the Literacy Heritage of Kerala—is a self-funding organization which has campaigned to help ordinary people struggle for their rights and has intervened not only in school and adult literacy programmes but also in their homes, by taking to them books and pamphlets written in Malayalam, in association with their own literacy work. In collaboration with other voluntary organizations it organized Bharatiya Jan Vigyan Jatha, a nationwide movement to create social and scientific awareness.

Thus, in contrast with Bihar, here in Kerala we seem to have an example of literacy being seen as an essential part of a political self-help and self-improvement movement. Of course, there have been many parallel movements among working people in many countries at many periods of history, including the formation of the Workers' Educational Association and the Cooperative Movement in Great Britain in the nineteenth century. They have been widespread in India. They played their part in India's struggle for independence from the British, and today play it in trying to free the Indian peasantry from the exploitative triumvirate of money-lenders, traders, and landlords, and in fighting social evils and bringing fresh vigour to the rural peasant villages and the rural economy. B. Pavier (1986: 136–7) records of that movement that: 'Part of the programme in the liberated areas was a literacy programme which was certainly the first time that the peasants and workers would have had any chance to read and write. Illiteracy had been one of the instruments and symbol of their degradation—now they were acquiring skills that had been the preserve of their rulers.'

P. Sundarayya was himself active in this same movement; he writes (1972: 128): 'many illiterate persons in the squads etc. were able to read newspapers and books after a few months. Because of the political consciousness, many were ready to learn and they did it in quite a short time. This could be done successfully because it was looked upon as a political task.'

More recent Indian history has seen a number of such socio-political movements, politicizing discontent among both agricultural and industrial workers, and trying to establish self-help measures with often foremost among their aims the establishment of literacy centres, libraries, and schools among socially disadvantaged groups. The achievements of some of these groups have in the short term been remarkable, carried along by the enthusiasm of those involved; the problem has been in sustaining them over a longer period unless tangible economic gains can be seen.

It is clear that in Kerala the left-wing orientation of the state government once contributed to the comparative success of literacy programmes by harnessing such enthusiasm. However, it has always been difficult to find motivated volunteer teachers and other helpers. Since there is now, since the Gulf War, massive unemployment, some people have agreed to work for various voluntary organizations for rather small wages. This has given them the opportunity to gain some work experience; in addition, some school and college students have been very happy and proud to be associated with such voluntary work. Since the literacy centres have been informally monitored by the local people, and also visited regularly by dignitaries and officials of the government, the young instructors have been keen to excel in their work. Women taking part have come out of their cloistered surroundings and improved their self-confidence.

5.8. *Delhi*

When we turn to Delhi we find the Ambedkar Nagar Experiment setting out to emulate the Kerala model. The least-literate part of the Delhi population, with a literacy rate for the 15–35 age group of 55.7 per cent for Ambedkar Nagar as against 79.5 per cent for this age group for Delhi as a whole, is concentrated in the resettlement ('JJ') colonies of Ambedkar Nagar, Mangol Puri, Nand Nagari, and Jahangir Puri. There is a long history of sustained exploitation behind the formation of these 'JJ' colonies—millions of rupees having been spent to create what are in fact ghettos of poverty, crime, and unemployment. (In this respect, of course, Delhi is little different from many other large cities, worldwide.) The Delhi State Committee of the Bharat Gyan Vigyan Jatha (BGVS—'All India March for Science and Literacy') and the Ministry of Human Resource Development decided to form the Delhi Saksharta Samiti (Delhi Literacy Mission) to eradicate illiteracy from Delhi over the next five years. Following the Kerala model, they decided to adopt a campaign-based approach involving intense community participation. Before launching the actual teaching programme it was decided to motivate learners, school students and teachers, members of the community, and its leaders through street plays and songs, poster exhibitions, and on-the-spot poetry and painting competitions.

Social Consequences and Political Philosophy

Agnihotri and Khanna interviewed nearly 100 learners on the programme. The experiment was then only a few months old, and it was difficult to make any valid generalizations from their observations. It was clear that the members of the Mission, in collaboration with a large number of governmental and voluntary organizations, had succeeded in involving the community in its literacy drive. In a place like Delhi, where the rental value of even very small rooms is very high, many people had willingly donated space, rooms, furniture, etc. for literacy work. A large number of the teachers came from local schools and colleges. They also participated actively in preparing and producing teaching materials. Most of the people interviewed felt that the general atmosphere of the neighbourhood had improved considerably—gambling, 'eve-teasing' (i.e. pestering women), drinking, wife-beating, petty crimes, and so on had declined. Many women with the help of Literacy Mission volunteers succeeded in convincing their husbands that going to literacy classes was a worthwhile exercise. Many women felt that learning to read and write improved their interaction with their children. They could also shop and travel about more confidently. It was with a sense of great pride that most volunteer teachers talked about their role in bringing about a change in the social milieu of the neighbourhood. A considerable part of this overwhelmingly positive response to the Mission must be set down as the initial exuberant response to the momentum built by intense social interactions, door-to-door canvassing, street plays, and so on. We shall have to wait to see if over the coming years there are any lasting and sustained consequences of such a campaign-based 'mission for literacy', or whether these initial responses are as transitory as many religious conversions.

Agnihotri and Khanna (1992b) feel that there are several aspects of the Indian social structure which *could* be exploited in the interests of literacy. The extended family unit and the network of rights and obligations it subsumes might go a long way in sustaining literacy initiatives. There is also a philanthropic streak in the Indian social ethos; people of quite modest means may sometimes happily join in by making rooms, furniture, materials, and so on available. They report (Agnihotri *et al.* 1991) that the current thrust of the NLM is to abandon all centre-based (or institution-based) programmes in favour of the campaign approach. Admirable though the harnessing of enthusiasm undoubtedly is, it is difficult to avoid the conclusion that literacy schemes which rely upon this strategy without doing a great deal more to create employment and alleviate poverty are a cheap escape route from social responsibility. If there is a political philosophy involved it seems to be that literacy itself will help to generate greater prosperity by leading to better job qualifications, entrepreneurial activity, greater social confidence, greater social mobility, a route out of the ghetto.

But similar schemes elsewhere have not solved the underlying unemployment, poverty, and exploitation. Without capital resources to draw on, entrepreneurs

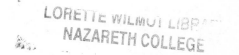

are undercapitalized and cannot survive, or are driven into the arms of the money-lenders, even if their enterprise is only selling ice cream. If jobs are available and literacy is a requirement, then the school system is failing if it cannot meet the needs. To say that is not in any way to decry the Delhi literacy initiative.

All the instruction was for literacy in Hindi in the Devanagari script. For those who came from elsewhere—the Tamil-speakers for example—the classes were lessons in Hindi as well as in literacy, which was a possible bonus for them. There appears to have been little demand for instruction in any other vernacular; the 'function' of literacy was how best to cope with one's surroundings. It is clear that the level of literacy aimed at or in prospect is scarcely such as to lead to the spread of radical ideas, and that unless the efforts of the unpaid or low-paid volunteers really are sustained over a much longer period than is usual—over the full five years of the programme at least—the political and social and economic fallout may be small. Were the level of literacy achieved in fact much more advanced and employment still not available, the programme might be helping to create a more explosive situation than already exists.

The Indian economy has been state-dominated, a mixture of private enterprise and nationalized industries, currency controls and controls on overseas investment. Since independence there has been massive state investment in industry, behind a protective tariff wall. In 1991 the government had to borrow a total of $US4.5 billion, taking its foreign indebtedness up to $US71 billion. At the end of February 1992 the Finance Minister, Manmohan Singh, announced a new and liberalizing budget. According to Reuter's correspondent in New Delhi (London *Independent*, 3 Mar. 1992) he 'eased open India's state-dominated economy . . . proposing to allow some free trade in the rupee for Indian foreign-exchange earners, to simplify taxation and to attack the black market by legalising the demand for gold. He cut public sector subsidies, proposed more sales of shares in profitable state firms and made modest starts on banking reforms and opening stock markets.'

Surendra Rao, of the National Council of Applied Economic Research, claimed that the budget was the most dramatic in India's history, and would release a lot of energy. He added the comment that the left-wing politicians had a valid complaint in that the budget did little for the 40 per cent of Indians living in poverty: it posed long-term dangers in the world's most populous democracy. Many opposition politicians, intellectuals, and students have complained that this liberalizing economic policy would virtually sell the country to the multi-national corporations. (In the case of somewhat similar economic measures taken in another country with a high rate of population increase, Mexico, although risk capital is now expected to flow back into Mexico and greatly strengthen the country's manufacturing and financial base, it will not necessarily do very much for the vast army of the very poor and unemployed, since modern industry is capital-intensive rather than labour-intensive. The few jobs that are provided by

a new industry are likely to be for quite highly qualified technicians and managers; basic literacy is quite inadequate.)

The one area in which fairly basic literacy may make a difference is in family
planning and population control; obviously this is a critical area for governments, but people living in subsistence economies have children to provide for
their old age.

The Government of India seems to be caught in an all-too-familiar trap. The
unity and integration of the country—multiethnic and multilingual and multifaith
—and the defence of its borders require high expenditure, with the result that
there is not enough to provide for adequate education; thus the population continues to increase at a greater rate than literacy and employment; the illiterate
population will continue to increase as long as it is caught in poverty and without adequate education, in a society which has no great need for additional
unskilled labour.

Within such a context, debate about the efficacy of education in 'the mother
tongue' as contrasted with a language not used in the home comes to seem very
academic. Possibly every effort should be made to use mother-tongue television
and radio programmes to get the family-planning message across. The vernacularization of literacy, however, may well continue to be a political issue in support of minority movements for recognition, as already in the case of Maithili in
Bihar, Rajasthani in Rajasthan, and for some of the tribal languages.

6. AFRICA

6.1. *Post-Colonial Africa*

In Chapter 7 the motivations and attitudes affecting the success or otherwise of
literacy campaigns are addressed in relation to four former colonial countries of
Africa: Kenya, Tanzania, Nigeria, and the Central African Republic (CAR), with
a glance also at its neighbour Cameroon. Here we will be concerned with the
political and economic aspects of the colonial hangover, in particular with those
African states of la Francophonie, comparing them with the former British colonies. Cameroon today provides us with a convenient bridge between the two groups
of states, since it incorporates a formerly British as well as a (much larger) formerly French sector. (The subject of Cameroon Pidgin English is discussed in
Chapter 6.)

The argument most strongly urged in favour of a revolutionary as opposed to
an evolutionary approach to social change is that the matrix of the old social order
must be smashed so that it does not persist in the institutions and stereotypes
of the new. A complaint frequently heard about the educational hierarchies of
the post-colonial states is that they are the old hierarchies with some new faces.
The new have been educated by the old, and share the cultural stereotypes and

know-how of the old regime; and as long as they go on using the language of the old regime this state of affairs will persist. Malaysia and Tanzania are two examples of states which have tried to switch their education systems wholly into an indigenous language of the new state—Bahasa Malaysia and Swahili respectively—using this switch as a major part of a programme to correct what were seen as pre-independence social ills (although of course the language used is in a symbiotic relationship with, rather than being the root cause of, those ills). Generally the former colonial powers have tried to cling on to political influence and economic advantages by fostering education in the medium of their own languages. In the British case they sedulously promote examination systems as an export; for example, the Cambridge Local Examinations Syndicate runs English-language examinations, widely used and recognized by the Education Departments of former colonies and accepted as entrance qualifications for English-medium universities all over the world, while the British Council organizes 'Trade Fairs' abroad to attract fee-paying candidates into British colleges and universities.

The cases of Nigeria, of Tanzania, and of the CAR are discussed at greater length in Chapter 7, although we must also mention them briefly here. But no former colonial power has exported its cultural stereotypes about education more for its own advantage than France, and here we will compare Senegal, Cameroon, and the CAR within the framework of la Francophonie.

6.2. *La Francophonie*

La Francophonie is an informal organization of states in which French has some official status or is in acknowledged use. (A government office for it, attached to the prime minister's office, was established in Paris in 1992.) In a speech in 1974, Valéry Giscard d'Estaing spoke as follows:

There is an interdependence between the economic power of a nation and the radiation of its culture. I mean interdependence advisedly. This means not only the material presence of a nation opens the way to its intellectual presence but also that this, in turn, thanks especially to the vehicle of language, contributes to economic dynamism on world markets. This is why the radiation of French culture in the world must be ceaselessly reinforced and extended. This is why this linguistic and intellectual community one calls Francophonia must be considered an essential element in our political policy.   (Battye and Hintze 1992: 55, from Gordon 1978)

Battye and Hintze continue: 'The success of *la Francophonie* is . . . perceived by speakers of French as a vitally important factor in maintaining the prestige of the French language on the international political stage; it is a living symbol of the perpetuation of France's traditionally important role in international politics. It is also an important symbol of France's cultural and linguistic independence from the English-speaking world.'

Eyamba G. Bokamba (1991) has discussed at length French colonial policies in Africa as they affected education. His is an important study by an Africanist who has been publishing work on language and literacy in sub-Saharan Africa since 1976. He shows how French internal language policies—the unifying of France through compulsory universal education in a standard French, the examination system which has placed great emphasis on showing a command of that French, an employment hierarchy in public life which in turn placed great emphasis on passing those examinations—were exported to the French colonies so that the colonized were encouraged to be assimilated to French cultural values and to take the same view of metropolitan French as the essential gateway to employment and public life. The carry-over of colonial educational patterns into post-independence political and cultural thinking has, as we have said, certainly not been confined to the Francophone countries, but Bokamba shows how much more pronounced the neglect of indigenous African languages and literacy in those languages has been in the Francophone states as contrasted with, for example, the former British colonies, where generally it was customary for primary schooling at least to begin in the vernacular, and where there are fewer direct subsidies to the education systems which are tied to the use of any particular language.

Bokamba compares the literacy rates, the school drop-out rates, the numbers reaching secondary school and tertiary education in the former French colonies and protectorates in Africa with the figures for the Anglophone countries. He cites at length (from Turcotte 1981: 65–8) the arguments often advanced in favour of the retention of French and the exclusion of African languages from public life, and concludes:

It is precisely this type of attitude that has permitted the perpetuation of the French colonial language policy . . . While there are undeniable short-term advantages, the long-term disadvantages . . . far outweigh the present benefits . . . While initial admission in primary one is open to all eligible children on the basis of space availability, promotion from one grade to another is strictly dependent on the pupil's performance in French. A consequence is the disproportionately high wastage rates found in Francophone Africa. (Bokamba 1991: 190–2)

(It must be stressed that many of the criticisms Bokamba makes—for example, the forced reliance on a parrot-like command of rote learning by the pupils— have been made also of former Anglophone countries in Africa and elsewhere —see, e.g., Le Page 1968a: 441.)

6.3. *Senegal: Literacy in Wolof and the Other 'National Languages'*

Senegal has shared with other countries along the southern fringes of the Sahara (including Northern Nigeria and Northern Cameroon) contact with a much older model for literacy than France: the vast Arabic-speaking empire of North Africa. The importance of Senegal to the Arab slave trade was that it lay at the end of the coastal caravan route around the northern edges of the desert, and this trade was well established in the hands of Mandingo merchants by the time the Europeans arrived on the scene and the French eventually displaced the Portuguese on the Senegal River (see Le Page 1960: 22–3). Today, primary and secondary education in Arabic is on the increase even if it is still subordinate to French, and it is preferred by certain ethnic groups—probably including the Mandingos— who are much influenced by Islam. The Arab states provide a great deal of aid to encourage education in Arabic among Black African communities.

Six African languages—Diola, Mandingo, Peul/Poular, Serer, Soninke, and Wolof—have been declared 'national' languages. University linguists actively engaged in the description of these are agreed about the need to develop them for literacy and education; but the former Directorate for Literacy had very little contact with these scholars. However, the *idea* of teaching in the national languages is gaining ground. But, despite lip-service on the part of the government towards introducing 'les langues du milieu' as media of instruction in infant and primary schools, training teachers, producing materials, and so on, there has been no real political will to get these things done, and, according to Juillard's reports in 1988 and 1990 to the IGLSVL workshops (see *Abstracts* 1988, 1990), at a political level very little has been done.

Experimental work runs out of steam for the usual reasons: lack of adequate preparation and training; lack of sustained support; parental worries about children missing out on French-medium examinations and the passport to a non-menial job. There have been scattered non-governmental initiatives in adult vernacular literacy: by Roman Catholic and other Christian missions using their own rather than the official selection of varieties of Serer and Diola and their own orthographies, and by various developmental agencies such as the World Bank. These are spotty and uncoordinated.

The use of Wolof as a spoken language is spreading throughout Senegal, especially in the towns. (This has long been noted as an urban phenomenon—for example, by Tabouret-Keller 1968: 111–12.) Social promotion was until recently obtained through jobs in the public sector, which demanded proficiency in oral and written French, but today in Dakar there is a new class of prosperous merchants who promote Wolof as their working language. Exogamous weddings, frequent in the towns, and labour migration to the towns, are important factors in promoting Wolof as a general lingua franca.

Juillard, who has carried out sociolinguistic studies in the southern town of Ziguinchor since 1985, points to the economic crisis and unemployment as two factors downgrading the value of education in French there (Juillard 1988). Most young people have no prospect of employment; most will not use their French if they leave school at the end of the primary stage. Particularly in the town (at present not so much in the rural areas) it is Wolof which unites people in their African culture, despite their differences. The Wolof, and those who in the town assimilate to the Wolof, have confidence in their commercial and ethnic success, and do not need (as other ethnic groups have needed) to form an ethnic group association to protect their interests or to push for literacy. It is principally an urban social élite who are interested in perpetuating a system of selection based on proficiency in French. Differences of ethnic origin are being replaced by differences of linguistic identity.

There are some initiatives to promote vernacular literacy. Some are from the Division of Literacy of the Ministry of National Education, which wanted to eradicate illiteracy by the end of the century, starting with mass literacy in the national languages. However, they have been denied adequate resources and lack any effective political support for this. Some initiatives begin in the villages (as opposed to the towns); young people organize and ask for literacy classes; if these contribute to some rural development project, it helps to keep young people from migrating to the towns, but there is no post-literacy follow-up for them.

Some initiatives begin with the various ethnic group associations collaborating with the governor, the local administration, local radio, and so on in a 'national literacy week'. But the enthusiasm generated is difficult to sustain for more than a month or two. Of the ethnic groups which have formed associations, the Soninke are well advanced with literacy projects in their own region (as well as in France itself), while the Diolas, Serers, and Mandingos have also started such projects. It is the Peul (Poular) speakers who are the main competitors of the Wolof, however. They are at the Atlantic end of a chain of tribes dispersed across sub-Saharan West Africa, whose eastern end are the Fula (Fulani) of Northern Cameroon. They have had an active association since 1980, and are strongly represented in the government. Juillard (1988) concludes that competition between the Peul and the Wolof is important for future decisions about the use of the indigenous languages in education and the administration, and that the economic evolution of the country, problematic at present, will be a determining factor.

6.4. *The Central African Republic*

The case of the CAR is discussed in Chapter 7 with particular reference to social attitudes; we refer to it here as another example of the seeming inertia and the persistence of the old status quo within la Francophonie. It is a country of about 627,000 square kilometres, thinly populated by approximately 2.7 million people, part of the former French empire, and surrounded, except to the east, by other Francophone countries. Cameroon is its immediate neighbour to the west, somewhat smaller (475,000 square kilometres) but more populous (c.10 million people). Cameroon subsumes two former colonies: the larger eastern part was French, the much smaller western part British, sharing a frontier and some tribal affinities with Nigeria. In addition to their African vernaculars and their use of French and of English respectively in each of the former colonies or protectorates, they have in common the widespread use in each of an indigenous, originally pidgin, lingua franca, Sango in the CAR, and Pidgin English in Cameroon.

Although they have been described, and used by missionaries from time to time, none of the African vernaculars of the CAR has a sufficiently large population base to appear viable as a language of wider communication within the country. That role is filled in spoken use by Sango, originally a trade or market Central African pidgin which seems to have come into existence in the latter part of the nineteenth century, no doubt partly as a result of increasing urbanization. As early as the 1920s both Protestant and Roman Catholic missionaries were making use of it. It was never used by the colonial French government; instead, it became associated with the independence movement, and since independence in the 1960s its symbolic role has been recognized. Since 1991 Sango has been one of the two official languages, alongside French. It has been used experimentally in education both by the missions and, very briefly, by the Education Ministry. Apart from religious literature, however, there is very little written in it; a grammar was published in 1963 (Samarin 1963) and two dictionaries have appeared so far—Taber (1965) and Bouquiaux *et al.* (1978).

When we speak of 'Sango' we are in fact focusing through the lens of a single name a very diffuse linguistic situation. The nuclear *modus operandi* of a trade language provides the common core for what is variably influenced within a multidimensional space by the African languages of the speakers, especially in rural contexts, and by the French of educated speakers, especially in the capital, Bangui. (The 'KiSwahili' of Tanzania and neighbouring countries is comparable in this respect, if we substitute 'English' for 'French'.) Sango is diffuse over time and generation also, and changing as a result of urbanization and radio use. Although there is a strong sense of proprietorship towards the language in the CAR, there is as yet no stereotype as to 'correct Sango', though the Bangui varieties have prestige for speech. Spoken Bangui Sango may be full of Gallicisms, but educated speakers would prefer to see the written language 'cleansed' of these. There is considerable disagreement as to the 'best' orthography, particularly between those who, like Diki-Kidiri, want to mark tone both to avoid ambiguity between homophones and to mark the 'Africanness' of the language in its written form, and those who feel that the context almost always disambiguates homophones and that marking tone creates unnecessary difficulties for the learner (see *Abstracts* 1986, 1988 for discussion.)[4] Despite its present diffuseness, we

---

[4] Discussion of orthographic problems generally is to be found in Ch. 3 of this volume. Here, however, we may note the arguments put forward by Bernard (1992), which ran as follows: (i) Linguistic diversity and plurality is a symptom of a cultural diversity which is essential to the healthy survival of man as a species. (In pursuing this argument Bernard makes a familiar confusion between the vehicle, language, and what is being carried, the culture, implying that the latter could not be carried except by a particular language.) (ii) Unwritten languages are being lost without trace at a great rate. (iii) It is essential to devise means to get native speakers to write literature in their own hitherto non-literary languages so as to preserve them as both spoken and written vehicles of their culture. (iv) His experiments have shown that this can best be achieved by devising the simplest orthography that native speakers can be taught to use using modern word-processor programmes. (v) His experiments have also shown that the marking of tone for tone languages is an unnecessary complication in such orthographies. (On this point, however, see Baker in Ch. 3.)

must regard Sango as the national vernacular of the CAR, just as we regard KiSwahili in this way for Tanzania, and probably also Krio for Sierra Leone. As with KiSwahili, there is a small, at present, but growing number of native speakers of Sango, many of them the children of ethnically mixed marriages in Bangui. Attitudes towards the use of Sango for education are analysed in Chapter 7.

At the First International Conference on Sango in Cologne in September 1992, Diki-Kidiri emphasized that, while Sango will in time take over occupational functions, that will not be possible until the lexicon has been expanded with the terminologies for modern occupations, and standardized.

By 1990 the Ministry of Education had reached an agreement with the American Summer Institute of Linguistics, or Wycliffe Bible Translators (the initials SIL are reinterpreted in the CAR as Société Internationale Linguistique), that allowed SIL to undertake 'development work' on Sango while at the same time doing work on the ethnic languages. Gerbault commented: 'the notion that initial literacy in Sango might facilitate literacy in French and subsequent learning has never been voiced officially in the Ministry of Education' (*Abstracts* 1990: 10).

A fresh experiment in the use of the language in primary education was due to start in 1993 or 1994, so that perhaps this last comment may be out of date. We must await the outcome of the experiment.

6.5. *Cameroon, and West African Pidgin English*

In Cameroon the large number of African languages spoken, and the existence of several regional vehicular languages such as Fulani in the north, together with the fact that Cameroon has inherited territory and administrative practices from two different colonial powers, France and Britain, create a context distinct from that of the CAR. Cameroon in its western, 'Anglophone' provinces possesses a creolizing 'pidgin English' related to general West African pidgin, which, according to Todd (1984: 96) forms the most useful link language between young and old, educated and uneducated, 'Francophone' and 'Anglophone', 'in spite of the fact that 90 per cent of all Cameroon children are being educated in both official languages', French and English, and that the Francophone provinces make up by far the greater portion of the country. Todd shows the pidgin in widespread use in the Anglophone west, but Carole de Féral (1989) says that it serves as a vehicular language also in some of the Francophone towns. Both Cameroon Pidgin and Cameroon English are susceptible to the influence of French on their lexicons, and Cameroon Pidgin (CP) is also diffuse in the same way as Sango, varying according to the African languages spoken in any locality and to the level of education of the speaker. Todd (1984: 98) distinguishes also between:

Liturgical CP, used by the Roman Catholic church. It is both spoken and written; its orthography approximates to that of Standard English, which makes it look like a substandard version of English.

Grafi CP, the CP of the Bamenda 'grassfields', and the basis of the most widely-used variety today. The Société Biblique used it, with a consistent, phonetically-based orthography, for their translation of St. Mark's Gospel; yet most Cameroonians find it much harder to read than the inconsistent orthography in Catholic translations.

Francophone CP, found in use in the Francophone areas, mostly in Douala and other towns. Mainly spoken, but occasionally written, in a small grammar and in humorous newspaper articles.

Coastal CP and *Bororo CP*, two regional varieties, spoken, each with distinctive grammatical and lexical features.

Makro CP, a secretive urban argot based on CP but using many words from other vocabularies.

CP is spreading at the expense of tribal languages; but, although it clearly has some of the same potential as Sango and some of the same record of use, it has lacked any political symbolism and is nowhere taken seriously in the running as a language of official literacy. Both Yaoundé, the capital, and Douala, the main port and economic centre, are in the Francophone provinces. Official policy is to promote unity for the country as a whole by promoting 'bilingualism', which means in French and English. The political authority has consistently clung to a policy of encouraging either all ethnic languages, or none; in practice this has meant none, for fear of arousing ethnic rivalries and disturbing the fragile hold of the central government. This may be wise bearing in mind ethnic incidents which have occurred since the country was thrown open to a multi-party system in 1991. CP, of course, would at least be free from this disadvantage.

Some moves have been made to encourage research into and experiments in the use of African vernaculars in education. For example, the programme PROPELCA was set up in 1978 'to develop curricula and materials to enable each Cameroonian entering school to read, write and count in his mother tongue, and to express himself in a vehicular language different from his mother tongue, to speak French and English fluently, and read in the two languages at the end of secondary school' (Gerbault, p.c.).

This would seem to be an exacting programme. It has been experimental for primary education in private schools since 1981. At first there were just two participant schools, and two vernaculars taught; by 1986, eleven schools and four languages. But there seems to be no government initiative to carry PROPELCA beyond the experimental stage. Gerbault cites M. Krieger (1991) to the effect that apparently 'Cameroonian multilingualism is safe as an area for research, but too dangerous for research to be turned into policy and implementation.' Those involved with PROPELCA push for greater government involvement and use of the programme, without much success. More than twenty tribal languages now have an orthography, a grammar, and a dictionary, and seventy more are being so described, but literacy in these languages is a purely local activity (see also Féral 1989).

Fear of ethnic fragmentation of the country, each of the fragments focused through linguistic separatism, is compounded by fear among the governing class of losing their privileged status bestowed on them by their French- or English-medium but bilingual education. This fear is very common, not only in post-colonial countries: hence the use of the education system to mould a self-perpetuating élite. The language mould must then not be broken. Meanwhile there seems to be little economic incentive for literacy for most of the ordinary people of Cameroon, and virtually none for vernacular literacy, which would not lead to any job or to any income-enhancing activity or any literature for reading. The economic life of the country remains largely in European hands, and the French in particular wish it to remain so.

There is nevertheless a slowly growing popular literature which links Cameroon with the other West African states in which the pidgin or its creolized indigenized form developed, often alongside a more standard but distinctively local educated English: Sierra Leone, Liberia, Ghana, and Nigeria. There have been active groups pursuing the use of Sierra Leone Krio in drama and written literature, some of which is dealt with in Chapter 6; they have often had to contend with fierce politicized opposition, as have the protagonists of Creole literacy in the Caribbean (see Chapter 2). The situation in Sierra Leone has been described in Jones *et al.* (1992), in Liberia by Singler (1990) and Tonkin (1990); in Ghana, by Sey (1973); that of Nigerian Pidgin English by Barbag-Stoll (1983). Written materials have been produced in each case; the whole coast is surveyed by Holm (1989: sect. 10), and the different varieties have been extensively described.

The respective cultural attitudes of the British and the French, coupled with the history of the slave trade and of post-slavery colonization, were described in Gilbert Schneider *et al.* (1974) to explain the emergence and use of varieties of Pidgin English—but not of a pidgin French—by missions and traders in his *Workbook* produced for the training of American Peace Corps volunteers in Cameroon in 1974. Other descriptions and collections of written materials include Schneider (1960), Dwyer (1968), Todd (1974), and Féral (1989). There is thus no lack of primary written materials as possible models in Cameroon Pidgin, should what Ndukwe has called the 'disassociation syndrome' ever be broken. This might just conceivably happen as a way around the political fears of fragmentation of the country through the support of one or more ethnic languages for education, referred to above.

6.6. *The Former Anglophone Countries*

By comparison with the former French colonies, both Nigeria and Tanzania, each the subject of a special report in Chapter 7, have for a variety of reasons had a head start in vernacular literacy. Indigenous languages had been both widely studied and described by both the Germans and the British, and used in education at least to lower primary level during the colonial period. That does not mean to say that the progress of literacy has not faced considerable problems.

Ayo Bamgbose has been studying and writing about Nigerian—and African —language problems since the 1960s. His book *Yoruba Orthography* appeared in 1965. He is committed to the case for vernacular literacy and argues it at length and in depth in, *inter alia, Language and the Nation* (1991). As we have already noted, not all of his arguments appear valid to us—we will return to them in our conclusion; but he is correct when he portrays the former colonies as still to a great extent the prisoners of colonial practices over the language and the organization of education; there the mould has not been broken:

African countries divide neatly into two groups which reflect the colonial practices. Mother tongue education is not practised in the former French and Portuguese colonies, and this is simply a survival of their colonial policy of assimilation which encouraged their own languages and discouraged African languages. Mother tongue education is practised in the former British colonies (with the exception of Sierra Leone), and this is in accordance with the educational policy of the British which encouraged mother tongue education in British territories. Although the Belgians also encouraged the teaching of African languages in their former colony of the Congo, the country now known as Zaire has . . . opted for education through French.

Where mother tongue education was practised, its role was limited to initial literacy, a medium of instruction at the lower classes of the primary school, and/or a subject at primary and higher levels. Adult literacy was also typically conducted in an African language. This is precisely the prevalent situation in Africa today.   (Bamgbose 1991: 70)

Ndukwe (1984) makes the further point that, even when, in the Igbo-speaking areas which were included in the former East Central State, there had been a policy shift towards giving more time and importance to Igbo, still far greater time and importance were attached to English; and what was actually going on in classrooms was far from being an effective implementation of policy directives. In the teacher-training colleges there was no provision for the methodology of teaching Igbo, while that for English was taught assiduously.

In relation to both Nigeria and Tanzania we must re-examine the concept of 'an African vernacular'. As already noted in the case of India, multiplicity of indigenous languages—estimated at 400 for Nigeria alone—makes the provision of resources for full literacy in all of them a formidable undertaking, and, where choice between them may also be politically invidious, the temptation to settle for a regional lingua franca is very strong. It might be that a greatly improved teacher-training programme for primary-school teachers, led from linguistically very sophisticated university centres, could provide them with the understanding to improvise *ad hoc* 'starting' writing systems on a very small scale without bothering about any prior standardization or other aspects of language planning; but such an initiative-led concept tends to run against the grain of teacher-training in most countries, bedevilled as it is by concepts of 'correctness' and the demands of examination systems; the idea is therefore probably pie-in-the-sky.

Moreover, the needs of at least regional, if not national, unity seem to most politicians to take precedence; and, as we have seen, literacy in a 'small' vernacular often seems to its speakers to be an economic dead end, however much it might be demonstrably a route to faster learning in an international language. In the case of Tanzania the problem has been resolved (if not solved) by the use of the Bantu-based lingua franca, KiSwahili. In the case of Nigeria there are alternative possibilities to be examined: concentration on one of the major regional languages, underlining the regional hegemony of, for example, the Yoruba speakers, the Hausa speakers, the Igbo speakers; or concentration on 'Nigerian English' —a solution favoured by, among others, A. E. Odumuh (1986); or the use of an undoubted lingua franca, Nigerian Pidgin, considered at length by Charpentier in Chapter 6.

Nigeria

Ndukwe (1984) examined two Nigerian languages—one of the Big Three, Igbo, and one comparatively less well-known language of the North, Kanuri. He was concerned with language planning as a contribution to standardization and the imposition of norms for the teaching of literacy. In neither case did he find the outlook very promising. The imposition of norms implies the intervention of some purpose-driven agency in promoting literacy. He referred to (the former) Czechoslovakia as a country in which planning had been very strict and norms rigidly enforced, in contrast with the French Academy which had lacked the means to enforce its norms (although in fact the French examination system has been very successful in this respect). Some ideology about education must drive such efforts. In the present-day UK (1996) a right-wing government, supported by the supposed needs of industry and commerce for clear indices in regular school examinations of 'correctness' in the use of written English, has set its face against the supposed laxity of previous left-wing attitudes towards norms in the written language and is busy reimposing them. Le Page and Tabouret-Keller (1985: ch. 5) examined at some length the stages through which stereotypes as to 'correctness' in language evolve. As we shall see, it is an important feature of resistance to the idea of vernacular literacy that some vernaculars cannot possibly be 'correct'.

   In Ndukwe (1984) neither Igbo nor Kanuri was seen as being well-focused as a written language. Their orthographies were far from being well defined, their vocabularies were standardized only for specialized technical terms; grammar was virtually untouched by standardization. Their speakers were contrasted in one respect: educated Igbo-speakers were reluctant to use their language in public and regarded concern about it as a time-wasting concern with the past, whereas the Kanuri felt fiercely attached to their local dialects and under no compulsion to identify with any prestige dialect.

Nigerian English.   We have already mentioned the solution, favoured by, among others, A. E. Odumuh, of accepting 'Nigerian English' as the best solution for education and advanced literacy, legitimizing what is the *de facto* usage of many classrooms and offices. It would be recognized as a semi-autonomous local mode, although Odumuh acknowledges that it would be difficult to make an autonomous description of it (*Abstracts* 1986)—this is true of all languages in contact situations. Such solutions tend to arouse strong hostility to what is regarded in a very paradoxical way as patronizing neocolonialism. Thus a proposal to prepare a dictionary of Central African French is denounced—there are already dictionaries of good French, why prepare a dictionary of bad French? The Government of Singapore, which has probably devoted more resources per head to resolving its 'language-of-education' problems, in favour of Standard British English, than most other states, has emphatically rejected any local solution, the Minister of Education in 1982 denouncing the 'Caribbeanization' of the language (see Anna Kwan-Terry, Chapter 8 in this volume).

Nigerian Pidgin English.   Nigeria shares with the other former British colonies of West Africa from Sierra Leone to Cameroon a lingua franca Pidgin English. The Sierra Leone variety, Krio, is the mother tongue of about 2 per cent of the population and is in widespread use otherwise. It has a number of regional, social class, and age-group varieties, but has been championed, as noted above, by some writers and dramatists and scholars as a vehicle of literature, of which there is a small but growing amount, both translations and original work. The orthography has been standardized and a dictionary published (see Jones, Sandred, and Shrimpton 1992; Fyle and Jones 1980). The Cameroon varieties are in written use as described above. Nigerian Pidgin has been the subject of a number of studies (see e.g. Barbag-Stoll 1983). It has been made lively use of by the nationally and internationally acclaimed Nigerian novelist Chinua Achebe; in *A Man of the People* (1966) nearly all the characters, from the Minister of the Government down to the cook, can speak it, and Achebe uses it to point up, without comment for the most part, the political and social significance of his characters' words. There is a very small literature and some unpublished plays in it. But the 'disassociation syndrome' would apply very powerfully to the idea of literacy and education in the pidgin—the general stereotype being that almost by definition anything labelled as a pidgin cannot possibly be correct, and education must be targeted towards correctness, whatever some intellectuals may urge about self-respect.

Pupils as Candidates for Employment.   The political ideology driving education policies is likely to marry the need for state unification and cultural standardization with the need for a docile and employable workforce and employment for that workforce, and to raise productivity. This at least is the mould which has been exported by the colonizing countries and reinforced by the policies of such development agencies as the World Bank and the International Monetary Fund. Where the state is itself the largest single employer and the main white-collar employer, the political will for vernacular literacy is likely to be weak. (The Malaysian government, however, has married the political will to Malayize the education system as a whole with that to enable Malays to compete successfully in the economy with the Chinese and Indians, who were until the 1960s the main entrepreneurs. This conjunction of political and economic ends through the imposition of a single medium, Bahasa Malaysia, has proved a winner, although the government has taken care to make ample provision for scholarships for study at schools and colleges in English-speaking countries for approved Malays, who then on their return home form part of a new élite.)

Vernacular Initiatives. Nigeria, however, unlike Malaysia and Tanzania, lacks today any single candidate for the role of most-favoured language group. It is usually referred to as one of the African nations committed to mother-tongue literacy. In his report (*Abstracts* 1990) Ndukwe describes various initiatives towards this end and tries to account for the present uncertain state of affairs. Two strands may be distinguished, as also in Tanzania: an ideological commitment to the Africanization of education, particularly on the part of some university teachers; and a failure of political and administrative energy in seeing that policy decisions are carried into effect. In the background one detects the apathy or vested interests of an English-medium educated élite, and the economic opportunities associated with a command of English.

Current national policy includes the stipulations (*a*) that pre-primary and the first three years of primary education shall be 'in the mother tongue' or 'in the language of the immediate community', and (*b*) the requirement that every Nigerian secondary-school student should offer as a subject one of the Big Three languages and should have as a core subject a Nigerian language and its literature.

There have been a number of research and development programmes which are discussed in Chapter 7 (Ndukwe). Such studies as have been done suggest a preference ranking for the medium in which parents wish their children to be taught to read and write:

English
regional language
mother tongue

Various explanations have been advanced:

(i)   English is used in higher education, and primary teachers have to prepare their pupils for this as soon as possible.

(ii) There is too much reliance in the teacher-training colleges on foreign models of training.

(iii) Inherited colonial practices are still adhered to.

(iv) There is a lack of ideological commitment on the part of government officials, leading to a divergence between policy and practice.

(v) The policy-makers and officials may extol the virtues of vernacular literacy and appear to be fully committed to it in the public sector but nevertheless send their own children to private English-medium schools.

But the economic argument must be a very powerful one. As long as all the people with the best jobs in the government and in large corporations expect to operate in English, aspiring parents will want to have an English-medium education for their children and it may well be difficult to convince them that the best route to that is through a vernacular-medium primary school unless the quality and preparation of its teachers are clearly outstanding.

Administrative Weaknesses. In the absence of overt political bias against vernacular literacy, maladministration seems to be the main enemy, as of the social services in general. Odumuh (1992) has described the gulf that separates government pronouncements from achievements. The government's vocabulary, he says, is dominated by such attractive phrases as 'Health for All by the Year 2000', 'Food for All by the Year 2000', or 'Education for All by the Year 2000'. There have been attempts by government to 'wipe out illiteracy completely from every nook and corner of Nigeria'. Campaigns were mounted to educate citizens about the dangers of illiteracy, especially about its negative effects on national development efforts. The citizens responded by sending their children to school and themselves attending evening classes in large numbers. And yet in December 1991 the Minister of Education, Professor Aliyu Babatunde Fafunwa, in an address to the first forum for the Post Primary Teaching Service Commission, drew a depressing picture of mass illiteracy and of education 'in a mess' because of a yawning gap between policy decisions and implementation. Oil revenues, squandered in the boom years, were now diminishing, while school populations had increased rapidly; the Local Government Education Authority Decree 3 of 1991, which reversed a decision of 1988 and made Local Government Councils wholly responsible for primary education, had created confusion and despair. The job opportunities to which literacy was supposed to be the gateway did not exist.

During the oil-boom years there had been a tremendous expansion in higher education—from five universities in 1969 to twenty-four in 1988 and thirty-one federal universities by 1992. In addition there are state-owned universities, polytechnics, advanced teachers' colleges, and colleges of education. In most of these, English—in practice, Nigerian English—is the medium of instruction. This huge apparatus fails to provide sufficient well-trained primary-school teachers.

Universal compulsory primary education has been the national policy since 1976. Today Nigeria has 14 million children in 19,000 primary schools employing 350,000 teachers—nominally, an average of forty children to each teacher. There have been many political initiatives; there has been since 1981 the switch to a mother-tongue literacy programme. But what looked like promising progress has, in the Minister's words, become 'a mess'. Some blame has been placed on the switch to mother-tongue literacy itself. Odumuh and others would like to see more emphasis placed on literacy in Nigerian English. But, he says, the comment of a weekly Nigerian news magazine on the health programme can be equally applied to education and literacy efforts: these are victims of 'a well-known game of statistics. Progress is measured in arcane figures designed to impress. There is more noise than achievements; more promises than fulfilment . . . there are no patterns, no goals, no ends, save cheap political ends' (Odumuh 1992: 14).

Thus the weakness of genuine and sustained political will to achieve the goals set up; moving the goalposts; dwindling resources; inability to face up to solving difficulties in teacher-training and the provision of materials: none of these factors is by any means peculiar to Nigeria, but they have all contributed to setting back what at one time looked like a promising programme to achieve universal literacy in the country using the vernaculars at least as the primary stepping stones. Nor are the present political uncertainties of the country helpful.

A More Hopeful Prognosis. Some 'hopeful signs' are discussed by Fasold in Chapter 7. Here we may note what appears to be happening at the academic level.

Bamgbose (1991: 99–100) accepts that weaknesses in African literacy programmes stem from the poor economic climate and the poor pay for primary teachers, who are also expected to take on the adult literacy classes. He sees hope for the long-term future of vernacular education, however, in the efforts of tertiary education institutions, notably the universities, whose departments of linguistics and African languages have carried out the necessary research and description and are busy training the teachers of the future; so that in Nigeria it is already possible to take not only first degrees but higher degrees also in Hausa, in Yoruba, and in Igbo:

For instance, the first graduates of Yoruba were produced at the University of Ibadan in 1969. All of them went into teaching. Between that year and now [i.e. 1991], tremendous improvements have been felt in Yoruba teaching in schools . . . All the innovations referred to earlier . . . the use of Wolof in primary education in Senegal, the use of Mende, Temne and Limba as media of instruction in the first three years of primary education in Sierra Leone, the use of Cameroonian languages in initial literacy, the Rivers Readers Project and the Six Year Primary Project—owe their existence to the initiative of Departments of Linguistics and/or Education in the relevant universities. The paradox of mother tongue education in many African countries is that while it is negligible at the primary level, it seems to flourish at university level. If any changes are to be expected . . . they are likely to be induced from the top of the educational system rather than from below. (Bamgbose 1991: 100–1)

Tanzania: Historical and Political Background

Political organization and development in Tanzania are both designed and predicated not upon the spread of literacy in any one of the hundred or more Bantu and non-Bantu vernaculars but upon universal education in Swahili, which is what we shall be referring to as 'the vernacular' in this case. To quote Abdulaziz (1971: 164): 'Swahili has played a very significant role in the development of political values and attitudes in Tanzania. Its integrative qualities have influenced the style of Tanzania politics, especially its non-tribal and egalitarian characteristics. All movements of national focus have used Swahili as an instrument for achieving inter-tribal unity and integration.'

The history of the use of written Swahili in East Africa goes back to Arab contacts with the coast over a period of several hundred years and the consequent use of an Arabized Bantu lingua franca by the people of the coastal and Zanzibari settlements, the Swahili. Its use written with a Roman orthography goes back to the Christian missions of the second half of the nineteenth century, and its official status to its use as an administrative language by the German colonial government before the First World War, and by the British. As a lingua franca it has the great advantage of its structural and lexical similarities to the Bantu languages of the region. Between the two world wars the British administration and the Christian missions set up an East African Committee to standardize written usage as far as possible in the British-administered territories of Kenya, Tanganyika, Uganda, and Zanzibar, and the Institute of KiSwahili Research in the University of Dar es Salaam inherited and has carried on the work of that committee.

In the face of the multiplicity of Bantu and Nilotic vernaculars, Swahili was the obvious choice to help unify a newly independent country in 1961, when it was declared the national language. It had long been a trade language, used along all the trade routes from the coast into the interior. The concomitant disadvantage is that there are as many varieties of Swahili as there are vernacular languages among its users. It has been the medium of all government primary-school education since the 1960s and the official plan, whose implementation has recently had to be postponed, has been to make it the medium of secondary education also and to provide for tertiary education in it. The Institute of KiSwahili Research and its associated bodies have been charged with the tasks of standardization, of creating the necessary technical lexicon, producing a dictionary, and so on. There has been no doubt of the political will behind all this, led by a president, Julius Nyerere, who has himself translated *Julius Caesar* into Swahili.

Ten years later, and thirty years later.   Russell's report to IGLSVL (*Abstracts* 1990: 111–15) considered 'the concept of development and the vernacularization of literacy' in relation to Tanzania. Many of the points made have economic and political significance.

She refers to the policies which stemmed from Ujamaa, or 'cooperative living', the underlying philosophy of the party led by Julius Nyerere which took power at independence. These included the collectivization of the rural population, previously scattered, in villages, and the political organization of the population through village, district, and regional committees to the Central Committee of the government. 'The assumption was that everyone involved in decision at every level of political organization . . . would be competent in Swahili—spoken and written' (*Abstracts* 1990: 113).

Assumptions were also made, contrasting with those of a Westernized urban society, about the meaning of 'development'—not in terms of conventional economic indicators, technological advance, individual wealth, but in terms of the ethnic traditions of East Africa, minimizing cultural and technological dependence on the industrialized world and concentrating on improving the lot of the majority of the population. Instructions as to how to achieve these aims and harness the work of individuals for the common good were circulated from the centre in the written Swahili of discussion documents meant to be discussed in every village—but these documents were in fact very little understood in many villages. Russell quotes Von Freyhold in a passage which she says seems to 'encapsulate some of the major problems involved in the acquisition, maintenance and function of vernacular literacy in rural developing areas, particularly in highly multilingual states such as many of those in sub-Saharan Africa' (*Abstracts* 1990: 111).

In one of the new villages which Von Freyhold had visited in 1971 when the adult literacy campaign was just starting:

Some villagers, including youths, could barely speak Swahili, and illiteracy was very high . . . There was also a need for political education. The chairman and secretary had attended a leadership seminar held in the division, and when they came back they read the Mwongozo [policy discussion document] to the villagers, but the villagers complained that they could not understand it because of the difficult Swahili. In any case the chairman by his actions contradicted many of the conditions both of Ujamaa and of the Mwongozo. (Von Freyhold 1979: 155)

Thus, in the case of Tanzania at least, the ideal of democracy taking the form of discussion, at each political level, of policy documents written in 'the national vernacular' has not been achieved.[5] This failure has been adduced by Russell as among the important reasons for the failure of the 1979 villagization policy, and for some of today's concomitant political and severe economic difficulties. In implementing collectivization an unrealistically heavy burden has been placed

---

[5] Definitions of literacy, of course, vary from the barest ability to sign one's name to one of reading and writing and of understanding written material in the target language. Definitions of 'democracy' vary, as we have already said. The Tanzanian democratic model might have worked better if there had been a highly educated teacher in each village able to read and understand policy documents written in the sophisticated KiSwahili of the centre and to translate and explain them in the rural vernacular. See Arnove and Graff (1987: 21–8) for discussion of the general problems, especially p. 21: 'Literacy itself is too often viewed in only a dichotomous way: either a person is literate or not. But literacy may also be viewed along a continuum: a set of skills that may become more complex over time in response to changing social contexts, shifting demands on individuals' communication skills, or individuals' own efforts at advancement. Only in Tanzania did the campaign actually define as many as four levels of literacy acquisition that involved increasingly more complex uses of reading and writing skills.' Clearly, four levels were not enough.

on the written language, which is in any case, like written Batua in the case of the Basques, not only not anybody's native language written down (even for those people who are native speakers of Swahili), but very much a language and style created by the educated coastal urban élite. Aspects of the style are frequently blamed on their English-medium advanced education, using as it does an English-like rather than a Bantu-like syntax. As for the technical lexicon: Mwansoko (1990) in his research tried to establish how far from the centres of dissemination the use and understanding of the terms sponsored by the Institute of KiSwahili Research extended; penetration into rural areas was very limited.

The 1991 Report.   Carr-Hill's 1991 Unesco report on the efficacy of literacy campaigns in Tanzania, discussed and enlarged upon in Chapter 7, assesses the functioning and effects of the Tanzanian literacy programme after a mass adult literacy campaign had been in progress for twenty years. It was based on systematic studies in four locations reflecting a variety of socio-economic environments. It throws up several marked parallels to the case of Nigeria. The first is the unreliability of given statistics. Reports made to the government about the success of the campaigns in attracting, retaining, and teaching learners proved to be very misleadingly 'optimistic'—in one case having to be described as lies. The second is the importance of teacher-training, teacher motivation, and rewards. The third was the importance of the socio-economic environment, and hence the motivation of the learners in each location, to the degree of success achieved.

In spite of the strong ideological commitment of the government, it appears that the campaign has declined substantially since the enthusiasms of the seventies. The teachers were ill-prepared, and paid very little. They had no infrastructural support, and most were heavily involved in earning income elsewhere and little effort could be expected from them. Most of the participants saw little connection between literacy and their development problems. 'Compounded with the economic crisis, this had led to a general lack of motivation among both learners and teachers' (Carr-Hill *et al.* 1991: 319).

7. LATIN AMERICA

Archer and Costello (1990) report on fieldwork in eight Hispano-American countries: Bolivia, Chile, Ecuador, El Salvador, Guatemala, Honduras, Mexico, and Nicaragua. In each country, locations—three in the case of Nicaragua, one in each of the others—*barrios* with poor communities, were studied in some detail in regard to efforts to release the people through cooperative self-help from gross political and economic oppression. Communicative skills were among the aims in each case, although in some instances television and radio assumed more importance than literacy. To a large extent it was assumed that literacy and education would be through the medium of Spanish. There are, however, several case histories of attempts to achieve literacy and education through the medium of an Amerindian language.

7.1. *Guatemala*

One such case is that of the Mayan Mam of Guatemala—a country in which the Hispanic settlers and their descendants have been practising genocide against the Indians since the sixteenth century; 'massacres of whole villages became a standard counter-insurgency tactic' (Archer and Costello 1990: 137) both for the contemporaries of the missionary Las Casas and up to, during, and since Le Page's fieldwork in Belize in the 1960s and 1970s (Le Page and Tabouret-Keller 1985). In most of Latin America both the economic and the political oppression have been propped up by economic and political agencies of the USA. In Guatemala, 'the only government to have attempted any serious land redistribution, that of Arbenz, was overthrown in a US-backed coup in 1954. Since then, anyone referring to land reform is branded communist by the landed elite and suffers at the hands of the military' (Archer and Costello 1990: 136).

The Mam have been progressively deprived of their lands, but the community studied, in Cabrican, have resettled themselves on poor mountainous land where they have maintained their language, beliefs, and customs, working the land and the limestone quarries on a communal basis. There is a small two-streets-and-a-plaza Spanish-style town with two Roman Catholic churches on a ridge overlooking the Mam villages; in the town, the Mam are second-class citizens, and the schools taught only in Spanish until 1987. In the early 1980s the national literacy programme was committed to the hispanicization of the children and of their national identity.

In 1986 a new 'democratic' government took over from the army, although the army continues to absorb 75 per cent of the national budget, and education only 2 per cent; power effectively remains with the army and the landowning élite. Nevertheless, in 1987 a semi-autonomous organization (CONALFA) was set up to design a literacy programme. The emphasis has been very much on 'functional' literacy—programmes designed to help combat, for example, soil erosion, or maize pests. The enabling law ostensibly offers the choice to the speakers of literacy in Spanish or in their own indigenous language. There is a parallel programme (PRONEBI) of bilingual education for children, set up with donations and loans from USAID. 'The syllabus includes literacy in Mayan languages, maths, oral Spanish and civic education' (Archer and Costello 1990: 141).

However, the underlying racism, corruption, distrust, and fear continue, as in other parts of Latin America; and the poverty of the provision made for the implementation of PRONEBI intensifies the suspicion of the Mam that the whole programme is operated for the benefit of *los ladinos*. 'PRONEBI has had little impact. The Ministry of Education supervisor told us that recently he asked for a bilingual teacher and was sent one who spoke Quiche, another Mayan language

... as unrelated to Mam as French is to Greek. In one village school there were two PRONEBI-trained Mam teachers. They admitted that they were being used to teach children Spanish so that they were not too far behind when they joined first grade' (Archer and Costello 1990: 143). One rural teacher found he had 150 children in his class. In general, the covert aims of the programme seem to have been the integration of the Mam into *ladino* culture and the Spanish language. For some of the Mam this became a desirable end; for others, it was destructive.

A more productive and creative programme seems to have been that of Radio Mam, using a transmitter largely funded by Oxfam. It was found that the community did not want to use it for programmes aiming at literacy in Spanish; instead 'what was necessary was a cultural reclamation to combat the racism of the *ladinos* by using the radio to promote Mam culture' (Archer and Costello 1990: 145). The transmissions were in a mixture of Mam and Spanish. People became no longer ashamed to be heard speaking Mam in public. Discussion groups were organized around educational radio broadcasts in the villages; the discussions were recorded and themselves broadcast. But when the 'disappearances', political arrests, started, the groups were too frightened to meet. Today there are plans to extend this purely oral education programme, giving the villagers an opportunity to discuss and record and transmit their histories, lives, and problems throughout the Mam community. We will return to the point of to what extent such programmes make literacy redundant when we turn to Chile; but it is to be noted here that, whereas there are at least seventeen recognized dialects of spoken Mam, work is going on to produce a standard written Mam and educational materials in it, which it is hoped will unify all the Mam peoples in a way which the radio broadcasts cannot.

These activities have been organized by the Mam cultural association ACU-MAM. In addition to its 'radioliteracy' and adult literacy work, the association had, for example, organized the building, on a self-help basis, of a school in the village of Buena Vista. They were sent a *ladino* teacher by the Ministry of Education, but insisted instead on having their own Mam teacher. The Ministry did not recognize her; the villagers therefore paid her themselves. When the fieldworkers visited the school, all of the sixty children knew and could write their own language. Thus democracy at the local level both stimulates and is made possible by pride in and literacy in the local language. 'The focus of ACUMAM's work is the rejection of the colonial language, Spanish. What they are attempting is the creation of a regional alternative, to develop Mam as the main local language in order to force the state's recognition of Guatemala as a multi-ethnic nation. Literacy is one of the first steps' (Archer and Costello 1990: 149).

Conflicting Unities—Local, Regional, National; Class and Community

We see, in many of the cases that we are examining in this chapter, conflicts of identity, of political and economic interest, of group unities, having expression in the linguistic symptoms of the interaction between individuals and groups (as provided for within an *Acts of Identity* theoretical framework) and between local and regional and national groups, rural and urban groups, and so on. In the case of the Mam, Archer and Costello set out the arguments for and against the strategies adopted by ACUMAM. Clearly 'the state's recognition of Guatemala as a multi-ethnic nation' has the obverse implication of recognition of Guatemala as the state legally enshrining the powers of that nation—in other words, ACUMAM does not represent a separatist movement; it does, however, set out to enable a Mam population literate in Mam to organize itself independently of the Spanish-using government. Secondly, ACUMAM's 'radioliteracy' programmes are effective by coordinating the use of broadcasting and written materials. But 'some political groups have argued that a cultural reclamation strategy is divisive: there are at least 21 different Mayan languages so that to promote regionalism in Guatemala is to create a cultural isolation of each group that can easily be exploited by a unified, ruling, Spanish-speaking élite' (Archer and Costello 1990: 149).

This argument only has power if literacy and education stop at literacy in Mam; the argument against it is that 'of course' one must go on to make provision for literacy in wider regional standards, Standard Mam, Standard Maya, and then for national unity and interaction through Spanish; but that, unless one *first* provides for literacy and self-identification through the mother tongue (in this case, Mam), the wider unities are built on sand on an inherently non-democratic social fabric, within which most of the population will be doomed to illiteracy and non-participation. On the other hand, it is argued, expecting people to become literate in three languages—mother tongue, regional, national—sets them too hard a task to be achieved *en masse*, and sets the state too hard a task in organizing the teaching resources and providing some of the motivation, particularly when the instincts of the ruling élite are in any case anti-democratic and anti-Indian. (Some of these arguments are rehearsed by Laitin 1992, see especially chapter 6. He argues for what he calls a '3±1 language outcome', a stable language outcome that gives an important role to indigenous languages in the state-building activities of post-colonial Africa.)

7.2. *Bolivia*

In their discussion of the case of the Aymara nation, in Bolivia, 'the third-largest Indian nation in the Americas', Archer and Costello (1990: 170–1) again confront a conflict of unities, this time between social class unity and racial unity:

Despite the limitations of CDA's [Centre for Self-manager Development's] work, it is clear that their policy of teaching literacy in Spanish is more popular amongst the women of El Alto than the teaching of Aymaran. Those who learn to speak the language of power at least have the tools to be able to assert their rights. But it is by no means simple. Behind the language of power lies a culture of power, embedded in a social and political system that dominates and exploits the Aymaran people in a way that can be described in both race and class terms . . . [But the CDA has a vertical, centralized structure.] At the *barrio* level there is a low level of active participation . . . Individual women are given individual skills but are not encouraged to organize or assert their rights. As a result, none of the CDA women in El Alto has succeeded in joining the local councils of each *barrio* . . . The Aymaran people have become guinea pigs for those who want to organize their communities for them . . .

7.3. *Chile: By-passing Literacy through the Broadcasting Media*

Nearly all of the initiatives for communal self-help in the *barrios* studied by Archer and Costello have literacy, though only rarely literacy in anything other than Spanish, as a prime aim.[6] In the case of Chile, however, the major initiative they describe is one using television to break what Paulo Freire had called the culture of silence by which people are prohibited from creatively taking part in the transformation of their society. The prior written literacy campaign is illustrated from the work of the TAC (Cultural Action Workshop) with, among others, the women of a populous *barrio* of Santiago, Lo Hermida, who had formed themselves into a self-help movement after Pinochet's *coup* in 1973 and the subsequent economic depression, and with the help of the local church had set up a laundry as a source of income. However

For all its successes, TAC's use of literacy work to recover culture and strengthen organization faces the serious problem of lack of motivation . . . The written word doesn't play a big role in urban daily life because other forms of communication have displaced it. In *barrios* like Lo Hermida, television is everywhere. While only half the homes have a sink for washing dishes, four in every five households own a television. Average television viewing in Santiago is 28 hours a week.   (Archer and Costello 1990: 118)

It is against this background that the arguments for and against the educational, and also the propaganda, values of television are put. Against the fears of the educators that television undermines reading is set the argument that people can be helped to 'read' television critically, and can be helped and can train themselves to make use of the medium constructively. Something akin to the processes of training in practical literary criticism is envisaged. Accordingly, a group known as PROCESO (i.e. Legal Process) began making videos in 1982; a research group of academics known as CENECA (i.e. Centre for Cultural and Artistic Research and Expression) had already since 1977 been monitoring and evaluating the national media, which since Pinochet's *coup* had been under control of the military; but now, videos were made and shown on a local basis. In 1985 PROCESO and the women's group MOMUPO (i.e. Popular Movement for Women) made a documentary about the history of popular women's organizations under Pinochet. It became widely seen. From this beginning, networks of

---

[6] Since this was written, Richard Gott (1995*a*, *b*) has reported at length on the astonishing rate of popular conversions by numerous evangelizing Protestant sects in Chile, and in Latin America generally, with an accompanying cultural Americanization.

do-it-yourself television groups have grown up, supporting human-rights groups and helping to educate them in evaluating what they see on the television screen. In the 1988 campaigns for the referendum as to whether Pinochet's term as president should be extended, TELEANÁLISIS (now called Nueva Imagen) and PROCESO were able to make sophisticated use of their constitutional right to some access to national television in order to swing the vote decisively to NO. Not unnaturally such movements are seen as a threat by the ruling élites.

We have seen political use being made of videos and television in India also. We must try to take stock of the media revolution in relation to the basic postulates about democracy set out at the start of this chapter. Where the television and video revolution has taken hold, clearly it has enormous potential to influence both political and economic processes; clearly also the language medium used on television influences the language of those who watch it; and clearly, 'education' in these circumstances needs to include training in a critical ability to 'read' television images just as much as to read books and newspapers.

It has been represented to us that a combination of pictures and spoken words does not necessarily communicate messages more effectively than the written word. This is partly because the written word has a longer life, and moreover is not readily discarded by illiterate people before they have found somebody to tell them what it says. But, more importantly, illiterate people may also have great difficulty in interpreting pictures, just as some highly literate people have difficulty in 'reading' strip cartoons. In the West, children's books tend to be lavishly illustrated so that children learn to interpret pictures as they learn to read. In culturally rich but economically poor societies like India, or even Haiti, children also have plenty of opportunity to learn to interpret images as they grow up, but this is in many African countries not the case. Even if every village in Uganda were to have a public television set, a successful anti-AIDS campaign on television would have to take account of the way the public interpret images they see on the screen (Baker, p.c.).

The political health of nations, and the economic and physical health of people, may well depend upon them becoming critically aware of manipulation through images. The act of making videos for themselves seems to foster self-confidence in political and economic debate where it has been tried in Latin America.

7.4. *Nicaragua*

The Caribbean Coast of Nicaragua

In contrast to some extent with the Mam of Guatemala, one of the effects of the much-praised Literacy Crusade of 1980 in Nicaragua was to reinforce demands from the 'Atlantic' (Caribbean) coastal Creoles and Miskito Indians and other indigenous peoples for autonomy. These demands must be seen against the declared intention of the Vice-Ministry for Education after the Sandinistas took

power to use post-primary education in Spanish as a unifying instrument throughout the country.

The main literacy campaign, carried out in the five months up to late August
1980, was in Spanish, the vernacular of the urban communities. The agents were
primarily middle-class urban students of both sexes enrolled in six 'brigades'
totalling more than a quarter of a million who went to live and work among the
campesinos. The claims made for success were considerable (as they had been
also in Tanzania in the 1970s and in Cuba in the 1960s): illiteracy reduced to
about 13 per cent of the 'teachable' adult population (i.e. those without any mental
or physical disability for learning); urban and rural populations integrated through
the contacts, through shared knowledge and understanding; young people committed to a new revolutionary future; the status of women very markedly raised;
mass organization (and hence democracy) strengthened; an indigenous publishing industry established. (For a discussion of all these aspects see Arnove 1987.)
A follow-up campaign in 'English', Miskito, and Sumo, as the main languages
of the Caribbean coastal peoples, was intended to help integrate them into the
country-wide community.

The sociolinguistics of the Caribbean coast of Nicaragua is fairly comprehensively dealt with, in historical and more recent terms, by John Holm (1978, 1989).
As in Belize (see Le Page and Tabouret-Keller 1985) and Honduras, the close
contacts between Indian tribes of the Miskito coast and English- and Creole-
English-speaking maritime 'interlopers' into the Spanish-Central American empire
must be seen in the context of Spanish hostility towards those contacts going
back to the British conquest of Jamaica in 1655 and lasting right up to the present claims of Guatemala to the territory of Belize. There has also been among
the Spanish-speakers a high level of general ignorance about the nature of the
indigenous Indian languages and of Miskito Coast Creole. Holm quotes a Spanish description of the latter as 'el inglés de los piratas del siglo diecisiete'.

Arnove reports (1987: 280) that:

Many of the indigenous-speaking people who opted to acquire literacy in Spanish did so
in order to participate in national institutions and communicate with the rest of the
country. It also appears that the more pro-Sandinista inhabitants were those who sought
literacy in Spanish.
By the end of the National Literacy Campaign, there were still a substantial number
of *costeños* who were illiterate and who preferred to participate in literacy classes conducted in English, Miskito and Sumo. Over 12,500 people participated in and completed
the indigenous campaign, which took place between October 1980 and March 1981.

By recognizing vernaculars other than Spanish the Sandinista government
hoped to lay the foundation for a programme of unifying 'revolutionary' education in Spanish once immediate vernacular literacy had been achieved. In spite
of the very careful efforts put into the 'indigenous' campaign, however, one outcome was that a Miskito leader used it to promote demands for autonomy for the

coastal people; when he was arrested in 1981 for threatening the unity of the country, many of the Miskito Indians withdrew from the campaign. When he escaped to Honduras in May 1981, many Miskitos went with him, and the Honduran–Nicaraguan coastal border became a war zone and a base for the 'Contras', many of whom were Miskito Indians.

The Nicaraguan process illustrates the point made by Agnihotri and Khanna (see above, Section 5.1), that the significance of literacy lies in its potential as a tool of change rather than being itself the reason for change. The major change was the ousting of the tyrannical and corrupt president, Somoza. The attempts to rally the whole population behind the Sandinista government through revolutionary education in Spanish had something of the effect that Franco's hispanicization drive had had in the case of the Basques and the Catalans: the focusing of the opposition around alternative linguistic identities. Something of the same effect was achieved in Belize (see Le Page and Tabouret-Keller 1985) by the external threat to the newly independent country from Guatemala: the focusing of the population around a new 'Belizean' identity, speaking Creole and literate in English.

The Nicaraguan Revolution and the Literacy Crusade as a Whole

The lesson that Archer and Costello drew from their detailed examination of political and economic developments in Nicaragua since 1980 is that (as has often been observed) a successful revolution necessarily contains the seeds of its own destruction, and that the literacy campaign was what watered the seed. In so far as the crusade and the programmes which followed it were successful and led on to a generally higher level of education among the people, it was they who in turn voted the United Nicaraguan Opposition (UNO) into power in 1990 with 54.7 per cent of the vote, the Sandinistas gaining 40.8 per cent:

The vote . . . was not one of uneducated, manipulated masses; that would have been a failure. Rather, it was an educated, pragmatic vote by people who understood the international arena enough to know that the crisis would not end while the Sandinistas were in power . . . Any attempt by the new government to dismantle the democratic structures established by the revolution will be met by strong opposition from the same people who voted for UNO. On the other hand if a democratic path is followed then the revolution is far from over. The struggle for the survival of popular education [as opposed to traditionalist, school-centred education] mirrors the struggle for the survival of the revolution. (Archer and Costello 1990: 53)

The vote for a UNO government as a peace-bringing solution must be seen against the background of the devastation, economic hardship, and loss of life caused by the US-backed counter-revolution, and longing on the part of many for the more stable and traditional institutions which are part of what is remembered from pre-revolutionary days, just as there are longings today in the former USSR for what are thought of as the old communist certainties.

8. SOME TENTATIVE CONCLUSIONS

A comparison of the case histories of this chapter shows each to be unique in some part of a complex of factors: ethnic or racial, geographical, demographic, political, religious, economic, and in terms of cultural history and beliefs. In the chapters which follow, some of these relevant factors are examined in greater detail.

The caveat with which we opened must be repeated in any summing-up: in many of the countries which we have not considered, and in some which we have, political and ethnic and economic and religious turmoil is at present so great that academic prognoses about literacy are likely to remain academic; and the academic community, with its Unesco and other conferences, resolutions and recommendations, seems frequently to operate in a sealed world. Under warlords, education of all kinds whether for self-realization or social good is a casualty; in time of drought and famine and forced migrations there are relatively few Josephs. Former President Bush's new world order, and the authority and potential of the UN, have disintegrated in a general despair. Television and radio are the nursemaids of this despair; people do not need to be able to read to experience it. Illiterates do not need to be able to read to operate Kalashnikov rifles, though the gun-makers may need to. Rather similar feelings were expressed by the monks of Peterborough as they wrote up their vernacular Chronicle for the reign of King Stephen in twelfth-century England. But these monks provided most of what education was available, transmitting knowledge about the world to subsequent generations who outlasted the anarchy. It is our own task to be acquainted with the past and to turn a clear critical and imaginative eye upon our own time.

In spite of the multiplicity of factors involved it is economic motivation which appears the most powerful in affecting vernacular literacy—for the landlords and moneylenders and rulers and priests who may feel threatened by it, the entrepreneur publishers who wish to exploit it, or the poor illiterates who may need it or prefer some other skill for their survival or advancement. Most societies can show us some rich or powerful illiterates as well as many literates who have remained poor. Literacy is to some extent a by-product of prosperity and this makes it appear to many the only escape route from poverty at least for their children; whether vernacular literacy will provide as effective an escape as literacy in some other language is often a puzzle, so complex is the interplay of conditions. Moreover, the political and religious and economic realities can change so dramatically that one generation's answer may seem useless or irrelevant to the next, as has happened with the current large-scale population movements and the collapse of seemingly impregnable regimes.

What is certainly true is that a literate vernacular, replacing a previous language of dominance, is often, as with the Basques, the leading banner around which those seeking a power base focus nascent ethnic identities and nationhood. Yet in spite of the very considerable efforts made among the Basques, the Welsh, the

Irish, and the Scots to encode national identity in their languages, labour migration and the economic pull of other languages make their successes seem very limited and temporary while their nationalism and hunger for power becomes more threatening.

There are at least two nascent developments which we have not been able to discuss in this chapter but which are likely to have profound political and economic implications for the future of mass literacy. The first is the shift of industrial and hence also political power to the countries of the Pacific Basin, in particular to China. The second is the development of the women's movement in many countries, but in particular in India and the other countries of South and South-East Asia and Latin America, perhaps the most important political development of the new millennium.

2

Social Contexts Conducive to the Vernacularization of Literacy

LAWRENCE D. CARRINGTON

with contributions from H. Devonish, R. W. Fasold, J. Gerbault, C. Juillard, and E. Tonkin

I. INTRODUCTION

Vernacular languages can remain unused for literate purposes for either *technical* or *societal* reasons. Technical reasons would include lack of a writing system, or of a standardized spelling system, or of linguistic descriptions that would allow ready development of these. Societal reasons would include the demographic and structural and political characteristics of the community, the legal status and political and economic affiliations of its languages, the attitudes towards them of members of the society, the educational processes, and the availability of literacy instruction. In this chapter we seek to identify the contexts that might be conducive to the vernacularization of literacy by focusing on the societal interfaces between literacy and vernacular languages. Of course, technical factors eventually become part of the societal discussions, but here we recognize their suitability for separate treatment with limited reference to the social environment.

For purposes of this discussion, it is best to work with a neutral definition of literacy as a skill that allows the creation and interpretation of written records. This is necessary because implanting literacy within non-literate environments is complicated by the ways in which views of literacy in such environments are entangled with the associations it bears in literate environments. There is a widespread unstated assumption that the applications of the skills of literacy should be similar wherever they are introduced; this thinking certainly pervaded the 1953 Unesco monograph. To free ourselves of the pre-judgements it would be appropriate to invoke Gudschinsky's definition of a literate person. She writes (1968: 146): 'That person is literate who, in a language he speaks, can read with understanding anything he would have understood if it had been spoken to him; and can write so that it can be read, anything that he can say'. Her definition compresses into a single quotable statement the critical element of reciprocity between oral and written competence together with scrupulous neutrality in respect of the area to which the skills of literacy are applied. For these reasons, the definition is applicable to any culture.

Part of the reason for the assumption that the applications of literacy should be similar wherever it is introduced is that literacy is not generated anew in each cultural or linguistic environment but tends to pass from one society to another. For a society to have a method of writing, it must either develop a method itself or adopt one—usually also adapting it. Most societies that use writing have adapted systems from other societies. Although today it is less likely than in the past, the notion of writing may not have existed in a culture until it came into contact with another that had writing. The notion of a community having one language as its oral medium and another, of limited oral distribution, associated with writing is therefore not unusual. What may be less common is the adoption of the technology of writing *without* the adoption of its vector language. It has, however, been historically common for a writing system to be adapted from a vector language for use with a hitherto unwritten vernacular—for example, from the Semitic languages to Greek, from Greek to Latin, from Latin to the Germanic languages, and so on.

In many ways, the coming of literacy to a society has resembled the coming of television. Television penetrates a receiving culture as a message system long before it surrenders its technology. Its messages are embedded in its technology sufficiently deeply for there to be an enduring assumption that the only permissible messages are those that accompany the importation of the technology. Manipulation of the technology as a neutral medium to convey messages created by the borrowing or penetrated society is a later development, and its products frequently suffer unfairly by false comparison with the imported material. Technologies circumscribe their application much more sharply when they are transferred into new cultures than when they do in the culture of origin. Often, the technology may not be *used* so much as it is *paraded* by the receiving culture. In like fashion, literacy and writing systems transferred from one culture to another trail their baggage behind them. It has been common, for example, for literacy to be part of the baggage brought by religious missions and to have remained for a time confined to religious writing before being adapted for secular indigenous purposes. The functions to which literacy is applied in the receiving culture do not readily change from those that it had in the vector culture. One might look at the connection between literacy and education systems. Contemporary literate cultures show a strong bond between literacy and education. It is often assumed that education did not exist before literacy and is impossible without it. It is further assumed that literacy will fulfil the same functions in any new environment into which it is introduced, chief among them being 'education' in the same sense as before, whereas we know of many cases (for example, among eighteenth-century Efik traders in Nigeria) where literacy has been acquired directly from and in order to trade. Television itself has been widely used for educational purposes, sometimes bypassing literacy, sometimes as a direct spur to the acquisition of literacy, as in a recent BBC campaign.

We might use the term *adoption of literacy* where the purposes of literacy are transferred from the vector culture. In this case, literacy can become a mechanism for unwelcome cultural impositions. *Vernacularization* ought to transcend these limitations and empower the receiving culture to decide its own agenda, assigning importance to functions that may be different from those in the vector culture. Writing down a prior oral literature, without being rebuked for sacrilege (like the Anglo-Saxon monk who, having written down pre-Christian lays, was asked 'What has Ingeld to do with Christ?'), would be one example. Sometimes, as with the transcription of collections of folk tales, this activity has preceded general literacy.

A parallel set of principles influences comparisons between languages of non-literate cultures and languages of literate cultures. The functions of language in the latter are assumed to be necessary in the former. We can observe the proposition that a given language 'may not have a vocabulary sufficient for the needs of the curriculum' (Unesco 1953: 50). The proposition carries with it the notion that a universal curriculum exists independently of the language culture in question and that the purpose of education is to implant that curriculum. When the University College of the West Indies was first established in Jamaica in 1948 it was under the tutelage of London University, and it was assumed that the content of the curriculum should be that of London. It has always been a common feature of colonial education that it has exported to the colonies the curriculum of the colonizers. Indigenization has often been a very slow process. Study of the 'classics' has usually meant Greek and Latin rather than native mythology, even in the Congo.

Clearer thinking might prevail if literate and non-literate cultures existed separately from each other. However, they do not; they frequently occupy the same geographical space, coexist within the same political units, and interact within the same economic networks. Equally often, they relate antagonistically to each other, with literacy itself as one of the contentious issues. Understanding the contexts in which vernacular literacy might flourish calls for a delicate appreciation of the case-specific interactions of favourable and unfavourable factors. It demands that no rules of thumb be created or dogmas adopted but that judicious informed experimental approaches to the processes of the vernacularization of literacy be developed within any environment where the technical supports are available. In what follows, we shall examine some considerations that would determine the contexts conducive to vernacular literacy.

2. THE SHARED LANGUAGE

In those most favourable cases where the literate and the non-literate members of a community already share the same language, with no very considerable dialectal differences between them, no technical problems arise and there is little question of needing to standardize the vernacular before spreading literacy from the minority to the majority. This was the case of Spanish in most of Nicaragua before the major offensive to establish literacy after the Sandinista overthrow of the dictator Somoza, or in Cuba before Castro's revolution.

However, the notion of 'sharing the same language' can be the subject of dispute. It may be challenged by reference to the differences between the norms of the written language and its spoken form on the one hand, and those of the oral, vernacular culture on the other, so that the two tend to be compartmentalized as separate entities (as is often the case in the Creole-speaking West Indies). It may be that the former literate élite have cultivated as a norm a 'High' written style (in the terms of Ferguson's 'diglossia') far removed from that of plain speaking, so that the use of spoken norms for writing is stigmatized as 'ignorant'. This, according to Gwyn Williams, was the case in eighteenth-century England (see Chapter 1). However, there is little doubt that in those environments where both the literate and non-literate share the same language or languages of literate reference (that is, languages generally recognized within the community as ones to be used for writing), where the wider spread of literacy in a language of literate reference would not meet competition and resistance from other languages, positive community values may attach to that spread. Indeed, the distinction made earlier between the *adoption* and the *vernacularization* of literacy may be irrelevant here. The applications of literacy may then be determined by other considerations—for example, the need for a literate labour force, or electorate, or for an army or an administration depending upon mass literacy for the spread of knowledge of general importance. Today, of course, some of these latter functions are performed to some extent by broadcasting and films.

3. THE PERCEPTION OF LITERACY IN THE VERNACULAR AS IMPORTANT

We move to the more common type of case in which the literate and non-literate do not share the same language. Among the principal considerations would be the absolute necessity for a community to perceive literacy in its vernacular as valuable. Ideally, the controlling group in the society should share that view. Fasold (*Abstracts* 1990) makes the point in respect of US Vernacular Black English and he sees the principle as having relevance to what he cites as 'Fourth World' languages, using a concept from Rigsby (1987: 360). Fasold represents Rigsby's formulation of Fourth World as consisting of 'indigenous dispossessed minority peoples encapsulated within modern nation states'. The 'modern nation state' (i.e. the controlling state) may be a First, Second, or Third World state. The group referred to as Fourth World is characterized as having no realistic hope of sovereignty and as conceding that their best path forward is the use of the written language of those who already control the institutions of the society, as would be the case for most speakers of Black English in the USA. But the concept can usefully be extended beyond 'minority' situations. The term can stand, but there are cases where the vernacular belongs to a majority in which similar lack of hope of sovereignty and resignation to the adoption of an alternate tongue would inhibit the pursuit of literacy through their vernacular. Such would be the case of Jamaican Creole, the vernacular of a majority who appear to acquiesce to the dominance of English as a written medium. The cases of the French overseas departments in the Caribbean would also fit. There, the mass of the society enjoys oral competence in Antillean Creole, but it is only a minority of the society that believes vernacular literacy would serve useful purposes. Included in the minority are the linguists and scholars who have elaborated the technical prerequisites to the literate use of the vernacular. However, neither the political directorate nor the masses who might be empowered by vernacular literacy appear to recognize the point of it.

The expression of the views of the masses and those of the controlling minority may be deceptive. The truth of their attitudes may lie behind a façade of agitation on the one part and apparently responsive official action on the other. For example, the fluctuating pressure for political autonomy in the French overseas departments of the Caribbean has been accompanied by agitation for the recognition of the creole vernacular within the education system of each country. In apparent response to this, the French state passed legislation allowing the use of vernacular languages within the education system for a specified range of purposes. Yet, there has been no rush to embrace the opportunity. Those few experiments undertaken have faced a number of factors militating against their success, such as lack of parental enthusiasm, and children dropping out. The legislation permitting and constraining the experiments has reflected the reluctance of the administration to open up the education system in any significant fashion.

In this case the unitary, centralized nature of the French state places ultimate responsibility for such decisions in a metropolis distant from the mass of speakers of Antillean. However, the same explanation cannot hold for Haiti, where similar decisions to use the vernacular, Haitian Creole, within the education system have also been unsuccessful. There, the explanation seems to be that the privileged classes do not wish to change the order of the society. They prefer to maintain the language filter that restricts entry to their class and access to the control systems of the society. Consequently, the state has not pursued the matter with vigour and the permissive decisions could be interpreted as tokenism by the state given its poor record of concern of the plight of the masses. Mistrust of officialdom based on experience is probably also a powerful factor in explaining popular misgivings about the intentions of a policy that would establish the use of the Creole in the education system; it would be seen as fobbing the people off with second best, as being dismissive of them.

Writing about Wolof and other vernacular languages in southern Senegal, Juillard (*Abstracts* 1990) makes a pertinent point when she refers to 'the social elite' as interested in reproducing a system of selection through the learning and the knowledge of French. Tonkin (*Abstracts* 1990) comments similarly on Liberia, where the ruling class of repatriates falls into the same category of resisting vernacular literacy, although the languages in question (Gleboe, Kru, and Vai) have established orthographic systems. In respect of Sango, Gerbault (*Abstracts* 1990) expresses the parallel view that the middle and upper classes of the Central African Republic (CAR) are not willing to change anything in the system that produced them; local educators and linguists are among those reluctant to bring pressure on the authorities to promote Sango seriously as a medium of literacy. Such reluctance is not restricted to Africa. It is indeed an almost universal characteristic of educated élites. Obstructive behaviour by the establishment can be triggered even by actions of instrumentalization or concession on a less formal level than vernacular literacy. Carrington (*Abstracts* 1986) provides evidence of adverse responses to a syllabus document that explicitly advocated that the vernacular of Trinidad and Tobago, an English-lexicon Creole, should be a factor conditioning approaches to the teaching of the English language. In the 1950s there was a good deal of resistance on the part of the (then) University College of the West Indies to the idea that cognizance should be taken of Caribbean Creoles when setting and marking examination papers; the proposal was seen as 'lowering of standards'.

There is little doubt that resistance to vernacular literacy can be high among the privileged classes of a society and rationalized by them in a variety of ways, as we see from some of the Indian cases cited in Chapter 1, but it may also be high among the lower classes and among the non-literate themselves. The non-literate and other members of a society marginalized by not sharing competence in its dominant language frequently demand access to the dominant language and to literacy in it in preference to literacy in their own vernacular. Given the choice between primary education in their own African languages and in English, many Kenyans moved their children to the private schools claiming to be 'English medium', however poor the teaching was (see Gorman 1968, 1971). Many reasons can be suggested. Most important is the economic advantage, clearly illustrated in the shift for demand from French to Wolof as white-collar unemployment has taken hold in Senegal (see Juillard in *Abstracts* 1990: 12–14, 23); next, there is the self-evident advantage of controlling the power language of a society. Apart from the principle itself, there is the fact that the applications of literacy within the society are all associated with the power language. Often also, speakers of other languages in a society frequently have some knowledge of the power language, but they underestimate how much knowledge and effort it takes to use any language at a level that would allow the development of literate skills in it. Consequently, they believe that they are more ready for literacy in the power language than their real skills would allow. The power languages may or may not be the same as the language of economic power, as we see from the case of Basque in Chapter 1; Le Page (1964) also showed how in Malaysia at independence (1962) three languages each had their own power base: Chinese, in business; Malay, in religion and politics; English, in the colonial administration.

English has now been replaced by Bahasa Malaysian in administration and education, but has retained its importance in higher education and the international sphere.

4. LEGAL STATUS AS A NATIONAL LANGUAGE

Literacy through a vernacular language may be favoured if it has the status of official or national language, although not necessarily so where that status is largely symbolic. Whatever level of success has been achieved in Tanzania with Swahili literacy campaigns since 1971 is partly due to the fact that the language had been going through the process of standardization for educational use since the 1930s and was made the national language with independence in 1961. It is, of course, a vernacular only for a minority, mainly the coastal Swahili; elsewhere it is a lingua franca or else a purely school-and-government language (though certainly indigenous). Carr-Hill shows (in Chapter 7) how exaggerated some of the claims made for literacy campaigns in Swahili in the non-native speaking parts of Tanzania have been, especially now that a new 'literary style' rooted in their English-medium education had been evolving among the scholars of the Institute of Swahili Research and the civil servants in Dar es Salaam.

The status of national or official language does not necessarily guarantee that the relevant vernacular will become an accepted medium for literate activity. Gerbault (*Abstracts* 1990), treating Sango in the CAR, draws attention to the lack of action towards accelerating the instrumentalization of Sango in the domain of literacy, although it enjoys the status of official language (see Chapter 4). Similarly, the official status of Haitian since 1987 has not led to significant acceleration of the development of literacy in Haitian. The military *coup* which derailed Haiti's recent move towards democracy has curtailed the possibility of success for the vernacular literacy programme and has highlighted the fact that other factors apart from legal status need to be harmoniously auspicious.

The contrast between the Tanzanian case, on the one hand, and those of Haiti and the CAR, on the other, suggests that real status is achieved when official action confirms an already existing situation in which significant objectives of official recognition are already operationally in place. For instance, the grant of official status to Papiamentu in 1985 in the Netherlands Antilles came long after the literate use of the language was established in several newspapers, in public notices and signs, and so on. As we see from the cases studied by J.-M. Charpentier and his collaborators in Chapter 6, prior literate use of a vernacular may be a useful introduction to a more general literacy.

The decision to accord a language national or official status can be used negatively and may be intended to have effects that the wording of relevant legislation might not suggest. When officialdom does not make decisions on language standardization and related matters, activists in favour of such developments can continue their agitation. When the decisions *are* made, it is more difficult to mobilize efforts to pursue the matter because the rallying point is undermined. Thus, change of status can be used as a political instrument to neutralize those pressing for a change in the status of a language by reducing the rallying power of their cause.

Changing the status of a language can also allow blame for failure to pursue its instrumentalization to be attributed to normal bureaucratic sloth rather than to any official antipathy towards literacy through a vernacular. Failure to execute decisions or to follow up initiatives may have a more damning effect than not making the decisions at all! The point is related to the neutralization of activism mentioned above. A decision can be reduced to pure symbolism by the ways in which a government, or an agency—even Unesco itself—pursues it or fails to pursue it. The Irish Republic's institution of Irish Gaelic as its national language has had the effect of ensuring that it is taught in all schools, but apart from the Gaeltacht—the narrow strip of land along the Atlantic coast where the language is still spoken—the population has Irish varieties of English as vernacular speech and more standard varieties of English as the vehicles of literacy. Writing in Irish Gaelic has not very much general currency. Thus, genuine literacy in Irish Gaelic declines steadily. This state of affairs can be compared with that in the Basque country of Spain, described in Chapter 1. There, the regional government has devoted great effort and funds to try to ensure a general literate currency for the language. Even in the case of Basque, however, the economic pull of Spanish is so great that these efforts are in danger of being nullified. In many parts of the world politicians pay lip-service to the egalitarian ideals of vernacular literacy at international conferences and then find the economic factors too powerful for them to do very much to realize those ideals in practice.

5. CREATING THE ENVIRONMENT

How then do we direct our efforts to create a decent societal climate for vernacular literacy? There is little doubt that a revolution would be a good starting-point. 'History has shown', says Lê Thành Khôi (1976: 125), 'that, up to the present time, revolutionary regimes have been the only ones capable of organizing successful literacy campaigns.' That this claim is not universally true may be seen from the non-revolutionary cases of Scotland and Protestant Northern Europe in Chapter 1 (unless of course one treats the Reformation as a revolution). However, the success of Nicaragua and of Cuba in spreading literacy to nearly all of their populations lends support to this claim. Any period of ideological transformation of a society, such as was created in Tanzania through Nyerere's philosophy, would also be a propitious time to engage in vernacular literacy.

Fomenting revolution (possibly bloody) to achieve literacy through vernaculars raises ethical problems of means and ends. Other means ought to be found.

Three broad strategies for creating a favourable environment for the vernacularization of literacy can be extracted from the cases studied. The strategies are not intended to limit the scope of action in vernacular literacy but rather to provide the most favourable platform for its initiation and implantation. Literacy in the vernacular is a goal worth pursuing only if there are people whose everyday existence can benefit from it. The proposition is virtually axiomatic and it suggests the following as a first strategy:

> Seek and act in those areas of the lives of the users of the vernacular language in which they can recognize that their everyday existence can benefit from literacy in their language.

The strategy is not new. It is an extension of the standard practice of literacy facilitators in motivating learners at an individual level to desire and pursue literacy. However, it must not be interpreted in a static fashion as referring only to the preliterate perceptions of the vernacular speaker. The users of a vernacular, while believing that there is some value in being literate in their vernacular, may not at the outset recognize that value as extending beyond private individual purposes. It is highly likely that they may desire to be literate in their language to read and write private letters or to read a holy book. However, these functions are restricted in that they do not readily lead to communal development of literacy. Initiatives in the vernacularization of literacy must open the possibility for benefits that transcend the original motivators, fostering recognition that the benefits go beyond the individual and expanding the perceptions of the vernacular among the non-literate. The initiatives must accentuate the advantages and implant those perceptions required for success.

In a dynamic interpretation of the strategy, the key issue would be to increase the information available in the vernacular at a rate that expands its concrete utility to its speakers. Hence, reading materials developed to support the venture must go beyond the initially perceived area of application of literacy to create a progressive expansion of the areas in which literacy is profitable. The neo-literates must see themselves as having access to the goods of the already literate society via their own language by tapping into knowledge and information that was previously privileged. Even so, a dynamic interpretation must respect the distinction made earlier between the adoption of literacy and the vernacularization of literacy. Wholesale translation into a vernacular of material available in an established language of literate expression would merely effect a transference of the agenda of the literate to the vernacular society. At the same time, the creation of a separate domain of language use for the newly literate vernacular could undermine social cohesion that is critical for the success of the process of vernacularization. A fine balance must be struck between the agenda of the literate and of the non-literate.

This leads us to a second strategy which can be stated as follows:

Identify and act in areas where the common good for the citizenry is sufficiently uncontroversial that the medium for transmission of messages is not seen as threatening by the literate social establishment.

This strategy finds persuasive exemplification in Carrington (1988*a*). Within the context of Antillean French-lexicon Creole, he identified news and information dissemination, agricultural information, and health education—which should, of course, include hygiene, diet, and sex education—as the areas for vernacular action before, or in close association with, literacy initiatives. He considers that the state has a responsibility to equalize access to information by deliberately communicating in the vernacular with both the literate and the non-literate on topics that are readily identifiable as non-partisan and beneficial to all. In essence and beyond his example, the benefits of vernacularization to both sectors of the society must be clearly established. We have noted that the literate social establishment is willing and able to sabotage the processes of vernacularization. It is imperative, therefore, that the areas in which the initiatives are attempted should not threaten the literate establishment so overtly that they are curtailed before they justify their continuation.

We can state a third strategy associated with the identification of areas for action:

Seek and exploit the pathways by which the relevant vernacular has been filtering into the linguistic domains that are primary domains of the official language.

Using the case of Jamaica as a starting-point, Devonish (1992) favours, as one strategy for instrumentalization, imitation of the pathways by which creole languages have been shown to enter public or formal domains. He draws attention to the functions to which literacy is put by literates whose dominant language is Jamaican. These citizens have control of the concept and the mechanics of writing; they apply those skills to their vernacular to effect written communication with readers having similar skills and language exposure. They write signs offering goods and services and inviting participation in the activities of the dance hall and other popular entertainment. The application of literacy to the vernacular is also in evidence in the writing-down of vernacular songs and 'dub' poetry. Devonish considers such literates, with little formal exposure to English, to be a potential vanguard in the application of writing to the vernacular and he argues that the evolution of vernacular literacy should be guided by the functions to which they put their writing skills. In his view, the entire process of vernacularization of literacy should focus on helping them in a process on which they have already embarked, making use of their limited exposure to the written form of the 'High' (in diglossic terms) variety of their vernacular. (This process is, of course, made easier where the vernacular is commonly felt to be a variety of the standard language already written, so that something similar to the same orthography can be used and recognized. The songs and poems of some published Jamaican writers such as Louise Bennett have created a model in this respect for less literate poets and casual signwriters.)

Related to the matter of infiltrating the domains of the official language is the issue of whether developmental action in vernacular literacy should be initiated in domains that are within the control of the state or outside its control. The issue is important because it can affect the status of the language in question. Starting with a discussion of the Creoles of Jamaica and Nicaragua, Devonish (*Abstracts* 1990) suggested that, in the Caribbean, any effort at language planning should aim at improving the efficiency and effectiveness of the vernacular language usage in the domains *outside the control of the state*. In contrast to this, Carrington (1988*a*), discussing Antillean (French-lexicon Creole), argues for the process of vernacularization to exploit domains that fall *within the control of the state*. The strategies proposed here straddle both these avenues. Their formulation allows them to override the importance of the question of whether one attempts vernacularization in domains inside or outside the control of the state. It may be, of course, that what is being advocated by Devonish will be seen as partial literacy, the creation of a new diglossia; it is necessary to ask whether contexts conducive to this will also favour the uses preferred by Carrington.

The strategies suggested here are quite prosaic and appear to lack reference to the deeper psychological reasons for attempting vernacular literacy. Whatever the psychological impact of literacy on an individual and on a population, the cases examined show that the motivation to be literate, whether in one's vernacular or in another language, does not derive from the deeper psychological justifications. Preliterate people would not be conscious of those justifications and have to be drawn to literacy by more practical considerations.

The creation of a favourable environment for the vernacularization of literacy cannot be based exclusively on societal factors. Technical considerations must be part of the equation and these are treated elsewhere in this book. Our discussion would suggest that, whatever the effect of technical considerations on policy formulation, ultimately decisions on pathways must be conditioned by the identity of the activists, their perceptions of the goals for vernacularization, and the stage which the process has reached. In other chapters of this volume, we recognize fully the difficulties which face such activists; here we have attempted to alert them to ways which may improve their chances of success.

3

Developing Ways of Writing Vernaculars: Problems and Solutions in a Historical Perspective

PHILIP BAKER

with contributions from R. K. Agnihotri, A. L. Khanna, and N. Shrimpton

I. INTRODUCTION

The 1953 Unesco report devoted only a short, three-page section to the Choice of Writing System and this was concerned largely with the need to be able to reproduce texts in the chosen orthographies on printing presses and typewriters without great difficulty.[1] The section concludes with the following words:

To summarize, where the attitudes of the population towards their orthographic traditions permit a choice in matters of orthography, we should prefer:

1. Spelling in conformity with contemporary pronunciation.
2. Agreement with phonemes of the language.
3. Simplicity in typography (available types, limited numbers of characters, etc.).
4. Letters without diacritics (if equally satisfactory).
5. Digraphs in preference to new characters unless they cause ambiguity.
6. Derivation of new characters from prevailing scientific usage.
7. Agreement between different languages of the region or country, especially with the national or official language. (Unesco 1953: 62)

Point 1 assumes that the particular variety of the language for which a writing system is to be designed has already been determined. This is generally the case today but it was not always so in the past; for example, missionaries in the nineteenth century were apt to base the orthographies they designed on the speech of those living close to their mission without necessarily determining its

We are grateful to R. B. Le Page and A. Tabouret-Keller for their detailed and helpful comments on earlier drafts of this chapter.

[1] In this chapter, we employ *writing system* to signify any means of representing graphically any language or group of languages. The word *orthography* is employed more narrowly to mean a writing system specifically intended for a particular language and which is either already in regular use among a significant proportion of that language's native speakers, or which is or was proposed for such use (even if not yet, or no longer, in established use).

place in the spectrum of speech varieties to be heard in the wider environment. The examples of Fiji and Zimbabwe will be mentioned later.

Points 2 to 6 inclusive appear to assume that an alphabetic script is to be preferred over any other kind. While this is widely thought to be the case, not least by those whose own language is written alphabetically, there is in fact some evidence that children acquire syllabic and logographic systems, initially at least, more easily than alphabetic ones (Romaine 1984: 58; Gleitman and Rozin 1977). Indeed, even in the case of alphabetic scripts, children often learn, and are taught to read, by using techniques of whole-word recognition. In such cases words function, initially at least, more as pictures than as combinations of letters.

The identification of the phoneme as the smallest unit of sound capable of distinguishing words of different meanings dates from the late nineteenth century. From the 1920s until at least the publication of Chomsky and Halle (1968), the principal of representing each phoneme by a single letter was regarded as an orthographic ideal. Against that background, 'agreement with phonemes' in point 2 may be intended to suggest that phonemes might be represented by a digraph, rather than by a single letter, in some cases.

Simplicity in typography (point 3) would seem to be desirable more on the grounds of cost than for pedagogical reasons. However, in an age when typewriters are fast being replaced by desktop computers, and in which printing methods are rapidly changing, simplicity in typography is perhaps becoming a less important consideration than it was in 1953.

As worded above, the meaning of point 4 is obscure. The preceding text says: 'For ready recognition and ease of writing, diacritics are best avoided except for the indication of accented (emphasized) syllables or for tone' (Unesco 1953: 61–2). It is not immediately obvious that a special character such as ɛ, or a digraph such as **eh**, is significantly easier to recognize or to write than è. There is also an underlying supposition here, for which no justification is offered, that it is of less importance to mark tones than phonemic contrasts.

The assumption of point 5, that digraphs are preferable to 'new' characters, probably stems from the authors' underlying concern about the cost and/or difficulty of equipping printing presses and typewriters with such characters.

With regard to point 6, it must be assumed that the authors wished to discourage the invention of *ad hoc* characters. If 'prevailing scientific usage' is taken to be a reference to the International Phonetic Alphabet (IPA), it has to be pointed out that many of its characters are merely letters of the Greek alphabet, or Roman letters turned upside down.

Points 4, 5, and 6 should perhaps be interpreted collectively as recommendations for what to do when a language has more phonemes than there are (suitable) Roman letters, i.e. 'use digraphs in preference both to diacritics and special characters. If you have to use special characters, choose from those already in use elsewhere.' Expressed otherwise: be wary of innovation. Before leaving this matter, we should mention two kinds of innovation which the 1953 report ignores:

assignment of unusual or unprecedented values to otherwise unwanted Roman letters and the use of punctuation marks and other non-alphabetic keyboard characters in the representation of particular phonemes. These are discussed in the section 'Alphabetic systems', below.

Point 7 is of an altogether different nature. The words 'agreement between different languages of the region or country' may be intended to mean 'harmonization between the orthographies of the different languages of the region or country'. In adding the words 'especially with the national or official language' the authors may have had in mind the particular case of Haiti, to which they devote considerable attention elsewhere in the report, where a basically phonemic orthography for its (lexically) French-based Creole had then recently been replaced by one which resembled the spelling conventions of French, the official language, far more closely. A broader, alternative interpretation of point 7 might be that the authors were conscious of the fact that certain scripts are very closely identified with particular political units, as is most notably the case in China and Ethiopia. As will become apparent below, there is often very considerable political, ideological, cultural, and/or religious significance attached to particular scripts.

All of the above points will be discussed in more detail below, but first we wish to review briefly the history and geographical spread of the world's principal scripts.

2. HISTORICAL BACKGROUND (TO AD 1600)

There are four main kinds of writing system which have been applied to the world's languages in the past and which remain in use today: logographic, alphabetic, semi-syllabic, and consonantal.

The earliest known forms of writing, the Sumerian and Egyptian dating from 3000 BC or earlier, were *logographic*, consisting of graphic signs (logograms), each of which represented a complete word. By AD 1600 the only major written language employing a truly logographic system was Chinese, but, in some neighbouring countries, Chinese logograms were adopted for the representation of syllables, as in the Japanese katakana and hiragana syllabaries. Some mixed systems—part logographic and part syllabary—were also developed using Chinese logograms, including the Vietnamese chu nôm and the Japanese kanji scripts.

The earliest known *alphabetic* system of writing is the Greek (from *c.*1100 BC). From this, the two most extensively used alphabetic scripts, Roman and Cyrillic, are both derived. The Roman alphabet dates from about 600 BC and had become established throughout most of western Europe by the sixteenth century, often with minor local modifications—digraphs, diacritics, some special characters—although, in the main, such conventions did not become standardized until later. The Cyrillic script dates from *c.* AD 900 and was used by the Eastern Orthodox Church for what was then the common language of the Slavonic peoples

TABLE 3.1. *An illustration of some of the basic principles underlying the semi-syllabic scripts*

Language/Script	Base form	Base form with vowel suppressed	Base form + lowest vowel	Base form + high back vowel	Base form + high front vowel	High front vowel after **m**	High front vowel after **p**	High front vowel after **l**
Approximate phonetic value	kə	k	ka(ː)	ku	ki	mi	pi	li
Hindi	क	क्	का	कु	कि	मि	पि	लि
Tamil	க	க்	கா	கு	கி	மி	பி	லி
Burmese	က	ကဲ	ကာ	ကု	ကိ	မိ	ပိ	လိ
Ethiopic	ህ	ህ	ሃ	ሁ	ሂ	ሚ	ጲ	ሊ

Notes:

- All such scripts have a series of base forms, each of which represents a particular consonant or semivowel followed by the most recurrent vowel which in most cases is a low central vowel.
- Where required, the above vowel can be suppressed by a diacritic to represent the consonant alone. In Hindi, this is positioned below right of the character. In the other three cases the diacritic is positioned on or just above the base form.
- Representation of vowels other than the most recurrent one which is inherent in the base form is achieved either by modification of the base form and/or by placing an additional character next to the base form.
- Modifications of base forms for other vowels tend to be fairly systematic: i.e. if [i] is represented by a small oval shape placed on top of the base form (Burmese) or by an extension to the lower right of the base character (Ethiopic), all other characters representing consonant + [i] will usually have essentially the same modification.
- While the overall direction of writing is always left to right, where vowels are represented by an additional character placed next to the base form, 'next to' does not necessarily mean 'to the right of'. In some cases this can be above, below, or even to the left of the base

(Old Church Slavonic). (Slavonic peoples who adopted Roman Catholicism— Poles, Czechs, Slovaks, Croats, etc.—employed the Roman alphabet for their languages.) With the notable exception of Romanian (see below), the Cyrillic script was not used for writing non-Slavonic languages until comparatively recent times. Other alphabetic systems which were current in AD 1600 include Armenian and Georgian.

The *semi-syllabic* (also called *alpha-syllabic*) scripts of Asia and Ethiopia are basically syllabaries in which most characters represent a sequence of a consonant and a vowel (CV).[2] Each set of characters sharing the same initial consonant generally has an overall similarity of shape but with individual modifications indicating the particular following vowel. Special characters may be required for initial vowels. A feature of many of these scripts is that the vowel of one particular set of vowel modifications can be suppressed by a diacritic, thus allowing for the representation of CVC and CCV syllables by two characters. In the case of languages such as Thai and Burmese, these modifications also indicate tones. Some examples from semi-syllabic scripts will be found in Table 3.1.

The oldest semi-syllabic script is probably the Brahmi script of India, known from Buddhist texts of the fifth century BC. The diffusion of Buddhism went hand-in-hand with the spread of semi-syllabic scripts, most of them designed for the representation of a single language. More than 200 such scripts are known to have been used in India, Nepal, Tibet, Sri Lanka, and throughout South-East Asia (with the exception of northern Vietnam, which was under Chinese rule). The only semi-syllabic script not directly linked to the diffusion of Buddhism is the one used by Christians in Ethiopia for the Ge'ez and Amharic languages from about AD 350.[3]

Consonantal scripts originated among the Semitic languages and the earliest inscriptions date from around 900 BC. The Arabic script, known from only AD 512, is thus a comparatively late development. Although it does make limited provision for the marking of vowels, the Arabic script is basically consonantal in that the diacritics for marking vowels are not normally written. (Exceptionally, they are usually written in the Koran to assist Muslims in reading the text aloud.) By the sixteenth century, this script was not only established throughout the Arab world but was also applied to some non-Semitic languages following the conversion of their speakers to Islam, including Turkish, various languages of central Asia, Urdu, Malay, and several African languages including Fulfulde (Fulani), Hausa, and Swahili. Malay had previously been written in a semi-syllabic script. Use of the Arabic script started in the fourteenth century. As Islam spread through

---

[2] The system used for modern Hindi is somewhat atypical in that (*a*) it has some graphemes representing CCV syllables and (*b*) **r** is represented in a bewildering variety of ways, often as an appendage to another grapheme (Agnihotri and Khanna 1992*a*).

[3] The possibility that the development of Ethiopic from an earlier consonantal script into a semi-syllabic one (written left to right, unlike consonantal scripts of other Semitic languages) may have been inspired by trading contacts with people using semi-syllabic scripts in India and/or Sri Lanka is discussed in Baker (1996).

most of Indonesia during the next two centuries, there was some writing of religious texts in local vernaculars in Arabic script, but no established semi-syllabic script was abandoned as a result of this. However, the Arabic script was subsequently adopted for some languages without an established written tradition, notably in Borneo and parts of the Philippines.

3. CHANGES FROM AD 1600 TO THE SECOND WORLD WAR

During this period, Europeans brought ever-increasing areas of the world under their political control. This meant that, in so far as writing systems were designed for previously unwritten languages, they were almost always adaptations of the Roman alphabet. Another consequence was that some languages previously written in a non-Roman script had romanized orthographies designed for them. Examples of the latter will be discussed below according to the system in use prior to (proposals for) romanization.

3.1. *Logographic Systems*

In this period, we have not found any examples of logographic systems being adopted for previously unwritten languages, while in both Vietnam and China romanized transcriptions were proposed as alternatives to logograms.

Christian missionaries arrived in what is now Vietnam early in the seventeenth century, and a dictionary using a romanized transcription of Vietnamese was soon published (Rhodes 1651). At that time, there was no intention that the Vietnamese should themselves adopt romanization. Vietnamese had long been written both in Chinese logograms (as if it were a 'dialect' of Chinese) and in the mixed logographic/syllabic script known as chu nôm. The romanized form of writing Vietnamese, subsequently known as quôc ngũ', did not become a serious rival to the other writing systems until after French occupation in the second half of the nineteenth century, and did not replace them until well into the present century. The ultimate success of quôc ngũ' has nothing to do with its missionary beginnings—90 per cent of the population remain Buddhists—nor much to do with the fact that romanization had at one time been favoured by the colonial government as a stepping stone to French. A more important factor appears to have been nationalist hostility towards the Chinese, who had dominated them, culturally and politically, for centuries (see DeFrancis 1977*a*).

Many different romanized transcriptions have been proposed for (varieties of) Chinese since the nineteenth century. The earliest were primarily concerned with the needs of foreigners wishing to learn the language, but, in the 1920s and 1930s, there were Chinese-designed systems promoted with the eventual aim of replacing Chinese characters (DeFrancis 1977*b*). These accepted that each major variety of Chinese (the so-called Chinese 'dialects') would have its own orthography but also proposed that Mandarin should be promoted as the national standard. However, the provision of separate orthographies for the various 'dialects' was seen by some as a threat to national unity, while the traditional logographic writing system, identical for speakers of all varieties of Chinese, was felt to promote national unity (DeFrancis 1977*b*: 123). This caused the romanization movement to fade away, but it was to be revived in the post-war era. (See also the extended discussion in Chapter 8.)

3.2. *Alphabetic Systems: Roman*

In the wake of European explorers, missionaries went out to spread The Word. Their aim was nothing less than mass conversion to Christianity. They quickly identified the need to be able to preach and conduct religious services in local languages as an essential step towards achieving this. Working with informants, they wrote down what they learned, gradually developed orthographies, set about translating religious texts, and taught people to read and write in their own languages. Finding people who wanted to acquire literacy in their own language appears not to have been a problem. There are many accounts of non-literate people being fascinated by the ability of foreigners to communicate with one another by signs on paper and there were thus many disposed to acquire this skill. There are also accounts of economic spurs to literacy, as, for example, in the case of the Efik coastal traders in eighteenth-century Nigeria.

While it is clear that early missionaries unquestioningly regarded literacy as 'a good thing', their principal aim was mass conversion to Christianity rather than mass literacy as such. They concentrated their efforts with regard to both conversion and literacy on local rulers because success with the latter might encourage their subjects to do likewise. This may have helped to create a literate élite but it is not apparent that missionaries intended this.

The first people to establish a mission in a territory often arrived there without any prior knowledge of the wider linguistic situation into which they had ventured. In their haste to produce religious texts in the local language, they were apt to assume that the variety spoken in the immediate vicinity of the mission was an appropriate one on which to base an orthography. Such was the case among each of the various and geographically dispersed missions in Zimbabwe, and this had, and still has, many unfortunate consequences for efforts to establish a standardized orthography for the language now generally known as Shona (Chimhundu 1992).

In many of the smaller Pacific islands, an orthography based on the speech of those living near the mission might often prove suitable for the entire population, but not in Fiji. As described by Clammer (1976), the first missionaries to reach Fiji had already spent some years in Tonga, where they had acquired considerable fluency in its relatively homogeneous language. Arriving in Lakeba in 1835, they immediately set to work on the local variety of Fijian. Over the following months and years they became increasingly aware of the extent of dialect variation within the island group, at one point concluding that they might need to produce religious materials in fifteen different dialects. It took ten years for them to identify the dialect of Bau, on political rather than linguistic grounds, as the most appropriate for their needs.

The influence of missionaries on the processes of literacy is still felt strongly in Third World countries even today, especially with regard to languages which are used only sparsely in literature or the media. In such cases it often happens that most texts are of a mainly religious nature and that these are the ones which the newly literate will most often encounter.

In designing orthographies for previously unwritten languages, the general practice was for missionaries to begin by adopting various conventions from their own languages. Thus Anglophones represented the semi-vowels as **w** and **y**, the French wrote [u] as **ou**, while the Spanish and other speakers of Romance languages opted for **c** (before **a, o**, and **u**) and **qu** (before **e** and **i**) to represent [k]. Because of the lack of consistent values associated with vowel symbols in English, Anglophone missionaries early adopted the policy of 'consonants as in English, vowels as in Italian'. These conventions were tolerably adequate for languages with a small phonemic inventory, but most of the languages which the missionaries encountered contained sounds or contrasts not occurring in their own. This forced them to innovate, but, in so doing, they could also draw on the strategies devised in previous centuries as the Latin alphabet had been adapted to other European languages. By the middle of the nineteenth century, four main types of innovation can be identified.

(i) The use of digraphs and trigraphs

European missionaries unhesitatingly adopted digraphs and trigraphs from their own languages, representing [ʃ], for example, as **sh**, **ch**, or **sch** according to whether their first language was English, French, or German. Such people also borrowed digraphs from other European languages and from romanized transcriptions of non-European languages, resulting in the use of, for example, **gh** for either a voiced velar fricative or an aspirated velar plosive. For previously unfamiliar sounds, such as the contrasting voiceless and voiced lateral fricatives of a number of southern Bantu languages, they were forced to innovate, choosing, for example, **hl** and **dl** for the latter pair. Other examples include **fh** and **vh** for bilabial fricatives. Note that most of these di- and trigraphs representing single consonant phonemes make use of the letter **h**. Modest use has also been made of **h** in the digraphic representation of vowels such as **eh** for [ɛ] and **oh** for [ɔ] by Anglophones in some seven vowel systems, but in general diacritics have been preferred for the representation of additional vowel phonemes distinguished by height or lip-rounding. Another widespread use of digraphs has been the doubling of letters to represent long vowel phonemes, such as **aa** for /aː/ and **ii** for /iː/, as well as, more rarely, long consonants, as in the Finnish orthography.

(ii) The use of diacritics

As with (i), European missionaries whose own languages employ diacritics had no hesitation in using these in similar fashion in the orthographies they designed. It was no doubt the absence of diacritics on their printing presses which led many Anglophone missionaries to prefer solutions of type (i) or (iii).

In the middle of the nineteenth century, Lepsius (1855) proposed a systematic approach to designing orthographies for previously unwritten languages. The most striking feature of this was the very extensive use of diacritics; in some cases, he proposed marking a single letter with two superposed diacritics. He illustrated his ideas by setting out alternative writing systems for many of the orthographies which missionaries had only recently designed. Although Lepsius predates the phoneme era, his proposals came very close to the phonemic ideal of a single segment for every contrastive sound. However, the proposed use of two diacritics with some letters has generally been regarded as unacceptable on both technical and aesthetic grounds. One of the very few well-established orthographies in which vowels may bear two diacritics is the Vietnamese quôc ngũ'. Vietnamese has eleven vowels, six of which are distinguished from the other five by a diacritic, and six tones,[4] five of which are written with a diacritic above the vowel and one written with a diacritic below the vowel. The details are set out in Table 3.2. Both the need to position two diacritics above a vowel and the fact that several of the diacritics are unique to the quôc ngũ' orthography did create technical problems, but, according to DeFrancis (1977*a*: 209), quoting a Vietnamese calendar and almanac published in 1932, 'the problem has been solved without too much difficulty by casting special fonts and by adapting typewriters [with e.g. dead keys for diacritics]'. One objection to the orthography raised by its opponents early this century was that tones could not be represented in telegrams, but this was solved by the use of letters which could not otherwise occur word-finally, as is also illustrated in Table. 3.2. There will be additional comment on the quôc ngũ' orthography below.

In spite of the Vietnamese experience, the general view remains that no segment should bear more than one superposed diacritic. This has led some to argue that superposed diacritics should not be used for the representation of vowel phonemes in tone languages because diacritics are needed to mark tone. However, subscript dotted letters, which were proposed by the Church Missionary Society in 1848 as a way of expanding the Roman alphabet (Tucker 1971: 620), are compatible with superscript diacritics marking tone. Subscript dots were adopted by Crowther (1852) for his Yoruba orthography, e.g. ọ for [ɔ] (ọ́ with high tone, ọ̀ with low tone), ẹ for [ɛ], and ṣ for [ʃ]. Crowther was a Yoruba and

---

[4] Here and below, when a language is said to have a particular number of tones, this should be understood as meaning 'tones which require overt marking in the orthography'. There is generally also a 'neutral' tone which is not signalled in the orthography (other than by the absence of any mark).

TABLE 3.2. *The Vietnamese quốc ngữ orthography*

Vowels	Front Unrounded	Central Unrounded	Back Unrounded	Back Rounded
	i (y)		u'	u
	ê		o'	ô
	e	â	â	o
	a			

Tones	Diacritic	Example	Telegraphic alternative	Example
Mid	a (unmarked)	ma 'ghost'	(unmarked)	ma
High rising	á	má 'mother'	q	maq
Low falling	à	mà 'but'	f	maf
Mid-low	ả	mả 'tomb'	j	maj
High rising glottalized	ã	mã 'horse'	w	maw
Low	ạ	mạ 'rice seedling'	z	maz

Consonants	Labial	Dental	Retroflex	Palatal	Lateral	Velar	Glottal
Nasal	m	n		nh		ng	
Occlusives voiceless	p	t	tr [ṭ]	ch		k (c, q)	
aspirated		th					
voiced	b	đ					
Fricatives voiceless	ph [f]	x [s]	s [ṣ]			kh [x]	h
voiced	v	d [z] (gi)				g [ɣ] (gh)	
Liquid					l		

... IPA values where these might not be obvious; parentheses contain orthographic variants.

may have been the first African to design an orthography for his own language using the Roman alphabet. It is worth noting that his orthography has survived to the present day whereas almost all other orthographies proposed for African languages in the first half of the nineteenth century have been considerably revised if not abandoned altogether.

There was also limited use of diacritics for new orthographies in Europe in the nineteenth century. A case in point is Samic (Lappish). The Danish linguist Rasmas Rask spent five months with a Same (Lapp) and a missionary, teaching the latter to distinguish the phonemes of Samic so that he could devise a suitable orthography. The resulting system, which formed the basis for later developments, made extensive use of diacritics.

(iii) Assigning unprecedented values to Roman letters not otherwise required

The best-known example of this kind of innovation is the choice of **q**, **x**, and **c** to represent, respectively, the dental, lateral, and palatal clicks of Xhosa and Zulu. Similarly unconventional, but less well known, is the use in the Fijian orthography of **g** for the velar nasal [ŋ], **q** for the prenasalized stop [ŋg], and **c** for the voiceless interdental fricative [θ]. Other unusual examples are to be found in the (now obsolete) Meeker orthographies designed for Ottawa and other indigenous North American languages which include such things as **f** for the velar nasal [ŋ], **h** for the affricate [ʧ], and **l** for the fricative [ʃ] (Anthony Grant, p.c.). Many other such innovations which would have seemed unusual in the nineteenth century no longer appear so today because familiarity with the IPA has altered our perception of the typical values of Roman letters.

(iv) The use of punctuation marks in the representation of phonemes

The most striking example comes from southern Africa, where, for Nama and other non-Bantu languages, /, ≠, !, and // were adopted for, respectively, the dental, alveolar, retroflex, and lateral clicks.

The apostrophe has been widely exploited to represent three different phonemes or series of phonemes: (1) the glottal stop (various languages of the Pacific and Africa); (2) glottalized and/or ejective consonants, for example, **b'** and **k'** for contrasting glottalized or ejective varieties of **b** and **k**, and (3) palatalized consonants, for example, **t'** and **k'** for contrasting palatalized varieties of **t** and **k**. A fourth use of the apostrophe is found in Swahili, Xhosa, and a few other Bantu languages of East and southern Africa where the sequence **ng'** represents the velar nasal phoneme [ŋ]. (In Swahili, **ng** without an apostrophe represents the phonemic sequence [ŋg].)

Other non-alphabetical characters which have been used include the ampersand (**&**) for an alveolar lateral fricative in Inuktitut (Mallon 1985) and the underline bar to distinguish a uvular fricative <u>x</u> from a velar fricative **x** in Okanagan (Hébert and Lindley 1985). These are indigenous languages of Canada.

TABLE 3.3. *Suggested representation of consonants in Vietnamese orthography, avoiding digraphs, diacritics, and non-alphabetic characters*

		Labial	Dental	Retroflex	Lateral	Palatal	Velar	Glottal
Nasal		**m** /m/	**n** /n/			**y** /ɲ/	**g** /ŋ/	
Occlusives	voiceless	**p** /p/	**t** /t/	**q** /ʈ/		**c** /tʃ/	**k** /k/	
	aspirated		**ç** /tʰ/					
	voiced	**b** /b/	**d** /d/					
Fricatives	voiceless	**f** /f/	**s** /s/	**j** /ʂ/			**x** /x/	
	voiced	**v** /v/	**z** /z/				**r** /ɣ/	**h** /ɦ/
Liquid					**l** /l/			

Note: The choice of **r** for the velar fricative would have been appropriate because this resembles its pronunciation in French. **Ç** would have been available on French typewriters and presses. Its use here for the aspirated voiceless plosive, and that of **q** and **j** for the two retroflex consonants, is arbitrary.

Most of the new orthographies of the nineteenth and early twentieth centuries were designed by missionaries without any relevant training. Apart from the influence of the written form of the language(s) they already knew, their choice of graphemes was constrained by the printing equipment and, later, typewriters they were sent from headquarters. Given such circumstances, they did a reasonable and sometimes remarkable job of identifying the 'significant sounds' of these languages—this was the pre-phonemic age—and finding ways of representing them. However, in hindsight the choice of graphemes in many of them seems somewhat arbitrary and/or to lack internal consistency. One such example is the Vietnamese orthography set out in Table 3.2. This in fact originated in the mid-seventeenth century but has probably experienced a number of revisions since then. The letter **h** has no consistent value in the digraphs in which it is employed, while the digraphs themselves seem to have been adopted from the orthographies of various European languages—for example, **nh** from Portuguese, **ch** from English or Spanish, etc. Particularly curious are the choices of **ph** for /f/, **x** for /s/, and **d** for /z/—with the consequence that /d/ requires a bar through its ascender—**đ**—to distinguish it from the latter. Although the eleven vowels and six tones of Vietnamese present an enormous problem for the designing of an elegant romanized transcription of this language, its consonant system is relatively simple. Using strategy (iii) above—assigning unusual or unprecedented values to Roman letters not otherwise required—its consonants might have been represented, without digraphs, diacritics, or non-alphabetic characters, as in Table 3.3 (cf. Table 3.2).

The consonantal system of Xhosa presented missionaries with a far greater challenge than Vietnamese. The solution they devised included many di- and trigraphs

TABLE 3.4. *The orthography of Xhosa*

		Labial	Alveolar	Lateral	Palatal	Velar	Glottal
Nasal		m	n		ny	ng'	
Explosive	ejective	p	t		ty	k	
	aspirated	ph	th		tyh	kh	
	voiced	bh	d		dy	g	
Implosive		b					
Affricate	ejective	f	ts	tl	tsh	kr	
	aspirated		tsh		tsh		
	voiced	v	dz	dl	j		
Fricative	voiceless	f	s	hl	sh	r	h
	voiced	v	z	dl		gr	h
Lateral				l			
Trill			r				
Click	voiceless		c	x	q		
	aspirated		ch	xh	qh		
	voiced		gc	gx	gq		
	nasalized		nc	nx	nq		
Semivowel		w			y		

as well as the assigning of unprecedented values to three otherwise unwanted letters. The current and long-established orthography is set out in Table 3.4.

The essential problem is that Xhosa has more than forty consonant phonemes, double the number of consonant symbols in the Roman alphabet. The choice of **h** as the final element in the representation of all the aspirated consonants conforms to a well-established practice. Unfortunately, however, **h** was also selected as one element in the representation of three non-aspirated consonants: **bh**, **sh**, and **hl**. The choice of **bh** for /b/ and **b** for implosive /ɓ/ seems quite arbitrary. In choosing **sh** for /ʃ/, the designer was merely following English precedent, but the consequences are in this case serious because they result in no fewer than three phonemes being represented by the same trigraph, **tsh**. As the palatal ejective fricative, **tsh** represents /tʃ/ (i.e. **t** + **sh**); as the alveolar aspirated fricative, it represents /tsʰ/ (i.e. **ts** + **h**); while as the palatal aspirated fricative /tʃʰ/ it ought logically to be written **tshh** (i.e. **t** + **sh** + **h**). Note that the digraph **dl** and the letters **f** and **v** all represent both a fricative and an affricate. The second element in the affricate written **tl** corresponds to the fricative written **hl** and might therefore logically have been written **thl**—were it not for the fact that this orthography uses **th** for an aspirated plosive. The letter **r** is selected for two even more contrasting roles, a trill and a velar fricative. Note also that no graphic distinction is made between the voiceless and voiced glottal fricatives, both written **h**.

It is widely accepted that, in an orthography using digraphs, the two letters chosen to represent a single phoneme should never occur together in any word in that language in which the two letters separately represent individual phonemes. As Xhosa lacks consonant clusters, none of the digraphs discussed so far conflicts with this. However, there is just such a problem with the nasalized clicks. Xhosa has both nasalized clicks, and syllabic nasals followed by non-nasalized clicks, occurring in the same environments. The choice of **nc**, **nx**, and **nq** to represent the former has forced the orthographer to innovate to distinguish the latter series from them. This has been achieved by inserting a gratuitous **k** between the **n** and **c**, **x**, or **q**. In this way, *nqonqo* 'spinal cord' is distinguished from *nkqonkqo* 'single one'. This particular problem might have been avoided by reversing the letters representing the nasalized clicks—i.e. *qnoqno* vs. *nqonqo*.

While it might be possible to dispense with some of the internal inconsistencies mentioned here by assigning some of the Roman letters to different phonemes, it is obvious that twenty-six letters are simply inadequate to cope with a language having about twice that number of phonemes. If it were practicable to design an entirely new orthography for Xhosa today, a more economical, more internally consistent, and perhaps more elegant orthography might be designed with the aid of diacritics and/or special characters.[5] However, Xhosa has been written essentially as set out above for a century and a half and thus any proposed major changes would almost certainly be resisted. The best that might be hoped for is that minor reforms could be introduced gradually.

Although it was not until the latter part of the nineteenth century that the phoneme was identified as such by Baudouin de Courtenay, most of the orthographies designed by missionaries were basically phonemic. While it is not difficult to find examples where they failed to distinguish between two phonetically similar phonemes or, conversely, where allophones of a single phoneme were given separate graphic representation, in hindsight it is more often the way in which they chose to represent the phonemes graphically which reflects their lack of linguistic training, as various examples above and below indicate.

The orthographic principle of 'one character per phoneme' appears to be attributable to Daniel Jones. He exemplified this in *Sechuana Reader* (Jones and Plaatje 1916), but this Setswana orthography, which employed a number of special characters, failed to become established. Nevertheless he set a modern precedent for designing orthographies which were not limited to the twenty-six letters of the Roman alphabet and diacritics, and this was to find favour with Westermann and other linguists in the following decades.

The precedent for augmenting the Roman alphabet had been set by the Romans themselves. In adapting the Greek alphabet to Latin, the Romans found no use for five letters (Θ, Ξ, Ω, Π, and Ψ) but reintroduced **F** and **Q** which had

---

[5] For an orthography of Xhosa using *african reference alphabet* characters, see Mann, Dalby, *et al.* (1987: 216).

been dropped from Greek at an early stage. They also developed both Γ and Y into two separate letters, respectively C and G and V and Y. Somewhat later, variants of I became established as independent letters, I and J, while V was ultimately developed into three characters: U, V, and, by reduplication, W. In applying the Roman alphabet to the Germanic languages, two letters were added, þ and ð, although only Icelandic retains both of these today. Other special characters added to various European orthographies include ç, œ, æ, and ø. Various European languages also extended the Roman alphabet by use of diacritics, including (illustrated with a unless not known to occur with this letter): à, á, â, ä, å, č, ż, and ã.

In 1926 the International Institute for African Languages and Cultures was founded and took an immediate interest in the design of orthographies. The Institute was persuaded by Daniel Jones of the need for additional characters for the adequate representation of African languages and in 1930 it published *Practical Orthography of African Languages*. This proposed a basic set of thirty-six letters, of which eleven were additions to the Roman alphabet.[6] It also espoused the principle of one letter per phoneme. Some of these letters, such as ʋ and ɛ, were already established in the IPA. Some proposed by the Institute were subsequently adopted for the IPA, such as ɣ and ɗ, while others, such as ƒ, for which the IPA used ɸ, were not. The Practical Orthography became known as the Africa Script, and, with the help of Westermann, its additional characters soon became established in the orthographies of various languages in Ghana, Togo, Sierra Leone, northern Nigeria, and the Sudan. Such use of special characters constitutes a fifth innovative tendency in addition to the four identified earlier.

Another important development in the years before the Second World War was the growing acceptance by British and some other colonial governments that literacy should be taught in the first instance in an appropriate vernacular. This meant that orthographies were no longer a matter for missions alone. Orthographies had to be standardized for the production of printed materials. Standardization was usually achieved by committees set up by colonial governments on which vernacular specialists would be represented. In some cases this meant that differences between rival orthographies associated with different Christian sects had to be resolved. While orthographies using Africa Script characters were approved in some parts of West Africa, such innovations were largely ignored elsewhere. For example, the standardization of Swahili was entrusted to the Inter-Territorial Language Committee for the East African Dependencies. On completion of its work, the Committee published *A Standard Swahili–English Dictionary* in 1939 which continued to use the nineteenth-century missionary innovation of **ng'** for the phoneme /ŋ/.

---

[6] The letter q was not included in the Africa Script. The additions were either adopted from Greek or variants of existing Roman letters.

A group of languages which, for the most part, received very different treatment in the nineteenth century are the creoles. Wherever creoles coexisted with their lexifier language, there were very few, if any, serious attempts to design autonomous orthographies for them. Instead they were largely written as if they were substandard varieties of the lexifier language, the language of the colonial power to which the territory 'belonged'. Even where catechisms and religious tracts were published in such spellings, it would generally be wrong to assume that literacy was being taught in Creole. On the contrary, such texts were intended only for those literate in the European language so that they could read them aloud to the illiterate. However, in some creolophone territories where there had been both a change of colonial power and a withdrawal of the first colonists and their descendants, as in Surinam where the English-based creole continued to survive after the territory passed into Dutch ownership, creole languages were treated like other previously unwritten languages in Africa and elsewhere and some progress was made towards designing autonomous orthographies for them.

3.3. *Alphabetic Systems: Cyrillic*

From the eighteenth century, orthographies using the Cyrillic alphabet were designed for Russian and other Slavonic languages spoken by populations who belonged to the Eastern Orthodox Church. Cyrillic had been used for writing Church Slavonic for several centuries but, in some cases, the phonologies of these languages demanded more letters than had been needed for Church Slavonic and this was solved by creating additional characters. Six were adopted for Serbian in 1818 and, with one minor modification, these have remained in use ever since. By contrast, Romanian and its close relative Moldavian, written in Cyrillic since the sixteenth century, switched to the Roman alphabet in c.1880.

Following the establishment of the USSR, orthographies using the Cyrillic script were designed for some previously unwritten languages in Siberia and elsewhere. A policy requiring most of the languages of Soviet Asia which had been written in the Roman alphabet in the 1920s to change to the Cyrillic script was implemented from the late 1930s. For details of how this applied to the Turkic languages, see below. Furthermore, Cyrillic orthographies were designed for all the Caucasian languages (with the exception of Georgian which had had its own language-specific alphabet for many centuries), regardless of their previous orthographic history. As Caucasian languages are noted for their unusually large inventories of consonant phonemes—as many as eighty in the case of Ubykh (Comrie 1981: 204)—Cyrillicization posed many problems. Solutions were found with a mixture of special characters—fourteen in the case of Abkhaz —and in the use of di- and trigraphs on a massive scale. One of these languages, Kabara, has what may be the world's only example of a tetragraph: кхъу for a voiceless aspirated labialized uvular plosive (Comrie 1981: 199).

3.4. *Semi-Syllabic Systems*

In general, the semi-syllabic scripts were too firmly established in the societies which employed them to be threatened by Arabic or romanized transcriptions that those seeking to convert their populations to Islam or Christianity might favour. The Indonesian languages are something of an exception. As indicated above, the Arabic script had begun to replace the semi-syllabic script for Malay from the fourteenth century. Competing romanized orthographies were introduced for Malay (alongside the Arabic script) and related languages including Javanese (alongside the traditional semi-syllabic script) in the nineteenth century. In India, with its multiplicity of both languages and scripts, there were occasional proposals to impose romanization throughout the subcontinent. One such proposal, dating from 1834 (Trevelyan *et al.* 1854), advanced five reasons for doing this, three of which stressed the advantages this would bring to Indians and expatriates alike in learning each other's languages and in encountering a single script wherever they travelled. The fourth reason revealed missionary aims.

All the existing Mahammadan [*sic*] and Hindu literature will gradually sink into disuse, with the exception of such portions of it as are worthy of being turned into the new letters. This would produce a great moral change in India in the course of a generation or two. Nothing keeps India in a state of moral and intellectual debasement so much as the false religion, false morals, and false science contained in the sacred and learned books of the Mahammadans and Hindus; and by getting rid of these we shall stop the polluted stream at its source. (Trevelyan *et al.* 1854: 40)

The fifth reason concerned the advantages a knowledge of English literature would bring. The 'greater rapidity with which the Roman character can be written [and] the superior distinctness of both the printed and written character' were also mentioned as minor additional advantages.

Burmese is written with a semi-syllabic script which takes account of tones. In 1832 an alphabetical script using Burmese characters was proposed by US Baptist missionaries for the distantly related minority languages of the Karen people. The script has been in use ever since. Publications include several grammars and dictionaries as well as religious tracts. An advantage of this situation is that the Karen can acquire literacy in both Burmese and their own language without having to master an entirely new writing system (although each character represents a syllable in Burmese, whereas each member of the subset of Burmese characters used for writing Karen represents a single phoneme in the latter).

3.5. *Consonantal Systems*

In the early 1920s modified and 'improved' versions of the Arabic script were adopted in Uzbekistan, Kazakhstan, and Kirghiz. The changes suited the languages concerned and were well received, but in 1925 the importation into the

USSR of all materials in the Arabic script was banned. Romanized transcriptions of these languages, such as had already been successfully introduced for Azerbaijani the previous year,[7] were encouraged. A Unified Turkic Latin Alphabet was adopted in the USSR in 1927 and, with very minor differences, this was the same as that imposed by Atatürk in Turkey in 1928, replacing the Arabic script. Unusual features of the Turkish orthography include ç for [tʃ], c for [dʒ], ş for [ʃ], and ğ for [ɣ]/[j], while (undotted) ı represents a high, back, unrounded vowel. (The upper-case version of the latter is I; Turkish also employs (dotted) i with its usual IPA value, for which the upper case version is (dotted) İ). All printing in the Arabic script was banned in Turkey in 1929.

Christian missionaries were generally less disposed to accept established Arabic transcriptions of non-semitic languages, because of their associations with Islam, than they were to accept the semi-syllabic scripts of the Horn of Africa and South and South-East Asia. In the case of at least two languages, Malay and Hausa, this led to romanized orthographies providing a serious challenge to transcriptions in the longer-established Arabic script.

3.6. *Other Scripts*

Entirely independent of missionary activities or political factors, a number of indigenous scripts were designed for African languages within this period (Dalby 1967, 1968, 1969). The earliest known is the Vai script which dates from the 1830s and which its originator claimed was revealed to him in a dream. This is a syllabary which was quite extensively used in Liberia in the nineteenth and early twentieth centuries. About a dozen other indigenous scripts for languages of West Africa are known from the early decades of the present century, for the most part also attributed to dreams. Most of these were also syllabaries but, unlike the Vai script, none of them has been extensively used.

Two points are worth noting about these indigenous scripts of West Africa. First, although all the scripts were designed for tone languages, only two of the scripts provide any representation of tone (Mann 1969: 107). This provides some marginal support for those who consider tone-marking to be less important than the indicating of phonemic contrasts. Secondly, in comparison with just about any of the semi-syllabic scripts, all these syllabaries lack internal consistency. In the semi-syllabic scripts illustrated in Table 3.1, it can be seen that, for each language, characters representing the same initial consonant (plus any or no vowel) have an overall similarity of shape, while characters representing a syllable containing any consonant but the same vowel are modified in a similar way. By

---

[7] For a fuller account, see Henze (1977). Languages such as Azerbaijani which are spoken both in what was formerly Soviet Central Asia and in either Iran or Afghanistan to the south continued to be written in the Arabic script in the latter countries. In Soviet Central Asia, the use of the Roman alphabet for Azerbaijani was subsequently replaced by the Cyrillic alphabet (see Sect. 3.3 above).

contrast, the Loma syllabary in Table 3.5 lacks such similarities both horizontally and vertically.[8]

The Santhal people form the largest tribal group in India and live in several of its states. In the state of West Bengal only, their Santhali language (a member of the Munda family) has been written in the Ol Chiki syllabary for more than fifty years. As in the case of the West African indigenous scripts, the Santhal believe that this script was divinely revealed to a member of their group in a dream (Annamalai 1979).

In North America in the first half of the nineteenth century, a number of syllabaries were designed for indigenous languages, including Cherokee, Ojibwa, and Cree. The latter is still in current use (Anthony Grant, p.c.).

4. CHANGES SINCE THE SECOND WORLD WAR

Significant changes affecting orthographic design since the Second World War have resulted, directly or indirectly, from the dismantling of European colonial empires. This has meant that orthographic decisions of all kinds have increasingly been made within ministries of education of independent countries, by people who speak those languages natively, rather than by expatriate civil servants and missionaries. Another more gradual change is that orthographies have increasingly been designed by people familiar with phonemic principles, although many of them have not upheld the ideal of one letter per phoneme.

4.1. *Logographic Systems*

Since about 1950 it has been the policy of the government of Taiwan not to permit literacy teaching in any of the Malayo-Polynesian languages of what are known as the 'high mountain' peoples through anything other than Chinese characters. Missionaries have surmounted this problem for one of these languages, Sediq, by designing a phonemic orthography using a (Chinese character) phonetic script developed in China earlier this century. This is an alphabetic, not logographic, system which has been used for a small number of mainly religious publications in Sediq in the past forty years.

In mainland China, plans for the romanization of Chinese were revived in 1956 with the publication of the pinyin orthography. In contrast to the situation in the 1920s and 1930s, it was now proposed only to romanize the putonghua 'standard vernacular or common speech', i.e. 'the northern dialect' (Seybolt and Kuei-ke Chiang 1978: 20–5). Although some Chinese argued for the gradual replacement of traditional logograms by pinyin, support for such a radical change

---

[8] We have chosen to illustrate the Loma syllabary because it has fewer phonemic contrasts than Vai. The Mende syllabary displays a greater degree of internal consistency than either of these.

TABLE 3.5. *The Loma syllabary*

	i	a	u	e	ɛ	ɔ	o	NASAL VOWELS	LONG VOWELS	DIPHTHONGS
p									pee	pei
w								wẽ / wã		wei
b								bẽ	bii / baa / bɔɔ / bee	bue / bɔi
ɓ										ɓai [?] ɓai / ɓue
kp										
gb								gbã		
ʼv										
f									faa	
v									vaa	tie / tui
t										
l									lee	lea / lui / lue / lue

DIPHTHONGS

diē
diū
due

sue

sie
sue

yie
yai

kai
kei
kue
kui

gie

mēi

ŋie

LONG VOWELS

saa
see
see

kas

gee

mū
mūu
mee

mɔɔ

ŋēe

SYLLABIC NASAL [1]

sɛ̃
sɛ̃

gɛ̃

agɛ̃

õ

ɔ

ɛ

ɛ̃

ũ

ã

ĩ

ĩ

NASAL SYLLABLES

p

s

z

y

k

ɣ

g

ŋg

-

m

n

ŋ

Source: Dalby (1967: 46–7).

seems to have long since evaporated. Others saw more restricted roles for pinyin, notably as an aid to learning logograms (Seybolt and Kuei-Ke Chiang 1978: 21–2, 342–4), and this appears to be the dominant view today. However, if the prospects for the replacement of logograms by pinyin romanization have receded for Chinese, romanized orthographies for the non-Chinese minority languages of China, also proposed in 1956, appear to have been accepted wherever such languages did not already have some other established orthography. (For a more extended discussion, see Chapter 8.)

The Mayan Institute in Guatemala proposed to resurrect a number of Mayan logograms for use in an otherwise romanized orthography of Mam. These included ✳ (which meant 'sun' as a logogram) to represent the glottalized velar plosive written **k**' in Kaufman's orthography for this language (Archer and Costello 1990: 152 n.).

4.2. *Alphabetic Systems—Roman*

There have been significant post-war orthographic developments in Africa, the Americas and Asia, as well as considerable activity in the field of pidgin and creole languages. Elsewhere, there has been little change apart from some minor orthographic reforms which do not warrant discussion here.

Africa

In spite of the efforts of missionaries and others in the nineteenth and early twentieth centuries, orthographies had been designed for only a minority of the more than 2,500 indigenous languages of Africa (Mann, Dalby, *et al.* 1987) by the Second World War. Since then, and particularly after decolonization, new orthographies have been designed for a great many languages which previously lacked one, while many of the orthographies used by missionaries and others for many decades have been revised, often on more than one occasion. The changes have been particularly dramatic in the former French and Portuguese territories of Africa, where, prior to independence, literacy teaching had been largely confined to the European language. In most of these territories, new orthographies have since been, or are currently being, designed for all but the most minor of their indigenous languages. The problems have been particularly acute in West Africa because of the large number of separate languages spoken in each state and because many of these languages are spoken in two or more countries. This international dimension led to a series of meetings, beginning in Bamako in 1966 and continuing into the 1980s, in which orthographic problems were discussed. At one of these meetings (at Niamey in 1978), tentative agreement was reached on a fifty-seven-letter *alphabet de reference africain* as a successor to the earlier Africa Script. Eight of these letters were distinguished from others only by the presence of a subscript dot. This was something which went against

TABLE 3.6. *the african reference alphabet*

a	α	ʌ	b	ɓ	c	ƈ	ç	d	ɗ	ɖ	ð	e	ɛ	ə
f	ƒ	g	ɠ	ɣ	h	ɦ	i	ʔ	j	ɟ	k	ƙ	l	λ
m	ɱ	n	ŋ	ɲ	o	ɔ	p	ƥ	q	r	ɽ	s	ʃ	t
ɛ	ƭ	θ	u	ɷ	v	ʋ	w	x	y	ỿ	z	ʒ	ɜ	ʔ

the spirit of the Africa Script, which had favoured only superposed diacritics, and only for marking tone. The International African Institute (formerly International Institute of African Languages and Cultures) was at that time working on its own successor to the Africa Script, which it launched in 1982 as the african reference alphabet (a.r.a.) and which has sixty letters, as set out in Table 3.6.

A meeting in Niamey in 1984 subsequently approved the design of a keyboard layout, to be known as the Clavier international de Niamey, on which there were fifty-six lower-case only letters. These included most of the letters in the a.r.a. Eight a.r.a letters were rejected. In the order they appear in Table 3.6 these are ʌ, ʔ, ɟ, λ, ɱ, ƭ, θ, and ɷ. Four other characters were added: æ, œ, þ, and ŋ. The preference for thorn (þ) over theta (θ) is curious given that the former is currently used only for Icelandic and there is some risk of confusion with **p**.

The designers of both these augmented alphabets were conscious of the limitations of keyboards and proposed dispensing altogether with upper-case letters, which were described by a participant at one of the above meetings as 'un luxe culturel et décoratif'. In presenting the a.r.a., Mann, Dalby *et al.* (1987: 207) list six general principles for its application which broadly reflect the views expressed at the above-mentioned series of meetings concerning the design of orthographies in West Africa.[9]

(i)   Each phoneme shall be represented by a single unique grapheme, i.e. by a specific letter.

(ii) Letters should be maximally distinct.

(iii) The same sound should be represented by the same letter in languages within a single country.

(iv) A language spoken in several countries should have an identical alphabet to represent its sounds in each country.

(v)   In the interests of harmonization, the same sound should be represented by the same letter within each subregion of Africa.

(vi) Diacritics should be avoided as far as possible.

With regard to (i) and (ii), the advantages of an augmented alphabet are particularly apparent for languages with an unusually large phonemic inventory such as Xhosa, discussed earlier, and Venda. The current (South African) orthography

---

[9] Mann, Dalby, *et al.* (1987: 208) also set out nine other principles relating to the selection and form of a.r.a. letters.

TABLE 3.7. *Two Venda orthographies*

	Bilabial	Labio-dental	Inter-dental	Cerebral	Labio-alveolar	Palatal	Velar	Glottal
Current orthography								
Nasal	m		ṋ	n		ny	ṅ	
Plosive ejective	p		t̰	t		ty	k	
aspirated	ph		t̰h	th		tyh	kh	
voiced	b		d̰	d		dy	g	
Affricate ejective		pv		tz	tzw	tzh		
aspirated		pf		ts	tsw	tsh		
voiced		bv		dz	dzw	dzh		
Fricative voiceless	fh	f		s	sw	sh	x	h
voiced	vh	v		z	zw	zh		
Lateral			ḽ	l				
Rolled				r				
Semivowel	w					y		
Proposed a.r.a. orthography								
Nasal	m		ɴ	n		ɲ	ŋ	
Plosive ejective	ɓ		θ	ɛ		c	ƙ	
aspirated	p		t	t			k	
voiced	b		d	d		ɟ	g	
Affricate ejective		ɓf		ɛs	ɛʃ	ɛç		
aspirated		pf		ts	tʃ	tç		
voiced		bv		dz	dʒ	dj		
Fricative voiceless	*f*	f		s	ʃ	ç	x	h
voiced	*v*	v		z	ʒ	j		
Lateral			λ	l				
Rolled				r				
Semivowel	w					y		

of Venda is set out in Table 3.7. This uses four letters marked with the same subscript diacritic, eighteen digraphs, and seven trigraphs. (A different orthography is used in Zimbabwe, where Venda is also spoken.) This is followed by an alternative proposed by Mann, Dalby, *et al.* (1987: 216) using the a.r.a. The a.r.a. orthography has no diacritics or trigraphs but digraphs represent the twelve affricates.

One of several West African countries to have adopted a common alphabet for the representation of all its national languages is Senegal.[10] This has forty letters, of which twenty-four are Roman (**v** and **z** not being required for any Senegalese languages), eight are special characters (ɓ, ɗ, ɖ, ɠ, ŋ, ɓ, ɛ, ƴ) seven consist of a Roman letter and a diacritic (à, é, ë, í, ñ, ó, ú), while the remaining one is the apostrophe (to represent the glottal stop). This means that each letter has broadly the same phonetic realization in as many of the orthographies of that country's indigenous languages as it is required. The latter include four West Atlantic (Wolof, Sereer, Pulaar, and Joola) and two Manding languages (Malinké and Soninké). No major compromises are made with the orthography of the official language, French,[11] and thus **c**, **q**, and **x** have their IPA values.

Although potentially in conflict with principle (iii), some limited progress with (iv) has been achieved in recent years in West Africa with regard to the writing of the Manding languages which are spoken in thirteen countries of the region. By contrast, the desirability of having a single orthography for languages spoken across political borders in southern Africa has so far scarcely been recognized (Mkanganwi, in *Abstracts* 1990). Recent political changes in South Africa have led to a call for new, harmonized orthographies for both the major groups of Bantu languages spoken within the Republic: Nguni (Zulu, Xhosa, Ndebele, and Swati) and Tswana-Sotho (National Language Project 1992: 13). However, this proposal does not mention the needs of speakers of (varieties of) the same languages located in Botswana (Tswana), Zimbabwe (Ndebele), Swaziland (Swati), and Lesotho (Sotho).

A recent case of deliberate lack of harmonization is the choice of orthographers of the 'Afar language of Djibuti to reject the precedent of the national orthography of Somalia by adopting **x** for retroflex **d** (Somali **dh**), **c** for the voiceless pharyngeal fricative (Somali **x**), and **q** for the corresponding voiced pharyngeal fricative (Somali **c**). Parker and Hayward (1985) attribute this to the desire of the 'Afar people to 'express their emerging ethnic identity'.

The sixth principle has sometimes, perhaps correctly, been regarded as a particular prejudice of Anglophone linguists. For a language in which tone is marked by diacritics over vowels (see Sect. 5), there would seem good reason to avoid using superposed diacritics to mark vowel quality. Apart from such cases, it is not apparent that there is anything intrinsically undesirable about the use of

---

[10] On the meaning of 'national' in this context, see Sect. 7.3.
[11] [e] is written **é** and contrasts with [ɛ] written (plain) **e**.

diacritics to extend the limited range of letters in the Roman alphabet, provided that they are (made) available on keyboards and printing presses.

Americas

Post-war orthographies of the Amerindian languages of Central and South America generally have **k** for /k/ instead of both **c** and **qu** in complementary distribution as in Spanish, as was formerly often the case. This has released **q** (without a following **u**) to represent the uvular plosive in orthographies for a number of these languages.

Kaufman's practical orthography for Mam (see Sect. 4.1) includes some interesting features. Apart from the glottal stop, Mam has no fewer than sixteen plosives and affricates (England 1983). Eight of these are written **p**, **t**, **tz** (alveo-fricated), **ch**, **tx** (retroflex), **ky** (palatal), **k** and **q** (uvular). These contrast with a corresponding glottalized (ejective or implosive) series written **b'**,[12] **t'**, **tz'**, **ch'**, **tx'**, **ky'**, **k'** (written ✱ in the Mayan Institute orthography, as was mentioned earlier), and **q'**. Having used the apostrophe to mark ejective series, something else was needed for the glottal stop and Kaufman has opted for **7**. This appears to be without precedent. If this does not blend particularly well with Roman letters—consider **ku7k** 'squirrel', **ri7t** 'solid', **xkoo7ya** 'tomato'—many might feel that the same could be said of the corresponding IPA symbol **ʔ**. Three phonemes occur only in words adopted from Spanish: **b**, **d**, and **g**. Spanish influence is also apparent in the choice of **j** for [x] and **ch** for [tʃ]. Since neither **h** nor **c** represents an independent phoneme, the only justification for this digraph is harmonization with Spanish. However, by representing the corresponding ejective and fricative as **ch'** and **xh**, respectively, Kaufman at least succeeds in establishing **h** as a common visual element in the representation of all three alveopalatal consonants. (The letter **h** does not occur independently—i.e. there is no /h/ in Mam. The letter **x** by itself represents a retroflex fricative; the two other retroflex phonemes are occlusives written **tx** and (ejective) **tx'**.) Among other Amerindian languages with revised post-war orthographies is that of Quechua, which now has official status in Peru. In addition to plain and ejective occlusives, Quechua also has an aspirated series, marked by a following **h**. A consequence of selecting **ch** for [tʃ] is that the corresponding aspirated affricative is written **chh**. Such usage has a precedent in nineteenth-century romanized transcriptions of Indic languages, in which for example, Hindi [atʃtʃʰaː] 'good' was written **achchhā** (Forbes 1859). Today **c** alone is more commonly used for [tʃ] and **ch** for [tʃʰ] in such transcriptions—i.e. **acchā**.

Asia

A policy of introducing romanized orthographies for most of the indigenous, non-Chinese languages of China, including those which straddle the (former)

---

[12] **b'**, **t'**, and **q'** are implosives; the rest are ejectives. The choice of **b'** (rather than **p'**) for the bilabial glottalized occlusive is curious because, in all other cases, only the following apostrophe distinguishes the glottalized occlusive from the corresponding plain occlusive.

USSR–China border and which are written on the non-Chinese side in the Cyrillic script, was adopted in the 1950s and subsequently implemented.

Pinyin was adopted as the official romanized form of Chinese in 1958. Although it has been used by Chinese primary-school children on an experimental basis as an aid to learning characters, there has been no clear indication that this is ultimately intended to replace the logographic system. Pinyin has also provided foreigners with an officially approved romanization of Chinese proper names. As an orthography, it assigns unusual or unprecedented values to five Roman letters: **q** [tɕʰ], **j** [tɕ], **r** [ʐ], **x** [ɕ], and **c** [tʃʰ].

In 1973 a unified romanized orthography for Malay/Bahasa Indonesia was adopted by the governments of Malaysia and Indonesia, ending the use of separate English- and Dutch-influenced orthographies in those countries, and effectively eclipsing the use of Jawi (Arabic script) for Malay after several centuries. Other languages of Indonesia, most of which have their own semi-syllabic scripts, are today increasingly written in romanized orthographies.

Pidgin and Creole Languages

In the period 1940–5, the McConnell–Laubach orthography was developed for Haitian Creole with a view to conducting what was probably the first mass literacy campaign for any creole language. This employed one trigraph and four digraphs: **tch** (for /tʃ/), **dj** (for /dʒ/), **ch** (for /ʃ/), **gn** (for /ɲ/), and, gratuitously,[13] **ou** (for /u/). If these were intended as compromises with French orthography, the use of the circumflex to mark nasalized vowels clearly was not. (It appears to have been chosen as a substitute for the tilde from among the diacritics available on local (French) typewriters and printing presses.) All other phonemes were represented by a single segment. Though used with government support in the 1940s and 1950s, this orthography was opposed by the Francophone élite (who, being already literate in French, had nothing to gain from written Creole). Pressoir, a member of that élite, launched a rival orthography in 1947 which resembled French spelling much more closely. He proposed that /w/ be written **ou** (which meant that it had the same graphic representation as /u/) and that, instead of using the circumflex, nasal vowels should be written as sequences of corresponding oral vowel + **n**. A consequence of this was that nasal vowels had sometimes to be disambiguated from sequences of oral vowel + **n** and this was achieved with the hyphen—for example, **ban** /bã/, **bann** /bãn/ but **pa-n** /pan/. He also proposed that /ẽ/ (**ê** in the McConnell–Laubach orthography) should be written **in**,[14] necessitating the writing of, for example, /fin/ as **fi-n** to distinguish this from **fin** (/fẽ/). (An alternative possibility, proposed by Hazaël-Massieux (1994) for the

---

[13] **U** was not assigned any independent role. Haitian, like other French-based Creoles, lacks the front rounded vowels of French. **U** was thus not required for [y] and might instead have represented [u], as in Mauritian.

[14] Although **in** is arguably the least ambiguous representation of this phoneme for literate Francophones, in French orthography /ẽ/ is also written **im**, **ain**, **aim**, **en**, **ein**, **un**, **um**, **ym**, etc.

Antillean French Creoles, would be to write **e** 'muet' following a nasal consonant pronounced as such—for example, /fin/ as **fine** and /fẽ/ as **fin**.) A deviation
from phonemic principles shared by both orthographies was that yod was written **i** between a consonant and a vowel but **y** in other positions. Several other
orthographies have been proposed more recently but the differences between
them are small. All of them use **w** and **y** for the semivowels in all positions but
keep **ou** for /u/. They follow Pressoir (and French) in using **n** both to indicate
that the preceding vowel is nasalized and for the nasal consonant, but all reject
Pressoir's use of the hyphen in the representation of words such as /pan/ and
/fin/, adopting a variety of strategies to cope with this.[15]

Since the 1960s substantially phonemic orthographies have been designed for
virtually all the other French lexicon creoles. Mauritian uses **u** for /u/, but **ou** is
used in all the others. As in Haiti, there have often been two or more competing
orthographies within the same territory, varying mainly in their representation
of nasalized vowels, the affricates, and the palatal nasal /ɲ/. Whether in spite or
because of these competing orthographies, there has been a substantial increase
in the number of texts published in these languages in recent years. However, only
in the Seychelles has literacy in a French-lexicon Creole been taught at school.

In recent decades, there has been widespread agreement among academics
that the English-lexicon Creoles require substantially phonemic spelling systems,
and that the inadequacies of English spelling should not be inflicted on their
speakers. Furthermore, the essential groundwork for designing orthographies for
the English-lexicon Creoles of the Caribbean area was done long ago (Cassidy
1961, 1978[16]), although other authors have proposed some minor refinements
more recently.[17] In spite of that, scarcely any popular writing has been published
in Creole in any of these territories. This contrasts with the experience of the
neighbouring territories in which French-lexicon creoles are written and spoken.
With reference to his own system for Jamaican, Cassidy (1993: 136) says that it
has not been used outside academic circles 'because there is no demand among
readers for a consistent system'. However, unless or until popular reading matter
in Jamaican Creole written in a consistent system is published, it is difficult to
see how the views of 'readers' (those already literate in English) can be assessed,
nor can it be discovered whether the existence of such texts might encourage
some of the less literate to learn to read their own language.

Substantially phonemic orthographies have also been developed for a number
of English-lexicon pidgins and creoles spoken outside the Caribbean area, includ-

[15] Where /ẽ/ is written **en**, as in most of these orthographies, the problem largely disappears.
Valdman *et al.* (1981) uses a diacritic to indicate that a vowel is not nasalized by a following
(graphic) **n**, but Baker (1991) argues that this is unnecessary because there are in fact no ṼN/VN
contrasts in Haitian.
[16] A noteworthy feature of Cassidy (1978) is that it proposes a single orthography for the
Anglophone Caribbean in which each letter and digraph representing a vowel or diphthong is chosen
to take account of their differing phonetic realizations throughout the region.
[17] See Devonish and Seiler 1991 and the references in Cassidy 1993.

ing Tok Pisin (Papua New Guinea), Bislama (Vanuatu), and Solomons Pidgin in the Pacific as well as Krio (Sierra Leone), Nigerian Pidgin, and Cameroon Pidgin in West Africa. In the Pacific territories, quite a lot has been published using such orthographies. In the case of Krio, considerable effort has been put into developing a standard orthography for this and other (non-creole) languages of Sierra Leone in recent years, and there has also been an experimental programme for introducing these into the primary school. Orthographies for these proposed using ɛ, ɔ, and ŋ, but financial constraints have delayed their availability on typewriters and printing presses, thus severely limiting the production of written materials in these languages. There will be further comment on this in Section 7.1.

4.3. *Alphabetic Systems—Cyrillic*

From 1939–40, a policy of replacing romanized transcriptions with Cyrillic orthographies for the languages of Asia in territories which then formed part of the USSR was implemented. (Romanization of many of these languages, replacing Arabic or other scripts which had long been used, had been forced on most of them only fifteen years earlier.[18]) The intention was that speakers of such languages would find it easier to learn Russian, and that the assimilation of Russian words into them would be facilitated (Henze 1977: 381). Consistent with this aim, no Cyrillic letter which was not required for its usual phonetic value in Russian was assigned any other value. Instead, additional letters were preferred. Azerbaijani, closely related to Turkish, required eight additions. Four of these were achieved by adding marks to existing Cyrillic letters—for example, Ғ for Turkish ğ. Lower case h (for /h/) was adopted from the Roman alphabet, as also—or from Greek?—was upper case Y (for a front-rounded vowel), while the choice of the apostrophe for the glottal stop has many precedents. The remaining addition was an elongated version of ə, from IPA. Conventions such as these differed from one Turkic language to another, the political aim being to emphasize differences between these peoples and between their languages. As a result of these changes, as well as those noted earlier, the only languages still using the Roman alphabet within the USSR after the Second World War were those of the Baltic States (Latvian, Lithuanian, and Estonian). Under pressure from the USSR, the Cyrillic alphabet was also adopted, with minor modifications, for the writing of Mongolian in 1946. Mongolian had hitherto been written in the Uighur vertical script, an alphabetic system which is still used in Inner Mongolia.

The disintegration of the former USSR has brought into question the continued use of the Cyrillic script for languages previously written in the Roman alphabet or the Arabic script in a number of territories which have recently (re-)gained

---

[18] For a fuller account including the political considerations underlying these changes, see Henze (1977).

their independence. Coulmas (1993–4: 36) notes that the decision that Moldavian should revert to the use of the Roman alphabet, bringing it into line with its close relative, Romanian, was taken in 1989. It is expected that the Cyrillic script will soon be superseded throughout central Asia but the choice of replacement is complicated because of the rival claims of the Arabic and Roman scripts. Arabic script stands for 'pan-Islamic unity', while the Roman alphabet is associated with 'modernity and secularism' (Coulmas 1993–4: 37). As stated above, almost all the Turkic languages were written in the Unified Turkic Latin Alphabet as recently as the 1930s. Coulmas reports that, in 1992, Azerbaijan decided in favour of the Roman alphabet while Tajikistan opted for the Arabic script.

4.4. *Semi-Syllabic Systems*

Few previously unwritten languages appear to have had semi-syllabic orthographies designed for them in the past fifty years and most of these are probably due to the work of the Central Institute of Indian Languages (CIIL) in Mysore. The CIIL has developed writing systems for a large number of tribal languages, primarily with a view to providing initial literacy in the child's own language with a subsequent gradual transfer to the language and writing system of the State. As Annamalai (1979) points out, there are often up to four possibilities for the choice of script: Devanagari, Roman, the local State script, or an entirely new script. (Where the language of the local State is written in Devanagari or, in the case of Konkani in Goa, the Roman alphabet, the number of possibilities is reduced to three.) The CIIL has no authority to impose any writing system on a tribal community, but it does try to persuade such communities to adopt one of the scripts already in use locally. However, the ways in which controversies regarding the choice of script get resolved vary from situation to situation. In the case of Christian tribals, the desire to opt for the Roman script is very strong because of its association with religion and international status. It is also claimed that, compared with the Devanagari and most local State scripts in India, the Roman script is linear,[19] simple, and easy to learn. The protagonists of Devanagari advocate its use on the basis of its phonetic character, its association with Sanskrit, and its potential for bringing tribal communities into the mainstream of national life. Those favouring the local State script similarly emphasize the potential for this to promote harmonization of tribal peoples with other local communities. In

[19] Linear in the sense that the order in which letters are written corresponds to the sequence of sounds they represent. In Devanagari, the order in which characters are written similarly corresponds to the sequence of spoken syllables. However, while the core of each character represents a consonant, the position of the modifications representing vowels or **r** relative to the central consonantal element is not an indicator of its position in the corresponding sequence of sounds. For example, the modification for short **i** in the character representing the syllable **ki** precedes the consonantal element, whereas the modification for long **i:** follows it. Other modifications are variously written above and below the consonantal element.

yet other cases, the quasi-magical bond between the written image and reality may decide the choice of script (Hagège 1990). As noted above, the Santhals of West Bengal have been using their own Ol Chiki script for the past fifty years, rather than one of the three other options discussed above. In India, it is not unusual for people to acquire literacy in more than one script for the same language. Traditionally, traders have had to do this. Sindhi is one language whose writing systems have had a chequered history (Khubchandani 1969). The greater part of Sindhi literature is written in the Perso-Arabic script, but several Indian educational institutions teach Sindhi in the Devanagari script. Those with a serious interest in Sindhi literature are thus obliged to master both scripts. Prior to the partition of India and Pakistan, it was common for people in the extended Hindi-Urdu-Panjabi community to be bi- or multi-scriptal in the Devanagari, Perso-Arabic, and Gurmukhi scripts.

It was mentioned earlier that the Karen people of southern Burma have been using Burmese characters to write their language alphabetically for more than 150 years. A minority of the Karen live in the adjoining parts of Thailand. Some of these speak a variety of Karen very similar to that spoken on the other side of the border and they have also long used the Burmese-derived script. However, a further 17,000 Karen speak a variety 'which differs strongly from that for which literature has been prepared in Burma' (Smalley 1964: 89). For writing the latter, missionaries have adopted the Thai script, making limited use of 'digraphs' (two different characters from the Thai syllabary) in order to cope with a few Karen phonemes not occurring in Thai. The advantage claimed is that such limited opportunities for education as are open to the Karen are through the medium of Thai and thus that this orthography will help them in that respect. Note that this is written semi-syllabically as is Thai, whereas the Karen to the north of the border write their language alphabetically (even though with characters adopted from a semi-syllabic script).

4.5. *Consonantal Systems*

Anuak is a Nilotic language spoken on both sides of the Ethiopia–Sudan border. There are about 40,000 speakers in Ethiopia and some 10,000 in Sudan (Smalley 1964: 100). In recent years it has been the policy of the government of Ethiopia that all the country's indigenous languages should be written in the Amharic script, while the government of Sudan's policy has been to use the Arabic script for all its languages. Anuak has no fewer than ten vowel phonemes so cannot be adequately represented in either of these scripts without considerable modifications. It also has five consonant phonemes which have no equivalents in Arabic and which have thus required the invention of new characters (achieved by adding a dot to, or subtracting a dot from, existing Arabic letters). Smalley (1964: 99 n. 30) mentions an alternative proposal for using what in effect are

Arabic digraphs to represent these phonemes.[20] Similar ingenuity has been used
to devise a system for writing Anuak in the Amharic script. Both of these systems for writing Anuak fail to take account of phonemic tone contrasts (Smalley
1964: 101).

With the exception of southern Sudan, we are not aware of any increase in the
number of languages written in the Arabic script since the Second World War.
However, recent political changes in central Asia could well lead to proposals
for the Turkic languages of this area to return to either the Arabic script (used
for many years prior to the establishment of the USSR) or to the Roman alphabet (adopted with little variation for all the Turkic languages in the 1920s) and
the abandonment of the Cyrillic script (forcibly adopted during the past half
century).

Apart from Malay, we do not know of any languages which were previously
written in the Arabic script but which have abandoned this in favour of romanization since 1940.

4.6. *Other Systems*

A late addition to the indigenous scripts of Africa is that of Nsukka, a dialect
of Igbo. Like most others, this is a syllabary and is said to have been revealed
to its originator, Nwagu Aneke, in a dream. It is currently the subject of a
research project at the University of Nigeria.

5. THE REPRESENTATION OF TONE

It is generally accepted that tone must be marked wherever otherwise phonetically identical words belonging to the same class (nouns, verbs, etc.) are distinguished solely by tone. Languages meeting this criterion are mainly restricted to
two geographical areas: (i) China and South-East Asia, and (ii) Africa south of
the Sahara.

When written logographically, the problem of tone-marking does not arise in
any variety of Chinese because every word has its own unique representation.
However, tone-marking is essential for romanized transcriptions of Chinese. For
example, the six tones of Cantonese may be illustrated as follows: (1) **yan**
(unmarked; high level tone) means 'because', (2) **yán** (high rising) 'patience',
(3) **yàn** (high falling) 'a seal (inanimate)', (4) **yān** (low level) 'man', (5) **yǎn**
(low rising) 'to lead', and (6) **yân** (low falling) 'pregnant'. From Wade-Giles to
Pinyin, tone has usually been marked with diacritics on the vowels, but the
Gwoyeu Romatzyh system, designed by Chinese scholars in 1926, is remarkable

---

[20] This is the only example of the use of digraphs in the Arabic script that we know, but it seems
likely that there are others.

in that it employs no diacritics whatsoever but gives instead 'different internal spelling to all vowels in all four tones [of Mandarin], or where this is impossible then to initial or final consonants' (Newnham 1971: 171). The system is for Mandarin only, but it might be possible to devise a comparable system for the six tones of Cantonese. Finally, it should be noted that the marking of tone does not eliminate all ambiguities in romanized transcriptions of Chinese. There are many morphemes which are identical with regard to both phonemes and tone. For Cantonese, Meyer and Wemp (1947) list, in addition to the examples given above, at least six other morphemes pronounced **yan**, one other **yán**, one other **yàn**, four other **yān**, three other **yǎn,** and ten other **yân**. Each of these has its own unique logogram in written Chinese and is an indication of the limitations of what romanization can achieve for the Chinese languages.

Most other languages of the region which require tone-marking have semi-syllabic scripts. In languages such as Burmese and Thai, the basic character representing the syllable is modified to indicate not only the following vowel but also the tone. In Bodo, a minority language of India, high tone is marked by visargah (which closely resembles the colon and is employed in Sanskrit to mark a final aspirated vowel), while **o** (zero) is used to mark low tone. At least two tone languages of the region have romanized orthographies. The system of marking tone in one of them, Vietnamese, was discussed and illustrated earlier. Another is the Naga group of languages of north-east India, in one of which high tone is marked orthographically by doubling the vowel, as in **aa**, **ii**, etc., whereas low tone is indicated by the vowel + **h**, as in **ah**, **ih**, etc. (Other languages of this group, such as Angami-Naga, have as many as five contrasting tones.)

In Africa, the need for tone-marking has long been recognized for many of the Kwa languages, including Twi, Fon, Yoruba, and Igbo, some of the Manding languages, and at least Hausa among the Chadic languages. Most of these languages distinguish two or three tones. That tone-marking is essential in such languages can be illustrated by disyllabic words which contrast all possible combinations of tones. The following examples, in which high and low tone are marked, respectively, by the acute and grave accents, come from two Nigerian languages, Igbo (Hyman 1975: 213) and its close relative Izi (Meier and Bendor-Samuel 1975):

Igbo				Izi			
ákwá	'crying'	ákwà	'cloth'	ọ́kú	'fire'	ọ́kụ̀	'fowl'
àkwá	'egg'	àkwà	'bed'	òkú	'a bird'	òkụ̀	'heartburn'

In these examples, the superposed diacritics marking tone carry vital information in an economical way. Note that they are compatible with the subdotted vowels (indicating retracted vowels) in the Izi examples.

In Igbo and Izi, as in Chinese and other tone languages of south-eastern Asia, tone-marking relates to the tone level of every syllable so marked. (Tone level is generally relative rather than absolute.) There are at least two other ways of marking tone, both of which are more economical, although neither is suited to all languages. In some languages, there may often be sequences of several syllables each carrying the same tone level. In such cases, it may be convenient to mark only the first syllable carrying a particular tone. In this way, a diacritic marking tone applies not only to the syllable containing the vowel over which it is placed but also to all subsequent syllables until another tone marker is encountered. A system of this kind was adopted by Christaller for Twi in the nineteenth century. The other possibility, explored by Mann (1969) with reference to Bemba (a Bantu language of Zambia), does not mark tone level as such but changes in tone level or 'tone contrasts', while the diacritics marking these tone contrasts are placed between syllables rather than over vowels, e.g. *u˘mucele, umupe˘ni*.

The tone systems of many of the languages of central and southern Africa have yet to be studied. Even among those which have been adequately studied, the questions of whether and to what extent tone-marking is needed seem rarely to have been resolved. Those specializing in the study of the same language may sometimes disagree among themselves. In the case of Sango, for example, Diki-Kidiri (1988) feels that tone-marking is so important that it must be given priority over marking the distinction between mid-high and mid-low vowels, while Samarin (1992) dislikes diacritics and fears that their use for tone-marking may retard the acquisition of literacy in this language. Samarin also claims that potential ambiguities resulting from the lack of tone-marking are almost always disambiguated by context. He does not reject the marking of tone in all circumstances, but suggests rather that, like the diacritics for marking vowels in Arabic, they might be written in some circumstances but not in most. We shall return to this below.

From the Sango dictionary compiled by Bouquiaux *et al.* (1978), it is clear that there are some pairs of words distinguished only by whether they have a mid-high or a mid-low vowel, e.g. /èrè/ 'peel (verb)' vs. /ɛ̀rɛ̀/ 'withdraw', some which contrast both tones and mid-high/mid-low vowels, e.g. /dō/ 'hole' vs. /dɔ/ 'axe', and a far greater number which are distinguished by tones alone, e.g. /kúā/ 'comrade' vs. /kūā/ 'hair' vs. /kùà/ 'work' vs. /kúá/ 'corpse'. Starting from the assumption that French diacritics offer the only practical means of *either* distinguishing mid-high from mid-low vowels *or* marking tones, Diki-Kidiri is correct in so far as the marking of tone would disambiguate far more words that the marking of mid-high/mid-low vowel contrasts. It is nevertheless possible to indicate both tones and mid-high/mid-low vowel contrast, as the above examples demonstrate, by using diacritics to mark tones and special characters for the mid-low vowels. (An alternative possibility would be to use subscript dots to mark the mid-low vowels, as is done in the orthographies of a number of Nigerian languages.)

The great majority of languages spoken in central and southern Africa belong to the Bantu group. Some of these, including the best-known member of the group, Swahili, are non-tone languages. In some others, tone plays a major role in determining the precise meaning of the verb. In Bemba, six or more different tone patterns may occur in the base (radical + suffix) of a verb according to tense, modality, and aspect, as in the following examples illustrated by the verb 'explain' (written in a tone-contrast orthography):

-**londolola** in 'that they might explain'
-**lon`dolola** in 'they explained earlier today'
-`**londolola** in 'they will explain'
-**lon´dolola** in 'they have already explained'
-`**londolo´la** in 'which they will explain'
-**londolo´la** in 'which we have just explained' (Mann 1969: 105)

Without tone-marking, all six forms of the base would be written identically as **londolola**. In many cases, the precise sense might be clear from the context. However, there are circumstances in which it would be important to avoid any possible ambiguity and where this could be achieved only by tone-marking. These include (*a*) legal documents of all kinds, and (*b*) all texts intended to be read aloud. The latter comprise announcements and bulletins to be broadcast on radio and television, speeches, plays, poetry, and sacred texts.[21] In all such cases, we believe that it is essential for the orthography to make provision for tone-marking, but the choice of whether or not to indicate tone in a particular text should be left to individual choice and popular demand. To the extent that we are suggesting the need for standard forms of the written language both with and without diacritics (representing tone levels or tone contrasts), we agree with the analogy Samarin draws with Arabic.

Apart from the Gwoyeu Romatzyh system for Mandarin mentioned above, all the examples discussed so far have marked tone with superposed diacritics. An alternative possibility, mentioned briefly but not illustrated in Mann, Dalby, *et al.* (1987: 210), is linear equivalents of diacritics. For example, if / represents rising tone and \ falling tone, the six tonally contrasting forms of -**londolola** given earlier might be written:

-**londolola** -**lon\dolola** -**\londolola** -**lon/dolola** -**\londolo/la** -**londolo/la**

If we add to these ¯ for high and ˍ for low, all four might be used in combination to represent the six tones of a language such as Cantonese. In a monosyllabic language such as this the tone marks might (*a*) precede the letters, (*b*) follow the letters, or (*c*) the starting tone might precede and the direction of travel might follow the letters. All three possibilities are illustrated in Table 3.8.

---

[21] Mann (1969: 107) notes 'there are frequent reports of . . . Africans having recourse to an English Bible before being able to read aloud a translation in their own language', attributing this to non-representation of tone in the latter. Bernard (1992) claims that speakers of tone languages can usually discern the correct tones from context, drawing a false analogy with the lack of stress marking in English (which is rule governed). A good test might be whether a speaker could supply the correct tones on the first reading aloud of a previously unseen test.

TABLE 3.8. *Three ways of marking tone in Cantonese using linear equivalents of diacritics*

Tone	Pre-posed (*a*)	Post-posed (*b*)	Pre- and post-posed (*c*)
High, level	⁻yan	yan⁻	⁻yan⁻
High, rising	⁻/yan	yan⁻/	⁻yan/
High, falling	⁻\yan	yan⁻\	⁻yan\
Low, level	_yan	yan_	_yan_
Low, rising	_/yan	yan_/	_yan/
Low, falling	_\yan	yan_\	_yan\

6. ON THE RELATIVE MERITS OF WRITING SYSTEMS AND THEIR 'LEARNABILITY'

It is widely assumed in the West that alphabetic writing systems are superior to all other kinds. The factors which underlie this assumption probably include the following:

1. that alphabetic systems evolved later than logographic and syllabic ones and are thus associated with a more advanced stage of human development (see Moorhouse 1946: 16; Abercrombie 1967: 38);
2. that it has long been considered that orthographies should give separate and unique representation to each phoneme of the spoken language, and this can only be achieved with an alphabetic system;
3. that alphabetic systems are more economic than other systems, in that they require far fewer characters;
4. that the individual letters in alphabetic systems tend to be simpler in design and more easily distinguished from one another than is the case with other systems.

Each of these factors requires comment. (1) and (2) overlook the semi-syllabic scripts. These in fact postdate the earliest alphabetic systems by at least 500 years but, so far as we are aware, no one has yet suggested that this makes them more advanced (with regard to human development) than alphabetic systems. It is also the case that semi-syllabic systems are not inherently less phonemic than alphabetic systems, although the former do give less graphic prominence to vowels than to consonants (see Table 3.1 for some examples). As for (3), while it is true that alphabetic systems rarely need more than forty characters, semi-syllabic systems often require 200 or more, and logographic systems demand several thousand, in practice the differences of scale are not quite so great as this implies. The Roman alphabet is generally said to have twenty-six letters, but there are distinct upper and lower case forms of each of these as well as separate cursive forms. Thus, even without taking account of the diacritics and/or special characters used in many orthographies, it could be said that literacy in a language using the Roman alphabet demands the ability to recognise about 100 distinct handwritten and printed characters. By contrast, semi-syllabic scripts normally have but a single form of each character. Furthermore, the modifications for particular vowels can be virtually identical regardless of the consonantal character (cf. Ethiopic illustrated earlier in Table 3.1). In such cases, it could be argued that the learner has only to acquire as many consonant characters and vowel modifications as there are phonemes. In terms of the number of graphic forms to be acquired, semi-syllabic systems are thus not necessarily more demanding than alphabetic systems.

The acquisition of 2,000 logograms is generally considered the minimum requirement for basic literacy in Chinese (Crystal 1987: 200). This is undoubtedly a far more arduous task than learning to read and write any semi-syllabic or alphabetic writing system. One important indication of this is the fact that the Chinese government publishes figures for literacy only for the population aged 12 years and over (Howes 1992: 6), in contrast to most other societies where literacy rates tend to be published for people aged 7 years (or less) and over. While it undoubtedly takes considerably longer to acquire literacy in Chinese than in languages written in alphabetic or semi-syllabic systems, the logograms themselves are, graphically, not quite so difficult to learn as they might at first seem in so far as there are 214 radicals (basic character forms) and all other logograms consist of combinations of (reduced forms of) two or more of these radicals. Note that the number of radicals is thus similar to the total number of characters in semi-syllabic scripts.

Factor (4) relates to the simplicity of design and distinctiveness of alphabetic characters. While any view on this must be partly subjective, we are not aware that anyone has ever claimed that any semi-syllabic or logographic system has a set of characters which is simpler or more distinctive than that of the Roman, Greek, or Cyrillic alphabet. We also do not know of any research which has been done comparing the learning difficulties associated with different alphabetic or semi-syllabic systems. Among the latter group, Février (1948) suggests that the Tamil script is particularly easy to read, in part because of its lack of ligatures. It might also be argued that its particular mix of angular and rounded characters makes them more easily distinguishable than is the case with most other scripts of the Indian subcontinent.

In our Introduction we mentioned that there was some evidence of children initially acquiring logograms more rapidly than syllabograms, and the latter more quickly than alphabetical letters. The emphasis here must be placed on the word 'initially'. Although we have not been able to consult the full account of the experiment, references to it seem to indicate that it was of limited scope and duration. (It seems inconceivable that parents anywhere in the world would willingly allow their preliterate children to take part in a lengthy experiment involving three different writing systems where knowledge of two of these would not subsequently be required for their education.) If we accept that a group of children in the USA more readily acquired a number of logograms than a similar number of syllabograms, and the latter more rapidly than a similar number of letters of the alphabet, it does not follow that any logographic writing system (as a complete system) is easier to learn than any syllabic system, nor that the latter is more learnable than an alphabetic system. The child who has acquired twenty logograms can read and write only twenty words and cannot use this knowledge to predict how any other word should be written or what any other logogram might mean. Such a child still needs another 1,980 logograms for basic literacy and perhaps a further 4,000 to be considered really well educated. (According to Wu Yuzhang, cited by Seybolt and Kuei-ke Chiang (1978: 21), Chinese children typically learn only about 1,000 logograms during six years of elementary schooling.) By contrast, the child who has acquired twenty syllabograms can potentially use this knowledge to read and write a small but significant proportion of his/her vocabulary (but he or she will still need to learn 180 or more other syllabograms to master the whole system), while the child who has acquired twenty letters of an alphabetic system will have the potential to read and write much if not most of his or her entire vocabulary. Thus, even if children can initially grasp the concept of characters representing individual morphemes more readily than characters representing individual syllables, and grasp the latter concept more readily than that of characters representing individual phonemes, there can be no possible doubt that complete alphabetic systems are acquired more quickly than complete syllabic systems, and that complete syllabic systems are acquired far more quickly than even basic literacy (2,000 characters) in logographic systems. (Note that, by syllabic systems and syllabograms, we refer in this paragraph to syllabaries such as that for Loma (Table 3.5), where neither shared initial consonants nor shared final vowels are reflected graphically. In semi-syllabic systems such as those illustrated in Table 3.1, where the representation of particular consonants and vowels is substantially constant throughout the system, we would not expect the time required for learning them to be greater than that needed for alphabetic systems except in so far as the characters themselves are more complex.)

7. GENERAL TRENDS

Most orthographies designed for previously unwritten languages in the past fifty years have used the Roman alphabet. While speakers of some minority languages in India have themselves opted for non-Roman scripts (see above), in most other cases where non-Roman scripts were adopted this was due to governments forbidding the use of the Roman alphabet rather than to the wishes of the orthography designers and/or users (in e.g. former Soviet Central Asia, southern Sudan, Taiwan, and Ethiopia). While the discussions which follow are primarily concerned with adaptations of the Roman script, we believe that the general principles invoked are also relevant to other scripts.

At the beginning of this chapter, we listed the orthographic preferences contained in the 1953 report. There were seven in all. The first, 'spelling in conformity with contemporary pronunciation', is so basic and uncontroversial that it requires no further comment (although, of course, it immediately raises the question of 'whose pronunciation?'). If account is taken of the remarks in the Introduction to this chapter, the same is true of the second, 'agreement with phonemes of the language'. The third, 'Simplicity in typography (available types, limited numbers of characters, etc.)' highlights an area which has changed enormously in the intervening forty years and will be discussed below (Sect. 7.1). Preferences 4, 5, and 6 all relate to the choice of characters to represent particular phonemes, a question examined in Section 7.2. The seventh preference was for 'Agreement between different languages of the region or country, especially with the national or official language' and this is discussed in Section 7.3.

7.1. *Technical Considerations*

In 1953, the principal technical constraint on orthography design was the range of characters available on typewriter keyboards and printing presses. Unless requested in advance to do otherwise, typewriter manufacturers supplied machines with keyboards suited exclusively to the requirements of the official (usually colonial) language of the country concerned. Although, even in 1953, printing establishments often had fonts which could cope with several of the principal European languages using the Roman alphabet, typewriter keyboards used in government offices were the more immediate, and constraining, influence on those who designed orthographies for indigenous languages. Furthermore, even in those colonies where there was a disposition to provide literacy initially in one or more of the indigenous languages, the purpose of schools was seen as providing a version of the educational system of the colonial power taught through the colonial language. Nevertheless, even when typewriters without special characters were purchased, it was not an expensive matter to adapt them. Writing thirty years ago, Smalley (1964: 14) commented:

But along with cultural imperialism it is easy to fall victim to a mechanical imperialism. The limitations of a typewriter's keyboard sometimes bear more weight in the development of a writing system than do the phonemes of a language. I can make all of the following characters on my typewriter, and it cost under $10 to have the typewriter changed to include all of these characters without eliminating any of the letters of the English alphabet: ɑʌɪŋæʊɔɔɛʔ. In addition, ˆ ˝ ˜ ` or ´ may be typed with a dead key so that they do not advance the carriage. They therefore show over the letter which is typed after them, giving é è á à etc. Yet the principal reason for not using ŋ in many languages has been that it was not on a missionary's typewriter!

Given the circumstances sketched above, considerable difficulties faced those who worked to develop orthographies for their own indigenous languages. If they felt the need for additional letters or diacritics in order to represent a language adequately, they were likely to face objections from the expatriate officials, whose approval they would require, on the grounds of alleged technical difficulty and/ or cost. Such officials would probably not even speak the language and might well believe, if not actually say, that it ought to be possible to represent any language with the twenty-six letters of the alphabet alone. (It is surely not necessary here to demonstrate either (a) that neither English nor French is adequately represented with the Roman alphabet, and that only a minority of their native speakers master their respective spelling 'systems', or (b) that, in so far as other European languages may be said to have better orthographies, this has been achieved partly by extending the possibilities of the Roman alphabet with diacritics, special characters, digraphs, etc.) In fact, it was never either technically difficult or expensive to replace one character on a typewriter with another or for printing works to obtain fonts containing such characters. The only serious problems were (a) geography: the people able to make such changes quickly and cheaply were based in London, Paris, or New York rather than Freetown or Djibouti; and (b) prejudice or lack of motivation on the part of government officials (expatriate or local). That these problems were far from insuperable, even in colonial times, is shown by the examples of Ghana and Togo (additional characters and diacritics for tones), Nigeria (subscript dots to create additional letters and superscript diacritics for tones), and Vietnam (diacritics, some specially designed, for vowel quality and tones).

The typewriter and, to a lesser extent, the printing press remained important constraints on orthography design everywhere until the late 1970s. Then the new technology began to change things in the Far East, Western Europe, and North America. By c.1985, the word processor or desktop computer had largely replaced typewriters in many of the richer countries and computer technology was rapidly ousting 'hot-metal' type for printing presses. At the present time (1994) a desktop computer, often with double the range of characters available on a typewriter, costs considerably less in real terms than a good electric typewriter of a decade earlier. These changes herald the end of almost a century during which the limitations of typewriter keyboards have been the major constraint on orthography design. The fact that the new technology has not yet replaced the old in much of the rest of the world does not mean that the new technology can be resisted. Most of the typewriters in offices around the Third World are no longer manufactured. Spare parts and ribbons will rapidly become more difficult to obtain and repairs increasingly problematic. Eventually they will have to be replaced and there is unlikely to be any realistic alternative to acquiring computer technology.

The rapidly approaching end of the typewriter era does not mean that orthographers should do nothing until they have access to the new technology. On the contrary, it means not only that they can design orthographies with fewer constraints than ever before, but also that they should do so *before* the new equipment is ordered so that they can be sure that it will meet all their requirements when it arrives. In order to obtain maximum value from the remaining life of their existing equipment, they may also need to devise transitional orthographic arrangements. This possibility merits further attention.

During the past 200 years, orthographies for previously unwritten languages have generally been designed by people who wanted them to be used as soon as possible. This was another reason, in addition to those mentioned above, for accepting the limited choice of characters which were immediately available. Today, while there is both more experience and a wider range of characters to draw on, the designer of an orthography may still opt for a less than ideal solution which can be reproduced on a twenty-year-old office typewriter rather than face the argument and delay that might result from an orthographic choice requiring new equipment. There will be comment on the financial aspects of this below. With regard to the problem of the delay between choosing an orthographic solution which requires new equipment and having such equipment available for the introduction of the orthography, we believe that this can generally be overcome by finding short-term alternative ways of representing the characters which are awaited.

German provides a well-known example of orthographic alternatives. In the standard orthography, there are three letters which occur with the umlaut: ä, ö, and ü. There exists, however, a long-established alternative tradition of writing these as **ae**, **oe**, and **ue**, respectively, wherever German is written on equipment which lacks this diacritic, in both upper and lower case. German orthography also features a special character, ß, but similarly provides for this to be written **ss** on equipment which lacks this character. By these means, German can always be written satisfactorily, even on equipment which lacks its single diacritic and special character. A recent example of orthographic alternatives comes from Senegal, where ŋ was adopted as one of the letters of the national alphabet ten years ago, and where children thereafter learned to read and write this at school. Unfortunately this letter did not exist on many of the old typewriters but the problem was solved by adopting ñ as a permissible alternative. This simple decision made it possible for the new alphabet to be taught without delay. For the children concerned, all this meant was that ñ was an alternative representation of ŋ.

We believe that wherever an orthography is proposed which makes use of characters (including diacritics and other non-alphabetic elements) not available on all the keyboards on which the language might be written, it would be advisable to provide an alternative way of representing those characters. For example, in Sierra Leone at the end of 1990, the Indigenous Languages Unit of the Ministry of Education possessed only one functioning typewriter equipped with the characters ɛ and ɔ (Johnson 1992: 55–6). These form part of the official orthographies of Krio and the three other important indigenous languages of the country. The extremely limited availability of these characters was thus a major constraint on the teaching of literacy in these languages. However, for Krio at least, there exist long-established digraphs for these phonemes, **eh** and **oh**. There would seem no obvious reason why the latter should not be used as alternatives to ɛ and ɔ until such time as all the necessary equipment possesses the means to reproduce the latter pair.

7.2. *Phoneme Representation*

The 1953 recommendations mentioned three ways of representing phonemes for which there were insufficient (suitable) individual letters in the Roman alphabet: diacritics, digraphs, and special characters. They also indicated a preference for digraphs over the other two possibilities, but this was in part related to their concern for costs, given the limitations of the technology then available. Elsewhere in this chapter we have noted two other strategies, neither of which had or has any implications for cost: the use of non-alphabetic keyboard characters in the representation of phonemes, and the use of letters not required to represent any of the phonemes with which they are usually associated in unfamiliar and even unprecedented roles (e.g. **q** to represent either a click, as in Zulu, or the voiceless pharyngeal fricative, as in 'Afar, now written Qafar in the latter's orthography).

In our experience, orthography is a subject on which many people hold firmer convictions than they are able to justify intellectually. We nevertheless think it is possible to identify, non-controversially, some practical advantages and disadvantages associated with each of the five strategies for extending the Roman alphabet mentioned in the preceding paragraph. These are listed below. There are also a few principles of good orthography design which, we believe, are widely accepted and these too will be set out below.

Digraphs and Trigraphs

The great advantage of digraphs and trigraphs consisting exclusively of letters drawn from the Roman alphabet is that they can be typed on any keyboard. The only certain disadvantage of orthographies which make extensive use of combinations of two or three letters to represent a single phoneme is that considerably more printing space is required than with orthographies in which every phoneme is represented, through use of diacritics and/or special characters, by a single segment. In extreme cases such as Xhosa (Table 3.4) and Venda (Table 3.7), one-segment-per-phoneme orthographies could produce economies of space in excess of 30 per cent. It seems likely that the saving in typing, typesetting, printing, and paper costs would very quickly far outweigh the costs of providing the equipment to cope with diacritics and special characters. Another likely disadvantage of extensive use of di- and trigraphs, though so far as we are aware it has not been studied, is that they complicate literacy teaching in that learners must identify clusters of letters as well as individual letters.

Apart from the above, it is often difficult to devise an orthography using digraphs (and/or trigraphs) without falling foul of some of the most widely accepted principles of good design. These include:

(*a*) The two or more letters chosen to denote a single phoneme should not co-occur elsewhere in the language where they represent individual phonemes. English orthography conflicts with the principle in words such as hothead and hogshead where both **t** and **h** and **s** and **h** are to be independently articulated and do not represent the digraphs **th** and **sh**.

(*b*) The two or more letters chosen to denote a single phoneme should provide some indication of its mode and place of articulation. By this criterion, **ny** and **ly** are reasonable digraphs for, respectively, a palatal nasal and palatal lateral, whereas **gn** (as in French) and **lh** (as in Portuguese) are not because neither **g** nor **h** relates to their place or mode of articulation.

(*c*) The orthography as a whole should be internally consistent. If a language has contrasting plain and aspirated occlusives, and if the latter are given digraphic representation consisting of the letter representing the corresponding plain occlusive + **h**, it is internally inconsistent to employ **h** in other digraphs representing non-aspirated phonemes.

Non-Alphabetic Keyboard Characters

Like digraphs, the immediate advantage of standard non-alphabetic characters is that they are available on all keyboards and printing presses. The main disadvantage is that their use in the representation of phonemes may mean that they are no longer available to fulfil their usual function.

The non-alphabetic character most extensively used in the representation of phonemes is the apostrophe. In some languages, it is used alone to represent either the glottal stop or, less often, a pharyngeal fricative. In other languages, it is the second element in the representation of either glottalized or aspirated occlusives. If used in any of these roles, it is inconvenient also to use it to signal elision (as in English *can't*, *I've*; French *j'y*, *l'a*; etc.) or as a quotation mark (although double quotes might be used instead). Other non-alphabetic characters used in the representation of phonemes in some orthographies may similarly impinge on their established roles as punctuation marks or numerals.

New Uses for Otherwise Unwanted Alphabetic Characters

As with digraphs and non-alphabetic characters, the advantage of using Roman characters not otherwise required to represent entirely different phonemes is that no technical problems or costs are involved because the letters are available on all keyboards. There are no certain disadvantages to this policy, although it seems reasonable to suppose that if, in a multilingual state, a single letter such as **x** or **q** were assigned different values in three or more languages, some confusion would result.

Diacritics

The advantage of superposed diacritics is that they can be used with any letter which lacks an ascender (that is, all vowel symbols as well as **s**, **c**, **n**, etc.).[22] A diacritic can greatly change the appearance of such letters, making them visually distinct, single-segment representatives of individual phonemes. Various disadvantages have been claimed for superposed diacritics. It has been said that they pose technical problems. In fact, any equipment designed for Portuguese has always made provision for the acute, grave, trema (umlaut), circumflex, and tilde and, in contrast to French practice, for use with upper- as well as lower-case letters. Such facilities are readily obtainable on modern keyboards. A more justifiable claim is that they are inconvenient to type, requiring at least two key strokes each. It is similarly claimed that they are cumbersome to write, since the pen must either leave the paper, interrupting the left-to-right flow, or they must be added after the rest of the word has been written, with the risk that they may get omitted. (These comments apply equally to lower case **t** and **i**.) These two objections clearly have some validity, but they apply exclusively to writing, not to reading. Another claimed disadvantage of superposed diacritics for distinguishing phonemes is that diacritics cannot then be used to mark tone. We share this widespread view and, while acknowledging that the Vietnamese quốc ngữ’ orthography demonstrates that, with specially designed equipment, it is technically possible to use superposed diacritics for both purposes, we consider Vietnamese usage an example which few would wish to emulate. While accepting that, in languages requiring tone-marking, diacritics should be reserved for that purpose, we can find no important practical reason for not considering their use in other circumstances.

Subscript diacritics are also employed in quite a wide range of orthographies, including those of several Nigerian languages. As noted earlier, these are compatible with the use of superposed diacritics for tone. Equipment and software for subscript diacritics is considerably more difficult to acquire than for superscript ones, but Nigeria has demonstrated that they can be obtained.

Special Characters

The one certain advantage of special characters over other strategies is that they can provide a unique character for every phoneme. The disadvantage of special

---

[22] All these letters also lack a descender. Superposed diacritics are occasionally used with certain letters which have a descender, notably **g** and **j**. (Depending on the characteristics of the particular font, the dot of both **j** and **i** can restrict the choice of superposed diacritics. This problem is mainly restricted to typewriters; computers generally dispense with the dot when another diacritic is superposed, e.g. **î, í, ì, ï**, etc.)

characters has been their absence on traditional keyboards. However, as indicated in Section, 7.1, such characters are less expensive and less difficult to obtain than has often been suggested. The fact that Togo and Ghana have been employing such characters for more than sixty years is a further indication of this.

Strong objections to the very idea of using special characters in orthography design are sometimes held by otherwise rational people, and seem to stem from a deep-rooted conviction that the Roman alphabet is somehow inviolable. The actual arguments advanced against special characters tend to be relatively trivial and include (i) that people don't like them, (ii) that there are no 'proper' corresponding capital letters for them, (iii) that they are difficult to write cursively, and (iv) that it is difficult, expensive, and time-consuming to obtain such characters and have them fitted to existing equipment.

In so far as (i) has any validity,[23] it seems to reflect the general unwillingness of those already literate in a prestigious language to accept major orthographic innovation in a language they regard as less prestigious.

Argument (ii) is not strictly true, in that the Africa Script provided both upper- and lower-case varieties of all its characters, and these have long been used in Ghana and Togo. What is true is that upper-case special characters have generally been far more difficult to obtain than the corresponding lower-case ones. In contrast to the Africa Script, the designers of the a.r.a. took the radical view that the use of majuscules was entirely unnecessary, opening the way to keyboards with a basic set of up to sixty characters, sufficient for the adequate representation of all known languages.[24] In fact, the conventions for using upper-case letters differ greatly from one European language to another, the only widely shared conventions for use of upper-case letters being (*a*) the first letter of the names of people, towns, and countries, and (*b*) the first letter of the first word of each new sentence. In order to demonstrate that lack of capitals does not make text more difficult to read, Mann, Dalby, *et al.* (1987) is printed entirely in lower-case letters.[25]

With reference to Argument (iii), the designers of both the Africa Script and the a.r.a. have published suggested cursive forms for all their characters. While literate adults might experience some difficulty in accommodating new letters into their established cursive style, there is no reason to suppose that children first acquiring literacy through an extended alphabet would find the new characters any more or less difficult than the old.

Finally, the claim (iv) that new characters are difficult and/or expensive to

[23] In our limited experience, this view is rarely expressed by native speakers of the language concerned.

[24] Languages with an exceptionally large phonemic inventory, such as Venda (see Fig. 3.5) and some of the Caucasian languages (see Sect. 4.3) would still require some digraphs or diacritics. However, the a.r.a. has twelve letters for vowels and this is probably sufficient for all languages without recourse to diacritics, in sharp contrast to the mere five of the Roman alphabet.

[25] With the exception of the cover and title page, where the use of capitals was imposed by the publisher against the authors' wishes.

obtain was discussed and rejected earlier. It was also pointed out that the real cost of adopting digraphs was, over time, far greater than that of introducing special characters (see above). While it must be acknowledged that the delay between deciding to use special characters and possessing all the necessary equipment ready to reproduce them can be considerable, this problem can be overcome by adopting alternative representations of certain phonemes, as suggested in Section 7.1.

7.3. *Harmonization*

The notion of harmonization was implicit in the 1953 report in the preference expressed for 'agreement between different languages of the region or country, especially with the national or official language' (Unesco 1953: 62). In 1953, 'official language' often meant 'language of the occupying colonial power'. At that time, the influence of the official languages on the design of orthographies for indigenous languages was still strong. In British colonies, the rule 'consonants as in English, vowels as in Italian' was fairly rigidly applied with **ch** for [tʃ] and new digraphs created for non-English sounds. In French territories it was not unusual, in the 1950s and 1960s, to publish grammars and dictionaries of indigenous languages in which the latter were written entirely within French orthographic conventions with, for example, [tʃ] represented as **tch**, **ty**, or **ti**, [g] as **gu** before **e** or **i**, and [u] as **ou** even in languages with just five oral vowels. Today, with the exception of pidgins and creoles, the conventions of (European) official languages have minimal influence on the design of orthographies for indigenous languages; in most orthographies proposed for African languages since the 1970s, [u] is written **u** and [tʃ] generally as **c**, entirely regardless of what was the language of the former colonial power.

In 1953, 'national language' had two distinct definitions: (1) 'officially declared to be the national language of a state' and (2) 'language of a nation'. In the colonial era, (1) was frequently and not always accurately interpreted as meaning 'the indigenous language spoken by the majority of the population' in contrast to the 'official language' of the colonial power. The meaning of (2) varied according to one's definition of the word 'nation'. In more recent times, in Africa at least, 'national language' has come to be applied to any indigenous language in which literacy is encouraged by government. Senegal, for example, has six 'national languages' and has developed harmonized orthographies for all of these, as was indicated earlier. Collectively, these are the first languages of some 94 per cent of its population (Mann, Dalby, *et al.* 1987: 197). A dozen other languages spoken by small minorities are denied 'national' status. Similar policies are pursued by other countries, particularly in West Africa.

Harmonization of orthographies across international boundaries has so far made little progress, largely because of political considerations. Where the contrasting writing systems of a language spoken on either side of an international border are both based on the same (Roman, Arabic, etc.) script, the literate will normally have little difficulty in reading each other's publications, even if there are important orthographic differences. Such is clearly not the case where entirely different scripts are adopted, as in the examples of Anuak (Sudan and Ethiopia) and Karen (Myanmar and Thailand) discussed in Sections 3.3 and 3.4.

Both within and across national boundaries, orthographic harmonization has important implications for the five strategies which have been employed so far to extend the possibilities of the Roman alphabet. The difficulties of selecting suitable letters for the digraphic represention of a particular phoneme in a language were noted earlier. Such difficulties are considerably increased when it becomes necessary to choose digraphs which are appropriate for, or not in conflict with, the phonologies of all the other languages in a multilingual country. Harmonization of orthographies within multilingual states similarly imposes severe constraints on the possibilities of finding satisfactory solutions which involve either non-alphabetic characters or assigning unusual values to established letters of the alphabet. The two strategies best able to cope with the demands of harmonization are those with the greatest number of single segments available for the representation of single phonemes, achieved through the use of diacritics or special characters. It is precisely these two strategies which are becoming more readily available through the new computer-based technology.

The above paragraphs concern the harmonization of orthographies for languages without their own indigenous script, without a long written history, and for which no alternative to an orthography based on the Roman alphabet has been proposed. The situation is very different in the parts of Asia where semi-syllabic scripts are dominant and where most languages with a long written history have their own language-specific script. In such cases, the language-specific script tends to be identified as an integral part of the language itself, and there is consequently no pressure for change or even discussion of the possibility of harmonizing, and thus reducing the number of, the different scripts. Nevertheless, as was noted in Section 3.3, the policy in India is to encourage (but not to oblige) speakers of hitherto unwritten languages to adopt orthographies based on an established script of the region, rather than to devise a new script.

8. SUMMARY AND CONCLUSIONS

One thing which emerges from this historical and geographical review is that orthographies, particularly those written in an alphabetic script, are rarely fixed once for all time. They may be changed for many different reasons:

- The phonological analysis of the language on which the orthography was originally based may have been faulty in some respects.
- Ideas concerning the particular variety of the language on which the standard should be based may have altered.

- Changes in the available technology may suggest other ways of indicating particular phonemic or tonal distinctions.
- It may be desired to harmonize the orthographies of several languages spoken within the same country, or to merge two or more orthographies for the same language where this crosses international borders.
- The phonemic inventory of the language itself may change, perhaps as the result of adopting vocabulary on a large scale from another language which has a rather different set of phonological contrasts, or simply through normal 'drift'.
- In some cases, changing political circumstances may even require that a language be henceforth written in an altogether different script.

As indicated in Section 3, most orthographies designed in the past 200 years for previously unwritten languages employ the Roman alphabet. The following remarks apply mainly but not exclusively to such systems.

While orthographers cannot be expected to predict the future, Section 7 and the above list of reasons for change suggest that it might be worthwhile at least considering the implications of possible future moves towards orthographic harmonization both within the country and, if the language is also spoken there, across its borders. Section 7 also suggests that orthographies might usefully be designed not only for the typewriters and presses which are currently available but also for the more sophisticated equipment which will almost certainly replace them over the next decade or two (by which we mean the equipment which has already replaced the typewriter in North America, Western Europe, and parts of Asia). Where the new technology offers more satisfactory solutions to orthographic problems than are currently available locally, it may be advisable to opt for the preferred solution while devising alternative representations for as many characters as necessary as an interim solution so that an immediate start can be made with introducing the orthography on existing equipment.

In the past, the representation of tone was often not considered until after an orthography reflecting only the segmental phonemic contrasts of a language had been designed. In our discussion of the relative merits of writing systems and their 'learnability', we concluded that all orthographies for languages in which tone plays a significant semantic role in the lexicon and/or syntax need to provide a means for marking tone. While we acknowledged that, with some languages, it might prove essential to mark tone only in specialized contexts such as legal documents and texts to be read aloud in public, we took the view that the system of marking tone should take priority over deciding how individual phonemes would be represented, because, if superposed diacritics were chosen for the former, they would not then be available for indicating vowel quality.

In Section 7.2 we discussed five strategies which have been employed in orthography design where there are insufficient suitable Roman letters for each phoneme to be represented by a single letter. We do not believe that any one of these strategies is intrinsically better or worse than any other. However, there are some practical advantages and disadvantages associated with each, as listed above. We also mentioned internal consistency which we believe to be a valid principle of good orthography design whatever the writing system employed. Beyond these things, there are matters of aesthetics which are not susceptible to rational discussion. We nevertheless suspect that the different orthographic preferences which people have are in large measure determined by the system(s) to which they are accustomed.

4

Pedagogical Aspects of Vernacular Literacy

JEANNINE GERBAULT

with contributions from D. Barton, L. Carrington, P. Christie, H. Devonish, R. B. Le Page, G. Lüdi, J. Russell, A. Tabouret-Keller, I. Tasker, G. Varro, and J. Warwick

I. PEDAGOGY REVISITED

At the forefront of debates in European countries as well as in many Third World countries, it is pedagogy—and in particular the teachers and how they teach—which has often been blamed for illiteracy. Although in this book one of the tasks has been to show that there are many other factors affecting the development of literacy, pedagogy seems to have become a serious concern, especially since the resources that many countries can afford have become scarcer.

In this chapter, our reflection on the theory and practice of vernacular literacy development will focus on the pedagogical means that have been put to work. In our examination of what has been tried, and achieved, and how, we will attempt to give an orderly account of pedagogical issues and problems, and possible solutions, providing concrete examples of curricula, teacher-training programmes, and materials.

Although the question of the desirability of developing vernacular literacy will not be discussed for its own sake, it will be addressed in connection with these pedagogical issues. They will be presented in such a way as to reflect both the present state of the art, and the extensive experience of literacy workers and of the contributors to this chapter. They will include specifically topics in the conduct of literacy campaigns, in the recruitment and training of teachers, in the methods and materials used for literacy teaching, and in the evaluation of (vernacular) literacy. As in the rest of the book, theory and practice will be combined, and we will try also to reconcile a backward-looking evaluative approach and a forward-looking, more broadly based, prospective approach.

2. PEDAGOGICAL CONCERNS AND THE ECOLOGY OF VERNACULAR LITERACY

In this treatment, the central goal will not be to advocate particular methods or assess outcomes of particular approaches, but, instead, to examine pedagogy through the filter of societal and linguistic environments. A number of decisions regarding the pedagogy of literacy are made, or are expected to be made, in response to various sociolinguistic challenges; they will depend on the characteristics of the learners, of linguistic communication, and of the society in which literacy is to be developed. They will also depend on the structure of the specific language(s) involved, the relationships between spoken and written language, and a number of other factors.

In our workshops (reported under *Abstracts* 1986, 1988, 1990) we have questioned the use of the general term 'illiteracy', on the ground that there are important differences among 'the states of not being able to read and write'; we have been concerned with literacy as a skill that individuals acquire, lack, or possess in specific social environments; in this perspective, the following distinctions may be useful:

- a child in a literate society who has not yet reached the point of learning literacy skills is *pre-literate*;
- a society in which the skill of literacy is of no consequence is a *non-literate* society;
- people who have failed to master generally accepted skills are said to be *illiterate*; their condition is generally viewed as an individual handicap; the term is also used to refer to people who have not maintained previously acquired literacy skills.

Of course these distinctions are arbitrary, and a number of other such distinctions have been proposed, but they are helpful labels pointing to the fact that different cultural/social backgrounds may call for different strategies with respect to the pedagogy of literacy.

It is true not only that literacy may mean different things to different people in different contexts, but that standards have changed over the years in most countries; for instance, at the beginning of this century, the ability to sign one's name was sufficient to identify a person in Europe as literate; today literacy tests given to new army recruits are of a much more elaborate nature. Even today, the levels of literacy required to 'function' in society may not be the same among, for example, women in Indian rural areas, on the one hand, and factory workers in industrialized Germany, on the other.

In 1987, in Hamburg, the Unesco Institute for Education proposed four definitions of literacy, which state degrees of literacy without specifying the condition of a person's environment: *basic literacy*, the ability to read and write in one's own language and to do simple arithmetic; *functional literacy*, which is more than basic reading and writing, and contributes to increased participation in civic activities and productivity; *literacy* as an ideal leading to more effective communication in general; and *post-literacy*, which aims at retention, continuation, and application of literacy skills. We will see that these differing degrees of ability to make use of the written word may call for different teaching strategies.

Our concern for the ecology of literacy will lead us to make a clear distinction between the school system as a road to literacy, and adult literacy programmes. We will also distinguish, within the school system, between the teaching of vernacular literacy as an end in itself, and as an introduction to literacy in another language. These distinctions affect arguments about orthography and materials. They also affect the teacher-training methods which ought to be developed in the three types of environment:

(*a*) children's primary vernacular literacy designed to lead on to literacy in another language;
(*b*) children's primary vernacular literacy designed to lead on to secondary and perhaps tertiary schooling in the vernacular language;
(*c*) adult vernacular literacy for its own sake.

3. THE PEDAGOGY OF VERNACULAR LITERACY: THEORY OR PRACTICE?

The pedagogy of vernacular literacy has borrowed principles from a variety of pedagogical theories, and it has also developed its own principles to cope with specific challenges in the practice of teaching vernacular literacy.

Unesco declarations about literacy have generated a great deal of pedagogical discourse since 1953, but there has always been a gap between the theory produced at the decision-making levels and what goes on in the classrooms (or in actual teaching outside traditional formal classes). In this section, therefore, we will try to present the theoretical aspects of pedagogy as they relate to the various stages of decision-making and of actual implementation of the teaching of literacy.

Approaches

Within a policy-making framework, three distinct positions have been held on the development of literacy. The *diffusion approach* posits that literacy will come gradually through universal elementary education, as literate children enter adult life; it has been the general theoretical orientation followed until the first quarter of this century. In the *mass approach*, literacy campaigns are conducted to make all adult men and women in a nation literate within a particular time-frame (Bhola 1984). Mass literacy campaigns are usually directed to out-of-school youth and adults, and are claimed to generate a truly collective momentum. They are also supposed to include the positive consequence of fostering parents' favourable attitudes towards the schooling of their children, and to remove the risk of social disruption involved in making children literate while their parents remain illiterate. Another theoretical option is the *selective and intensive approach* (also termed the 'programme' approach), in which occupational groups are selected to be taught literacy, and which focuses on specific development objectives. This approach aims at teaching skills which are relevant within the experience of individuals, thus providing effective motivation for their acquisition.

Distinctions

The theoretical distinction between *traditional* literacy and *functional* (or 'modern') literacy is also pedagogically relevant. The contrast here, which Street (1984) identifies as 'autonomous' versus 'ideological' literacy, is between an emphasis on the acquisition of the basic literacy skills themselves (the three R's) without specific reference to the contexts in which those skills are to be used (*autonomous* literacy), and an emphasis on the content and contexts of literacy (*ideological*). Traditional literacy is what schoolchildren are typically being taught, and, as Street points out, early efforts for the development of adult literacy were conducted in line with this approach. Traditional literacy has also usually been associated more closely with the mass-campaign approach, in which literacy skills are taught in all environments, while functional literacy may be more closely associated with a selective approach, where teaching of certain literacy skills is geared to a specific population. The theory underlying functional literacy is that 'there exists a relationship between the instrumental aspects of reading, writing, and arithmetic and the various motives conducive to acquiring those techniques' (Street 1986: 46). The concept of functional literacy was born in 1965 at the Unesco Tehran Conference, and it was put into practice in the form of the Experimental World Literacy Project (EWLP) between 1967 and 1973. The EWLP has had considerable influence on methods of literacy work (Experimental World Literacy Project 1976).

In today's 'modern' literacy pedagogy, which is an offspring of functional literacy, literacy teaching is claimed to be not about technical skills, but about a whole approach to the use of one's own language and the control of one's life. The basic assumption is that, whatever methods are used, the goal is to enable people to *do* things with the written language, to prepare individuals to perform certain functions in their society (Barton, in *Abstracts* 1990).

Srivastava (1984) reports that in South East Asia most adult education programmes are now characterized by what he calls 'modern' literacy, in contrast with 'traditional' literacy—that is, they do not merely bring the three R's, but provide human-resources development leading to more meaningful participation in society. In countries such as India, Bangladesh, Nepal, Pakistan, and

Sri Lanka, the goal of government literacy programmes today is to improve people's quality of life (a means for social change).

Continuums

The continuum *pre-literacy–literacy–post-literacy* has become a pedagogically crucial concept. As greater understanding has been gained of the elements that contribute to success or failure of the teaching of literacy—either in the school system or in the multitude of campaigns and programmes that have been undertaken—literacy specialists agree that mere instruction in literacy skills, regardless of the approach or method adopted, cannot be expected to meet the goal of developing literacy worldwide.

Pre-literacy activities are theoretically intended to stimulate awareness and motivation among the target population. It has become clear today that 'the target population' means both the illiterate and the literate portions of the society in which the teaching of literacy is to take place. The 'consciousness-raising' approach in Freire's theory, which will be presented below, can be viewed as one type of pre-literacy activity in a literacy campaign or programme.

The importance of the post-literacy phase of a literacy development enterprise has been brought to the fore by the observation of repeated relapses into illiteracy in various contexts, in both developing and developed countries. The principle underlying post-literacy activities is that, if acquired skills are to be maintained, it is necessary to create a 'literate environment'—that is, an environment in which new literates will need and want to use their skills; post-literacy is viewed as a stage in the consolidation of literacy and a factor in preventing relapse into illiteracy. Post-literacy activities are intended both for adult new literates and for young people having completed elementary school or having dropped out. It has even been suggested that it may be necessary to create that 'literate environment' before the pre-literacy activities (see e.g. Chapter 2).

Freire's Theory

The Brazilian educator's thinking on the philosophy of education was first expressed in 1959, and spread in the course of a few years, especially after the publication of *Pedagogy of the Oppressed* in 1970. In his view, the educator/ teacher's efforts coincide with those of the students to engage in critical thinking: education is of a 'problem-posing' nature; it is the action and reflection of people upon their world in order to transform it.

Literacy then is 'reading the world', and not simply a decoding of words. The participants learn to read and write what concerns them centrally in their own lives. This theory of education and of literacy acquisition has had a considerable influence in Latin America and in other parts of the world. Section 6 below, dealing with specific teaching methods, will present the main features of what has come to be known as the 'Freire method'.

Shifts in Focus

The recent shift in pedagogical theory from a focus on teaching to a focus on learning has implications for a number of theoretical positions regarding the pedagogy of literacy. Learners are not seen as passive recipients of knowledge; they actively participate in the learning process. This theory has been translated into a number of principles for the pedagogy of literacy, which Hamadache and Martin (1986) have labelled *functionality* (of skills taught), *participation* (in teaching/learning processes), *integration* (into action towards development targets), and *diversification* (to suit a variety of learning styles and rates). These principles apply to children's school literacy as well as to adult literacy acquisition.

The *learner-centred approach* to teaching has led to the open recognition of important differences between adult and child learners of literacy skills. Adult literacy needs are quite different from the skills imparted to children in schools (see the 'autonomous' model above); moreover, adult learners want to be viewed as adults, and their social role and dignity to be acknowledged; adults usually have a lower tolerance than children for the feelings of uncertainty and failure experienced in some learning situations. These characteristics deserve careful attention in a world context where more and more literacy activities are concerned with adult learners. Their application in the UK, for example, has led to the selection of reading and writing tasks that can be used as they are being taught, and in many countries to the production by adult groups of their own literacy materials.

Present Trends

The present trend in the pedagogy of literacy is that reading, writing, and numeracy skills must be *integrated*. Research has shown that reading and writing are complementary activities, mutually reinforcing for all types of learners (for example, that spelling exercises improve reading ability). Moreover, since adults need basic numeracy skills, it is important to provide them with the ability to write their arithmetic calculations as soon as possible. For adult learners, reading and writing should not be separated either from speaking or from each other; learners should 'write their way into reading'. Reading aloud plays a special role for the beginner; it acts as a link between speech and writing; it is seen as a transitional step to silent reading. In fact, arguments about the best way to teach literacy are often concealed arguments about the relation between reading and writing.

This approach is in contrast with the teaching of reading on its own, as, for example, in Bible-reading practices of the past centuries in Europe, or in our century's Christian missionary schools or Koranic schools in various parts of the world, where reading aloud or silent reading have not been primarily intended to lead to writing.

Literacy Acquisition is not Language Acquisition

A person can only learn to read in a language he understands. In the acquisition of literacy, as in all learning, it makes sense to go from the known (the spoken language) to the unknown (its written representation). The teaching of initial literacy, therefore, is in a language that the learner can speak. This principle has been central to Unesco's philosophy and to advocates of vernacular literacy in general.

We learn to read only once, whether in a first or in a second language, except where a new script is involved. In some cases, the bridge to a second language may be an integral part of the basic instruction. Ideally, in 'bi-literate bilingual' programmes, the first language (L1) is used for the teaching of reading and writing in the first year, while the second language (L2) is used orally; reading and writing in the L2 are introduced in the second year. Literacy skills can be transferred from the mother tongue to the L2. This theoretical position has important implications in many parts of the world, where the local language is chosen for fast acquisition of literacy, and then the switch is made to the official language or lingua franca, for access to employment. In Jamaica, for example, some educators think that literacy in Creole should be used as a bridge to literacy in English. Of course, a question that has to be addressed is how and when to move from the L1 to the L2.

Devonish (*Abstracts* 1990: 98) has argued that it is possible for vernacular literacy to feed on established literacy teaching efforts in the dominant language. The *transfer model* can be viewed as working both ways: literacy in one language can be extended across languages and writing systems. The model has been quite popular in India (Srivastava and Gupta 1990), and can be successfully applied, it is claimed, to most multilingual situations: initial literacy is in the mother tongue—because literacy presupposes control of oral skills, and is just an extension of language skills. Once literacy has been achieved, the skill is applied to other languages. The problem of what is meant exactly by 'mother-tongue literacy' has been raised in other chapters of this book (e.g. Chapters 1 and 3), and its pedagogical implications will be discussed in a later section.

The Nature of Reading and the Pedagogy of Literacy

The learning of reading and writing is not a built-in competence: there is no such thing as a language acquisition device (LAD) for written language. Of course, many children who are surrounded by written materials and by literate siblings seem to learn to read without formal teaching—for example, by associating word shapes on cereal packets with pronounced words. But in general, as Kavanagh and Mattingley (1972) have shown, reading and writing, unlike the spoken language, have to be taught. Children will normally acquire a language regardless of their social environment, but the acquisition of literacy usually involves conscious teaching and learning. Nevertheless, as Lee (1982) suggests, a parallel can be drawn between listening and reading skills (decoding) and speaking and writing skills (encoding): we should expect the reading ability of a normal reader to surpass his writing skill, and progress in writing to be slower than progress in reading; therefore, maybe more attention should be given to developing the skills of writing in the later stages of literacy acquisition, in situations where the writing ability is important.

Much of the research on reading in developed countries has been said to be irrelevant to Third World adult literacy problems (Lind and Johnston 1990); it is true that it often results in models of literacy based on psychological processes rather than on the social processes which are crucial for adults. However, the analysis of reading as a process involving not mere decoding of written symbols but also the knowledge of context and of the world around us for discovering their meaning (a 'psycholinguistic guessing game'), and of writing and reading as involving a decontextualization of language, has important implications for the teaching strategies to be used in different contexts.

4. LITERACY CAMPAIGNS

A large number of literacy campaigns have been conducted in various areas of the world since the beginning of this century. But literacy campaigns started well before this century. As Chapter 1 reports, the literacy campaign in Scotland may have been the first truly national campaign; after the Reformation, the Protestant and Nonconformist churches in Northern Europe wanted everybody to be able to read the Bible. Missionaries all over the world have followed the same line, and Koranic schools have contributed to the development of reading in Arabic.

The most spectacular and best-known mass campaigns of this century have been associated with political revolutions and the ideology they represented. (Chapter 1 of this book provides a number of examples.) Bhola (1984) has reported extensively on such cases. The campaign which started in 1919 in the former USSR is said to have been the ancestor of all modern mass-literacy campaigns. Those in Vietnam (1945–77), in China (1950s to 1980s), in Cuba (1961), in Burma (1960s to 1980s), in Brazil (1967–80), and in Somalia (1973–74) were all started as a consequence of a political and/or sociocultural revolution. They involved high mobilization of the masses and institutionalization of the government efforts from the very beginning. They were 'high-pressure' campaigns, which were sustained by feelings of urgency and combativeness.

On the basis of the analysis of the successes and failures in mass literacy campaigns, Bhola (1984) has suggested a general theory and technology, intended to be used as a model of 'How best to plan and implement a mass literacy campaign'. The basic processes are claimed to be the following, in chronological sequence:

- articulation of the political will
- institutionalization of the first policy initiative
- development of a comprehensive policy-making body
- study and diagnosis of the preconditions
- general mobilization of the public
- establishment of structures of mass participation
- development of inter-ministerial and agency structures (administrative and technical 'organizational responses')
- pre-operational preparation
- implementation of developmental and instructional actions
- evaluation of context, processes, and results
- establishment of post-literacy programmes.

Within this framework, the particular political culture will determine organizational, mobilizational, and technological choices.

In the mid-1960s, in contrast with these high-pressure campaigns, the United Nations Development Programme conducted a large-scale experiment in functional literacy in eleven countries (the EWLP). Lacking the urgency of the revolutionary campaigns, the failures that have been observed have been attributed to the failure to take into consideration people's own purposes and current communication practices. Lüdi (*Abstracts* 1990: 103) writes: 'many failures of literarization programmes are due to the fact that decisions have been taken top-down without taking into account on the one hand . . . the real need of the people concerned . . . and on the other hand . . . the acceptance of the decisions by those who have to realize [them]—politicians, teachers, parents, pupils.' Reporting about Tanzania, one of the EWLP countries, where the aim was to make everyone competent in spoken and written Swahili, Russell (*Abstracts* 1990: 111–15) mentions that, although there had been a laudable organization of decision-making structures from central to local levels, campaigns have failed because they have been 'founded on assumptions derived from the technological literate societies in which the policy makers' own higher education had been embedded'. At the most local levels people did not always understand higher level directives.

Literacy campaigns have also been conducted recently in Europe and the USA (Limage 1987). Although in principle state education for all has been the law for many years, various social circumstances have recently made clear the necessity to conduct literacy campaigns in developed countries. In the USA, the federal government became involved with adult literacy in the early 1960s. In France the first report calling for an adult literacy campaign for French nationals was published in 1981 (*Oheix Report*, reported in Limage 1987); it referred to an estimated 100,000 virtually illiterate school leavers each year. The voluntary body 'Aide à toute détresse-Quart Monde' (Aid to all the Suffering Fourth World) has focused on the illiteracy of poor people in Europe. Opération CLE (Compter, Lire, Écrire) was launched in France by various bodies in 1988 (advertised in *Le Monde* (17 Mar. 1988)), after an evaluation reported a surprising percentage of illiterates (persons who had forgotten their literacy skills). The most recent census of literacy in Germany revealed that 1,000,000 German adults were more or less overt or hidden illiterates. The first German Conference on Literacy was held in Bremen in 1980 (Lüdi, in *Abstracts* 1988). In the UK also adult literacy campaigns were launched in the 1970s. The Adult Literacy and Basic Skills Unit in the UK offers adults specific skills for special purposes, respecting their own perception of what they need; it stresses that literacy is 'doing', and only meaningful in practice. In Germany and the UK the television media were extensively used in order to sensitize and motivate illiterate portions of the population. The particular techniques used with the new media are presented below.

5. TEACHERS AND THEIR TRAINING

In almost every country teachers have been blamed for the lack of progress in literacy; they are certainly one of the cornerstones of literacy operations everywhere. HMI (1990) explicitly states that the single factor most hindering literacy progress in primary schools is weakness in the management and organization of reading within the class (i.e. the teacher's inability to teach). Well-planned progressive reading and writing activities are an important factor influencing the standards of reading, therefore teacher training is very important. 'Poor teaching' in general refers to the lack of mastery of the techniques of communication in classes or in small groups, and to inadequate use of teacher talk, poor organization, and sequencing of teaching activities. One crucial aspect of teachers' competence, as Adams (1990) points out, may also be their ability to stay tuned to the delicate interval between difficulty and ease for the learners.

Whether in children's school literacy education or in adult education, reports from all over the world have pointed to problems both in the number of available teachers and in the quality of their training. Among those that have been identified are not only lack of trained teachers, and a lack of motivation in teachers, but also the fact that in many countries the best teachers are likely to look for or to be put into administrative jobs. (See Le Page 1964: 81.)

5.1. *Recruitment and Motivation*

The question of teacher availability is often closely linked to government policy and practices: for example, in Nigeria, although a huge apparatus has been in existence in higher education, it has failed to produce sufficiently well-trained school teachers. The lack of success in the policy of literacy in the three official languages has for years been blamed on the lack of sufficient numbers of trained teachers. Ndukwe (1984), for example, has reported that no provision had been made for the training of teachers in the methods of teaching Igbo, one of the three official languages. But lack of political will and initiative is often responsible for this state of affairs (see Chapter 1).

The great variety of contexts in which vernacular literacy is acquired calls for a detailed account of how teachers are recruited. In contexts where there was a sense of 'urgency', it was not always necessary to offer incentives in the form of (additional) salary, because teacher motivation was high at least to begin with. But in cases where no such sense of urgency prevailed, it has often been difficult to maintain teacher motivation and attendance in the absence of reward.

In the 'mass-campaign' approach, all adults have usually been mobilized for teaching; this means that both professional and volunteer teachers have been used. For example, in the Jamaican campaign (JAMAL), literacy workers were all volunteers (Hamadache and Martin 1986). In the 1961 campaign in Cuba, literate factory workers were recruited for teaching, and paid their regular salaries. The school teachers' direct participation in the campaign was made mandatory. In the USSR campaign, teachers were offered suitable incentives; all school teachers were expected to take part in the literacy campaign, and all educated citizens serving as teachers were to be paid as teachers (Bhola 1984). In the Brazilian campaign (MOBRAL), teachers were chosen from the communities where the literacy classes were to be taught; they were semi-volunteers—that is, they received a small gratuity. In the Somalian campaign (1973–4), all schools were closed for one year, which made 20,000 literacy teachers available (students plus their teachers) (Mezei 1989); each teacher in the rural areas received a small daily allowance from the government and lived with a family (Bhola 1984).

In the cases mentioned above, motivation has been provided for teachers, and rewards of one kind or another have been sufficient to ensure that they stay on the job. But in many contexts, the problem of teachers' salaries has been a crucial element in their lack of motivation; teachers are either not paid regularly, or earn very low salaries, and find it necessary to earn supplementary income by being involved in other activities. In Tanzania (EWLP; 1967–72), school teachers were not given extra money for conducting work-oriented classes for adults after school hours, and had no real motivation (Street 1984). In the 1990 meeting in Thailand for the International Literacy Year, the fact was explicitly mentioned that two out of three teachers from developing countries earned less than in 1980. In China, professional teachers have been reported as earning less than factory workers and as leaving the profession (Tasker, in *Abstracts* 1990: 31).

The physical conditions under which many primary school teachers have to teach, especially in developing countries, where they are in insufficient numbers and where there is a shortage of school buildings and other materials, often play an important role in their poor motivation and the poor results of the teaching enterprise. In many countries of sub-Saharan Africa or Latin America the average size of a primary school class has swollen to over 100 children. Even an experienced teacher will have serious problems teaching basic literacy skills to children in such large classes, often without any materials, even chalk and slates. (Materials will be dealt with below; see also Agnihotri's comment on India quoted in Chapter 1.)

5.2. *Training*

In the USSR campaign, centres for training teachers in adult education methods were opened, and most of the mass literacy campaigns of the past fifty years have included an important teacher-training component at all levels. Where the campaigns were moved by revolutionary ideologies, the training consisted of political and ideological classes as well as classes on teaching techniques *per se*—the idea being that making instructors conscious of the revolutionary significance of their work is the best way of making them capable of overcoming the difficulties in their teaching. Bhola (1984) reports that in the Vietnam campaigns (1945–77), for example, teachers managed to improve their teaching methods and constantly innovated because they were enthusiastic about what they were doing. In Cuba, the one-week training programme based on *Alphabeticemos* had a political, social, and technical component. In Burma, teacher-training was done according to the 'multiplier' model: professionals trained at one level training those at the next level and so on, from the centre to the districts and then to fieldworkers.

However, the problem of the relatively low level of qualification of many teachers has been felt in many countries, and, as we shall see, it has a bearing upon the teaching methods that can be used. It has been particularly felt in Brazil (MOBRAL), where the turnover was high, and where, in 1972, a solution was devised by training 100,000 literacy instructors by radio under an agreement with the educational broadcasting service of the Ministry of Education. The training programme consisted of twelve broadcasts, thirty or sixty minutes long, supplemented by appropriate teaching materials and teacher manuals (Bhola 1984). The widespread use of the radio in Latin America for the spread of literacy in general and for the training of teachers will be mentioned further on.

In general, the training of literacy teachers has varied in length from one day to several weeks, depending on the available resources and on the initial level of the instructor or teacher. It has usually been found that initial training followed by periodical in-service training gives the best results. Instructions on how to train literacy programme directors, teachers, and writers of materials have been provided in the form of monographs or books (e.g. Laubach and Laubach 1960; Gudschinsky 1962, 1973; Unesco 1975, 1981).

Because of the wide variety of contexts in which literacy is taught (in school or out of school; to children or to adults; in literate or non-literate societies) and because of the recognition of the learner as central in literacy-acquisition operations, the importance and need of new types of teacher have been acknowledged.

Community work has been advised in many contexts: for example, teachers should go out of their schools and meet the parents to see what the children are doing in their home environment. It has long been seen as an important factor for teachers to belong to the same environment as their students—whether adults or children; experience in India, Tanzania, Jamaica, and Ethiopia, among other countries, has shown that instructors drawn from the milieu are often more effective than professional teachers. They may not be so good at pedagogy itself, but they are better at motivating learners. In Tanzania, there was resistance to teachers 'reaching out to ignorant farmers' to teach them literacy skills, and not taking account of their feelings and culture (Street 1984: 191). In the 1940s the Laubachs started their experiment in the Philippines, the 'Each One Teach One' way, where an individual learns, then teaches a friend, who himself teaches another friend; adult volunteers taught their illiterate friends at home at any hour of the day. Such an approach recognizes that the best way to learn something is to teach it. Similarly, for the adult literacy campaign of the 1970s in Great Britain, volunteer literacy workers had to be trained for one-to-one tutoring or small group classes. More and more in-group teaching has been done, and tutoring experiences have been in operation in various countries; in Indonesia the KEJAR programme, which operates entirely by tutoring (one literate person and ten illiterate persons from the same village meeting in homes), started in 1977 (Lowenberg 1984). Self-improvement groups have also become active all over the world. Important changes in the condition of women in many countries have also contributed to transforming the literacy teaching task; women have organized themselves as teachers to other women, a type of situation encouraging learning and participation; numerous cooperative animation groups have been created in many parts of the world among women.

Thus new teaching situations have been identified and new strategies reported. Creative solutions have been proposed; in South Africa, for example, the suggestion has been made to integrate non-teaching staff and parents into the life of the school to help in promoting vernacular language use and development (National Language Project 1991). Redfern and Edwards (1992) have suggested that partnership between school and parents is a valuable help in the teaching of reading skills. Wherever possible, parents must be encouraged to help their children with some language skill requirements; it is probably necessary in many contexts—if not all—to link primary-school activities with home activities. In several countries allowing children to take their books home has proved very effective. For them to read to their parents, even to illiterate parents, is a valuable stimulus.

These modern approaches to vernacular literacy would tend to suggest that teachers should be trained not so much in prescriptive methods, but rather in 'how-it-works' methods (if, in many contexts, the priority is to give children and adults a functional knowledge of the written word), and in having a positive, cooperative attitude to learners. Training should certainly be flexible and enable teachers to use as effectively as possible any method that comes to hand. The new approaches seem to call for a more systematic transfer of educational technology; if a community is to take over responsibility for literacy training, some of its members must be able to teach how to teach and how to develop materials. If functional content is to be an important element of literacy training (see the next section), it is also important in a number of contexts that teachers should be able to provide help in other areas of activity, such as health or agriculture. The constraints of production in rural areas often mean that literacy work is done only in certain seasons, both for schoolchildren and for adult learners, which can result in big gaps and relapses into illiteracy. In a country like Somalia, the problem of teaching nomadic populations had to be attended to. Teachers should be made capable of coping with such situations.

6. METHODS AND MATERIALS

Poor teaching methods and the lack of materials for literacy teaching have been reported in many countries. Although it has been evident, in this chapter and in the other chapters of this book, that motivational and mobilizational circumstances may be critical in the development of vernacular literacy, especially in mass campaigns, the question of 'how-to-teach' literacy skills is certainly not to be neglected; what goes on in the classroom is of central importance.

In Western societies 'poor teaching methods' are often today associated with 'parroting the alphabet' and rote learning. However, one should be sensitive to the ways of learning in traditional oral societies: any method must take into account such factors as the demonstrative nature of teaching in some societies; Greenfield (1972) has pointed out the contextual nature of the teaching of skills in some cultures, especially in African cultures. The place of repetition in Koranic schools in Moslem areas is well known. Street (1984) has discussed the value of 'Maktab' literacy for the acquisition of 'modern' literacy skills in Iran. The 'Maktab' is the traditional religious Koranic school, where whole passages of the Koran are recited by rote, often without reading—it also occasionally teaches vernacular literacy and numeracy. Street argues that the specific skills imparted by Maktab literacy (awareness of the way in which meaning is dependent on the layout of a page, familiarity with paper, representation of sounds with letters) are transferable to new 'modern' literacies.

Usually, teachers with limited or no training are able to reproduce in their methods only the way they themselves were taught, which means that in many areas the long-established rote way of learning is likely to be perpetuated.

Any discussion of teaching methods has to start with a definition of what the goals are, what it is that has to be taught. According to Gudschinsky (1962), people are literate when they can read and understand anything they would have understood if it had been spoken to them, and write anything they can say in such a way that it can be read and understood by other literate persons speaking the same language. There are three goals: independence (to be able to read and write without help), comprehension, and fluency; writing also requires creativity (the ability to write new messages). Of course these goals stand in sharp contrast with the practice in Koranic schools, which have concentrated far more on reading than on writing.

A related question is whether it is lower or higher literacy skills which have to be taught. Linguistic objectives must be defined clearly before pedagogical decisions can be made and materials elaborated. We may want to acknowledge, as Tonkin does (p.c.), that there are different levels of literacy, all of which may be relevant and necessary, but not for everybody. Dubin (1989) uses the term 'mini-literacy' to refer to partial literacy in the mother tongue in very specific contexts. It may be useful to make a distinction between the acquisition of literacy and schooling. 'School education' is a Western concept that has been exported and adapted to many parts of the world. But literacy training, which takes an average of one to two years, is not to be equated with school education, which can extend over a period of six to eight years. Tabouret-Keller (*Abstracts* 1988: 106), in connection with the marked decrease in school attendance in a country like the Ivory Coast, has also mentioned the need to separate the two notions. It is sensible to compare costs and benefits of the two types of learning in different societies, and to acknowledge that teachers, methods, and materials may differ for each type of education.

6.1. Methods

Basic Distinctions: The Synthetic and the Analytic Methods

The debate between proponents of the synthetic method and of the analytic method for teaching reading has been going on in industrialized countries for some decades. The *synthetic* method, in which individual symbols (letters and their names—alphabetic—or letters and their sounds—phonetic) are learnt first out of context, then put together in syllables and words, has been claimed to result in better recognition of letters and earlier independent reading. It has the advantage of being simple to teach (for instructors with limited qualifications, and with limited materials). But it is better suited for some languages—alphabetically and phonetically written—than for others, especially the non-alphabetic languages. (For further discussion, see Chapter 3.) The *analytic* method, in which learners start with units having meaning (words, phrases, sentences) before discovering word parts and syllables, has been claimed to provide more encouragement to beginning learners, who can see immediate meaning in what they read from the first day of class. This method is more universally applicable, but it requires better trained teachers, and is said to delay the recognition of new words.

The controversy about phonics (sounding the letters, synthetic) and about the look-and-say (global, analytic) method has been going on in the USA and the UK for a number of years. The phonics approach emphasizes the learning of letter–sound correspondences. The Initial Teaching Alphabet (ITA), which was developed by Pitman in 1960 to try to establish a one-to-one correspondence in English between grapheme and phoneme to help beginners in reading, has been used in several programmes in the USA and the UK. Other attempts at simplifying English spelling have been made, but have encountered a lot of resistance and have not brought about the expected results (Lamb and Arnold 1980). Reforming alphabets or spelling systems is among the most difficult of cultural changes —the reform in Turkey in the 1920s is a noteworthy exception.

Research has shown that no one teaching method is really superior overall. This has been confirmed by a survey conducted in British primary schools in 1989–90 (HMI 1990). While a method may be more effective from the start for a specific language, factors other than methods influence learning in both adults and children. In any case, one has to be aware that not only research results, but also the vested interests of publishing houses, affect the manner in which reading is taught. Cato and Whetton (1991: 6) report that 'experimental and psychological investigations of reading have had little impact on those concerned with the literacy education of children' (i.e. on the development of methods).

There is no single teaching method pre-eminently suited to child or to adult literacy. However, if one considers that adults have a lower tolerance of ambiguity and for drills than children, a variety of the analytic method may be more appropriate for them. It may also be easier for people to learn to read by the 'look-and-say' method if they are taught with texts (e.g. biblical texts) with which they are already familiar in their oral form.

In many contexts an *eclectic* method, i.e. a mixture of the synthetic and analytic methods, has been in use. It tries to find the proper balance between emphasizing meaning and emphasizing code. In Burma, for example, the sounds represented by the five or six most frequent characters are taught first and immediately put to work in combination with the three tones of each vowel sound, which gives the adult a sense of achievement on the very first day. In Vietnam, in contrast, a traditional synthetic approach has been used, beginning with the eleven vowels and diacritics to mark the tones, and then going on with the consonants. In languages where the writing system is more complex, as in Chinese, the emphasis is on calligraphic skills: lines, curves, and strokes are taught prior to teaching the real characters, and functional content is introduced later. (The specific problems of literacy in Chinese are dealt with in Chapter 8.)

6.2. *Methods at Work*

The Gudschinsky method, also known as the 'whole-language' method, has been widely used. Gudschinsky's *Handbook of Literacy* (1962) and *Manual of Literacy for Preliterate Peoples* (1973) have presented this method and also provided suggestions for the preparation of primers and reading materials, and instructions on how to teach them in class, how to train national instructors, and other activities necessary in literacy operations. In this analytic method, one does not start with anything smaller than a word (something, therefore, with a meaning). The word is broken down into syllables, and syllables are practised through an algorithm of 'search, match, contrast, identify, read'. 'Keywords'— very commonly occurring words—are made links between the real world and that of literacy. Basic criteria for determining the progression of the introduction of elements in the teaching programme are their productivity, position, and contrasts.

The Laubach method uses a combination of phonics and keywords, associating the shape of a letter with an object, the name of which begins with that letter. Each lesson contains a page of words (to teach syllables) and a simple story with those words. It is claimed to be easy to teach—that is, particularly appropriate for use by teachers with little training. Because of the increasing number of teachers with little or no training, teaching methods and instructions in materials development have been devised specifically for their use. Rauch's (1969) *Handbooks for the Volunteer Tutor* are examples.

Freire and the 'Psycho-Social Method'

Freire's ideas and methods have been quite popular in South America since the 1970s. The learner's immediate experiences, environment, and needs form the basis of every pedagogic decision, from the selection of teaching items to the definition of goals in a literacy programme. This 'consciousness-raising' approach encourages participants to act on their milieu. The teacher is the coordinator, and learners are 'participants'. This approach is also known as the 'psycho-social' method, and it has great motivational power.

The method, which has been widely used, centres on the 'generative word', which is selected from the environment and has to be highly emotive. It is pedagogically similar in function to the keyword in Gudschinsky's method; the word is broken down into syllables, which in their turn are used to make new words. Although the implementation of this method may not always be easy, in particular with non-phonetically written languages, this pedagogy has contributed to improving the understanding of literacy learning among adults. Numerous programmes have been built on this model, especially as an alternative to Unesco's functional literacy programmes, which were more or less overtly teaching ideology and were consequently resisted in many parts of the world (as in Tanzania, where new ways of cultivating the land have been forced upon the peasants together with literacy).

Freire's methods have also inspired non-governmental organizations (NGOs). The need has been recognized in numerous contexts to design literacy programmes as part of an integrated rural development that keeps the participants operating in their own environment. In various developing countries NGOs and government agencies employ a substantial network of specialized personnel, who are responsible for laying out programmes to motivate local communities towards participation in development projects. Quite frequently the objective of their activity is not to impart skills through technical assistance, but to get members of the community to exchange ideas, to understand a specific problem, to find one or more solutions to it, and to determine a programme with a timetable, using specific materials. The personnel working in such 'operational pedagogical approaches' act as 'motivators', and one outcome among others is the development of vernacular literacy, if the need for it has been identified by the community involved. In general, as can be expected under those circumstances, the teaching methods are very flexible, and are to some extent determined by the strategies used to trigger the teaching of literacy.

But whatever technical methods are used with this socially integrated and functional approach, experience has shown that there may be a problem in integrating literacy training with training in other functional skills: that is, if one tries to achieve too many things at the same time, the risk is that none of the objectives can really be reached. The claim has been made by literacy workers that unambiguous goals are needed, and there have been arguments for teaching reading and writing as the core objective: functionality in a programme should not 'dilute' this objective; it should be taught in a second phase.

The new kinds of teacher that we have mentioned in the preceding section, who belong in the same social networks as the literacy learners, certainly need to develop their own methods for these alternative ways of transmitting literacy. In the Ivory Coast, for example, where a number of economic and social factors have led to a decrease in school attendance, there are informal ways of acquiring literacy in vernacular French (the local lingua franca) outside school; there exists a demand for literacy—but not for school education, which requires time and money, and no longer gives access to improved standards of living. In such contexts, methods will build upon whatever skills have been picked up in everyday activities, and emphasize and encourage cooperative learning (Tabouret-Keller 1988a). Such cooperative work in 'parallel' literacy networks has been reported in other parts of the world, and it has developed in similar environments, especially among women's groups and between young adults and their children.

Eclecticism of methods and flexibility of strategies have been major characteristics of several of the programmes mentioned so far. In the China campaign, any methods and strategies could be used that would satisfy the people's needs, possibilities, and customs; in adult basic literacy, this resulted in a lot of flexibility, with many methods and strategies:

- in the Qi Jianhua's Quick Literacy method, 1,500 to 2,000 characters were to be learnt in about 150 class hours;
- in the collective teaching method, all the learners in the village were brought together to a class for distribution of lessons, and then study was interspersed throughout the working day;

- literacy billboards were located in every village, mutual dictations were given, various quiz and game systems were played, etc.;
- 'circuit teaching' was practised—that is, a teacher stayed in a village for four or five days, leaving interim teaching to 'little teachers', who taught their own families (Bhola 1984).

6.3. *Materials*

Preparation of Materials

In mass literacy campaigns, instructions on how to prepare teaching materials have often been provided. A number of books have been published to help in the preparation of pre-primers, primers, follow-up, or post-literacy materials. The Unesco Regional Literacy Workshop held in Udaipur, India, in 1979, resulted in a series of four monographs, *Literacy Curriculum and Materials Development* (Unesco 1981), which present a complete package for the development of literacy materials. The recommended approaches are objective-oriented, and the content is to be directly related to the everyday life of adult learners. Motivational materials as well as follow-up materials are included; both will be discussed below.

Lee's *Literacy Primers: The Gudschinsky Method* (1982) is a detailed presentation of ways of developing materials following the Gudschinsky method, and is intended as a tool for the trainers of literacy primer writers. Laubach and Laubach (1960) also provided instructions for materials development that were usable even by instructors with little training.

In preparing a literacy primer, Gudschinsky (1973: 2041) recommends starting with the preparation of language data, which consists in the 'analysis of linguistic structure of oral and written language, and the specification of the relationships of these structures to each other and the writing system'. Ideally, the structure of a language at every level (phonology, grammar, semantics) should be known by the teacher.

In contrast with this position, Tadadjeu (1977a) insists that a complete linguistic description is not a prerequisite to the teaching of literacy and to primer development. The assumption in this case is that, if teachers have received adequate training, they have the capacity to prepare reading lessons without bothering about complete linguistic descriptions of the language being taught.

Readability of Materials

How can one decide upon the quality of literacy materials? What makes them comprehensible and readable? Laubach and Laubach (1960) report on a number of formulas to measure readability; they are usually based on such criteria as the number of 'hard words', sentence length, the number of references to persons, and the proportion of personal sentences. But there are no universal formulas.

Concern for readability led to the establishment of other formulas intended to measure the 'human interest' of a piece of writing. The readability of literacy materials has also a lot to do with their relationship to the learners' spoken language (consequently, the readability of literacy materials prepared in a language which is not the mother tongue of the learners will be low), and with interaction between the text, the reader, and the total communicative situation. As Carrell and Eisterhold (1988: 79) write, 'much of the meaning understood from a text is really not actually in the text, *per se*, but in the reader'. Materials should be derived from the culture rather than imposed upon it; folk tales and fairy tales are appealing to children because of their high emotional content, whereas discontinuity between oral discourse styles and written language seems to decrease the readability of literacy materials. (This issue will be taken up again later.)

Availability of Materials

Although a lot have been developed since 1953, the shortage of adequate materials for both school teaching and for adult literacy teaching is still a major handicap in many places. A serious shortfall in both quantity and quality has been reported for the Somali language, which was unwritten before the 1973 campaign. In the Local Languages Literacy Project of Southern Sudan initiated in 1976, there were problems in the development of materials because of the lack of trained personnel (Cowan 1984). Sometimes, as with the lack of teachers, a solution may be found when there is a greater commitment to the development of literacy on the part of the national or regional authority. A lack of materials in Krio or other indigenous languages has been reported to hinder the development of vernacular literacy in Sierra Leone: very few textbooks are available there. This problem is also felt outside Africa; though some original writing has been published in the Caribbean, Carrington (1988a) reports that there are few teaching grammars for creole languages, except in Haiti, where most effort has been made, and where some post-literacy reading materials can also be found.

Lack of financial resources has plagued the development of materials in many countries. Some language groups are not big enough to sustain the cost of developing materials. In South Africa, as elsewhere, funds are not sufficient to give all languages status at school (National Language Project 1991). The resources needed for teacher-training, development of materials, or sustaining acquired literacy skills may not be available even among large groups. In the Philippines a shortage of non-formal education materials was reported in 1979 (Unesco 1981).

Characteristics of Adequate Materials

It has often been the case that materials were translated from another language and were culturally inappropriate; in India, for example, imported materials have been found not to work well. At various periods and in various parts of the world, literacy campaigns have been seen as interesting markets for materials produced in developed countries—often in dominant languages rather than in vernaculars; the concern was more to sell a product than to provide adequate teaching materials for the receiving population. This was particularly true in Africa in the years that followed the independence of countries in the early 1960s. In industrialized countries, also, the complaint has been voiced that the commercial reading materials of publishers and their 'experts' have had a negative influence on teaching practices (Shannon 1989).

Ideally, as Tadadjeu (1975) points out, teacher trainers, textbook writers, and student teachers should work together in preparing textbooks and teachers' guides. But, largely because of lack of communication between these specialists, this does not always happen. Moreover, in many Third World countries the reliance of élites on Western cultural values and the maintenance of imported standards for formal education have blocked or delayed the search for original solutions to the question of school literacy education; this has often led to the importation or development of materials without consideration for indigenous values or patterns of learning. We have present-day instances of imported materials being used to teach literacy and basic numeracy skills, whereas, with a reasonable amount of financial support, excellent materials could be produced locally.

Instructional materials are designed to guide teachers in planning their teaching; they include a sequence of lessons and help for effective teaching. Ideally, they are graded, have appropriate reinforcement exercises, have properly chosen vocabulary and sentences, are well printed, in the right language, include teachers' guides, and so on; they are characterized by cultural relevance, linguistic adequacy, and attendance to psychological considerations. They can be developed all at one time for the whole curriculum or progressively in the course of the teaching operation; sequential preparation of materials allows for better adaptation to the demands of the teaching situation, but it requires well-trained teachers.

Materials for Specific Learner Groups

Although it is difficult to use children's materials for adult literacy—as mentioned earlier, the social and educational objectives and the interests are different—in some countries today adults are taught with primary-school materials. In the early stages of adult literacy campaigns in the USA, where the materials and methods used were similar to those used in schools, adult learners dropped out because of failure and discouragement. The experience has also been that the traditional teacher-taught relationship expressed in the materials of formal child education does not work too well in adult education (adults need self-reliant learning). One may add that differing sensory preferences of individuals may be attended to in instructional materials; whereas formal education tends to call upon only two senses, hearing and vision, motion and tactile operations also may be used in adult education (e.g. representing the shape of letters with parts of the body, or having adults touch the shapes of wooden or cardboard cut-out letters).

Readers, including those for adults, have often been in big print. The use of pictures may not always be appropriate; it facilitates learning among non-literate adults only in cultures where pictures can be 'read'—that is, where there is familiarity with printed two-dimensional representations. In non-literate societies there may be a failure to understand pictures—that is, difficulty in recognizing pictures of objects because of limited pictorial experience; there has to be training in 'reading pictures'. Western-style graphics may not be appropriate, since the symbolic world may be different. Cook (1981) has discussed the issue of interference with the intended message caused by pictures used in literacy primers, posters, health manuals, and other printed materials.

It may be necessary to develop separate materials for men and for women, for adults in urban and in rural areas, or in vernaculars as opposed to standard written languages, in cases where such a distinction is maintained (see below). In Brazil, among the Karaja, different morphological forms are used by men and women speakers; the materials used by government bilingual education programmes have texts in both styles on each page, to accommodate male and female learners (Kindell 1984).

In various parts of the world, the necessity to adapt materials to the environment and the difficulty and cost of preparing new materials for each teaching situation have led to the development of 'prototypes', which provide a basis for materials which can then be developed according to the interests of each group of learners (farmers, fishermen, women, etc.). The 'shell' materials of the Summer Institute of Linguistics, which were first used in Papua New Guinea, are intended as 'skeletons' for the construction of literacy primers and post-primers: writers use a common core to which specific elements relevant to the various groups of learners are added; 'shell' materials are just beginning to be used in literacy work in Cameroon. They represent a compromise, reconciling the problems of teachers with limited ability with the need to personalize literacy materials.

Teams close to the situation of learner groups may be best equipped to produce primers. In a number of contexts, the subject content is determined directly with the learners prior to the development of materials. This approach was first proposed by Freire, and aims at raising the awareness and motivation of learners; it requires well-trained and motivated teachers. In Papua New Guinea, literacy specialists invited local storytellers into their classes, where their stories were put down on paper or written on the board and then used for later writing exercises (SIL 1990). A variety of teaching aids have been devised to suit particular teaching situations. In Burma, a 'teaching wheel' has been used to instruct in the sounding of consonant and vowel combinations. In Tanzania, a variety of materials were developed for specialized groups, with innovative methods, strategies, and structures. A single language was used, Kiswahili, with many different primers (twelve different sets: cotton, banana, home economics, fishing, etc.), each accompanied by a teacher's guide (Bhola 1984). The approach was eclectic, and integrated reading, writing, and arithmetic. In Benin, materials have been developed locally for basic arithmetic learning which take into account and use the experience of adults, instead of merely replacing their mode of calculation with a new one (Girodet 1983).

In Cuba, there was a single primer used for the whole country, along with a teacher's guide, *Vencerimos*; it was based on three realities: country, reader, volunteer teacher. Each of the fifteen lessons was based on a motivational theme linked with the economic and social reforms that were taking place (Bhola 1984). In Burma, where about twenty languages are spoken, literacy was taught only in the Burmese language, which has been the principal medium of literacy since the sixteenth century (Bhola 1984), and has its own semi-syllabic script. Only one curriculum and one primer were developed officially throughout the country; however, in the nineteenth century American Baptist missionaries used the Burmese script to write the language of the Karen, one of the hill tribes on the Burmese/Thai border, and translate the Bible into Karen (see Baker, Chapter 3 of this volume); literacy among the Karen, now fighting for their independence from the Rangoon government, is based on this work (Falla 1991). In the early mass campaigns of the USSR, the learner was free to choose his language of literacy (Russian or his first language).

The time required for the acquisition of literacy is to some extent at least a function of the pedagogical objective. Levels and norms must be chosen carefully: if the objective is too ambitious, adults can be discouraged; if too low, literacy will not last because it will not be firmly established. But research is needed to identify the stage of 'no return to illiteracy'. One may hypothesize that there exist different stages in different social contexts. Literacy acquisition may be easier in some languages than in others: Hamadache and Martin (1986) report that Arabic is said to take twice as long as Swahili; the learning of Chinese characters may take several years (see Chapters 3 and 8).

6.4. *More Constraints on Methods and Materials*

Speech and Writing

After the 1987 Education Act in Zimbabwe, phonemically written teaching materials were produced for minority languages as well as for Ndebele and for Shona (Mkanganwi, in *Abstracts* 1990: 72). But with languages with a long written tradition, the change to a more phonemic type of writing is not easy. We have noted earlier the failure in the UK of the Initial Teaching Alphabet, where children were first taught to read and write in an approximate morpho-phonemic representation of their speech, which was supposed to facilitate the acquisition of literacy.

The technical problems in adapting orthographies for pedagogical purposes and the problems of choice of script and choice of orthography are specifically discussed in Chapter 3; they involve scientific as well as pedagogical and psychological considerations.

In countries where there are ancient written languages, one may distinguish along a continuum between, at one end, those where the spoken language is similar to the written language, and, at the other end, those where newspapers and books use a language not used in speaking. Arabic has been cited (Ferguson 1959) as a typical case of diglossia where the written language is the classical language of the Koran, very different from the numerous modern spoken dialects, but modern standard varieties of Arabic close to the educated spoken language of Egypt, Morocco, etc. are also written nowadays. The case of Chinese is more complex. Classical written Chinese characters were normally read with the values of the words as they would have been in Mandarin; modern written Chinese correlates with the spoken language, Putonghua, standardized for use in all Chinese schools; but of the eight major Han 'dialects', not all mutually intelligible, whose speakers make up 90 per cent of the population of China, some, and in particular the Cantonese of Hong Kong, have written characters to correlate with the local spoken pronunciation rather than with either classical Mandarin or Putonghua; and even the standard characters may be read as if Cantonese.

Norms

Before the production of instructional materials can begin, the decision has to be made about the language variety which will be used: first the dialect of the learner, then the standard dialect, since one of the principles of pedagogy is to start from what the learners know—the language spoken. But, as in the case of ancient written languages, problems arise with languages where the written and spoken languages are distinct. If there are differences between the variety of a language already available for literacy and the variety of the same language spoken by the target population, there should be special provisions in the materials and methods used. A related question, in both literate and less literate societies, is about the best way of passing from oral to written discourse. Differences in discourse styles have to be taken into account for the development of teaching materials. What style of language should literacy be taught in? The relationship between spoken and written forms and styles should be clarified, so that differences can be taken into account. In South Africa the proposal has been made to 're-standardize' the Nguni and Sotho language varieties into two written standard forms, referred to as *Nguni and *Sotho. This process of integrating varieties within a language cluster into one cohesive standard has been considered a necessary harmonization for literacy teaching purposes. But there is sometimes resistance, often political, to such blending of varieties where, for example, it may be felt that there is a loss of ethnic identity in what is being taught.

Which standard is to be recognized for teaching? How do teachers and literacy planners cope with cases of competing standards? A crucial question which we have discussed in our IGLSVL sessions is the possibility of accepting writing even in non-standardized forms. In South Africa, the suggestion has been made that coexisting (Zulu, Xhosa, etc.) forms should be permitted in written texts without penalty to school or university students. The decision has to be made as to whether the goal is to teach literacy in a standardized form, or to teach how to communicate in writing, even in non-prescribed forms. The answers may depend on a variety of social, psychological, and economic factors, upon which the ultimate goals of literacy development rest.

In Europe there is a great distance between the spoken dialect and written norms. Problems have been noted in the acquisition of literacy in German because of the difference between speaking and writing final dentals (devoicing) and between different dialects in speaking. In order to enable teachers to train children in bi-dialectal studies, a number of books have been produced contrasting standard and dialect. This has been judged a helpful approach (Dittmar, in *Abstracts* 1990: 87). In Greece, Katharevousa has been competing with Demotic; until the late 1970s, everybody who had gone through primary and secondary education would have been exposed to varieties of Katharevousa—the more 'classical' variety—and have had to impose its morphology on their writing. The learners claimed (Warwick, in *Abstracts* 1990: 79–81) that this diglossic situation was confusing and impeded their performance. The 1981 reform simplified the writing system in the direction of Demotic. In Switzerland, where there is a functional distribution of two varieties of German, children are taught to recognize the norms of one or the other variety. In Norway, the vernacular literacy project has also emphasized the learners' ability to identify varieties of language (this project, in which school beginners received all initial teaching in their vernaculars, is reported in Chapter 5). In India, the wide gap between the local vernacular and the standard language of education in both Indo-Aryan and Dravidian areas has been reported as creating problems for literacy education.

The literacy education of immigrants in Europe provides other examples of similar problems (see Chapter 5). Certainly different pedagogical approaches have to be devised according to whether immigrants are literate in their L1 or not, and whether they speak a standardized form of their language or not. When they are taught to read and write in their 'home' languages, it is usually in the national standard rather than in their 'mother tongue'; this has been reported by Varro (*Abstracts* 1990: 52) and by Gardner-Chloros (*Abstracts* 1990: 56) for such languages as Arabic or Greek. One has also to distinguish between the social and psychological condition of first generations of migrants and second or third generations. Teaching of written French to migrant workers in France has recently been done by the method *Lire la ville* ('Reading the Town'), with three levels, the first level intended for totally illiterate adults or adults with limited schooling in a language not using the Roman alphabet. In Germany, it has been known for immigrant children to be put into classes with handicapped children, which may not be the most helpful strategy. The specific problems of vernacular literacy among immigrants are dealt with in Chapter 5.

The question of which norms should be taught at school or in adult literacy classes has also been addressed in Europe for such languages as English or French. The answer to this question will depend to some extent on what the teacher is willing and able to teach. Recently teachers in European schools have seemed willing to make use of written norms closer to those of speech in order to make writing more easily accessible to child or adult learners. And in contexts where French has become a vernacular language in Africa (e.g. Ivory Coast, Cameroon) there has also been major criticism of the use of both exogenous and endogenous norms for literacy, but research continues in order to make the language of literacy and education closer to the spoken local norms (see e.g. Manessy 1991).

Multilingual Contexts

A multilingual context may be significant when dealing with vernacular literacy:

(*a*) if the child or adult has more than one vernacular;
(*b*) if the community shares a repertoire of different vernaculars;
(*c*) if the script used for one vernacular is different from that used in another;
(*d*) if (as in the Chinese case) the script established for use is non-alphabetic and is not a 'representation' of any of the vernaculars in use, but has to be learned as a distinct set of symbols.

When children have to learn more than one script, they have to devote more time to language learning in general (see Chapters 1 and 6). Is there one better way of teaching literacy in bi-scriptal contexts (e.g. in Singapore, Hong Kong, or in areas with Arabic as one language of literacy)? In India, where there are different scripts (Arabic, Bengali, Marathi, Gujerati, and so on), the learning load may be considerable for literacy acquisition. But as Verma (*Abstracts* 1988: 149) noted, one cannot establish any straightforward correlation between the number of scripts and of languages to be learned and the literacy rate. There are many other factors involved, such as the place of the written word in the environment, or the economic or psychological incentives.

In bilingual environments bi-literate bilingualism may be adopted as official educational policy, with initial literacy teaching provided in the mother tongue, followed by teaching in the official language. In the Nicaragua campaign, minority groups were taught literacy in their first language as a transition to Spanish, the official language (Street 1984). But is it always the right thing to do to initiate literacy in the mother tongue? There are situations in which there is a problem deciding what a learner's mother tongue is—we have had examples from China, with several home languages; there are many other cases in which a child may have more than one home language. In any situation where there are cross-cultural marriages, 'mother tongue' may be an ill-defined concept.

The mother tongue may be a minority language among other more important mother tongues. We have mentioned also some of the situations where the vernacular language in which literacy is taught is not the mother tongue, as in the case of Swahili for most users in Tanzania. Is the teaching of literacy via a lingua franca advisable? Are there cases where the learner's motivation justifies teaching him in a second language? (See e.g. Chapters 5, 7, and 8). It has generally been found that, for adults, initial literacy in a second language makes severe demands, learning both the written and the spoken language; and in many rural developing areas, there are problems involved in the acquisition, maintenance, and function of vernacular literacy, when children or adults lack oral competence in whichever language is selected as the medium of primary education or adult literacy.

In highly multilingual settings such as India or most parts of Africa, a trilingual pattern of literacy has been suggested. India's Three Language Formula has been developed to cope with the recent phenomenon conditioned by the administrative, political, and economic organization of various regions (Srivastava and Gupta 1990). In Cameroon, Tadadjeu (1977b) supports the view that most primary schools in Africa should be planned as functional trilingual schools and that adult literacy should ideally be planned as functional multilingual literacy capable of following the same trilingual pattern depending on the particular interests of a given group of adults.

Tadadjeu's plan for Cameroon may be appropriate in multilingual countries in general: it recommends a minimum of two standard handbooks per language: one for early primary school, with orthography, simple reading texts, vocabulary, basic grammatical patterns and exercises, and reading texts drawn from oral folk literature. The second handbook would be for adult literacy, and would include basic arithmetic, problem-solving procedures, and informative reading texts (health, civics, agriculture, etc.). For such multilingual contexts the suggestion is also to have bilingual books which could be used to teach literacy in two languages.

As we have noted above, the cost of developing and producing literacy materials for a large number of languages is often too high for some nations or regions. The twelve multilingual countries participating in the 1979 South East Asia Regional Literacy Workshop reported a lack of learning materials (Unesco 1981). In India and Pakistan, it has been found difficult to provide materials in the numerous dialects, while the motivation for acquiring literacy in standard languages is low. However, the new possibilities of 'desktop' publishing will certainly contribute to increasing the materials available cheaply.

6.5. *Motivational Materials*

Definition

Such materials are intended to motivate individuals or groups to participate in a literacy programme, and also to motivate influential non-participant literate individuals or groups, who may fear losing their own socio-economic advantages (see e.g. Chapter 1).

Creating social awareness in favour of literacy skills means sensitizing participants to the merits of literacy. It involves creating the desire to acquire literacy,
getting the illiterate to come to class, sustaining their interest, and persuading
them to use their literacy skills. It has only recently been undertaken in a systematic manner.

In South Africa the 1991 National Language Project Conference proposed a
two-track approach to mother-tongue instruction: on one track, there would be
popularization of the idea and its importance in terms of access to economic,
political (and cultural) power; on the other, the requisite research and development of appropriate materials and resources in the harmonized varieties. The
need for a Language Awareness Campaign prior to any campaign for vernacular
literacy has been emphasized. In Sudan, the absence of pre-teaching campaigning in order to 'persuade' has been seen as contributing greatly to the failure of
the literacy campaign (Cowan 1984).

The term 'pre-literacy activities' as used in most of the literature covers in
fact two different types of activity, of which only the first is motivational. In
this, more or less informal pre-literacy activities and materials are developed
in order to provide incentives—that is, to develop attitudes necessary for a person to learn to read; the written language, its usefulness, and its relationship to
spoken language are introduced into people's experience. The term 'pre-literacy'
has been used also to refer to formal 'pre-reading' activities; in this second type,
activities and materials which provide visual and motor training have been developed to prepare children or adults for reading and writing. In pre-reading the
learners are familiarized with two-dimensional symbols and specific tools, hand-
ling books, reading pictures, and manipulating a piece of chalk or a pencil. In
non-literate societies, everything in traditional cultures that calls on symbolic patterns, such as tattoo marks, or weaving patterns, can be used. Pre-reading through
a phonetico-gestural method, arms in positions to represent the shape of letters,
has also been found useful (Hamadache and Martin 1986).

The Need for Motivational Materials

In literate and non-literate societies alike, it has been found that linguistic awareness—that is, awareness of spoken phonemes, syllables, words, and sentences
—helps in acquiring literacy. 'Language-awareness programmes' have recently
been set up, which use language as a 'bridging subject' (Hawkins 1992). These
programmes are designed to use reading exercises critically to raise consciousness as to the nature of the language being used; they are rather different from
pre-literacy consciousness-raising about literacy, although of course they may
overlap. They are of use in teacher-training.

A prerequisite to the beginning of any literacy programme must be the provision of something worth reading. In some societies, as Hamadache and Martin
(1986) point out, the only written message is on bottles of beer or soda. Even
when newspapers are available, they are in a language that is unfamiliar to the

population. A body of literature the speakers of a language want to read is the single most important factor in motivation to become literate. The availability of easy and useful reading materials, such as posters, newspapers, and so on, influences motivation for literacy; the creation and use of a literate environment is part of pedagogy.

Preparation of Motivational Materials

The importance of motivational materials has been gaining ground as non-formal techniques of education are becoming more common; as the 1981 Unesco report underlined, the development of such materials requires specialized training, which is related to training in publicity and public relations. The choice of format will depend on factors such as local conditions, financial constraints, availability of appropriate materials, and so on. As in publicity in general, the purpose of motivational materials is to bring to notice a certain product (literacy), and to persuade a target population to procure the product or participate in the process. (For example, adults may be reluctant to join in literacy programmes, thinking that education is for children, and may not want to acknowledge openly that they themselves also need to learn.)

Motivational materials must employ, as far as possible, local resources, including traditional art forms and media. The language used must be that of the target group. More than any other kind of materials, they can exploit modern technology in various media. They must be brief, to the point. Film, radio, television, and traditional art forms such as folk songs and folk plays are considered best. The use of radio and television, whose potential has not yet been fully exploited, will be discussed below.

Follow-Up Materials

Literacy skills may be lost because of the lack of opportunity to develop and maintain them. Unesco now emphasizes the need to ensure the retention of reading, writing, and mathematical abilities by making provision to avoid relapse into illiteracy; effort and finance put into teaching people to read and write have been wasted because nobody took the trouble to provide materials for them to read and write once they had acquired the skill.

In many countries, literate persons have few materials on which to practise their skills. Although during the campaign in Tanzania there were numerous supporting motivational and instructional services (songs and jazz bands, textiles printed with literacy themes, diaries and calendars, radio broadcasts, correspondence courses, rural newspapers, and libraries (Bhola 1984)), Russell (p.c.) reports that today few newspapers are in fact passed around. In the CAR there exists no newspaper in Sango, although this language has had national status for several years (Gerbault, in *Abstracts* 1990: 8–9). In India, the lack of post-literacy support has been a major problem, particularly in rural areas. After the 1935–40 literacy campaign, acquired skills were not maintained because the gap between the primer and available literature was very great—there existed no specific post-literacy materials. There was nothing simple and interesting to read (Laubach and Laubach, 1960).

Ready access to follow-up materials provides learners with an opportunity to practise their literacy, particularly where there are few trained teachers and where little use of the written word is made in everyday activities. The materials must be easy to read and attractive; they have both a remedial and an extension function. There are various types, according to whether they are used for reading only, whether they are teacher-dependent or independent, and according to the medium used. But the lack of sufficient material is frequently due, as we have said, to financial constraints on its development. The best post-literacy activities are those that arise spontaneously from local initiatives (market accounts, local taxes, organization of cooperatives, sanitation, production of local news bulletins, etc.). It is often possible to associate the communities with the production and sale of cheap reading materials.

In Cuba, some reading materials were made available to the newly literate immediately after the campaign. Rural libraries were opened, and a Department of Workers' and Peasants' Education was created. A formal follow-up course was developed, *Seguimento*, with the goal of reaching the equivalent of the sixth year of schooling. A variety of instructional settings and structures were in operation: afternoon and evening classes, schooling in factories and work centres, family reading circles, and so on (Bhola 1984). A lot of effort has also been put into post-literacy in Brazil, including an important book production programme and an oral literature project, and the claim has been made that there has been a low degree of relapse into illiteracy in this country (Bhola 1984). In Senegal, there has been a National Literacy Week every year since 1985 (Juillard, in *Abstracts* 1990: 13). Although it has been reported not to be very effective to promote literacy at the national level, its main effect has been that ethnic associations have been teaching reading and writing in their languages to small groups.

The role of the press in the production of follow-up materials cannot be overestimated: the presentation of newspaper materials—headlines, advertisements, illustrations—is always attractive to the new learner. In Pakistan, radio and television have been used as follow-up together with textbooks, and mobile schools have been in use, with teachers moving in a caravan from place to place. In many places the public has been kept informed of the need and progress of literacy through the media and by means of posters and billboards (Bhola 1984).

Is there a *minimum amount of material* necessary for teaching and then maintaining literacy among adults and children? Certainly, the total absence of the written word in the environment will result in a more or less rapid decline of literacy skills. A variety of reading material has been recommended for primary schools, including books, signs, maps, lists, newspapers, posters, and so on. Necessary materials can be imported, produced centrally, or locally; besides reading materials *per se*, they include teaching manuals, pedagogical cards, technical booklets, radio broadcasts, films and cassettes, exercise books, pencils, paper, blackboards, benches, and oil lamps. In industrialized countries, the production of literacy materials for schools has become a vast commercial enterprise involving the publishers of traditional written materials as well as those who develop audio and visual materials. It has been claimed that good standards of reading cannot be achieved without adequate and suitable material resources. But the minimum amount needed depends on the context; on the level of literacy sought, whether for adults or children; on the presence or absence of written materials in the environment, and on the amount of motivation of teachers and learners. In the USSR campaign there was at the beginning a scarcity of all material goods necessary for the conduct of classes, but both teachers and learners were highly motivated and made up for the poor material conditions. In the rural areas of Cameroon, where women volunteers organize literacy classes for other women, there is no book and hardly any material of any kind to start with. But these women are highly motivated by their need to read prescriptions and to be able to do basic arithmetic, and they manage to acquire basic skills in spite of the adverse conditions. The question of the need for a variety of materials can be answered only in terms of specific programme characteristics (intended audience, financial constraints, logistics). Motivation is more important than the teaching materials used, but adequate pedagogy requires some attention to the mechanics of literacy, which can be acquired only by doing actual reading and writing.

7. LITERACY AND MODERN TECHNOLOGY

New questions related to literacy have been put to us by the development of new technology. We may first ask what place is left to traditional literacy and its teaching, in a world where audio and visual means of communication have gained so much ground and have become so effective. Charpentier reports (see Chapter 6) that tape-recorded oral messages have been seen to replace the written word in the South Pacific. Increasing use of the telephone the world over also surely threatens the use of written correspondence. With the spread of cheap transistor radio sets, the transmission of personal messages through the radio has become a familiar mode of communication in many African, South American, and Asian towns, villages, and rural areas. A major advantage of such systems is their compatibility with traditional oral message-sending (Christie, in *Abstracts* 1990: 127). In addition, this technology may perhaps enable societies to sidestep literacy in propaganda campaigns to educate (one purpose of literacy campaigns being to educate for politics, as well as for health).

But, in spite of extraordinary technological developments, a lot of distance communication will still have to be through writing. We have to reflect, then, on how technological advances (radio, television, video, tape recorders, computers) have affected or are likely to affect the conduct of literacy campaigns, the training of teachers, and the actual teaching methods. While it is true that we are very far indeed from the stage where every primary school will have a computer, and that traditional methods of teaching literacy are going to survive for some time, one has to examine how technology can help the development of literacy.

New possibilities for cheap printing have been mentioned in an earlier section. A number of book publishers are now also producing materials for the recent video and audio media that can be used for pedagogical purposes. In this section, we will focus on the use of radio and television.

Radio and Television

Radio and television can play a role at every stage of literacy operations: in motivating learners and other sectors of the population, in the training of teachers, in literacy teaching itself, and in follow-up. The 1981 Unesco report lists a number of advantages of radio and television: they permit communication with large audiences, which may be scattered over wide distances. While only radio can be said to be cost-effective, the vision–sound mode of television is very attractive, and it can, for example, show visually the hand movements involved in writing. Both are suitable for classroom and home instruction.

Radio and television cannot be stopped for clarification, although this is possible with audio and video cassettes. Also, the spoken message is transitory, unlike the printed medium. Where radio and television have been used for actual teaching of literacy, they have often been associated with printed materials and teacher supervision. It is true that for a wide range of tasks it may be easier to have an illustrated text by one's side as one performs the task than to listen or view part of a cassette over and over again. It has been argued too that, by its nature, television invites passivity, and can be used effectively only with other activities involving dialogue (Limage 1987).

For the vast majority of people in the world, it is radio rather than television that deserves to be called the universal medium of communication: radio can be used anywhere, and costs little compared with television. In *The Use of Radio in Adult Literacy Education*, Burke's (1976: 1) goal is 'to give "middle-level" literacy workers an understanding of the possibilities of radio in adult literacy programs and provide practical suggestions . . . to put these ideas to work'. Radio, which helps solve the problem of lack of roads, mail service, and of trained teachers, is not used more, according to Burke, because technological solutions to educational problems have often not occurred to those in decision-making positions today; radio is viewed as entertainment. Besides, radio uses sound, while reading and writing use seeing and doing, which seems at first sight to make radio incompatible with the pedagogy of literacy.

Radio and television have been used to present model classes to teachers; audio and video cassettes have also been used as teacher-training tools. The pedagogical possibilities are today increasingly exploited. Radio has been used in mass literacy campaigns in several countries of Latin America, both for promoting the campaign and for actual teaching. In Colombia, Accion Cultural Popular (ACPO) has been providing basic education through the radio since the end of the 1940s (Radio Sutatenza), and using newspapers, textbooks, records, and extension courses to supplement the broadcasts (Burke 1976). The materials were distributed free of charge to rural families, and a correspondence system with ACPO was organized to deal with questions and answers. 'Radiophonic schools' were started progressively in several countries of Latin America, and within a few years almost every country from Mexico to Chile had its own. Instruction becomes an integrated system, in which the radio plays a part while teachers use literacy materials. The master teacher is in the studio, while the monitor speaks to learners in classes. Various formats can be used: talks, or radio lessons, dialogue, interviews, discussions, dramatizations. In all cases, it is necessary to produce materials for learners and teachers which will supplement the actual broadcasts. In all cases, the radio must be able to establish two-way communication, between producers and listeners, and between listeners (Hamadache and Martin 1986). This can be made possible through written communication and tape-recording. This type of broadcast leads to group listening and to discussion and comments.

However, the use of all media aids is dependent on technical back-up (batteries, power supply, regular maintenance, etc.), which may not always be available in developing countries. This dependence is often as important in limiting the use of such technology as actual lack of funds.

Radio has also been used in countries such as Tanzania, Niger (radio clubs), and India (Radio Rural Forum). In Somalia a variety of innovative techniques were used to bring literacy to the masses: helicopters scattered leaflets displaying the new alphabet and slogans written in it. The language was taught by radio broadcasts based on printed materials in the newspaper. New alphabet symbols and word-division rules were announced daily by the radio and newspaper (Mezei 1989).

Television was used in teaching literacy to adults in Memphis, USA, as early as the end of the 1950s (Laubach and Laubach 1960). The use of television for educational purposes is now a worldwide phenomenon, and it can be used for all domains and all levels of education. US television productions such as *Sesame Street* or *The Electric Company* are well known, and have played an important part in familiarizing young children with print. In the Philippines, a comparable children's television series, *Batibot*, was started in 1983 (*Wall Street Journal*, 27 Oct. 1989); it appears to have been more effective for the spread of literacy in Pilipino, the national language, than all government efforts. In Europe, where television has become the most important source of news and information, literacy campaigns have been conducted through this channel. The best documented are those in the UK and Germany. British television (BBC) chose to stimulate rather than actually teach: the principle of the broadcasts that started in 1975 in North Yorkshire ('On the Move') was to give illiterate viewers the desire to acquire literacy, and the means to do so by informing them of available resources in their environment, and providing encouragement so that they would be willing to get in touch with the available help. In 1978 the series 'Make it Count' was started in order to improve adults' mastery of numeracy skills. Finally, 'Speak for Yourself' was developed for non-English-speaking adults (Highton 1986).

In Germany, the approach was similar, and the goal was also to sensitize the illiterate public and help them locate help. Various techniques were used: dialogues, interviews, discussions, and so on (Petrick 1986). In both the UK and Germany, television acted mainly as the starting-point for the viewer.

8. THE EVALUATION OF LITERACY PROGRAMMES

8.1. *Purpose and Scope of Evaluation*

It is now thought advisable to include an evaluation component in any literacy programme from the very beginning. Evaluation is required to compare the results obtained with the objectives set; it provides information necessary to adjust policies and procedures. Traditionally, two basic types of evaluation of literacy have been considered: one based on the number of years of schooling, and the other on actual results of literacy tests. But in a broader perspective, evaluation of literacy deals not only with actual literacy performance or achievement, but also with how a literacy programme is received, how acquired skills are used, and what the effects of literacy are on people's lives. We shall see later, and in Chapter 6, that this type of evaluation has been considered in Tanzania, and how it has failed to be completed.

8.2. *Problems in Evaluation*

Several problems may arise. First, considering that today the emphasis has shifted from mere measuring of literacy performance to evaluating changes in the lives of people who have acquired literacy, one problem has been a lack of clarity as to what the effects of a literacy programme might be. We have seen, for example, that the campaign in rural Somalia improved communication and changed the behaviour of people as a consequence of instructors from urban areas being sent out there; mutual comprehension between urban and rural populations was gained in the process. Today, drought and warfare and famine make any kind of long-term evaluation difficult. Evaluating changes in people's lives will rarely be straightforward. It requires not only clear formulation of expected outcomes in specific contexts, but also a longitudinal type of evaluation, which is more difficult than one-time testing of skills.

Secondly, since it is difficult to reach a satisfactory definition of literacy, there are problems with any measures and tests, although there have been attempts to establish a scale of literacy skills (see e.g. Unesco Institute for Education 1987). One cannot invoke a universal standard, a measure to be reached by an individual. Should the measure depend on the environment of the individual? Certainly testing must be based on practices in everyday life. How can one compare degrees of literacy? Carrington (1988*b*: 36) reports that, in a 1975 survey in Jamaica, a test was given in which the respondents were asked to answer in writing a number of questions such as how long they had lived in the area, whether they had any plans for moving, and so on. The goal was to classify them under one of four categories: 'Can read and write properly', or 'with difficulty', or 'with great difficulty', or 'not at all'. There was a problem in assigning people to categories according to whether they used features of Jamaican Creole rather than English.

We know how unreliable the figures based on the number of years of schooling or instruction have been in the evaluation of literacy worldwide. In many places, government categories for literacy count as literate someone who has had a specific number of years of schooling. For many literacy specialists, however, less than three years of instruction does not make a primary-school child literate. Moreover, people who can read when they leave school may not be able to read five years later if they have never had to read in the interval. Assessment must be related to the age of the person being tested; ideally one would break people into age cohorts, and then subdivide them by numbers of years of schooling. Carrington also mentions that census statistics in the Caribbean have not been consistent, the basis being quite different from one ten-year period to the next. Many censuses are taken by asking the head of the household how many people can read and write, and in what languages, which yields almost totally unreliable figures.

Thirdly, achievement tests may not be advisable in all cultures, because of different behavioural or cultural patterns. How can literacy be assessed then? Can self-assessment be trusted? As Le Page (*Abstracts* 1988: 75) points out, 'if you ask people if they can read and write, the chances are they are going to say "Yes" rather than "No" because you are challenging them . . . and even if you ask teachers in school how many of the children can read and write, they want to know why you want the information'. Sometimes the statistics will vary according to whether you ask 'Can you read?' or 'Have you been taught to read?'

In many contexts, literacy assessment has been with non-standardized tests, and has dealt with the ability to read and copy. In developed countries a number of standardized tests have been in use. The reading tests used in the UK for primary schoolchildren (Cato and Whetton 1991) can be classified according to the amount of understanding that is tested (beside word recognition), but none of them assesses how competent readers actually are in real life. In the UK tests assessing real-life literacy competence have been developed only for adults.

Shannon (1989) claims that 'objective tests' that substitute for the professional judgements of teachers dehumanize the social act of reading. Extreme caution has been recommended in dealing with the data collected with standardized tests even in the UK, because of disparities between different types of test and changes and inconsistencies over time in the ways the results have been collected.

Test results or procedures have sometimes been falsified to match expectations, as exemplified in Chapter 1. In the Brazilian MOBRAL campaign, the statistics on attendance and success were falsified by the teachers, who were paid according to the number of participants in their classes (Lind and Johnston 1990). Government literacy statistics have also occasionally been falsified when national literacy figures were needed to match expected levels of development.

8.3. *Evaluation in Action*

In the Cuban campaign there were initial, intermediate, and final tests. In Brazil, there has been no formal test of literacy, and the teacher has had complete authority to decide whether or not a student is literate: the students must be able to identify the content of what they read, write sentences that make good sense, solve problems involving the four mathematical operations with one or two figures, solve problems involving measurement of length, weight, volume, and time. In Tanzania, there were national examinations, which showed individual achievement and served as motivation for the continuation of the campaign. In Somalia, no formal evaluation has been available, and testing procedures have not been made clear; but the effects have been important in terms of social change. In Vietnam, the evaluation of literacy has changed during the life of the campaign; it has become more strict (reading, writing, numbers, dictation). There has been continuous evaluation of progress, with feedback into planning and implementation processes (Bhola 1984).

Large-scale evaluation may be very difficult in rural environments, and literacy statistics quite surprising. Baker (p.c.; see also Mitton 1976) mentioned that in Lesotho, many years ago, literacy was claimed to be 70 per cent; a random sampling system was used to test the percentage. It was found that the level of literacy among women was indeed as high as 70 per cent, but very much lower among men, who stayed away from school for long periods when very young, looking after the cows. One way of evaluating literacy more effectively in a variety of environments, including rural ones, may be by tapping parental attitudes towards what literacy can do for them and their children.

Carr-Hill in Chapter 7 reports on the testing of literacy in Tanzania by the International Institute for Educational Planning, the research branch of Unesco. The purpose of the project was 'to assess the functioning and effects of literacy programmes in developing countries'. Three kinds of effect were distinguished: (1) the actual learning of what was supposed to be learned, (2) the use actually made of what had been learned, and (3) the impact of what had been learned upon the participants' daily lives. Unfortunately the study did not assess the impact of literacy upon the lives of participants, which, it was realized, would have necessitated a complex longitudinal design. In Tanzania and elsewhere, measuring this effect (3) is now being seen as an important element in testing literacy. It is recognized that merely testing literacy and numeracy abilities, and even evaluating their actual use, are not enough. Not only must literacy skills be developed and measured within the learners' environment, but one must identify the changes that literacy has brought to specific individuals' lives and to specific societies over a period of time. It is hoped that such longitudinal studies will be undertaken.

9. METHODS AND NON-METHODS IN PRACTICE

So far we have given examples from numerous countries illustrating the pedagogical issues in vernacular literacy. In this section those in two highly multilingual countries, India and Cameroon, will be presented at some length.

9.1. *India*

Chapter 1 explains the important role played by political movements in starting literacy activities in India; for example, in the rural areas of Telangana and Jharkhand, Saxena (1990: 2) reports that 'because of the political conciousness, many were ready to learn [reading and writing] and they did it in quite a short time'.

   Some of the pedagogical aspects of these activities in India are of interest here. Night schools were opened in villages, where boys and girls came after the day's work. The teachers were generally youths with a few years' school education. Sympathetic school teachers were enlisted to help night school teachers improve their knowledge of pedagogy. The instructors were motivated because literacy activities were monitored informally by local people, but in some instances they did not even have lanterns and were not always provided with textbooks and slates. Women came to get out of their isolation and improve their self-confidence. Various non-political associations emerged to open literacy centres in the 1960s and 1970s, also opening libraries, reading rooms, and clubs. The Prime Minister of India observed that 'to relate [literacy] to the lives of the people, the mission would teach them in their own languages and dialects' (Mahapatra 1990).

   One problem for literacy in some Indian languages has been that a large number of tribal languages either did not have a script of their own or had once had a script now no longer in use. The Central Institute of Indian Languages, Mysore, has worked on the development of writing systems. First, a linguistic description is obtained or made. Secondly, the phonemic inventory is mapped onto the alphabet of the standard script of the language used at the state level; thirdly, a trilingual dictionary of about 2,000 words is prepared. Rules for the spelling system are evolved, and primers written. The primer and dictionary are handed over to the State Education Department for use in primary schools. The basic purpose is to provide initial literacy to the child in his own tribal language and to ensure a gradual transfer to the state's standard language and its writing system.

There have been problems in some Indian languages to evolve teaching strategies that will help teachers and learners to negotiate the extremely complex interaction that obtains between the spoken and the written form (Agnihotri and Khanna 1992*b*). In contemporary Hindi, for example, there is no phonological correlate of the different orthographic representations of '*r*', and learners face serious problems trying to learn writing conventions which look so complex and arbitrary. Intensive teacher-training seems to have been an important factor in the success of literacy work. In order to minimize the difficulties of learning specific scripts, teachers have been made aware both of the system and of the learners' difficulties, and initially accept non-standard spellings. A variety of interesting and cognitively challenging games and tasks have been suggested by Agnihotri and Khanna to accelerate the acquisition of writing systems: identification of words with a specific sound in an already learnt poem and their classification on the basis of different orthographic shapes of this sound, classification games based on the shapes of letters with or without vertical lines, and so on.

But, as Agnihotri (p.c.) writes,

the experimental work in the States of India often suffers serious setbacks as the political ideology of the changing governments in the States suggests different interpretations of history and social science . . . In general, the pedagogical aspects of literacy have been ignored in India—the principle being, use any primer and teach the basic literacy and numeracy skills. No attention is paid to the importance of learner-oriented and socially relevant materials, teacher training and appropriate classroom strategies. It is only recently that different organizations involved in literacy projects have woken up to the overwhelming importance of these variables in any enterprise involving literacy.

However, we have some examples of successful literacy activities in various areas of India: Agnihotri reports that neighbourhood libraries, on-the-spot story and poetry competitions, exhibitions involving reading and writing tasks, playing a variety of language games, and involving children in the process of producing their own local magazine as in the 'tree letter-boxes' experiment, have all shown considerable potential. In the campaigns of the 1960s, posters with charts of Hindi letters were used in the villages. Among the Adivasi-Oriya, 'gurus' have traditionally been the learned and wise men; 'guru groups', with a maximum of ten learners each, are used for literacy training in Adivasi-Oriya and in Telugu, the official language of the state of Andhra Pradesh (Gustaffson, forthcoming).

In one experiment, members of a voluntary group approached illiterate women without any materials to begin with. The idea was to talk to them about issues that concerned them and write out things that they wanted to see written. It worked quite well (Agnihotri, p.c.). In Kashmir, a province of Northern India, an experimental method used proper names as the basic materials for adult education: the written forms of participants' names were used as the basis for learning letters, and provided initial motivation (SIL 1990).

9.2. *Cameroon*

The PROPELCA project in Cameroon is one of the best documented and most complete examples of a literacy programme, including materials development, a teacher-training programme, and evaluation. The principles of PROPELCA (Projet de Recherche Opérationnelle pour l'Enseignement des Langues Camerounaises) are summarized in Tadadjeu (1990). It was born out of a collective idea put forward in 1977–8 by Yaoundé University linguists and educationists, with the goal of conducting research in order to improve school achievement in Cameroon. The underlying assumption was that success or failure in school is basically related to linguistic success or failure, and therefore local and official languages must be taken into account. The working principle is 'to use local languages as the initial instruments for scientific and technological training, using traditional games and the immediate environment', the assumption being that Africa can no longer attempt to found its development on borrowed (i.e. imported) values.

The theoretical position of PROPELCA, which holds that it is impossible to select a single language to be used for education for the whole country, resembles very much that of Indian educationists and policy-makers. Multilingualism is the rule in both countries and the problem of choosing which languages should be taught is considered 'a false problem'. There has to be official recognition of the elementary educational functions that any Cameroonian language must fulfil as a mother tongue, and a second Cameroonian vehicular language must be taught in school.

In the early meetings of PROPELCA the recommendation was made that existing practices of using the mother tongues (L1) for initial education should immediately be made official—that is, that Cameroonian languages should be used orally in the first three classes of primary education. The existing language committees were to be constituted into textbook preparation teams; 1978 was a very active year, with several official meetings and correspondence with representatives of the Ministry of Education.

At the time there were twenty-seven languages (out of the 236 Cameroonian languages) with developed writing systems available for teaching. In January 1979 the first staff training meeting was held in Yaoundé. The need was expressed to have publishing facilities to handle the basic materials for the first forty languages—that is, one pre-primer, two primers, one reader, three maths textbooks, one text for transition to the official language (LO).

The training of teachers was a very important aspect of the project. In order to be certificated, each teacher was to participate in three training sessions, each 12–15 days long in three consecutive years. The training programme, by project members and linguists, included information regarding the linguistic and socio-linguistic situation in Cameroon, information on PROPELCA, ongoing trainees' reports and discussions of problems encountered, writing in the L1 (orthography, grammar, tones, practice), methodology of L1 and LO teaching (theory and practice at the different grade levels), evaluation, and other topics (evaluation of new materials, monthly and weekly planning, visual aids, etc.).

Between 1982 and 1988 the number of trained teachers increased from three to eighty-seven (in four languages). Each subsequent year the number has been increasing steadily. Each training session was reported to be an occasion for progress, especially in terms of choice of content: better texts have been identified and used. In 1987, for instance, fourteen training sessions were organized, in Yaoundé and in the other provinces (decentralized training sessions are cheaper, more motivating, provide more information, and have more impact in the provinces). As in a number of other contexts, one problem has been that the trained teachers are likely to be appointed to other areas or to non-teaching positions at any time. Another has been that teachers feel frustrated because they are being trained while others are getting a paid vacation, and they receive no compensation for the additional work they put in.

In addition to the first four languages (Ewondo, Lamnso', Fe'efe'e, and Duala), there has also been informal and voluntary training for five other languages (Limbum, Kom, Mundani, Bagyeli, and Babungo). The training of school directors (to enable them to make administrative decisions concerning the project) has also been seen as an important component. (Unfortunately, the frequent displacement of directors is a major handicap to the effectiveness of such training.) The materials for training included the General Alphabet of Cameroonian Languages, a guide for the development of writing systems for African languages, and basic principles of language education in Cameroon, discourse analysis, semantics, and translation.

PROPELCA started as an experimental programme in Christian schools: in 1981 two Catholic schools started with two languages (Ewondo and Lamnso'), and by 1986 there were eleven experimental schools in four different provinces, in which a total of four languages were taught (the two above, plus Fe'efe'e and Duala).

9.3. *Methods and Materials*

The distribution and time of introduction of the L1 and LO are shown in Table 4.1.

For each language two primers and one reader and three maths textbooks were to be developed. Counting in all classes is done in L1. In order to facilitate distinguishing between the two languages, the children are made to write the L1 in

TABLE 4.1. *Distribution of languages in the first three years of schooling, Cameroon (%)*

Year	L1	LO	
1	75	25	(speaking only)
2	60	40	(speaking and writing)
3	25	75	

print letters and the LO in cursive handwriting. The general primer is intended to apply to all Cameroonian languages, and could be used for non-Cameroonian African languages too. Instructions are given in French and English at the bottom of each page. The teacher communicates the instructions in the children's language. Children are first taught to *look* (at images, shapes, letters, getting used to identifying small differences), *think* (understand that real life can be found in a book), and *do* (talk about a picture, answer a written question or problem). Primers are intended for the initial reading of a particular language by learners who have had no exposure to its written form. The synthetic method is used: shapes of letters and their sound values are taught, then the combination of letters into words, and of words into sentences. Tone is taught by means of pictures of children in standing (High), sitting (Mid), or crouching (Low) positions. Writing is initially practised with large gestures of hands (in the air or on the sand). The readers include texts representative of the various discourse types, and include difficult words, grammar exercises, spelling, pronunciation, and writing exercises, with French and English translations. Transition to the LO—French or English—is made using contrastive analysis. The development of materials for the teaching of numeracy skills seems to have raised special difficulties, and experimental testing of these materials for readability and rhythm of presentation of content has been a primary concern. Traditional games have been used for the teaching of numeracy skills.

The testing of children's performance in basic skills has been done each quarter or each year, both in the L1 (reading, writing, numeracy) and in the LO (speaking, reading, writing). Questionnaires have also been used to test how the programme has been received in the community.

Although the pedagogical approach of PROPELCA and its development by local specialists is exemplary in sub-Saharan Africa, it has met with the lack of involvement of official institutions typical of this part of the world. Only private institutions and local communities in general have been supportive of the programme since its initiation. Some of the reasons for official apathy or negative attitudes towards vernacular literacy have been discussed in other chapters; political reasons are well to the fore in Cameroon, where ethnic rivalries continue to threaten national unity.

In addition to the teaching of vernacular literacy by PROPELCA, literacy in a number of Cameroonian languages has been taught to young children for quite some time in an informal way outside school hours. As in other parts of the world, religious groups have played an important role in supporting such initiatives. Students and other adults literate in French or in English have taught themselves reading and writing in their mother tongues in order to be able to teach them in their villages. The NUFI programme for literacy in the Fe'efe'e language is a well-documented and successful example of such informal literacy networks (Tadadjeu 1977*a*).

The research conducted in North Cameroon in 1987 by Barreteau and Dieu (1991) is one example of a vernacular literacy project embedded in economic and social practices: the rice production society, SEMRY, was restructured, with technical and social reforms aiming at a larger participation of local peasant groups in a number of tasks related to rice production; this resulted in a total change in the communication system between managers and peasants, and it was necessary to identify a viable language for communication in the multilingual area of Maga. The opinion of the population was asked regarding the choice of the language which would be the 'working language', in which they would be taught to read and write in order to be able to take on their new role.

Literacy workers in Cameroon are continuing to work among small groups. Some of these groups live in environments which are still almost totally non-literate. For example, in West Cameroon, the Meta women, who are a highly motivated group needing literacy skills to read medical prescriptions and do basic arithmetic, have had no previous exposure to literacy materials and have no books to be taught from. The teachers are mostly women with a primary-school education, who get their training in six-month seminars. Classes are held once a week. A multi-strategy method is used; an extensive pre-reading period is necessary, in which individual letters are cut out of cardboard for the learners to hold in their hands (to make a bridge between the real world and the world of literacy). They are taught to recognize the shapes of letters, and to describe them using whatever vocabulary is at their disposal; then they learn to recognize the shapes of letters on letter cards. In a later stage, the teaching is conducted in small groups through some form of the global method: they are shown keywords, with the corresponding real objects—pictures are not used, because these women cannot 'read' them—and break them down into syllables and letters. These groups have been reported to be very eager to write, even before the teacher thought it advisable. After a year's learning, the women can buy a small locally made book.

10. CONCLUSION AND GENERALIZATIONS TO BE DRAWN

In this chapter we have related teaching practices to various aspects of the theoretical framework within which we have considered literacy pedagogy.

Unlike spoken language, literacy, in a vernacular or in a second language, is a skill that has to be taught. Therefore, once decisions as to the appropriateness and relevance of acquiring literacy skills have been made, pedagogy becomes of central importance. A lot of our examples of pedagogical initiatives have illustrated the point that, if literacy is embedded in social practice, pedagogical approaches (campaigning, teacher-training, teaching methods and materials, post-literacy materials) need to adjust to different audiences in different types of society.

Throughout the discussion of the various components of pedagogy, we have seen that the teacher factor is crucial: availability, motivation, ability to cope with diverse learning needs of either pre-literate children, or illiterate or non-literate youth or adults. The teaching enterprise is, of course, helped or hindered by the quantity of available and adequate materials, but it is the role of the teacher to motivate the learners in their own environment and show them the value of literacy as a social practice. Motivated learners can overcome many of the difficulties arising from method or materials.

One characteristic of present-day literacy pedagogy is that it must adapt to needs more diverse than ever in the past. Social changes of all kinds have opened new roads for the pedagogy of vernacular literacy: new types of teacher, more flexible methods, greater variety of strategies and materials, including those provided by new technology. While technical means for training teachers or developing materials are constantly improving, the actual conditions in which the teaching of vernacular literacy takes place also require constant adjustment of pedagogy.

The development of new power relationships and the need for communities to rely more and more on themselves have tended to operate a shift in responsibilities in many contexts; the most striking example is that of the action led by women's groups, in literacy development and in other areas of activity; women have played a role in the dissemination of literacy for specific purposes, such as contraception or hygiene (it has been noted that in many countries, such as India, if the illiterate population increase continues, the role of women will be more and more crucial for education in family planning).

This points to the need to consider with a great deal of attention specific cases of pedagogical adaptation to the environment, and the pedagogical means which have worked best. Maybe innovative small-scale approaches are more effective than many of the mass literacy campaigns that have been conducted all over the world. Today the real problem may be how to reconcile the two approaches, and translate those ideas (informal, small-group approaches) into large-scale campaigns, given the socio-economic conditions and political priorities.

As new questions concerning the spread of vernacular literacy are beginning to be addressed, new pedagogical challenges have come to the forefront: for example, devising means of spreading literacy without destroying or altering traditional ways in social and economic interaction, evaluating literacy by taking into account its actual impact in people's lives. The cases of two very different countries with complex literacy problems—India, where there is official commitment to the development of vernacular literacy, and Cameroon, where there is no such commitment—have been examined. A variety of examples of ways in which pedagogical resources have been developed and put to use in response to the problems in these two countries have been provided.

There may be no incentives (economic or other) for people to wish to acquire literacy skills, either in the L_1 or the L_2. This may occur in all kinds of environments, in non-literate societies but also in literate societies, among adults but also among schoolchildren; it may be extremely difficult to devise successful pedagogical approaches to literacy, when its attractiveness has received a serious blow from the deteriorating job market everywhere. Teaching literacy skills in the mother tongue if people want literacy in a lingua franca or in an international language may be a hopeless task; the literacy campaign planner, materials developer, or teacher has to answer the question of what people want literacy for.

At last it has been realized that provision for the maintenance of acquired literacy skills is a crucial aspect of pedagogy. Absence of the printed word outside schools or learning centres hampers the effectiveness of literacy programmes. If there are no signs, no newspapers, no books, people will not see reading as an integral and meaningful part of the environment. Some form of literature must be produced for the general population on a regular basis. But in industrialized societies also, where modern ways of communication are so developed, provisions to avoid relapse into illiteracy are necessary.

The need to reconsider the issue of the evaluation of literacy has been mentioned. If literacy is to be viewed as a continuum, there may be no universal standard of evaluation. Research in this area is badly needed. As in the other areas of pedagogy, it is suggested that major qualities of evaluation may be its flexibility (both in terms of content and in terms of frequency) and its relevance to real life.

PART TWO

Cases from Migrant Settings in Europe; East, Central, and West Africa; East, South, and South-East Asia; Pidgin- and Creole-Speaking Communities

5

Vernacular Literacy in New Minority Settings in Europe

PENELOPE GARDNER-CHLOROS

with contributions from T. Bull, G. Varro, and J. Warwick

I. INTRODUCTION

Vernacular literacy for migrant populations represents a further complication compared with vernacular literacy for indigenous groups. The 1953 Unesco report, which recommended that all children should have the right to education in their 'mother tongue', did not lead to any widespread implementation of the latter. Reasons for this range from a lack of theoretical precision as to what the concept of 'mother tongue' is intended to mean (see Introduction to this volume and Section 2.2 below) to the fact that a nation's resources to introduce new teaching programmes may be limited in proportion to the number of dialects or vernaculars in which such teaching needs to be conducted.

These problems are compounded when one considers whether and how the report could be applied to immigrant populations or communities. On the one hand, the problem of defining the 'mother tongue'—or tongues—is likely to be greater. Within a community coming from a particular country there may be a number of different varieties represented, none necessarily corresponding to the official language(s) of the country of origin, nor, consequently, with the variety used as the medium of education in the country of origin, in which the migrants may or may not already have been schooled.

On the other hand, resources for teaching facilities of all kinds are likely to be even more grudgingly granted by the host country to migrant groups than to native minority communities, particularly if they represent linguistically and geographically fragmented groups within the host-country society.

In this chapter we consider the question of vernacular literacy as it affects the education, the rights, and the ethnic identity of migrant populations in various European countries. After having clarified the scope and terminology of the chapter, we discuss a number of background issues relating to the host countries, their policies, and prevailing attitudes. We then illustrate the variety of problems and attempted solutions from a number of recent case histories. Next, we discuss theoretical and practical issues relating to these groups, an understanding of which is essential for appropriate policies to be formulated in this area. Finally in the last section we suggest some guidelines and principles which emerge for future action.

2. SCOPE AND TERMINOLOGY

Although there are, of course, both old and new minorities in those European countries which are not members of the European Union (EU, formerly EEC), most of our examples will be taken from countries which are members of the EU, in particular the UK and France, which were among the main recipients of a non-indigenous labour force in the 1950s, 1960s, and early 1970s. Within the latter we will refer mainly to the Greek Cypriots and various Asian groups in Britain, and North African, Spanish, and Portuguese groups in France. We will make a number of specific comparisons between the new minorities and the older established ones (sometimes called 'indigenous' minorities), and also with one non-EU country, Norway, with reference to how aspects of the indigenous language situation and older minorities have affected the treatment of and/or policies towards the newer minority groups.

Two of the problems one encounters in considering these groups are, first, the lack of comparable data from the different countries and, secondly, the lack of any consistent terminology, both of which make comparisons problematic. In order to get round the second problem we will therefore provide a brief discussion of some of the relevant terms used here.

2.1. *Migrants and Immigrants*

In several international institutions (EEC, EU, Unesco, Council of Europe), all foreign labourers (whatever their origin) in industrialized societies are referred to as *migrants*. The term in English does not carry any implication that the workers are temporary visitors, though it may do in certain national contexts—for example, in the French one. This is by contrast with the German term *Gastarbeiter* ('guest workers'), which is a euphemistic title for a class of workers who are not given the same rights as long-stay residents.

In the UK, however, both Commonwealth and south European workers are usually called *immigrants*. Each country tends to develop its own specialized terminology for describing sections of the migrant population. For example, migrant children are sometimes referred to in the UK as 'Section 11 children', after the name of an administrative provision regarding their education.

2.2. *Linguistic and Ethnic Minorities*

First of all it should be pointed out that the term *minorities*, in spite of its appearance of neutrality, is ideologically loaded to the extent that it implies that the nation state is the relevant unit of measure. In fact, in the case of the older minorities, at a regional level they may well constitute the majority of the population, and it is on that basis that their demands for autonomy can be justified.

Linguistic minorities generally refers to communities whose languages have been indigenous to the state at issue over a considerable period of its history (Welsh, Breton, Friulian, etc.), or whose minority status is the result of the redrawing of political frontiers (Alsatian, Macedonian). *Ethnic minorities* usually refers to the groups of more recent migrant origin which form the main subject of this chapter. To designate these groups, we refer here simply to old minorities and new minorities, following Reid and Reich (1992).

2.3. 'Mother Tongue'/Vernacular/Dialect/Standard/National/ Official Language

As pointed out in the Introduction to this volume and above in relation to the Unesco report, the term 'mother tongue' can have a variety of meanings. This confusion gives rise to two principal problems.

First, there is the mistaken assumption that the mother tongues spoken by migrants can be identified with the national or official language of their country of origin. An example of this would be the assumption that Berbers of Turkish nationality have Turkish as their mother tongue.

Apart from these cases where members of new minorities already belong to minority language groups in their country of origin, there are other cases where they do not speak the official language of their country of origin at home but a regional variety (e.g. Moroccan or Algerian Arabic), as opposed to classical or literary Arabic (which is the official language in Morocco and Algeria). It often makes little sense to view such vernaculars as regional variations rather than independent languages in their own right. In particular, speakers may have had little or no exposure to what is seen as the standard in their country of origin.

Secondly, there is the problematic assumption that migrants' mother tongues are set in stone for all time. The first generation's vernacular—what they actually speak—changes through contact with the host-country society, the language(s) spoken there, and contacts with other migrants. The second and subsequent generation's vernacular is usually different again, not only through increased contact with the host-country language, which may be more of a mother tongue to them than their parents' mother tongue, but also through lack of contact with the vernaculars *and* the standard current in the country of origin.

Terminological issues recur at various points in this discussion, as they impinge on, and reflect, attitudes which have a serious bearing on migrants' access to education and the type of provision which is made for them (see Section 3.2).

2.4. Education and Literacy

Since we have defined 'vernacular' here as the variety actually spoken by a particular group, we make no *a priori* assumption as to whether a given vernacular is written or not. For some people, a standard language is their vernacular and so their vernacular has a written form, though this may differ more or less from the spoken form (for example, it is often said that written standard French is more different from spoken standard French than is the case with English).

Ideally, in talking about vernacular literacy, we are therefore talking about whether people read and write in the variety which they speak. This should be distinguished at a conceptual level from the issue as to whether they are *educated* (i.e. schooled) in the language of their country of origin or that of their parents. A further complication, which will be discussed below, may arise when the vernacular spoken by certain groups is different from the language of literacy in their country of origin.

As we will see, in this context and at this stage it still appears idealistic to claim that migrants should universally be provided with the opportunity for literacy in their vernacular as such. The recognition that the languages spoken in their countries of origin should play a part in national education systems in Europe already represents a big step both at national and at European level. Inevitably, therefore, much of the discussion which follows still focuses on that first step rather than on vernacular literacy as such, though, as we will see, there is some progress in that area also.

3. BACKGROUND ISSUES

3.1. *Migrants in a Plurilingual Europe*

The Myth of Monolingualism

In Europe as in the USA, but not in Asia or Africa, a philosophy that monolingualism is the norm and multilingualism the exception manages to prevail in spite of massive counter-evidence available in our own back yard. Almost every European frontier can be shown to represent an artificial line whose path is determined by a series of historical coincidences, and which meanders through a continuum of dialects. The latter closely resemble their own neighbours and usually much less closely the national standard of the state in whose territory they fall (Chambers and Trudgill 1980). The advent of the twentieth century and the influence of widespread—though not always centralized—educational systems has led the speakers of these dialects to become increasingly bilingual or bidialectal in the state language and the local language. Only Belgium, Luxembourg, and Switzerland have several official languages, but their multilingualism, at least in the cases of Belgium and Switzerland, owes more to the competitive struggles of separate monolingual communities than to the harmonious plurilingualism of their populations.

To this plurilingual jigsaw one must add the array of regional languages for which often hard-won recognition has been achieved during the course of this century. While some of these have died out or are on the wane (like Scottish Gaelic or Occitan in France), others have been revived with renewed vigour and have reinforced their infrastructure to the point where they have increased their speakers and/or their domains of use (as in the case of Basque—dealt with in Chapter 1—or Welsh). Luxembourg children are taught in their home dialect, Letzebuergisch, on entering elementary school, and gradually move over to the two standard languages which are both part of their national heritage, German and French. This system, as we will see, has much to recommend it in the migrant context as well.

It is with this background in mind that one should consider the question of literacy in the mother tongue or the vernacular for migrant populations in Europe —the two terms having, as we shall see, different implications. One can legitimately argue that their arrival has done no more than bring to a head an issue which European governments should ideally have faced at the same time as compulsory education for all was introduced in the late nineteenth or early twentieth century. It is the same issue which the Bullock Report (DES 1975) raised in simple and memorable terms, saying that no child should have to discard the language of the home on entering school. At least in Europe, this apparently basic principle has more often been disregarded for ideological than for practical reasons. For example, the European Charter for Minority and Regional Languages of Maastricht (1992) makes no mention of the languages spoken by the immigrants established in Europe.

Recent Migration

Several factors are important in relation to immigration in Europe, of which the colonial legacy and the post-war economic boom are the most significant in terms of the number of settlers to which they gave rise.

In the UK, immigrants from the New Commonwealth had British citizenship and full rights to settle and work. In France the same applied to citizens of the Caribbean 'Domaines et Territoires d'Outre-Mer' and to Algerians born before Algerian Independence in 1962, as well as to their children. Citizens of former Dutch colonies had similar treatment. The Federal Republic of Germany did not consider itself a country of immigration in the same way and therefore classified foreign workers as *Gastarbeiter* with no permanent status in the country.

Immigrants to the other countries who fell outside the post-colonial provisions, in particular workers from the poorer Mediterranean countries (Italy, Greece, Spain, Turkey, Morocco, etc.), were not immediately granted full residence and working permits. Starting in the 1950s, the latter were recruited actively by governmental agencies and private enterprises in the industrialized northern European countries, in particular Belgium, France, the UK, the Federal Republic of Germany, and the Netherlands, to do the jobs which their own workers were overqualified or unwilling to do.

The recession precipitated by the oil crisis in 1973 led to a closing of borders to immigrants of whatever origin. Many workers, aware that if they left the country they would be unable to re-enter, sent instead for their dependants to join them, a policy promoted by the host countries. It is at this stage that the social and educational services of the host countries were called upon to provide for these new arrivals, who generally did not speak the local language. Owing to the type of labour for which there had been a demand, they represented the poorest and least educated sections of the population in their countries of origin, and the least likely to be literate. For example, one of the reasons for immigration from Cyprus in the 1950s and 1960s was the fact that peasants who did not own a sufficient plot of land to make a living came to build a new life in Britain.

Naturally the picture presented here is a simplified one and, within any national group, there are many possible reasons for emigration. For example, the first Cypriot wave was followed by a second one in 1974 when Turkey invaded Cyprus, and people from all walks of life who were made homeless sought refuge in Great Britain. The same split can be found among Indochinese immigrants in France: those who came over in the 1970s were frequently students or highly educated professionals, and may be contrasted with the second wave of immigrants from the same area who came over in the 1980s, refugees known as the Boat People.

The various educational systems of the host countries, centralized or decentralized, were unprepared for the arrival of these families. Any consideration of their needs for literacy in their languages of origin took second place to hastily set-up language tuition in the host-country languages.

The 1977 EEC Directive

One of the few official documents which set out directly enforceable policy specifically for the teaching of Europe's new minorities was the 1977 EEC *Directive on the Education of Migrant Workers*. The final version of this directive, as adopted by the member states of the EEC, suffers from several significant limitations. On the theoretical side, the directive studiously avoids any reference to the benefits of mother-tongue teaching (let alone vernacular literacy) for the children's broader educational needs. Its aim is restricted to making it possible for the six million children from other EEC countries to be reintegrated in due course with the schooling system in their country of origin. On the implementational side, the directive gave rise to intense debate and the setting-up of various pilot and research programmes, but the resourcing of actual teaching programmes in accordance with the directive was left to the member states. By way of example, we will consider below the projects which were set up in response to the directive in the UK. But it should be noted that there were huge and significant differences between the directive as it was finally adopted by the Council of Ministers and the proposals which had been put originally by the Commission of the European Communities on the basis of the work of groups of experts (Sneddon 1993*a*).

In what way did the directive as adopted differ from the original recommendations? First of all, the Commission had consistently referred in its proposal to migrant workers from non-member states of the EU as well as those who had migrated within it. This was justified by the Commission at the beginning of the proposed directive with reference to a Council resolution of 1974 which fixed as an objective equality of treatment for Community and non-Community workers and their families in terms of living conditions, along with the development of better opportunities for cultural and vocational training for both groups.

Secondly, the Commission's proposal had placed far more emphasis on the *educational needs* of the children of migrant workers, irrespective of their country of origin, than was carried through into the actual directive. Their need for education in their mother tongue was not reduced to the sole motive of facilitating their reintegration in a school in their country of origin, but was also related to the 'full development of the personality of children situated between two cultures'. In pursuance of this aim, the Commission wanted the member states to make arrangements for the mother tongue and culture of the country of origin to be taught in the school curriculum, gratis and throughout the period of compulsory education, in accordance with the educational standards normally applicable in the host country, as well as for appropriate teacher-training. None of these aspects was reflected in the directive in its final form (EEC 1977*b*; Boos-Nunning 1986).

There is, therefore, a considerable gulf between the experts' recommendations, as channelled through the Commission's original proposals, and the obligations which the ministers of the member states were, in the last resort, prepared to impose on their governments. But even in this watered-down form, the directive gave rise to extensive debate both in Europe and outside it. Its impact can be appreciated by the fact that, of the projects set up in response to the directive, some were organized in countries which were not members of the EEC, such as the Swedish bilingual programmes for Finnish children (Skutnabb-Kangas 1984), and some, although organized by the member countries, were aimed at non-Community nationals, such as the German programmes for Turkish children.

Reid and Reich (1992), whose use of the term 'new minorities' has been adopted here, evaluated fifteen experimental projects in a range of EU countries. While they found many of the projects innovatory and worthwhile in themselves, they regretted the lack of experimental design and evaluation that were built into them, and the lack of communication between research teams. All but two of the projects came to an end as soon as EEC funding was withdrawn.

Other work carried out by international organizations, such as the Council of Europe's Committee on the Education of Migrants, has led to numerous recommendations, but on the whole these have not been taken up by the member governments in such a way as to make any substantial changes in policy effective. The 'intercultural' approach was earlier much discussed by Unesco (Unesco 1983). Based not on language teaching but on the revalorization of the different cultures involved, it has been variously implemented, usually in experimental school settings in the host countries over the past twenty years. In Belgium, an apparently successful four-year 'intercultural' experiment which ran from 1988 to 1992 permitted pupils of three secondary schools in Brussels to choose their first modern language as they wished, and whatever their background, among classical Arabic, Turkish, Spanish, Portuguese, Italian, or Greek (Anciaux and Baucy 1993). Some national education policies are now attempting to incorporate its principles.[1]

3.2. *Host-Country Issues*

Apart from the transnational directives pertaining to migrant education and the existing linguistic picture, which includes the existence of, and provisions made for, the older minorities, vernacular literacy for new minorities is dependent on a range of legal, political, attitudinal, and practical factors in the particular host country where they find themselves. Far from amounting to a consistent set of principles and practices, in each of the countries one may wish to consider there are inconsistent and even contradictory tendencies and pressures.

Old and New Minorities: Issues in Common?

The majority of migrants, as defined above, are now permanent residents in the host country, as very few decided to return in spite of inducements offered by certain governments such as those of the Federal Republic of Germany and of France.

The drawing of distinctions between old and new linguistic minorities is therefore not connected with their degree of establishment but is primarily a political issue. In Section 6 we will touch upon some recent legal developments concerning the civic and linguistic rights of the newer and older minorities. Certainly there seems no objective reason why, for example, a second- or third-generation migrant—if this is not in itself a contradiction in terms—should have less right to be educated in his or her mother tongue than the speaker of a small and dwindling indigenous language.

It is a political question of which members of both types of minority are keenly aware. In spite of the similar basic problem which they face of having the principle of bi-literacy acknowledged, it is exceptional for the two types of minority to see themselves as united in a common struggle for the same rights—particularly where resources for teachers and teaching materials are scarce.

---

[1] The French government declared in 1986 that 'the new national programmes for primary and secondary education are opening up to other cultures, a necessary step in a world where everything is more and more on an international scale. From this point of view, the presence of foreign children in the classroom is a piece of luck for modern France. However, these pupils must neither be the only beneficiaries of this new approach, nor its only support; the new programmes must be applied regardless of how many foreign children there are in the class and whatever their nationality' (Directive no. 86–119, 13 Mar. 1986, in Saladin *et al.* 1993: 29).

The persistence of a difference in status is illustrated by the separateness of the two Finnish minorities in Norway, of which one is long established and the other is a recent migrant community. The indigenous group is made up of settlers who moved from Finland to the north of Sweden and the adjacent areas of Norway from the sixteenth century onwards (Vikör 1993). This group, known as the Kvens, retained their identity and language into the twentieth century in spite of the assimilationist efforts made until recently by the authorities. One of the villages, Börselv, has recently introduced a literacy programme in the Kven dialect. The more recent Finnish migrant community benefits from the teaching of standard Finnish, which is considered an immigrant language.

One can usefully contrast the policy in the Nordic countries with the lack of financial involvement of most EU members (see Section 4) and the aims set by the EU itself—the provision of mother-tongue instruction for migrants with a view only to their return to their homeland. In the Nordic countries, the official aim is that such groups should become bilingual in their mother-tongue and the host-country standard (or in one of its standards in the case of Norway) and public funds have been directed towards this end. Migrant children have the right to be instructed in their home language and to receive special support from teachers who know this language when they move over to the host-country language. The extent to which this policy is implemented is, however, said to vary within each of the countries, depending on resources and political will (Vikör 1992). On the whole, at least in Norway, mother-tongue literacy among newer minorities (from Pakistan, Vietnam, Turkey, Yugoslavia, etc.) is decreasing, whereas it is increasing among indigenous groups.

The prime example of increase is that of the Sámis (Lapps), who now have schools where one of the varieties of Sámi is used as a medium of instruction throughout compulsory schooling. Sámi was proclaimed an official language of Norway only a few years ago, but the movement for literacy in Sámi has been gaining momentum, in spite of generations of oral cultural transmission, as a means to counteract a general decline in the use of the language.

This degree of deliberate support for the language is more likely to be necessary in cases, such as Sámi, where the language has no nation state of which it is the official language. This factor may indeed be more significant for its general prestige and vitality than whether the language is associated with a newer or older minority. In France, among the languages spoken by economic migrants, those which are taught as part of the school curriculum (and *a fortiori* European languages) enjoy greater prestige than others. It is symptomatic, for example, that second-generation Portuguese are now studying Portuguese in French universities (Villanova 1988). The bicultural and bilingual accomplishment which this represents is connected not only with the status of Portuguese as a national language elsewhere, but also with the fact that it is standardized.

For the older minorities, on the other hand, it has not always been an advantage to speak a language which is recognized as being a national language elsewhere.

For example, in France, when the Loi Deixonne (1951) gave a measure of recognition for the first time to Breton, Basque, Catalan, and Occitan, the other
three major regional languages, Corsican, Flemish, and Alsatian, were ignored
on the basis that they were 'dialects' of other 'national' languages: Italian, Dutch,
and German.

Social and political considerations determine these distinctions, which are
arbitrary at a linguistic level. Even within the majority-language context, certain
varieties, especially if oral and/or unstandardized, are stigmatized by the wider
group. Derycke gives an example from a marginalized French community of
inland-waterway workers ('bargies') in the north of France, whose vernacular is
made up of a mixture of the northern dialect (especially Picard) and 'spoken
French', which is known to diverge in many respects from the written standard
(Derycke 1989, 1994). The group is described by Derycke (1989) as 'strangers
in their own land' owing to their illiteracy, the failure of their children at school—
for which they feel guilty—and their linguistic insecurity. Like migrants who do
not bring with them a literary tradition and whose spoken variety is unstandardized, the 'bargies' do not recognize the richness of their own linguistic baggage,
which, Derycke shows, includes constructions which represent stylistic enrich-
ments of the standard. The speakers themselves, when confronted with the two
options, chose the standard forms as being the correct ones. In all these respects
they can be compared to some of both the old and the new minority groups, also
marginalized and persuaded of their own linguistic inadequacy (Varro 1992).

Nationality and Citizenship

Following a series of transitional arrangements, EEC nationals from Southern
Europe have since 1985 had full freedom of movement and rights to settle and
work in all the member countries, so there are no longer the advantages which
there were in acquiring the nationality of their northern European host country
(EEC 1985). Nor are there the dilemmas which were involved in giving up one's
nationality of origin in order to gain practical advantages in countries which do
not permit dual nationality. This latter course has always caused administrative
headaches, especially in the area of military obligations, but it is now sometimes
recognized as providing the most satisfactory solution, at least at a personal
level, for migrants who feel allegiance to both their country of origin and their
country of residence.

There are considerable differences between European countries, both inside
and outside the EU, regarding the ease with which they grant nationality or citizenship rights. It is the practice for some well-informed non-EU nationals to
acquire nationality rights in countries such as Ireland where they are granted
easily, thereby also acquiring a passport which enables them to work in any of
the fifteen member states. Employment may then be sought in a country other
than that which provided the passport. Some countries such as Sweden, which,
as mentioned above, makes generous provision for mother-tongue maintenance,

regard the acquisition of citizenship as an aid to integration and have traditionally granted it quite easily. The UK has several tiers of citizenship which depend
on the individual's degree of connection with the country and confer different
types of residence and other rights. It has maintained a liberal attitude towards
multiple nationality. As for France, we have already mentioned some of the categories of people who were entitled to French nationality without having been
born and bred in metropolitan France. Until immigration began to be seen as a
political problem, France maintained a liberal attitude towards naturalization.[2]

But, whereas legally speaking certain categories of people may cease to be
treated as immigrants by virtue of gaining nationality rights, a society may not
accept them as anything other than immigrants for years or even generations
beyond that stage. Being accepted as a non-immigrant depends on a complex of
factors in all societies, of which command of the local language is only one.
Whether or not a foreign or naturalized resident is referred to as an immigrant
depends partly on their country of origin but also on other factors which reflect
their status in that society—for example, wealth.

Attitudes and Representations

The last point brings us back into the area of terminology which in turn is inter-
twined with attitudinal questions in the host societies. To the question of who
is an 'immigrant' one could add the question of who is 'bilingual'? The term has
come to be used quite differently in common parlance in the UK and France. In
France, among teachers in particular, it is used not of those who are categorized
as immigrants (*enfants de migrants*), but rather of middle-class children, who,
as it is thought, are able to add full fluency/literacy in another language to full
fluency/literacy in their own. It refers to those, in fact, of whom it is assumed
that their bilingualism is 'additive' rather than 'subtractive' (see Section 5).
'Bilingualism' is thus associated with the middle-class élite (Varro 1990: 33). In
the UK the reverse is the case, with 'bilingual' being used euphemistically to
designate educationally disadvantaged children of immigrant origin, just as 'ethnic
minorities' refers only to new minorities but not older ones.

It is not new to find that attitudes to socially disadvantaged speakers of a
language can be carried over into judgements about the languages themselves,
but it is none the less discouraging to find the same attitudes now to new minority languages as were expressed in a different form half a century or a century
ago with respect to the older minority languages of Europe. Whereas the latter
were looked down on then as being inadequate vehicles for intellectual advancement, the new minority languages are now often regarded as inadequate for social
and professional advancement. A teacher of Arabic at the prestigious École Poly-
technique of France recently referred to this status problem: Arabic is associated

---

[2] The new law effective as of 1 Jan. 1994 does not abolish the *jus soli* but rules out 'automatic'
acquisition of French citizenship for children born of foreign parents on French soil. Such children
must apply for it, if they so desire, between the ages of 16 and 21 (Costa-Lascoux 1993: 251–3).

with immigrants, by contrast with English, which is seen as the language of professional success (Bassam-Tahhan 1989).

Attitudes to the languages spoken by new minorities take their place within the prevailing discourse about language and languages in general, which generally speaking in the industrialized countries of northern Europe is still based on what I referred to above as the myth of monolingualism. Bilingualism of any kind is far more likely to be found among members of the minorities than among the majority. A Sámi speaker, for instance, will nearly always be fluent in Norwegian, Finnish, or Swedish, depending on his or her country of residence, as well as in Sámi. Romaine (1992) has pointed out that the varieties of language which are relevant in the lives of new minorities can be seen as being arranged in hierarchical order. For example, in the Greek-Cypriot community in the UK, at least for the second and subsequent generations, English is at the top of the pecking order, followed by standard modern Greek (the language used for education in Cyprus and consequently in Greek classes in England), followed by the Greek-Cypriot dialect which is spoken in the homes of the migrants, followed last of all by the spoken Cypriot dialect plus the English mixed vernacular of British-born Cypriots. Monolingualism, according to Romaine, is a luxury only those at the top of the hierarchy can afford. One might add that, conversely, the most creative forms of language, which emerge from code-switching and the mixing of the different varieties, are frequently produced by those at the bottom of the hierarchy.

In France, for over a century, in addition to the myth of monolingualism, the French language has been upheld as one of the major instruments of national unity and pillars of the Republic. This is ostensibly done in a positive spirit, with a special literary prize being attributed, for example, to foreign writers writing in French. In practice, it translates itself in the schools into an extremely uniform, de-vernacularized presentation of the French language. A survey in Alsace, for example, showed that primary-school teachers were prepared to tolerate some regional variation in pronunciation, but hardly any in vocabulary use, and even less in grammar. Seventy per cent thought that speaking Alsatian was a slight or a great disadvantage for pupils' ability to express themselves in French (Gardner-Chloros 1991).

Until now there have been no comparable overt principles expressed regarding the uniformity of English, and it is nowhere stated that English is the official language of the UK. But the introduction of the national curriculum with its emphasis on the learning of 'correct' English rather than on the development of pupils' *language*, and its heavily monocultural bias, is in practice a step in the same direction. If only the use of a highly normative version of the national language is condoned in the educational system, both children from linguistic minorities and indigenous children from working-class backgrounds, who on the whole are not exposed to that variety outside school, are put at a disadvantage. In the next section we will consider what further effects this has on vernacular literacy.

The maintenance of a myth regarding the existence of a correct, focused variety of the language to which everyone should aspire, often invoking great authors (such as Shakespeare in Great Britain—whose pre-standardization English was in fact full of inconsistencies of spelling, grammar, and vocabulary), is responsible for a crisis of confidence among many old and new minorities regarding the value of preserving and transmitting their own language.

In France the notion that a native language (whether standard or vernacular, indigenous or migrant), might be harmful to the non-French-speaking child, whose future lies in integrating with mainstream French society, is deeply ingrained. In Alsace as in other regional minority settings (Denison 1982; Gardner-Chloros 1991), the awareness that a language is not officially recognized may lead to a feeling that it is not worth transmitting, indeed that it is not 'a language' at all. Social workers, school heads, and teachers all report that immigrant parents and even middle-class foreign parents come to them for advice as to what to speak to their children. They see themselves as caught between the devil and the deep blue sea in having to make a choice between *bad* French and their *useless* native idiom. The sense of shame transmitted to the younger generation can lead to certain speakers denying they know how to speak their native language (Jerab 1988; Gardner-Chloros 1991). Conversely, renewed ethnic pride leads others to claim their parents' language as their own, even if they can hardly speak it at all (Dabène and Billiez 1987).

As linguists we no doubt have ourselves at least partly to blame for the degree of ignorance about the nature of standard and non-standard languages and bi / multilingualism which is prevalent even among some highly trained teachers, in France as in Britain.

The Politics of Ignorance

Ignorance about which languages are spoken by the minorities is more of a political question. In the UK, for example, the Department of Education and Science holds no statistics on how many pupils speak which languages, nor on which new minority languages are taught in schools. They are only able to give the numbers of pupils taking GCSE examinations in modern languages, some of which are also spoken by migrant groups. Sources of information on such questions are therefore unsystematized at any official level. To our knowledge, there has been no exercise elsewhere equivalent to the Linguistic Minorities Project (LMP), which was carried out between 1979 and 1983 with EEC funding and which aimed to give a picture of community language use in three areas with heavy immigrant populations in the UK.[3] As well as the Adult Language Use

---

[3] The Linguistic Minorities Project was set up to look at the changing patterns of bilingualism and mother-tongue teaching in England. Surveys were carried out mainly in Bradford, Coventry, and London. It was followed up with the Language Information Network Coordination (LINC) project, which ran until December 1984 and the Community Languages and Education Project from 1983 to 1985. All were based at the Institute of Education in London.

Survey, a Mother-Tongue Teaching Directory was drawn up which provided a survey of the provision in mother-tongue teaching offered by local authorities and a range of community groups (Khan 1984). Finally the project made recommendations for schools and educational authorities (Stubbs 1985). Until it was dismantled by the Conservative Government, the Inner London Education Authority also carried out bi-annual surveys of the languages spoken in London schools. The last survey in 1989 showed, for example, that 25 per cent of pupils spoke a language other than or as well as English at school, the most common other language being Bengali. As a very first step in setting up any sort of policy on the teaching of mother-tongues, a regularly updated survey of this kind as to which languages there are and how they are used would seem to be essential.

In France, no equivalent study has been carried out either (Varro 1992). Official censuses asked no question regarding language use until the 1992 census. The results of the latter are accompanied by the conclusion that 'the most general practice by far is that parents abandon their mother-tongue when speaking with their own children' (INSEE 1994: 58). (It may be argued that a census is an inappropriate method to collect the information; see, for example, the precautions which were taken in LMP to ensure that respondents did not feel threatened by the questions asked.) A presentation of twenty-five different sociolinguistic situations in France, including those of linguistic minorities and some new minorities (Vermès 1988), shows that official languages are often erroneously ascribed to people simply on the basis of their nationality.

The Indigenous Illiteracy Question

When we come on to the question of the degree of literacy of new minority groups, it is clear that information is even more difficult to come by. It is certain that we are not contrasting illiterate migrants with a perfectly literate native population. In the UK the consistent figures showing that around 10 per cent of adults have problems with literacy refer only to literacy in English. In 1992 newspaper headlines splashed the results of a government survey which supposedly found that 25 per cent of 7-year-olds could not read properly, though no details were given about the criteria used or the sample. Similarly, in France much has been made of the proclaimed 4 per cent illiteracy rate. There is doubtless an element of political expediency in the media 'panic' relating to this issue, drawing attention away as it does from the problems of teaching migrant languages. Similarly, in the Scandinavian countries, the enthusiasm which could be detected for the *bilingual* development of minority-language speakers in the 1970s has dwindled, at the very time when concern about native illiteracy appears to have reached crisis point.

The statistics regarding illiteracy in European countries are singularly unilluminating. We neither know who is illiterate and who is not, nor whether some who are illiterate in the host-country languages are literate in other languages instead. What is clear is that Western governments have apparently had their hands too full or their coffers too empty to concern themselves with research on effective methods for making people literate, regardless of their linguistic background. Literacy is not an all-or-nothing phenomenon, as the difference between the two French terms *illettré* and *analphabète* illustrates (Fraenkel *et al.* 1989). There is a scale from people who do not master all the skills (form-filling and decoding, etc.) necessary to function in a sophisticated industrial society (*illettrés*) to those who have never been taught to read or write in any form, who are rare in our societies (*analphabètes*). Until the twentieth century in Britain the test of literacy was whether people could sign their name on the marriage register. We demand a much more complex level of skill in the computer age, and the consequences of illiteracy are potentially more severe also.

4. ASPECTS OF VERNACULAR LITERACY IN THEORY AND PRACTICE

In this section we will look at some examples of action undertaken by host countries in the area of migrant education. As we saw above, these mainly involve general mother-tongue instruction rather than vernacular literacy *per se*.

4.1. *The United Kingdom*

Apart from the Linguistic Minorities Project (see above), the EEC funded two other projects in Great Britain during the same period, the Bedford Project, described in Tosi (1984), and the Mother Tongue Project, funded through the Schools' Council. The Mother Tongue and English Teaching project (MOTET) was also carried out in the late 1970s with funding from the DES.

The objective of the Bedford Project, along with its sister projects in Paris, Limburg in Belgium, and Leiden in The Netherlands, was to enable member states to examine 'administrative solutions and adaptation of language teaching methods and materials' with a view to implementing the EEC directive. Bedford was chosen because of its unusual concentration of migrants from the south of Italy, many of whom intended to return there and who spoke various dialects quite far removed from standard Italian. A second group was made up of Punjabi-speaking children who spoke a variety of Punjabi not too far removed from the standard. After consultation with the parents, children were taught the standard version of their mother tongue in mainstream schools with methods involving 'guided transfer'. Although the project has been criticized for deficient evaluation (e.g. no control groups) (Sneddon 1993*a*), the teaching of the mother tongue in mainstream schools was popular with parents and gave rise to greater involvement and support for the schools.

The object of the Mother Tongue Project (Schools' Council) was to develop appropriate teaching materials in Greek and Bengali for Cypriot and Bengali children, for use in community schools and in mainstream schools in multicultural classrooms. The problem of obtaining age-appropriate teaching materials, which also reflect the children's bicultural experience, is one that comes up again and again in discussions of vernacular literacy for migrants. Alongside the written materials, which were in the standard languages and designed to be transferable to other languages, a range of materials to develop oral skills in London Greek Cypriot and Sylheti—a variety of Hindi—were also developed (Tansley 1986). The project clearly fulfilled a need and the materials devised were widely disseminated through training courses for primary-school teachers. The project was less successful in its further aim to bring together the work of community and mainstream teachers. Differences of training, methodology, and working conditions were such that many community teachers withdrew, and the hoped-for partnership between the two types of teachers in the classroom did not materialize. The necessity of face-to-face communication between parents, communities, and teachers was further demonstrated (Sneddon 1993*a*).

The Mother Tongue and English Teaching Project (MOTET)

The third British project described here is the only one which was a true bilingual teaching project. It was carried out in Bradford and Keighley in the late 1970s with funding from the DES—unfortunately only for one year—and its design included provision for control groups and full evaluation.

The purpose of the project was to investigate the possibility of using Mirpuri, a dialect of Punjabi spoken in parts of Pakistan, as a medium of education alongside English for reception-class children. Both languages were given equal weighting, and the purpose of teaching in Mirpuri was not merely to facilitate the transition into English. Mirpuri does not have a written form and would not be used as a medium of education in Pakistan (where Urdu would be used instead). Nevertheless the project was strongly supported by the parents, who had high aspirations for their children and a strong commitment to maintaining their language, in spite of not having a high level of literacy themselves and not having much reading matter in the home. The results showed that the experimental group achieved better results both in Mirpuri and in English as compared with the control group, and that there was a transfer of skills from Mirpuri to English. A research project carried out with Turkish children in The Netherlands (Verhoeven 1987) showed that the use of a 'transitional' literacy—i.e. being taught literacy in the L1 and the L2 at the same time—did not lead to any retardation in the L2.

No further officially funded projects have taken place since the early 1980s in mother-tongue or bilingual education. Some local authorities have been very supportive with scant means—though, as mentioned above, the most supportive, the Inner London Education Authority, has since been dismantled—and individual teachers are still active in promoting children's mother tongues. But, whereas the Bullock Report had said that home languages should not be discarded at school, ten years later in 1985 the Swann Report (DES 1985) said that research evidence was inconclusive in this area and that mother-tongue maintenance was best achieved within the ethnic minorities themselves. It therefore concentrated on the provision of ESL (English as a Second Language) needs. The national curriculum allows for 'mother-tongue' literacy teaching only from the age of 12–13, by which time it is too late for it to take hold as the primary form of literacy,[4] although some voluntary classes can also lead to pupils entering for GCSEs in new minority languages. As for the adult literacy programme, it is limited to English, for migrants as for native English speakers.

4.2. *France*

Between 1973 and 1982 France signed a series of bilateral agreements with eight other governments[5] in order to implement the EEC scheme, known in French as ELCO (Enseignement des Langues et Cultures d'Origine (Teaching of Languages and Cultures of Origin)), with instructors being sent over and paid for by those governments. The languages taught under these schemes are the official national languages. Very recently, however, in a few public elementary schools, some teaching of vernaculars, especially those spoken by children of North African origin, has been tolerated and even encouraged by official reports which link the teaching of dialectal varieties to a more 'communicative approach' to language teaching (Prunet 1992: 41, 64). In various state examinations, such as the *baccalauréat*, candidates may now present dialectal Arabic as an option.[6]

The languages of more recent immigrant groups (e.g. West Africans, who have been arriving in growing numbers since the early 1990s) are not covered. As in the other countries, community organizations carry out teaching outside the state system, and some of this is in vernaculars, in the sense of non-official, non-national languages, e.g. Creole, Bambara, Sarakole, Peul, etc. and Berber (Djaffri 1983). Varro (1992) points to the fluctuating attitudes of the French government and public opinion in this area. After a period (roughly 1975–85) when there was an underlying conviction that migrants (and their children) would one day return home, and when their 'right to be different' was affirmed, a realization followed that a large number of *populations étrangères* (foreign populations)

---

[4] Urdu, Punjabi, Gujerati, and Bengali can now be taught from the first year of secondary school, either instead of or on top of the traditional modern languages, and Chinese is widely taught in voluntary classes. This information was kindly provided by the Association for Language Learning, 16 Regent Place, Rugby CV21 2PN, which is funded by subscriptions from its various member organizations supporting various languages.

[5] Portugal (1973), Italy and Tunisia (1974), Spain and Morocco (1975), Yugoslavia (1977), Turkey (1978), and Algeria (1982).

[6] In Belgium also, a mixed committee was recently (1994) set up between the ministry of education, research, and training of the French community, the EEC, and the Moroccan education ministry. Negotiations are underway for colloquial Arabic to be taught in the classes before introducing the classical language which is the only form currently taught by the Moroccan instructors.

were in fact in France to stay. Official policy expressly changed its aim to the 'integration' of these groups, which the prime minister of the time punned as their 'right to indifference' (*Le Monde de l'éducation*, 1989). This is thought to imply their satisfactory acquisition of French but not to include any publicly funded mother-tongue maintenance. The latter is left to the ELCO scheme referred to above, financed by the various states, and to the large network of voluntary associations of whom several organize native-language teaching for the members of their communities.

At the same time, in educational circles, the idea that the full development of a second language is dependent on the acquisition of skills including literacy in the mother tongue has gained currency. The setting-up of structures in the schools to make this second aim a reality is at odds with the underlying philosophy of non-denominational, free, and compulsory schooling for all, which includes a provision that French should be the only language of instruction. The result is that, as matters stand, very few state schools in France offer teaching in migrants' mother tongues, though bilingual sections offering reinforced teaching in German or English have become much more common (Boulot and Boyzon-Fradet 1987). The 1989 government decision to introduce early foreign-language instruction in primary schools has led to most parents (including migrant parents) requesting that their children be taught English (84.3 per cent of state school pupils choose English as their first foreign language at secondary school, and a further 14 per cent choose German (see Prunet 1992: 48)). But it has also led to the enhancement of the status of other languages such as Spanish, Italian, and Portuguese, which were also part of the 'Languages and Cultures of Origin' scheme in primary schools, but which are now coming out of the migrant ghetto and being learned by other children too. In the rue de Tanger state elementary school in Paris, where an international section offers bilingual education in Arabic and French to children, whatever their background, from kindergarten on, it is reported that 'Arabic has retrieved its social status', that 'the children are proud to speak it', and that this 'rehabilitation has had beneficial side-effects on other languages such as Italian, Spanish, Portuguese and Yougoslav' (*Le Monde de l'éducation*, 1990).

Apart from local groups in the large urban centres which provide social assistance and advice for migrants, and sometimes organize language teaching in their vernaculars, the public Fonds d'action sociale (FAS) funds a Liaison Committee for Literacy (CLAP) which organizes or gives teaching in the *langues d'origine* all over France. The teachers are usually students from the country in question studying at a French university and the methods and syllabuses are therefore diverse. In the case of Arabic, a pupil being taught some classes at school and some through this organization may well be taught two different versions of the language (e.g. classical or Egyptian) while the variety spoken in his or her home may be different again (e.g. Moroccan) (Vermès and Bazin 1991).

Overall, as in Great Britain, there is a need for a much better informed educational policy on the question of bi/multilingualism. This should take account of the fact that, as is evidenced by the existence of 'additive' bilingualism in certain pupils, it is never the fact of bilingualism as such which poses a problem for achievement (Tabouret-Keller 1988a, 1990b), but the conditions attendant on its realization (see below).

4.3. *Germany*

As in the UK, the reason given in Germany (then the Federal Republic) why widespread implementation of the EEC directive was not held to be feasible was the decentralized nature of the educational system, in this case devolving to the Länder. In practice some of the education ministries of the Länder adopted measures for the maintenance, outside the curriculum, of the migrants' mother tongues (Tosi 1984). Others established 'mother-tongue medium' schools, where children of the same nationality are taught almost exclusively in their national language (such as the Greek school in Munich), with relatively little German input. Although some have praised this system in particular in the context of its facilitating reintegration in the home country, educationalists have on the whole opposed these schools (Skutnabb-Kangas 1984), on the basis that their segregationist character leaves little room for the development of bilingualism with German.

4.4. *Scandinavia, with Particular Reference to Norway*

In Sweden, Norway, and Denmark, as Skutnabb-Kangas (1988) reports, it has generally been argued by educationalists that migrant children should be taught through the medium of their mother tongue, with the host-country language as a second language. Although migrant communities have generally favoured this system (which to a certain extent has been practised in Norway), in Sweden the 'submersion' model, whereby almost all teaching is in Swedish, and the 'compound' model, where only a small portion of the timetable is kept for the teaching of the mother tongue, are both still prevalent.

Although the other Scandinavian countries were influenced by Sweden's policies, the position in Norway is slightly different and provides a good example of how 'indigenous' issues can affect policies towards new minorities.

In Norway the total number of migrants is relatively small and insufficient to have an impact on the native linguistic configuration (for figures see Vikör 1993). But a high degree of awareness of multilingualism issues is derived from experience with Norway's older minorities (Sámis and Finns), along with an awareness of the standard versus dialects question, owing to the existence of two separate Norwegian standards. Unlike the situation described in Ferguson (1959), the two Norwegian standards are not in the complementary distribution position of a High and a Low. The one is derived for historical reasons from Danish and the other is a more recently created standard based on a 'common denominator' of Norwegian dialects. The aim of educational policy is literacy in these *two* standards—within which a high degree of variation is permitted, especially in the oral mode (Bull 1985). Vernaculars have high prestige and teachers are not allowed to correct the vernacular speech of a child.

Against this background, and bearing in mind also the Sámi and Finnish issues which were described above, it is more understandable that migrants in Norway should be, at least in theory, educated first in their mother tongue and then in Norwegian. As we shall see below, this is a policy which finds favour with certain educationalists in the field of bilingualism.

5. UNDERLYING ASPECTS OF VERNACULAR LITERACY FOR NEW MINORITIES

5.1. *Some Theories of Bilingual Development*

In a Unesco-funded study, Skutnabb-Kangas and Toukomaa (1976) criticized the assimilationist implications of both the submersion and the compound models outlined above. Their *educational* analysis of the problem in terms of 'semi-lingualism'—a state in which the child does not have adequate competence in either language—has, however, proved more controversial (Martin-Jones and Romaine 1985). Basically, the theory states that, where a sufficiently high level is not reached first in one language, the fact of learning another language can lead to a low level of competence in both. 'Semi-lingual' children may be quite fluent in everyday situations, but this fluency masks a deficit with respect to the more sophisticated structures of the language. Unfortunately, as far as the operational properties of this concept are concerned, the supposed deficit is only deduced on the basis of standard tests and academic results, which are likely to be inappropriate means of assessment for such children. In particular, such tests take no account of their socio-economic circumstances. In fact these can make the whole difference between the performance of bilinguals being as good as or better than those of monolingual groups, both from a linguistic and from a general academic point of view (Troike 1984).

In trying to explain how bilingual development could have either a positive or a negative cognitive outcome, Cummins (1979, 1981, 1991) placed much emphasis on skills connected with literacy. His hypothesis is that the development of competence in a second language is a function of the existing competence in the mother tongue. If a sufficient level has not been reached in the L1 when the L2 is introduced, its introduction will have a negative outcome for cognitive abilities, and a low level of competence in both languages might result. If, on the other hand, the L2 is introduced once a high level has been attained in L1, the effects of bilingualism will be positive.

What is particularly relevant to the question of migrant literacy is that Cummins claims that the cases of bilingual development which have a negative outcome are those where an L2 is introduced to children who do not possess the skills prerequisite for literacy. Literacy skills are known to be highly transferable from one language to another; teachers in France have remarked that previous schooling and having learned to read and write before immigrating are decisive for successful learning in the majority language.

There is, therefore, an argument in favour of migrant children first being introduced to literacy in their mother tongue, which one hopes would be a variety at least very close to their vernacular, before being taught the host-country language. In fact what usually happens in Europe is that newly arrived migrant children are first placed in preparatory or reception classes to teach them the host-country language at an accelerated pace (the EEC directive referred to 'crash courses'), and then integrated as soon as possible—one year is the official time allotted— with the majority classes. In their assessment of the EEC pilot projects, Reid and Reich (1992) pointed to the lack of suitable methods of assessment for migrant children's linguistic abilities. It is common for them not to have progressed beyond the acquisition of basic communicative skills in the L2 when they are expected to start becoming literate in it. This can lead to a cycle of educational failure, as in the case of children of Caribbean parentage in the UK, of whom a large number have been erroneously placed in special education (Edwards 1984).

Like Skutnabb-Kangas and Toukomaa (1976), Cummins remains silent on the effects of sociocultural factors other than language on cognitive development. Furthermore, he fails to explain what factors might influence the cognitive development of simultaneous bilingualism, which is very common for large numbers of bilingual children (Hamers and Blanc 1989).

In the work of Lambert (1972, 1977), an attempt is made to explain the role of the sociocultural environment in the bilingual child's development. Lambert conducted a series of experiments in Canada, where English-speaking children were taught through the medium of French ('immersion') and compared with matched groups who were simply learning French as a school subject. He found that the immersion classes could have entirely beneficial effects both at a linguistic and a cognitive level, providing there were positive sociocultural attitudes and support for both of the bilingual's languages by the parents and in the broader community. If these conditions were filled, 'additive', as opposed to 'subtractive' bilingualism would develop. Unfortunately Lambert's studies, though convincing, are correlational as opposed to explanatory. As Hamers and Blanc point out, we still know very little about the psychological mechanisms which intervene between the social and cultural environment and intellectual functioning. Neither is it clear how this kind of experiment could be extended to a substantial proportion of the new minorities. Nevertheless there is a clear echo from these Canadian experiments in the Mother Tongue and English Teaching project described above.

The importance of the mother tongue being taught alongside and valued equally with the environmental language appears to be crucial to the harmonious development of both. More fundamentally still, illiteracy or incomplete literacy in the L1 makes literacy in the L2 problematic. Klassen (1991) shows how such situations can lead to a double stigma, first within the migrant community, and secondly in the wider community, where job opportunities are restricted by an inability to function in a fully literate way in the host-country language. One need only think of the countless Cypriot or Asian women in England trapped as seamstresses doing part-work at home or in substandard factories, with no chance of improving their working conditions because of their low level of education. Whereas some so-called 'literacy' projects are in fact practical skills-related courses conducted orally, a few programmes have recognized this predicament, and for example provide literacy training simultaneously in English and Urdu for South-East Asian women (Hartley 1993).

5.2. *Understanding the Needs and Motivations of New Minority Groups*

As we have seen, in spite of the scale of recent immigration to Europe, both at national and supra-national level very little has been invested in research and on the formulation of policies regarding the specific educational problems of migrants. As with bodily health, a total lack of preventive measures results in the need for far costlier remedies. Forms of racist and religious conflict have exploded, in Great Britain in the Rushdie Affair, in Germany in arsonist attacks on the homes of migrant workers, in France in the *affaire du foulard*.[7] Tosi (1984) quotes estimates which say that, by the end of the century, one-third of under 35-year-olds in urban Europe will be of migrant origin—in France alone, there are potentially some 1.5 million speakers of Arabic (1982 Census)—and it is therefore high time that European governments took education for these groups more seriously.

First of all it is important to build up a picture of the communities in question, their educational profile and their needs. In spite of being grouped together, for example in the French school system, as foreigners (*enfants étrangers* or *d'origine étrangère*, also commonly called by the media *enfants de migrants, enfants immigrés*, or *enfants de la deuxième génération*), and in spite of the broad subdivisions used in the official statistics to define their origin ('Europe', 'Maghreb', 'Black Africa', 'Asia'), their characteristics vary widely and they do not constitute homogeneous groups. There follow some of the dimensions of variation which need to be taken into account.

[7] A much-publicized and repeated incident involving girls who kept their headscarves on in school, as religious (Islamic) symbols, in contradiction to the non-denominational principles of the state schools.

Literacy/Illiteracy

In some cases, illiteracy is likely to be associated with immigration since one of the reasons for emigrating is the inability to make a living in the country of origin, which is more likely to strike the less well educated members of society (as in the Cypriot example). However, as we have seen, there are also highly educated migrants and political refugees, who bring their own literacy with them, like the Overseas Chinese in Malaysia (see Kwan-Terry and Luke, Chapter 8 in this volume). It is therefore important to understand something about the socio-economic circumstances in the country of origin and about the immigrants' personal histories and itineraries as they pertain to the reasons for migration.

Literacy and Identity Maintenance

One must take account of huge variations in ethnolinguistic vitality between different groups of migrants. In the USA, children of recent immigrants from El Salvador are already speaking only English to their siblings (Fasold p.c.), whereas in southern California and southern Florida English-speakers feel that English is threatened by the Spanish of Mexican and Cuban immigrants. In France, one recent study shows that some young (9–11-year-old) migrant children of West African parents state that they can speak and understand their parents' home language, and several say they would like to study it if they had a chance (Heredia-Deprez 1989). In Australia, migrants of Greek origin have been shown to keep up their language and culture very effectively (Smolicz 1985), but in England, where contacts with the country of origin are theoretically much easier, the younger Greek Cypriots rarely speak their parents' language fluently, and one could therefore question whether it is appropriate from an educational point of view to persist in teaching them to write it. In France, a report compiled by the Inspectors of the French Ministry of Education in 1992 comes to the conclusion that, increasingly, the so-called 'languages of origin' have become foreign languages to the pupils, for whom French is the more natural medium of interaction, and should be taught as such (Saladin *et al.* 1993: 194). The same Education Ministry's report to the EEC (1992) calls for a review and reorganization of the way in which languages and cultures of origin are taught in schools (Prunet 1992: 195).

On the other hand, for some migrant groups, the teaching of the official language of the country of origin, as opposed to a variety closer to the vernacular which is actually spoken by the younger generation, is viewed as the most desirable form of identity maintenance. This applies, for example, to the parents of British-born Cypriots, many of whom struggle to maintain their children's literacy in standard Greek, which is the language of education in Cyprus as it is in the community schools in England. In Norway, Sámi literacy is mainly a post-war phenomenon, developed in response first to a growing fear that the language and culture would die out, and secondly to a realization that the Norwegianization policy prevalent until 1945 had been undemocratic and harmful.

Sometimes, it is through contact with the host-country society that the significance of literacy as a form of support for a language is realized. Whereas a generation ago the Punjab people were happy for their children to be literate in Hindi rather than Punjabi, Punjabi Sikhs in England now want their children to write in Punjabi for reasons of religious and cultural maintenance. Cases where vernacular literacy also has a full range of practical functions, such as that described by Saxena (1993) for Punjabis in Southall, are probably less common. Practical functions of literacy would more usually be tied up with the host-country language.

Vernacular literacy—or sometimes literacy in the official language of the country of origin—on the other hand, is tied up with identity in that it reflects and interacts with practices which form an intrinsic part of the original culture. This may be insensitively glossed over by the host-country society, which sees vernacular literacy as a straight alternative to literacy in the national language, with its attendant practical advantages. The whole conception of literacy may vary from that which is prevalent in the host society, as was shown when Australian Aborigines strongly disapproved of what they considered to be teaching children adults' language through a literacy programme. Culture-specific factors need to be taken into account when evaluating mother-tongue programmes: for certain West African groups, the symbolic values and social functions of the languages which they speak are not equally weighted, and individuals do not therefore always consider all their languages an important part of personal identity (Platiel 1988).

Saxena shows the range of types of literacy used by three generations of a Hindu Punjabi family in Southall over a twenty-four-hour period, and also shows how this community's literacy needs and practices have changed over the thirty years since the male workers first arrived. Developments which have made a difference to their literacy needs include the arrival of their families to join them, the setting-up of language classes and temples to cater for the children's education, and the setting-up of many small businesses in the 1980s which created a need for regular contacts with Asia. The ESRC funded a research programme for 1993–5, to investigate literacy practices among Gujarati-speakers in Leicester, using ethnographic methodology (Bhatt, *et al.* 1993–5).

Vernaculars, Standards, and Multiple Misunderstandings

As stated above, the myth of monolingualism in Europe is such that the first preconception which has to be put right is that migrants have a single mother tongue which they have brought over from their country of origin, which corresponds to what is taught in the schools of that country and which is a standardized variety which they need only 'maintain'. Observers have pointed to the dismay felt by pupils when handed a textbook called *Je parle arabe* ('I speak Arabic'), on discovering that the 'Arabic' in the book is not the one they speak at home. They may well infer from this that they 'speak neither French nor Arabic' (Valdman 1988). The myth that a single unified language is appropriate as a medium of education for such pupils is unfortunately usually reinforced by the existing contracts between the host country and the countries of origin.

In fact, most areas in the world are multilingual and this applies particularly to some of the main sender-nations—for example, of Africa and Asia. This need not only mean that the country of origin has several different language groups living within it, which it may well have (e.g. Turkish migrant workers in Germany may be Kurdish and not Turkish speakers), but also that the migrants themselves may already have several mother tongues when they arrive, as is the case, for example, with some South-East Asians or ex-East-African Asians in Britain.

Even when the language of origin is clearly identifiable, it may be associated with various different systems of literacy. We gave the example above of Punjabi speakers who may be literate either in Hindi or in Punjabi; each of these has a different script corresponding to it, Devenagari and Gurmukhi respectively, which carry different religious and ideological associations. The situation with Punjabi speakers' literacy is in fact highly complicated, a fact which may not be recognized by teachers and indeed not understood by the young pupils themselves. Punjabi speakers in Britain come from three different religious traditions, Sikh, Hindu, and Muslim. The Sikhs and Hindus originate from the Indian Punjab or from East Africa, whereas the Muslims come from the Pakistani Punjab or nearby areas like Azad Kashmir. Though all three speak varieties of spoken Punjabi, the Hindus may also speak Hindi and use it as their language of literacy and for the Muslims the language of literacy is Urdu, the national language of Pakistan. They may also have a range of literacy skills in Arabic, the language of the Koran (Khan *et al.* 1984). Pupils may report speaking Urdu because Urdu is the most prestigious language, or writing Punjabi when they in fact write Urdu (Schools Language Survey Manual of Use 1985: 121–5). They may in fact have no understanding of the spoken version of their 'language of literacy'. Nor do we have to look to exotic locations to encounter this problem. The Italian children studied by Tosi in Bedford spoke among themselves different regional dialects instead of standard Italian. In that particular research project account was taken of this in the teaching provided, but, as we saw above, in France the agreements between the French government and a range of sender-countries have resulted in children being mainly taught the official languages of their countries of origin; Catalan-speakers are taught Castilian, Berber-speakers are taught Arabic, etc.—though, as Varro (forthcoming) points out, there is some recognition now in schools of colloquial Moroccan, Algerian, and Tunisian varieties of Arabic, and a growing recognition in official circles (Intercultural Education 1992; Saladin 1993).

In some cases, as we saw above, the teaching of the standard language of the country of origin is in accordance with the parents' own wishes, and the language actually spoken is equally absent from the educational establishment in the country of origin. Thus children of Greek-Cypriot origin in Britain are taught in standard Greek, though they may otherwise never hear standard Greek in their daily lives either in Britain or on holiday in Cyprus. The Greek-Cypriot dialect is written only in the context of journalism or popular literature, neither of which is normally used for teaching children who attend Greek schools. Educational confusion, teacher corrections, and, at least to some extent, resulting demotivation for the pupils are the outcome.

The other side of the coin is that it is far easier to maintain and encourage forms of literacy which are associated with a standard language (Valdman 1988). Teaching materials and literary support are available, attitudes on behalf of both the host country and the migrants themselves are likely to be more positive, and there is less discrepancy between the aims of the governments involved and the users.

Lastly, we come back to the point which has come up several times regarding the mismatch between the needs and interests of a transplanted community and the teaching methods and materials provided by sender-countries. The success of the Mother Tongue Project teaching materials described above illustrates the importance of children being able to relate to the materials provided. Other problems can arise, either with the host community or with the migrants themselves, if the teachers sent by countries of origin on a temporary basis see it as their mission to support the home country's religious/moral/cultural values and institutions.

An article in the French daily *Le Monde* of 23 November 1989, during the *affaire du foulard* mentioned above (see n. 7), pointed out that in France, where the non-denominational character of public education is a jealously guarded (if still disputed) principle, Muslim teachers were 'suspected' of trying to put across religious propaganda (Varro 1992). In fact their teaching syllabuses, as put forth in the bilateral agreements signed with France, were quite explicit concerning their religious and patriotic aims. Turkish and Moroccan programmes, for example, include a religious instruction component which is intended to put across the principles of Islam. The article insinuated that French officials had just not read the agreements carefully—perhaps for lack of translations!

Nor is it a secret that the Greek classes organized by the Orthodox Church in London, as opposed, for example, to those organized by the Parents' Association, are intended to support Orthodox Christian values and religious practice. There may be contradictions which arise from the fact that a large number of pupils attend these classes and are then tested through the national GCSE examinations, set by a body essentially outside the community, whose aim is parity across a range of languages regarding skills and levels of language. The Cypriot community in Great Britain provides a good example of the conflicts involved in maintaining mother-tongue literacy in the second generation, as will be discussed below.

5.3. *The Second Generation*

It is important to recognize the needs of second and subsequent generations of the new minorities as fundamentally different from those of first-generation settlers, though this difference is by no means universally taken into account in devising teaching programmes (see the problem with materials discussed above).

Like the first generation, members of the second generation are confronted with at least a double literacy standard: literacy in the language of origin and in the host-country language. Very often there is a third element, the vernacular which they actually speak. It should be abundantly clear that one does not achieve 'vernacular literacy' by teaching minorities the official language of their country of origin. As with the South-East Asians, for example, there may be several other languages which have traditionally played an important role in their lives. Living in a new, totally different environment does not necessarily mean that these languages are cast off. Instead, owing to the absence of the corresponding reference groups or contexts where each of the languages might be spoken separately, the most likely development is that more individualistic forms of *mixture* develop within families or communities. Where members of the first generation come from a multilingual society where a fairly diffuse use of various languages is the norm, as in creole-speaking areas of the world, the most natural development is for the host-country language to be added as a further element to the melting pot. We now have ample documentation of the prevalence of code-switching among newer as well as older minorities all over Europe and in other parts of the world, and it is one of the most interesting challenges which face linguists today to investigate the workings of these mixed varieties (Poplack 1980; Auer and Di Luzio 1982; Chana and Romaine 1984; Agnihotri 1987; Denison 1987; Dorian 1988; Gardner-Chloros 1991; Deprez 1994; Sebba 1994; etc). In particular their implications for writing practices and literacy remain to be explored (Fishman *et al.* 1982).

In the case of the second generation one faces the further challenge of deciding how to translate their complex and developing linguistic background into meaningful teaching policies. Perhaps even more than for the first generation, being fully literate in the host-country language is a *sine qua non* of success in the broader society. The desire to preserve the culture of origin is not usually so pressing as it was for the first generation, though it can still elicit great loyalty, in particular during adolescence, when people generally go through a period of identity searching. That this loyalty exists is illustrated by the high take-up of subjects like modern Greek GCSE in Great Britain.

But as developments in several of the countries which we have discussed show, we are dealing here not merely with maintenance and survival but also with the emergence of new vernaculars, deriving from the old ones but encompassing new elements as well. Such vernaculars develop, initially at least, at an oral level. This can mean that the variety which the second generation has created for itself to express its identity not only has no written form, but also defines itself by contrasting with the host-country language and the written forms used by the parents' generation. The two examples we will give here concern British-born Greek Cypriots on the one hand and French-born Portuguese on the other.

'BBC (British-born Cypriot) Gringlish' is a name given to the code-switched variety of Cypriot dialect and English spoken by young second-generation Greek Cypriots in England. Superficially, it may appear to resemble the mixture used by their parents' generation, who have also adopted and integrated numerous English words into the dialect. But on closer inspection it appears that it is differently constituted. First, it contains a mixture of dialect features and the standard modern Greek, which is taught in community schools and which the younger generation often have difficulty distinguishing from the dialect. The mixing of English and Greek takes place at sentence level rather than at lexical level. It includes not only loanwords from English but also highly productive *ad hoc* creations such as operator verb (have/make) + noun combinations which replace other Greek verbs (Gardner-Chloros 1992). This latter technique has also been found in many other code-switched varieties (e.g. Punjabi and English, see Romaine 1987), particularly in circumstances of dense switching where the concept of focused, clearly discrete languages is unlikely to be affecting language behaviour. It seems unlikely, however, that this new vernacular will ever be translated in any serious way into a written form, even though elements of it may be 'caught in transit' every now and then in the form of theatre, poetry, and so on.

In France similar developments have been documented—for example, among Arab second- and further-generation migrants who are literate in French, but whose identity maintenance goes through the channel of oral transmission. The latter trend has been reinforced by the birth of free radio stations (1981) such as Radio Beur.[8] This station mixes French with North African expressions conveying the specific identity of second-generation children born in France of North African families. (The resulting variety is sometimes called *maghrébin*.) The fact that these new inventions are not purely the product of necessity is borne out by the emergence of a similar intra-community variety among the Portuguese, who, as mentioned above, have in France a relatively high level of literacy in the standard version of their mother tongue. The latter, as Muñoz (1991) reports, is seen as a way of mastering the history and culture of Portuguese, but not as a means of expression of their own identity. For this purpose they use *immigrais* (immigrese), by their own description a bastard Portuguese, including French words and colloquialisms, intolerable to purists but understood by the nearly 800,000-strong Portuguese immigrant population. In 1986 a group of Portuguese in France set up *Albatroz*, a literary review somewhere between surrealism and neo-realism and trilingual in Portuguese, French, and 'Immigrese'. In this they wrote:

Through no fault of our own, we're foreigners. But we have a tool: the Portuguese language contaminated by *positive pollution*. We write in both languages, copulating frenetically, with the outcome that literary and pictorial objects are pleasantly produced. It'll be fine. We respect none of the spelling or vocabulary rules of the immigrese language and

---

[8] The word *beur* comes from *rab*, '(a)rabe' pronounced in accordance with the dictates of 'Verlan', a young people's slang in which words are pronounced backwards.

although we may perturb, we demand that mistakes be acknowledged as a technique for exploring the ambiguity of a text or as a gimmick of polysemic amplification. Don't you agree? And while we're at it, let's do away with the cedilla! Irreverence, dear reader, irreverence . . . (quoted by Muñoz 1991: 71)

As Muñoz puts it (1991: 70–1), the irreverence subverts the instituted language, and bears witness to a capacity for creative acts. But, as the last part of the quotation shows, it may also constitute a rejection of conventions and stability, which are—perhaps somewhat unimaginatively—traditionally considered the *sine qua non* of a literate culture.

6. PROSPECTS AND CONCLUSIONS

Given the enormous political, practical, and economic difficulties attendant on introducing widespread vernacular literacy programmes for the newer minorities in Europe, linguists and educationalists need to concentrate their recommendations on a small number of principles well supported by the research in this area. There are two principal types of argument: an argument to do with fundamental rights, which politicians ignore at their peril at a time of unemployment, social disaffection, and protectionism; and an argument concerning the type of *linguistic* policies which will fulfil the minorities' legitimate claim to identity maintenance while giving them full access to the host community. On the latter question the results of some of the research on bilingualism should be consulted.

The Right to Literacy?

To what extent do new minorities have a right to instruction in their mother tongue or to vernacular literacy? However strong the moral argument put forward by the communities themselves or by idealistic linguists that they have such a right, we need to know whether it is enforceable through any existing framework.

Lawyers are in agreement that the only way to guarantee fundamental rights effectively is to restrict declarations as to what these rights consist in to the most basic and incontrovertible ones. It is, therefore, pointless to think that any number of grand declarations of policy on the teaching of vernaculars would be effective if they are not tied to a—preferably existing—legal instrument with an effective machinery for enforcement. We cannot necessarily look to the EU for such an instrument. As we saw in relation to the 1977 EEC directive above, the EU is reluctant to impose social policy obligations on the member states which might give rise to controversy and so jeopardize the EU enterprise at a political level. Unfortunately we cannot look either to the Council of Europe in Strasbourg, which, in spite of its enlightened work in this area, operates through intergovernmental cooperation and cannot impose obligations directly on its members.

There are, however, two areas where legal thinking is developing in a way which is likely to have direct results for the position of migrants. One of these concerns their civil rights and the other, which is relevant here, potentially concerns their right to be instructed in their mother tongue.

As far as civil rights are concerned, EU law is moving towards the granting of voting rights to migrants established for more than a certain number of years in their country of settlement.

Secondly, lawyers concerned with drafting provisions for minority populations, who are faced with the question as to how to define minorities in a practical way, are increasingly coming to the conclusion that special provisions can only be enacted on the basis of *linguistic* differences, as opposed to cultural, racial, or religious ones. The European Convention on Human Rights guarantees rights for all those *residing* in the territory of the signatory countries without distinction as to language, and this in turn means, for example, that court interpretation can be requested whenever it is necessary. It has been argued elsewhere that this provision has so far been under-exploited in practice by minority-language groups (Gardner-Chloros and Gardner 1986). For example, one of the rights guaranteed by the Convention is the right to education for one's children in accordance with one's philosophical beliefs, and, if this right were to be invoked without distinction as to language, the consequences would be extensive for the sort of provision that could be demanded of the twenty-one signatory states. In most of these countries, the Convention has been enacted as part of domestic law and its provisions can therefore be implemented much more rapidly through the domestic courts than where recourse to Strasbourg is necessary. So here we have one example of how new minorities could vindicate their linguistic rights in a practical way.

The Teaching of Vernaculars

As we have seen, in most of the European countries which have sizeable new minority populations, the principle of teaching them their mother tongues at all is still at too early and experimental a stage for any consistent overall policies to emerge on the teaching of vernaculars. The EEC directive was extremely restrictively drafted, and the projects to which it gave rise, albeit in many cases very valid, have not in the main been followed up, for lack of funding and political will. Where sufficient awareness exists for actual vernacular teaching in any shape or form to be practised, this is often due to particular local circumstances, such as those described in relation to Norway.

In general, the provision of any form of mother-tongue teaching is variable and patchy. It lacks a coordinated central policy at any level, relying instead on the countries of origin themselves (not necessarily the best judges of the needs of their transplanted nationals and above all of the bi-cultural second generation), local initiatives, and community associations, which often work in ignorance of each others' efforts.

There are two fundamental issues here on which research and experience with bi/multilingual communities can throw some light.

First, should literacy training for new minorities take place in the vernacular, or, more realistically, in a closely related written standard, *or* should it take place first in the standard of the host country, or in both, and if so in what order, for adults and for children?

At least as far as children are concerned it is useful here to refer back to Cummins's research on the need to acquire sophisticated linguistic and cognitive skills through one language first before being taught another. One need not necessarily agree with this theory, as we have shown above, since in any case it leaves some fundamental questions unanswered, in particular about the crucial role of the social environment, and about what happens when the two languages are, of necessity, introduced simultaneously in the child's environment.

What is clear, however, is that it is pointless to teach people to master sophisticated literacy skills in a language of which they possess only the barest tools. In the case of children, the problem may indeed be compounded if the introduction of the L2 and of L2 literacy is *at the expense of* the normal full development of their vernacular. This is most likely to occur where it is put across to them, however implicitly, that the vernacular is an inferior instrument, not worthy of developing in the same way as the L2. Successful simultaneous development has been shown to be possible,[9] and success can also be attained through a variety of methods which involve a staged introduction to the different skills in the different languages (see the Luxembourg model mentioned above, where school instruction is first in the vernacular, then in the most closely related standard, and thirdly in an alternative standard).

There is no single magic formula, but there are fundamental, common-sense principles to be followed. The most successful examples so far often involve expressly bilingual educational methods (e.g. the MOTET project). Their advantage, we suggest, is that they involve an implicit *valuing* of both the languages being taught. There are other ways of achieving this, such as when parents and community teachers are successfully involved in mainstream school activities. The ideal is probably for vernacular or mother-tongue teaching to take place within the school curriculum—without the pupils involved being put at a disadvantage by missing out on other desirable aspects of school life.

As many new minorities have realized, literacy in the national standard is a necessity if migrants are to play a full role in national life. Migrant groups have been known to reject vernacularization for this reason. But no one has yet shown that bi-literacy, any more than bilingualism, is a practical impossibility.

Secondly, which mother tongue should one teach: the national language of

[9] See e.g. the successful on-going bilingual education programmes in Turkish and German in state schools in Berlin and Frankfurt, or in Arabic and French in the rue de Tanger school in Paris (see Sect. 4.2), where all pupils in certain classes, whatever their nationality, are taught in both the majority and the minority languages.

the country of origin, the nearest standardized variety to the vernacular actually spoken, or, in appropriate cases, an unstandardized variety? One factor in this decision is that it is clearly not feasible for most national school systems to teach *all* the vernaculars involved. And what of the case where cultural transmission in the vernacular has traditionally been oral, and where there is no recent written tradition to draw on, as in the case of the Greek-Cypriot dialect?

Again, the answer is a complex one: unstandardized varieties can and have been taught, as is shown by the example of Norway (Bull 1985) and by creole-speaking areas such as Papua New Guinea (Romaine 1992). In some cases, as with Punjabi in Southall, that is what the community wants, and there are successful examples of the community language being taught in preference to a standard (e.g. Algerian/Moroccan/Tunisian Arabic in France). In other cases, like that of the Cypriots in Britain, the community may see their identity as being tied up with the same standard which is taught in their country of origin, and want bi-literacy in Greek and in English rather than the vernacular. However, it is both realistic and desirable to back the official recognition of dialect forms of official languages, such as that noted recently in France or in the context of the MOTET project in the United Kingdom.

The new vernacular creations of the younger generations should be free to develop. They may be fundamentally oral, as 'BBC Gringlish' appears to be at present, or may move into the literary mode, as was the case with the 'positively polluted' Portuguese journal from which we gave an example above. There is no inherent contradiction between the desire to maintain a standard, exogenous language for reasons of identity and literary tradition, and the development of a new vernacular which remains oral. In time, with the changing functions of literacy in general, the functions of standard-language literacy may become more specialized as well. The popularly held view, at least in the West, that the written language and the spoken language should be perfect reflections of one another may then gradually be dissipated.

In the interests of the new minorities, one should work for the acceptance of all these dualities: written/spoken, standard/vernacular, host country/country of origin, and for the acceptance of dual ethnic identities in Europe, which are already common in the USA: if one can be Italian–American, then why not Punjabi–British or Berber–French? Though there may seem to be little prospect at present of further immigration from the traditional sources, the situation may change and there is new immigration from other sources as well, such as the ex-Eastern European countries. In Germany, there is already work being done on linguistic differences between ex-East Germans and those from the West (Auer 1994) and the cultural misunderstandings to which these can give rise.

Overall, the question of vernacular literacy for migrants is highly symptomatic of the inadequacy of ideologies based purely on monolingualism and on standards. These ignore the fact that language is a living thing, consisting in many varieties, and that even 'majority' speakers experience and contribute to language variation. Such ideologies are inadequate to deal with the actual linguistic situations which arise all over the world, and not least with the complex situation of the new minorities in Europe, whose own linguistic patchwork is superimposed on the often equally complex tapestry to be found in their country of residence. The responsibility of linguists is not only to describe these issues but also to bring them to the attention of the interested parties and the relevant authorities, so that they can be reflected in appropriate policy decisions.

6
Literacy in a Pidgin Vernacular

JEAN-MICHEL CHARPENTIER

with contributions from P. Mülhäusler, S. Romaine, and L. Todd

1. INTRODUCTION

The 1953 Unesco monograph reflects the ambivalence of the time towards pidgin languages. On the one hand, pidgins do not appear at all in Appendix 1, a 'Tentative Classification of the Languages Spoken in the World Today' (Unesco 1953: 139–43); on the other, pidgin appears among the terms defined at the beginning of the report of the meeting of specialists (held in 1951): 'a language which has arisen as the result of contact between peoples of different languages, usually formed from a mixing of the languages' (ibid. 46), and one of the seven case histories deals with 'The Problem of "Pidgin" in the Trust Territory of New Guinea' (ibid. 103–15). The tentative classification is organized by divisions into main stocks and families, a model based on the genetic metaphor with common ancestors for the different families; such a view excludes in principle the presence of 'hybrid' languages. But the specialists were well aware of a vernacular literacy problem specific to pidgin situations, which they discuss in the following terms:

In some countries pidgin languages, such as Creole and Pidgin-English, are spoken. These languages are sometimes only used by a section of the population in commercial or work contacts with people with whom they have no other means of communication. But in other regions a pidgin tongue is freely used over a wide area as a lingua franca between peoples in habitual social contact, and the children become familiar with it from an early age. When this is the case, it can be used as a medium in the schools. There are however two objections to this: (a) when the pidgin contains elements based upon a European language, it is feared that the use of the pidgin in schools will make it harder for pupils to learn the European language correctly; (b) the people are often oppposed to it because of its association with economic and social subordination. (ibid. 54)

In the case study of New Guinea Pidgin, the ambivalence remains: the author (C. A. Wedgwood) stresses the Pidgin is a genuine language, a hybrid language, written as well as spoken, being used as an effective medium for thought and communication, and not just a broken form of English, used only as a trade language, 'not a degenerate or bastard form of English' (ibid. 109). But should it be given official recognition, and be used or taught in the schools and in adult education? Wedgwood examines a series of arguments for and against it. In the end, however, it seems to him that 'English (i.e. Standard English) should be taught in the schools as a "world language", and the sooner in a child's life that he can begin to learn it without overstrain or harm to his general intellectual development, the better. For English, it may be expected, will play much the same role in the Pacific that Latin played in Medieval Europe' (ibid. 115).

What is the situation today, in particular for vernacular literacy? We no longer simply class Creoles and Pidgins together but try to distinguish them. Creoles, the mother tongues of their native speakers, are associated with eponymous cultures and thus form part of the cultural identity of those speakers; they may legitimately be thought of as related to a culture in the same way as other 'minority' languages which suffer from a lack of official recognition and concomitant prestige. Although 'pidgin' is often today used in respect of a language which has in fact been creolized, for some speakers, as in the West Indies, traditionally the term has referred to those contact languages which are not yet anybody's 'mother tongue', not yet 'creoles', and thus cannot be said to have moulded minds or to have provided inspiration for literature or writing.

Pidgins usually differ from other languages by the extreme complexity of the sociolinguistic situation of which they form a part, of which we will be giving examples. A pidgin may be a simple 'trade jargon' of unstable structure and minimal lexicon, hardly capable of being written. It may, on the other hand, be used in nearly all walks of life, including the administration and officialdom. In pidgin-speaking areas it may be the mother tongue of a greater or smaller number of isolated individuals and a component of their cultural identity.

In this last case, the status *vis-à-vis* potential literacy poses particular difficulties, since the population is divided in its sociocultural membership. For some who have creolized the pidgin having learnt it as their mother tongue, the official language—usually English—will have become a model, with its orthography and literature; for the others, the local indigenous languages and the philosophy and world-view associated with them will have formed their way of thinking. In such societies the first group idealize the European orthography they have been taught and think that literacy in any other language is superfluous; the second group feel that, since the oral transmission of local culture has preserved it over the centuries, one can do without writing, felt to be foreign and another kind of interference in their local affairs.

Such cultural duality and polarization are characteristic of societies where pidgins are used (e.g. West Africa, the South Sea Islands), and make for specific problems when considering literacy in the vernacular pidgins, additional to those which arise when dealing with other vernaculars.

2. CHARACTERISTICS OF PIDGINS

The description of any pidgin cannot be given in purely linguistic terms or independently of the sociocultural context. In her article 'Ce que parler pidgin veut dire' ('What it Means to Speak Pidgin'), Carole de Féral illustrates one of the main characteristics of a pidgin, already stressed by Loreto Todd (1974*b*: 1): 'a marginal language which arises to fulfil certain restricted communication needs among people who have no common language.' 'Marginal' and 'restricted communication' emphasize best the particular nature of pidgins and the necessity to examine their implications for literacy.

2.1. *Sociolinguistic Differences between Pidgins and Creoles*

While pidgins necessarily exist in a multilingual context, creoles usually cohabit with an official language of European origin. In the latter case, both the Creole and the official language(s) may be pointed to as vehicles for literacy. Creole vernacular literacy then has to face rather different motivational and pedagogical problems.

Pidgins are used for interracial or at least inter-ethnic communication, they are not the expression of any ethnic culture (though perhaps they may underlie a fledgeling national culture). Creoles, on the contrary, are the vehicles of local cultures to which they have been indissolubly linked for a long time. Some of them have transmitted African oral traditions to the New World. However, the distinction between pidgins and creoles based on the relationship of the latter to particular cultures seems rather tenuous for West Africa.

Like creoles, which often are characterized by the presence of a continuum, pidgins also run a gamut from the basilectal rural pidgin of Melanesia (more or less equivalent to the *gros créole* of the French Antilles) through a mesolect to an acrolect. Where a pidgin and a creole have remained in contact with the language from which they derived most of their lexicon, if that is an official language, the pidgin and creole acrolects and the official language merge in a post-pidgin/creole continuum:

basilect—mesolect—acrolect/official language—post-creole continuum

It is at mesolectal level that pidgin and creole differ most. The greater instability of the pidgin arises from the fact that it is subjected to interference both from the official language and from the substrate languages in which speakers experience their cultures and their view of the world.

Creole languages are relatively stable, serving all the normal needs of everyday life; one cannot generalize in this way about pidgins, which do not form a homogeneous category. Their characteristics vary according to their role in their multilingual sociocultural context. Todd (1974: 5), who had lived a good deal in pidgin-speaking milieux, proposed a distinction between a 'restricted' and an

'extended' pidgin. Extended pidgins are good for all the domains of social existence: in administration, in political parties, in the technical field, and so on. Very
often, in the absence of another vehicle at the national level, they fill *de facto* the
role of an identity-linked national language and thus closely approach the creoles.

As we have suggested above, the difference *in situ* between pidgins and creoles
is somewhat arbitrary in many pidgin-speaking areas. Romaine (1992, 1993) examines in detail the emergent situation in the urban areas of Papua New Guinea,
whose hallmark is

> the presence of a significant concentration of non-indigenous people (and hence different
> language groups needing a common lingua franca) . . . In towns, Tok Pisin has become
> the ethnic vernacular for Melanesian in-group communication, particularly for the young-
> est generation, who often have no other language . . . Sankoff (1980: 26–7) wrote that
> although the distinction between the two languages was very clear, there were signs of
> an emergent post-creole continuum in urban areas. In town standard English, English
> spoken as a second language with varying degrees of fluency, highly anglicized Tok
> Pisin, more rural Tok Pisin of migrants and the creolized Tok Pisin of the urban born
> co-exist and loosely reflect the emerging social stratification. (Romaine 1993: 27–32)

This sociolinguistic situation resembles that of Port-Vila (Vanuatu) today.
Sometimes the confusion between pidgin and creole, as in the case of Guinea-
Bissau, is such that an auxiliary language used by most of the people as a second
language is called Creole, because it has originated in a neighbouring territory
(the Cape Verde Islands), where it is the first language of the whole population.
But in Cameroon and in Nigeria, even in the urban centres, the distinction between pidgin and creole is just as difficult to establish as the one that claims that
'language' and 'dialect' are two separate entities. In both cases, the difference
is sociolinguistic.

It is precisely at this level that the problem of going from the oral to the
written form arises. Literacy and literature are connected to sociolinguistic context at least as much as to linguistic form; to study the specific sociolinguistic
dimensions of pidgins within the context of literacy does not preclude those of
creole-speaking worlds.

2.2. *Two Large Pidgin-Speaking Regions: West Africa; Melanesia*

There are throughout the world many pidgins with distinct lexical bases: in
Africa, Sango in the Central African Republic (CAR), Pidgin Diola in the Ivory
Coast; in the Sudan, Pidgin Arabic, and so on. Here we will deal only with the
English-based pidgins of Melanesia and of the Gulf of Benin. Pragmatic reasons
for this choice are:

(*a*) Many studies in both English and French already exist of the sociolinguistic
context in each locale (see Bibliography).

(*b*) Despite the geographical distance that separates them, they are in many ways amazingly comparable. The same two official languages, English and French, are in use side by side in Cameroon and in Vanuatu, together with an English-based pidgin used by many indigenous linguistic communities. In New Guinea, as in Nigeria, the official language—English—is challenged, orally at least, by local pidgins, which tend increasingly to be written. In Nigeria, a pidgin-influenced form of English has been in use since the end of the eighteenth century (see Antera Duke's diary). Todd (1974) shows that the local Nigerian English has been more affected by the pidgin than in Cameroon, where English and Pidgin remain more distinct. The convergence in Nigeria seems to have been important when a written form emerged; an important literature in 'pidginized' English now exists in Nigeria, as we shall see in Section 5.4 below.

(c) Most interesting here is the fact that the pidgins both of Melanesia and of the Gulf of Benin have reached the 'extended-pidgin' stage, when the impetus towards a written form is strongest.

The problems specific to pidgins when going from the oral to the written forms will be the main focus of this chapter, but the problems encountered by the languages of the substratum cannot be ignored, since literacy concerns all of these vernacular languages.

3. THE WRITTEN AND THE ORAL WORLDS, ANTITHETICAL ENTITIES

Born of colonial expansion, present-day pidgins could hardly escape the influence of the philosophy and beliefs of Westerners confident in the superiority of their own civilizations. Far from approaching intrinsically the new sociolinguistic situations created by their arrival, the colonizers sought to solve the problems that cropped up in the colonies by applying remedies that had been successful in their own past.

The written word, and the discovery of the printing press, are, in the Western imagination, indispensable stages in technical progress and the spread of knowledge. All the problems raised by writing in Europe—norms, standardization, and so on—were transferred to worlds which for millennia had lived and prospered with speech and some graphics as the sole means of transmitting knowledge. Far from being merely a technique or a neutral graphic representation, writing has become an object of contention between two world-views apparently very hard to reconcile. Because of their mixed origin, contact languages were (and are) the target of a double set of prejudices. These prejudices have developed a good deal in the course of time, being especially affected by the degree of 'assimilation' or Westernization of the population.

For a long time, native speakers in Melanesia confused the pidgins with English. In many languages of Vanuatu, the term *Bislama* is translated as 'the white man's language'. The problem of writing these contact languages therefore did not arise at first. In West Africa, the confusion between Standard English and Pidgin is also common among unschooled people. Todd tells of an old man she recorded in Nkar in the north-west of Cameroon, who had learned Pidgin as a child before the Second World War. He called it 'Ingrese' /ingrese/. How can one convince populations of the need to write a language—the pidgin—when they were certain (perhaps still are) that it is already being written?

The Whites had their language (English/Pidgin); writing (seen as a drawing: the verb meaning 'to draw' in the local languages is often used to translate the new action of writing); and books. That was their world. The Melanesians had their own languages, they had their traditions (oral), making up a different world. Mixing the two worlds was tantamount to disturbing the natural order.

As Romaine puts it (1993: 15), literacy has from the start been at the heart of a profound misunderstanding: 'The promotion of literacy thus took place in a cargo-cult atmosphere, with indigenous people expecting access to wealth and status and Europeans hoping for an ample supply of converts or cheap labor.'

The intrusion of writing into their indigenous world only appeared with the desire of some missionaries to translate the Holy Scriptures into the local languages. But these local, ethnic languages were inseparably linked to oral tradition and to the customs it preserved and perpetuated. To write the language meant that all the uninitiated, be they White or Melanesian, as long as they knew how to read and write, would have access to the esoteric world of the ancestors.

Such a step could only be perceived as an attack on the sacred. The first texts written in the vernacular, far from being popularly acclaimed, were considered to be an intrusion of the White Man's world into local affairs. Writing in the vernacular was nevertheless best tolerated when, as was almost always the case during the first contacts between Europeans and Natives, it served to express the White Man's thoughts (e.g. translating the Holy Scriptures). Resistance to writing in the vernaculars has been manifest to this day in the face of scholars wanting to transcribe the oral tradition, compiling the traditions and beliefs of the Ancients. Such an approach was long felt to be a reprehensible interference, forced acculturation.

In 1976, in what was formerly the New Hebrides (today Vanuatu), when I was director of the Cultural Centre of the country, I began to record and transcribe the oral tradition in the local languages, which largely guaranteed its confidentiality. Certain informers baulked at helping with the transcription of their narratives, both from fatigue and from a desire to protect the ancestral heritage. Only the people of the community could have access to the narratives in the language of the ancestors. I was often forbidden to have them listened to by women or by the uninitiated. My successor (not a linguist) decided to have the recordings done in Pidgin. The main advantage, of course, was that he was able to understand them. Besides, the recordings could be put on the radio or listened to by outsiders.

Many of these recordings connected with initiation rites or with mortuary rituals were marked 'taboo' by the storyteller. Thousands of hours have thus been recorded and conserved, prohibited to all except the direct descendants of the author; theoretically, even his close relatives must have attained a social ranking equal to his in order to have the right to listen. Unless he gives his explicit permission, nobody will ever be authorized to write these texts; they must remain oral for ever.

For many of the elders, writing in the vernacular was simply useless, since for thousands of years tradition had been transmitted without any sort of written form. It is only, after many generations, since Christianization finally succeeded in abolishing the holy and secret nature of oral tradition, that transcribing what is left of it has been accepted, sometimes welcomed.

The collection of texts written in the Paama language (Vanuatu) by Crowley (1990) was well received and quite widely read, but it is the work of a European. No initiative of this sort has ever come from a Melanesian intellectual. Moreover, it was done in a context of thorough disacculturation. Literacy, a European concept, seems only to succeed in Melanesia where European thinking has totally submerged and erased the local cultures. This is again an example of the passage of one world to another; belonging to both is seemingly impossible.

Pidgins do present the advantage of not being directly connected to any particular local culture; they can be considered culturally neutral. In fact, because of their supra-local and inter-ethnic nature, they can be used without endangering the secret governing local cultures.

To try to perpetuate the oral tradition through the use of pidgins means making it available to all, and writing it down means giving it away beyond all control. (In Vanuatu, the Cultural Centre abounds in recordings of the oral tradition in Pidgin, since no director could possibly know the 106 local languages.) The local storytellers have often opposed making the texts available to the public; if they did so, they would take away one *raison d'être* of the Pidgin: its esoteric nature, its supra-local function.

3.1. *Nationality and Attitudes towards Pidgins*

Before the 1970s, when the countries of the South Sea Islands were to experience profound sociocultural change, only Europeans had attempted to write the pidgins. To do so, they had had to overcome a great many prejudices.

Pidgins had all the less prestige as they were unwritten and most often seen to be corrupt forms of English. In West Africa, many educated Anglophones called the pidgins 'Broken English', 'Bush English', or 'Rotten English'. In Melanesia, until the 1970s, many missionaries considered them unworthy to carry God's word. In Africa, at least in Cameroon, missionaries took a radically opposed view. Catholic priests from different countries—France, Germany,

Holland, Ireland—hardly felt they were 'deforming' English, since it was not their language. In the face of the great many languages present, Pidgin seemed to them an inestimable instrument for evangelizing the populations (as early as 1926, Monseigneur Plissoneau published a Pidgin Catechism). In the Pacific, it seems that the approach to and the verdict on Pidgin were directly connected to the missionaries' nationality or at least to their mission. The missionaries and the Protestant missions (except for New Guinea, which had belonged to Germany) were all English-speaking, and to them the Pidgin seemed a bastardized English improper for expressing the divine gospel. As for the Catholic priests and missions, mostly French, they hesitated to use what they considered to be a form of English.

The local vernaculars were an integral part of thousand-year-old local cultures; English and French were the languages of dominant, modern societies; pidgins, linked to no particular society or culture, could only be looked down upon. The lack of prestige made for little incentive in giving them a writing system. These 'handicaps' do not seem to have had the same dissuasive effect in Cameroon, probably because of the presence of Germans, who did not have the same compunction about 'deforming' English, not their own language. Besides, very pragmatically, they had only to continue the usage already established in Bamenda, where, well before the German annexation, different ethnic groups used Pidgin for business.

3.2. *The Extreme Complexity of Sociolinguistic Situations, an Obstacle to Literacy*

Some linguists, specialists of the pidgins and Melanesian vernaculars, are very strongly opposed to the writing of any of these languages. Mühlhäusler (1988: 54) notes that 'the most general long-term effect of vernacular literacy is language decline and death'.

It would seem that by being written these languages enter into a competition against the 'big' languages with literary traditions. The theory is that, when they learn to read and write their own language, the native speakers cannot help it competing with English, French, and so on. The existing diglossia (High/written–Low/oral) would then be displaced by a new configuration (High/written–Low/written), and the danger of seeing the Low language replaced by the High is all the greater as the intimate, familial, and convivial nature of the spoken language would then disappear. (Mühlhäusler's opinion does not seem to be shared by Todd, at least as far as West Africa is concerned.)

Though less outright in her condemnation, Romaine (1993: 3) denounces the ambiguity of the aims of those who promote policies of vernacular standardization: 'Thus, contrary to what is often claimed by supporters of literacy programmes, literacy (and by implication, language standardization) has seldom emerged as a response to needs inherent in traditionally oral societies, but has been used by outsiders to achieve certain objectives.'

Mühlhäusler (1992: 7) lists the objectives which, according to him, governed the introduction of vernacular literacy in the Pacific:

(a) cheaper missionisation in highly multilingual areas;
(b) facilitating effective government control through village chiefs;
(c) the means for transition to English. It should be noted, for instance, that Mihalic's Tok Pisin dictionary explicitly expressed the wish that this language would be replaced by proper English one day;
(d) as a means of unifying a New Nation state.

In the pidgin-speaking regions of Melanesia and West Africa it seems that only (a) and (b) have been implemented, and then only partially.

There is one respect in which Melanesian multilingualism cannot be compared with that of the Gulf of Benin, even though in each case European contact with it led to the emergence of Pidgin English as a vernacular language: Nigeria has almost as many, or even as many, indigenous languages as Melanesia, but it also has important African vehicular languages such as Igbo, Yoruba, and Hausa, which challenge the role of Pidgin English in some respects; Melanesia has no equivalent. Thus, in Melanesia, no local language dominates. Linguistic pluralism and the smallness of the groups involved guaranteed an equilibrium that Mühlhäusler (1992: 8) described in the following terms: 'Diversity provided a means by which small groups could signal and maintain their separate identities and, because of the absence of single, powerful groups or languages equality was found both between different groups and inside groups. Laycock (1987) and others have emphasized the role of diversity in maintaining democratic lifestyles in Melanesia.'

Familiar with the Melanesian world, and especially with Papua New Guinea, Romaine and Mühlhäusler perhaps do not sufficiently stress the fact that literacy, a danger in the Melanesian context, is not necessarily so elsewhere. True, writing one language, choosing it among others, makes it exceptional and jeopardizes the equality that prevailed among the various languages.

Of course, even when written, the chosen Melanesian language remains of modest dimensions: a few thousand speakers at most. Not so for the pidgins: with over 20,000 native speakers, Tok Pisin is by far the leading language of Papua New Guinea. In Vanuatu, Bislama, mother tongue for over 10 per cent of the population, is also without contest the most important language of the country. In both Nigeria and Cameroon the English pidgins are important languages but local inter-ethnic vehicular languages seem to be used by at least as many speakers. Although they are spreading, the pidgins there hardly threaten the linguistic balance.

At the 1988 York IGLSVL workshop I myself expressed many reservations about writing and teaching in Pidgin, and I argued that there existed 'the danger of creolizing' small states such as the Solomons or Vanuatu. This formulation left my friend and colleague, Lawrence Carrington, creolophone from birth, quite speechless! In his Antilles, creole languages and cultures have replaced imported African languages and cultures, but in the South Sea Islands creolization is taking place *in situ*. African languages and cultures in Africa are not threatened by creolization elsewhere, but in the Islands any extension of it outside the towns means a dwindling of Oceanic languages and cultures, and, in the end, their disappearance. Todd (1974) feels that even in Cameroon multilingualism in different African vernaculars may also be at risk, or at least is regressing, especially among educated families.

Thus in Oceania linguistic and cultural diversity is beginning to yield to national monolingualism; the omnipresent pidgins have the slums as their cultural reference; communication in the administrative and technical domains mainly takes place in Standard English (in French in Vanuatu). Already, the generalization of the oral use of pidgins has seriously damaged the remarkable linguistic balance of the past.

Taking advantage of the existing dialect channels, Melanesians used to be plurilingual and there was inter-comprehension between neighbouring communities. This plurilingualism is being rapidly displaced by the shared use of pidgins. Whereas in the plurilingual context the 'small' languages were known and used as second or third languages far more than one could have imagined given the limited numbers of their native speakers, today they have been cut down to strictly local size, which often makes one doubt whether they will survive.

3.3. *The Instability of Pidgins, 'Second Languages', a Check on Standardization*

Literacy in English-based pidgins has to contend not only with much psycholinguistic prejudice and the need to protect sociolinguistic situations, but also with linguistic problems *stricto sensu*, these being directly connected to their status as second languages.

For these languages, it is especially difficult to decide on any kind of coherent orthographic norm that would suit all the European users and the local populations, who each possess their own distinctive linguistic baggage. The first writings, in Africa as well as in Melanesia, were translations of the Bible. But the missionaries were not all of the same nationality. Each was thus tempted to write the pidgins using the form most familiar to him. Tok Pisin was written first German-style, and then English-style; Bislama first *à la française*, then *à l'anglaise*. It is enough to point out how, until Vanuatu independence in 1980—when a standardized orthography was needed to be able to name the pidgin—some Englishmen and Frenchmen wrote the name: some wrote 'Beach-la-Mar' or 'Bishlamar', others 'bichelamar', even though the most usual pronunciation had long been fixed as [bislama]. Each missionary gave it his personal touch. These orthographic

variations naturally are reflected in all the attempts to write the vernaculars, whatever they may be, but, in the case of pidgins, the variations are far more numerous. It is a fact that pidgins, as second languages, are locally pronounced according
to the various linguistic substrata. Only the need for inter-comprehension curbs
the variations somewhat. In Cameroon, the situation is even more complicated
because the Catholics chose a modified form of English script to write Kamtok
and the Bible Society (Protestant) chose a phonetic alphabet unrelated to English
script.

In Africa some indigenous languages cover relatively very large areas and
thus confer a relatively greater unity on the pidgins they affect.

For anyone wanting to write the English pidgins, several scripts are available:
one corresponds to an etymological orthography that takes into account the spelling of English etymons, another is phonemic, tending to make the pronunciation
of a grapheme correspond to a phoneme. Todd (1974: 72) mentions yet a third
script that the German missionaries set up for Pidgin, an independent system far
removed from any already existing orthography. She sums up the main advantages
and drawbacks of each of these choices:

> The etymological orthography is naturally best for the Anglophones but it makes the
> pidgin seem like a corrupt form of English. I may add that this orthography eases the
> transition from a pidgin to a local form of English, possibly not really desirable at least
> for the local élites. There is a great risk that the Anglophones may learn pidgin through
> the written medium. Recognizing the etymons, they will invariably pronounce them as
> they are pronounced in English.
>
> The phonemic orthography does not put anyone at an advantage but obliges each
> and everyone to learn it. Such an effort will probably greatly slow down the spread of
> literacy.
>
> The third system makes the pidgin look like a major and autonomous language, but
> there is a considerable risk of interference for anyone also learning English.   (Todd
> 1974: 72–3)

In fact, since no official policy exists in the countries we are discussing, the
emergence of a norm accepted by practically everybody has been a very empir-
ical process and has almost always been the work of missionaries. In Vanuatu,
the Council of Christian Churches established a norm for the writing of religious
texts and for correspondence between churches. This semi-official norm is by far
the best known in the Archipelago and hardly needs fear the orthography proposed a few years ago by the 'Komiti blong Bislama' made up mainly of Pidgin-
speaking civil servants. In Cameroon, as already mentioned, no such ecumenical
wind has blown which could have brought an agreed orthography to all the
missions.

In Papua New Guinea, missionaries have played the same decisive role as in
Vanuatu: Romaine (1993: 10) notes: 'Different standards were used by different
missions initially but eventually the orthography used in the *Nupela Testamen* has
come to serve as a de facto standard for Tok Pisin since its publication in 1966.'

It must be added that as early as 1943, Robert Hall had proposed a coherent system for writing Melanesian Pidgin.

In Nigeria, in spite of Pidgin being very widespread, Eze remarks (1980: 52): 'However, pidgin usage in the police and the army is still confined to oral conversation for there is not, as yet, a uniform orthography for it.' But the absence of a uniform orthography does not really prevent the police force and the army from writing their letters in pidginized English.

In Cameroon, the same deficiencies exist, as Todd (1974: 78) has noted: 'The lack of a uniform orthography and of standardized norms were considerable handicaps, but the advantages of employing such a medium outweighed the drawbacks.'

Far be it from us to deny the handicaps stemming from the absence of a norm, but perhaps norms are in fact less important than we Westerners, conditioned by our very standardized written languages, might assume. After all, our own standardization is only a product of the eighteenth and nineteenth centuries; however effectively Alcuin of York may have prescribed for Latin, for the vernaculars each scribe and each publishing house had their own conventions in Europe until printing had been established for at least two centuries.

Living as they do in polyglot societies, pidgin speakers are accustomed to linguistic variation; rarely are they biased towards one particular spoken, still less one particular written, norm of pidgin. Possessing usually a rudimentary knowledge of the conventions of written English, they are tolerant of, or indifferent to, variant orthographies for pidgin; unlike the European reader they are not always unconsciously looking for the English etymon or related graphic form.

During the last parliamentary elections in Vanuatu, in December 1991, I was struck by the ease with which the voters of the Islands glanced over and understood the different election posters, some written by Anglophones, others by Francophones. Unfettered by any rule, each author had freely used his imagination to render the modern or technical terms that the voters had never seen written but had heard on the radio. All the scripts were equally accessible: might it not be our European norm that becomes a handicap? By constantly prohibiting any deviation in our languages, we are put off when any disparity appears in languages which should be very familiar.

The extreme variability of the pidgins makes their writing even more uncertain than that of creoles, already difficult enough, as Valdman (1978: 97) notes: 'Creating an orthography poses particular problems in the case of French creole languages. Firstly, they are socially inferiorized vernaculars. As they are not accepted in any kind of employment conferring some degree of prestige (administration, teaching, etc.), their speakers can hardly be enticed to learn to read, much less to write, them.'

Valdman believes that literacy in contact languages is inhibited as much by the lack of any official function for it, an absence of any prestige, and hence adverse social behaviour, as by technical and linguistic difficulties.

Over the last twenty years, it has indeed been shown that the development of literacy and the emergence of a literature in a pidgin have always followed social change implying the extension of its use beyond the framework by which these languages are traditionally encompassed.

4. PIDGINS AND TEACHING

4.1. *Pidgins and Teaching Policies*

Even when they benefit from formal recognition by the state, as national or official languages, as particularly in the constitutions of Papua New Guinea or Vanuatu, the actual situation in the country remains ambiguous regarding the use of pidgins both in writing and in teaching. Among other things, this ambiguity stems from the fact that pidgins were promoted at the time of independence largely for lack of any alternative solution.

These countries were divided ethnically and linguistically. Religious differences compounded the divisions. The pidgin in Melanesia came to be seen as the only value shared at the national level.

In the case of Cameroon (a German colony from 1884 to 1916) and of Vanuatu, the shared colonization by the English and the French left behind English-speaking and French-speaking bureaucrats who were very seldom bilingual (English–French). Pidgin was thus the only means of communication in the higher administrative spheres. Using Pidgin was above all dictated by the fact that there were few indigenous people who could speak English. Contrary to what several linguists have declared, local management in Melanesia did not make a choice in favour of the pidgin; it was the lack of an alternative that dictated their choice.

On the other hand, two social and psychological approaches to the pidgin worked in its favour: despised, even attacked, by the Whites, it came to be seen by Melanesian nationalists as an anti-colonialist weapon. Since most of the neighbouring countries could not speak it, Pidgin became a major factor in the building of a new national identity.

The ambiguous nature of the attitudes to pidgins was revealed by the constitution of Papua New Guinea. In 1975, at the time of independence, the pidgin was not officially recognized but, according to Romaine (1993: 23): 'The constitution of Papua New Guinea calls for all persons to achieve universal literacy in Tok Pisin, Hiri Motu or English and in a tok ples (local vernacular language).'

Although no official norm of Tok Pisin nor any sort of standardization of the local languages exists, the promotion of literacy, envisaged in these languages, is a declared aim of the Constitution. But as soon as independence was obtained, as Romaine (1993: 23) remarks: 'After the Department of Education took charge of the schools, government assistance was given only to English-medium schools on the assumption that modern technology could not be easily expressed in non-western languages.'

In Vanuatu, although the pidgin Bislama was the 'official' and 'vehicular national language', it is also said in the constitution that 'the principal languages of education are English and French'. The adjective 'principal' allows one to imagine that other languages could be taught, in particular the local vernaculars. Those who championed the use of Pidgin at all levels of the state—'isn't Bislama spoken by (almost) everyone and isn't it a major ingredient of national unity?', they asked—dropped their projects for the promotion of the pidgin as soon as they became ministers. Only Mr Regenvanu (married to an Australian and whose children were sent to study in Australia) tried to impose the use of written Pidgin in his Ministry, when he was named Minister of Education. At the end of his term, he decreed that all the texts should be written in English or in French because the absence of a norm made for too many errors. Since independence in 1980, and though many of them boast the merits of the national language, no Minister has ever tried to promote teaching in the pidgin. However, unofficially, Bislama is not absent from the primary schools. The pupils speak it sometimes (when several local vernaculars are present) and the most isolated English-speaking teachers, lacking practice in English, have difficulty avoiding interference from Bislama.

As Todd (1974: 83) very astutely remarks, teaching in Pidgin is above all an affair of political choice in matters of education: 'It can no longer be seriously suggested that pidgins and creoles are incapable of being used as media of instruction . . . the debatable point is not whether they could be used but whether they should be.' The same author perfectly sums up the disadvantages inherent in literacy or partial instruction in Pidgin. The facts she puts forward were considered sufficiently 'dangerous' that no state to this day has dared officially to introduce literacy in the pidgin: 'If educationists decide to use such texts (in pidgin and creole) they face serious problems. If they use the standard English orthography they save money on printing but make the pidgin or creole appear at best dialectal, at worst inferior. And if they use a tailor-made orthography they teach a set of spelling conventions which will inevitably clash with those of standard English.'

We must stress the fact that it is not that the English pidgins are intrinsically inapt for educative purposes but that they coexist with English, from whom most of their vocabulary is derived. Unfortunately for the English pidgins, wherever they are in use English is an official language, leaving little room for their autonomous development.

4.2. *The Problems of Teaching in Pidgin*

The Latent Hostility towards all Teaching in Pidgin

In Vanuatu, hostility towards teaching in Pidgin is manifest in the whole teaching establishment, not least of course among the anglophone élites who master standard English very well. Very likely the memory of the difficulties they had to overcome in order to sort out the two codes (Pidgin/English) is at the root of this behaviour. The less an anglophone teacher masters the English language, the more he confuses the two codes, and the more inclined he is to consider the possibility of teaching in Pidgin. The reticence of francophone teachers regarding Pidgin is not of the same kind, their refusal is more political than pedagogical. They fear that teaching and generalized literacy in the pidgin may lead in the end to official English monolingualism.

Anglophone teachers frequently argue against teaching the pidgin by saying that the less pupils know Pidgin, the faster they acquire English. It must be noted that, for these Anglophones—very nationalistic and convinced advocates of Pidgin as a part of identity, as a principal ingredient of national identity—this code belongs to the realm of English-learning. All of them, in fact, give priority to English (the colonial language) for teaching and thus nobody, at any level of instruction, thinks of replacing the international language by the pidgin, though that would consequently make it become intrinsically autonomous and dynamic.

The Reasons for the Failure of Pidgin as School Subject and Medium of Instruction

The combination of English and Pidgin (or source language X and lexically X-based pidgin) seems to lead to a social, psychological, and pedagogical blockage, seriously compromising any passage to literacy. The children in particular cannot seem to figure out the respective roles and characteristics of the two codes.

From a social point of view, these two codes are often difficult to distinguish (especially in the middle of the continuum) and refer to the same semio-cultural world in which certain domains—agriculture, fishing, drinking kava (the local drink)—would speak in favour of Pidgin without however excluding the other languages. In domains where English tends to dominate, Pidgin is sometimes preferred. Of course, not all the children encounter the same difficulty in sorting out the two codes, since they are not all exposed to English in the same way and do not hear the same variety of Pidgin, depending on where they live. Most of them learn Pidgin late (though it is being learned at a more and more early age). Some are bilingual in a Melanesian vernacular and Pidgin. Living in rural areas, they learn the basilect, an only slightly anglicized Pidgin very influenced by the local substratum, and English will thus seem a quite foreign tongue to them. Others, born in the town to parents speaking different languages, usually learn Pidgin first, then a vernacular, before starting on English—which, however, they have always heard spoken around them. This is the trickiest linguistic heritage of all for those who want to master the two codes, because their subconscious system of reference will be in the pidgin, whose vocabulary is much more sparse than the English one. Some more privileged children (e.g. of high-ranking civil servants) learn English first, and then, as they grow up in the wider society, the pidgin. Here the risk of confusing the two codes seems to be less, except at the level of phonology, but in such a milieu the pidgin may well be despised.

Confusion between two codes, those of English and the pidgin, by children for whom neither is their first language, occurs when they have to learn the two simultaneously. The codes have more than 80 per cent of their lexical roots in common; a speaker of any non-Romance language would have a similar difficulty in trying to learn Spanish and Portuguese simultaneously. But in the English/ Pidgin English situation the children find it difficult to distinguish two discrete phonological systems within one diffuse system to some extent at least because psychologically they cannot admit the pidgin to the same systematic status as the source language. English/Pidgin bilingualism is neither 'compound' nor 'coordinate' and rarely balanced. It is a diffuse sociolinguistic situation in which everyone expresses themselves according to their own linguistic baggage, to what they feel, to what they think appropriate in the circumstance, and so on. It goes without saying that the experience of bilingual schools would be of little help in teaching English and Pidgin to linguistically heterogeneous classes where the children are seldom completely unfamiliar with these languages.

The Technical Problems that Arise in Pidgin-Medium Instruction

From a practical point of view, (eventual) literacy in Pidgin and using Pidgin and English as media of instruction in Vanuatu would, according to the teachers, create nearly insurmountable problems at the semantic and graphic levels. The National Council of Churches of Vanuatu has an orthographic system conceived more for people who already know how to read and write than for people having to be taught; this system, already well implanted and fairly universally known, is the one the children would probably be submitted to. They would thus be confronted with situations such as the following:

Many signifiers meaning the same thing are represented differently by the two codes: English *girl* is gel in Pidgin, English *boy* is Pidgin boe; in English *canoe*, in Pidgin kanu, etc. The young child must learn to memorize two graphic forms, and learning the semantic variations of apparently similar signifiers is even more complicated. In Pidgin,

'stesen' (etymon: *station*) means 'village'
'skul' (etymon: *school*) can be 'church or school'
'faet' (etymon: *fight*) means, apart from the English sense, that the pimento is 'sharp'
'plasta' (etymon: *plaster*) means that the earth is 'sticky', etc.

There are hundreds of examples of such semantic differences, adding to the difficulties a young child would have to overcome in learning to read and write. How can they help being bewildered by the fact that the English word *station* never means 'village' but that the word in Bislama, 'stesen', means just that? The confusion will be all the greater as they will need a lot of time to distinguish the two pronunciations, for it is unlikely that the teachers today would be native English-speakers. Children will have to learn by rote that the English signifier *school* can only mean 'school', never 'church', though in Pidgin 'church' is expressed by *skul*; that in Pidgin *faet* can mean both 'fight' and that the pimento is 'sharp'.

On the morpho-syntactic level, things become even more confusing: 'ol boe' in Pidgin translates as *the boys* in English. In the first case, the plural is expressed by a pre-fixed 'ol'. In the second case, the ending 's' indicates the plural. For one single function, the children will have to remember two totally different systems; imagine their dismay when they hear *all boys* in English and discover it is not the simple plural, as they might expect, but corresponds to 'olgeta boe' in Pidgin. These are extremely subtle difficulties; one need only listen to anglophone élites speaking Pidgin to see that most of them say 'olgeta boes' for 'ol boes', unconsciously mixing the two grammatical systems.

From these few examples we can understand why the strongest partisans for teaching Pidgin are expatriate Anglophones. On one hand, they often have ulterior motives of a political nature; on the other, the fact that they grew up speaking English makes them insensitive to the difficulties of having to learn standard English along with an English pidgin when both are foreign languages. The above examples, drawn from the Bislama Pidgin of Vanuatu, are just as apposite for other pidgin-speaking areas.

Attempts to Teach Pidgin and In Pidgin

Before Independence in Papua New Guinea, teaching was left to the missions: 'Orthographies were often first developed as a means for teaching literacy to religious converts' (Romaine 1993: 7). (Hall, who made orthographic suggestions for what he called Neo-Melanesian in 1955, is an exception.)

In Africa, no teaching in pidgin really developed, outside the narrow sphere of the missions, and they too hardly sought to create a specific orthography for pidgin before 1966. In the 1940s and early 1950s, when Cameroon was under British mandate, the British controlled the system of education. The vernacular-medium schools were deliberately neglected in favour of teaching in English.

Just before Vanuatu's independence in 1980, a teaching-in-Pidgin experiment started at the agricultural school. The pidgin Bislama was the obvious working language there, since the students came from English- and French-speaking primary schools and had to be taught together. The general level of education of these young people was modest and none of them was a French–English bilingual. The success of this programme seems to have been due to two factors of equal importance. First, the pidgin was closely linked to the semiotic domain of agriculture in which it originated. Much of the lexicon, designating flora and fauna, comes from the Melanesian substratum, and over time a vocabulary has evolved for agricultural techniques and products, their qualities, conservation, and so on. Europeans must borrow species terms from Latin; Pidgin has terms familiar to all Pidgin-speakers. The second factor stems from the trainees' generally low level of education: not being able to spell in English or French made it easier for them to accept graphic variation, their familiarity with the environmental context helped them to disambiguate each variant they encountered. Similar advantages ought to apply in the domain of fishing, but unfortunately no fishing school of comparable size has lasted long enough for the efficacy of Pidgin-medium teaching to be assessed.

Bislama Pidgin is studied as a subject in the University of the South Pacific in Port-Vila. Courses in Pidgin are also given to expatriates appointed in various parts of the country.

In Papua New Guinea, although the governments have invariably chosen an all-English teaching system since independence in 1975, Lutherans and Catholics continue to use Pidgin in their schools. On the whole, it must be admitted that both Pidgin-medium teaching and teaching the pidgins themselves face much technical difficulty and prejudice, and also suffer from the absence of a propitious cultural context where the pidgin could develop and transmit a national norm from generation to generation of pupils, a norm capable of surviving side by side with English. But, in spite of their own limitations or those which they are perceived as having, pidgins are far too much in use in everyday speech for Europeans not to have been, from very many years back, tempted to put them into writing, with the local westernized élites following their lead.

5. PIDGINS AND WRITING

Different types of literacy therefore developed as the functions of pidgins became more extended and diversified: in all the countries considered, the first stage was religious literacy; then in some countries a political-administrative literacy appeared, and, much more modestly, an attempt at literature.

5.1. *Christianization and the Use of Written Pidgins*

In the South Sea Islands, as in Africa, missionaries came up against local multilingualism. Where dialectal chains existed, as in Vanuatu, it was possible to some extent to choose certain of the languages and to write them or even teach them. From the beginning of this century, the Holy Scriptures were translated into Mota by the Anglicans and into Aulua and Nguna by the Presbyterians. Speakers of neighbouring languages learned these tongues. That explains why the Gospel only came out in Bislama Pidgin in 1975. Until then, the pidgin had been considered inappropriate and incapable of expressing the divine spirit. In Cameroon, the Baptists translated the Scriptures into Douala and Mungaka, but the Catholics decided to use Pidgin. The first catechisms in Pidgin date from 1926.

In Papua New Guinea, the German missionaries had underestimated the complexity of the sociolinguistic situation and had started evangelizing by writing in the local languages. They had to give that up rather soon and use Pidgin instead, which was therefore already written and taught before the First World War; but most of the texts were translations of the Bible. The European missions modulated their proselytizing according to the sociocultural context of the countries where they were established and adapted their work to the different colonizers.

5.2. *Administration and the Use of Pidgins for Writing*

The colonial bureaucracies had fluctuating policies as to the use of Pidgin for speaking, but they were consistently opposed to any form of written Pidgin. However, confronted with general ignorance concerning the European languages and the imperative need to communicate, actual practice challenged official positions.

In Papua New Guinea, during the Second World War, the allied troops dropped thousands of leaflets written in Pidgin for the local population. In all the countries with which we are concerned, posters giving advice on how to protect oneself against endemic diseases are also written in Pidgin. Because of the small number of people who know how to read English, election campaign posters and literature are also done in Pidgin. Using Pidgin for writing is all the more necessary where the country is officially bilingual, as are Cameroon and Vanuatu. In these two countries, when the administration wants to reach the entire population, Anglophones as well as Francophones, it has no choice but to use the local pidgin.

This was done by the former Residence of France in the New Hebrides, which in 1970 published its bulletin in both French and Bislama. The British Residence quickly followed suit. After independence the various administrations printed a trilingual weekly, semi-official, known today as the *Vanuatu Weekly Hebdomadaire*.

At the time of Vanuatu independence, Pidgin seemed to be a fundamental part of the national heritage and the favourite medium for citizens wishing to express their nationalism. From 1980 to 1984 there were several short-lived weeklies, all written in Pidgin. Their lifespan corresponded exactly to the spurt of nationalist feeling following the secessionist movements which accompanied independence. In the wake of this same nationalist current, there was also poetry, mainly the work of Sela Molisa. She spoke out against colonialism and racism; today, still using the Bislama Pidgin, she condemns corruption and the alienation of women. Few other writers, let alone Vanuatu writers, have been as persistent, most of the other writing being done by Melanesians at the request of European academics at the University of the South Pacific. An article 'Lanwis blong Nyus' published by the university (Ligo 1987), deals with information and the language problem. This sort of social criticism is also expressed in Cameroon Pidgin through songs or in the columns of the *Courrier sportif* and *Katakata for Sofahead*.

In Papua New Guinea, the Pidgin weekly *Wantok* has about 50,000 readers. As in Vanuatu, most of what is written in Pidgin is the work of Europeans, as, for example, the Catholic missionary Mihalic, author of a *Grammar and Dictionary of Neo-Melanesian* (1957), or Crowley (1990), who did the same for Vanuatu's Bislama (see also Camden 1971).

In West Africa spoken Pidgin is used in the administration, but not written, except in the health and disease information campaigns already mentioned. As in the various states of Melanesia, Papua New Guinea, the Solomon Islands, and Vanuatu, the written documents of government are always in English or French. In spite of orthographies being available for many of the vernaculars of both Melanesia and Cameroon, they are very rarely written by educated people, though in Melanesia Pidgin is at least recognized in the various constitutions.

Hall (1972: 150) wrote that 'Once a pidgin or creole has been used for semi-official purposes, informal use of its written form is likely to take root and spread. It is then only a short step to free creative composition.' Melanesia does not at present bear this out. The reason seems to lie in the continuing contact of Pidgin speakers with spoken and written English. Valdman (1978: 10) wrote that 'The crystallisation of a pidgin requires the social distance that separates the alloglots on the road to acculturation from the speakers of the base language.'

In Melanesian terms this would mean that only the élites would continue to be anglicized, while the masses remained confined within their traditional cultures. But in fact English is taught and heard in every region, even the most remote; all day, and everywhere, anglicized Pidgin pours out from the radio, and its influence on young people is undeniable. Having learned to write English in school, Pidgin-speakers prefer the certainties of English for writing to a vernacular they feel to be unstable and inferior. In parts of West Africa, on the other hand, where English has long been more solidly established, the broadcasting media seem to affect the English of educated people rather than affecting their Pidgin, better anchored as that is to an African cultural milieu (some young people show a distinct influence from American slang in their English.) In West Africa, as we shall see below, many texts are written in Pidgin and Creole, but more to express an African identity *vis-à-vis* the Western world than to express inherently ethnic cultural values.

5.3. *Pidgins as Vehicles of Fledgeling National Cultures*

In multiethnic, multilingual sociocultural milieux where an extended pidgin is in use, one cannot talk about Culture with a big 'C'. The beginnings of a supra-local culture associated with the pidgin must be added to the local cultures connected to the vernaculars of the substrata. Before acquiring any sort of national stature, this new culture develops locally, at the regional level.

In the South Sea Islands and in Africa, the new culture was first expressed by song. On the African continent, these songs were connected to work on plantations, house-building, road-breaking, and so on. In Cameroon, the first examples go back to the German presence. In Melanesia, in the midst of 'string bands', the young people sing about their feelings, their joys. As often as not improvised, these songs in Pidgin exalt the existence and the genius of a group that had previously remained unexpressed.

This original, outward-turning type of expression can be done only in Pidgin. Nobody would dream of singing or improvising in the local language (though sometimes bits of songs in the vernaculars find their way into the improvisations). After all, traditional folk songs already exist. The new songs show first of all that pidgins can fill other than denotative needs, and also that they can express personal feelings, as long as they are used in a new semantic field where neither the local languages nor the European languages have taken hold.

To conserve and transmit this innovative cultural expression, created outside the older vernacular oral tradition, two apparently complementary but rapidly competing ways were available to the young people. Writing the songs down was naturally a way of not forgetting them but so was recording them on cassettes which could also preserve melody and rhythm. Many string bands recorded themselves and sent the cassettes to Radio Vanuatu to be put on the air. A letter generally accompanied the cassette, usually in Pidgin (the broadcasters being English- or French-speaking), sometimes in English or French, or a message would be recorded directly on the cassette. Messages sent by cassette also developed widely outside this radio context and a lot of interpersonal and family exchanges took place in this way. Thus literacy became obsolete even before it ever really existed. The advantages of letters recorded on cassettes were several:

- they avoided the problems of writing;
- they could be 'read' even by illiterates;
- the recording could be done in any language, in one's mother tongue, thus recreating an in-group feeling with others from the same clan, however small.

This innovative system of oral communication seriously challenged fledgling literacy, but it practically disappeared with the coming of telephones into the countryside a few years after independence. In countries which do not have a tradition of writing and where universal education is relatively recent, any technique using speech is preferred to writing for informal exchange. However, such techniques can only replace literacy where they are available and cheap. In Africa this is not generally the case; one would expect the literacy option therefore to be reinforced there.

5.4. *Literature which exploits the Pidgin English–English Symbiosis*

In many creole cultures the writing-down or the creative writing of songs, poetry, drama, stories, collections of proverbs and sayings, and so on long antedated any standardization of the languages or the orthography. The *Bibliography of Pidgin and Creole Languages* (Reinecke *et al.* 1975) devotes a whole section of 103 items just to 'West Indian Dialect in Literature' from Michael Scott (1829), C. G. B. Allen (1893), and Tom Redcam (1903), to modern writers such as Derek Walcott, who has used both French patois and Creole English in his plays and poems. Baissac's (1880) *Étude sur le patois créole mauricien* contains twenty-one pages of Mauritian Creole proverbs; in his 1882 study of the Portugese Creole of S. Thomé, H. Schuchardt included songs and proverbs among his texts; in 1885 the Márques de Barros published a collection of thirty poems in the Portuguese Creole of Guiné; and so on. Of course, when published such texts were intended to be read by educated people already literate in another language. Educated Creoles have, however, in this way become habituated to reading an oral literature, written down in an orthography usually arrived at by adapting the conventions of writing the European base language. From this it has been a natural step for educated Creoles to 'compose' poetry, songs, and drama initially for oral 'publication' on the stage, and subsequently for publication in print; the theatre audience not needing to be literate to enjoy the literature, the subsequent readers needing some familiarity with the spoken Creole in order to interpret the orthography employed. As we saw in Chapter 2, some West Indian scholars as well as West African scholars see such processes as valuable steps towards mass literacy in various creoles. There is today a flourishing theatrical literature in the Krio of Sierra Leone as well as in the various patois of the West Indies, a 'pre-literacy literature'.

It has been suggested that pidgins, because of their inherent instability, are not likely vehicles for literature, but, as both Todd (1974) and Barbag-Stoll (1983) have pointed out, the symbiosis between Pidgin English and more standard English means that the entire English lexicon is potentially available to the creative writer, so that any subject may be touched upon, while speakers or writers can shape their texts according to their potential audience or readership, the characters they are creating, their dramatic needs, and so on. Barbag-Stoll illustrates convincingly how Nigerian writers such as Chinua Achebe, C. Ekwensi, and Wole Soyinka have exploited the Nigerian Pidgin English—Nigerian English—Standard English continuum for dramatic and stylistic purposes. In relation to Achebe she says: 'When examining his work chronologically one can observe a clear development in his use of pidgin. In *No Longer at Ease* he uses it half apologetically for humorous purposes, while in *Girls at War* it proves to be a handy tool for depicting his characters, as well as a successful medium of the writer's humour' (Barbag-Stoll 1983: 57). (Most non-standard dialects have of course frequently been regarded as inherently funny in themselves, and therefore used as vehicles for humour before any other literary use. For a long time the South Sea Islands pidgins were written by Europeans in fun, most recently in a 'tourist guide' by Tryon (n.d.).)

Quoting C. Ekwensi, Barbag-Stoll (1983: 110) shows how he has managed to compensate for the absence of a norm and reach a large readership: 'In his novel

Jagua Nana (1960) . . . Being aware of the fact that his books reach vast circles
of readers who may find it difficult to follow the dialogues in Pidgin English,
Ekwensi partly solves the problem by eliminating from pidgin those words
which are difficult to recognize for English readers.' However, this option, though
well thought-out, may lead to idiosyncratic forms of written Pidgin, far removed
from actual oral behaviour. Thus, to the already great variability of oral pidgins,
other variations, written and unconnected to the first, would have to be added.
Literacy in pidgins seems to some extent to have failed for lack of a teaching
norm; generalizing such a norm has even less of a chance if everyone writes as
they please and uses as sole model the English norm. These artificial texts in a
so-called pidgin cannot be called pidgin literature, but research in style. They are
not so much written Pidgin as exercises. Of Wole Soyinka's novel *Trials of
Brother Jero* (1964), Barbag-Stoll says (1983: 111): 'The proportion of pidgin
compared with English seems to increase in favour of the former with the degree
of informality of its speakers.'

Using Pidgin in this way for stylistic ends rather than for its intrinsic appro-
priacy may be a rather negative way ahead for general Pidgin literacy. It is reminiscent of the way some nineteenth-century European writers made use of
dialect and patois—to introduce local colour or reflect social class; the dialect
so used was not thereby enhanced as a vehicle of literacy. Mixing English and
Pidgin in writing leads to a kind of acrolect which will only be detected as non-
standard by somebody with a perfect mastery of the standard.

According to Barbag-Stoll, the main objective of these Nigerian writers is not
a pidgin literature but the adaptation of English to the semio-cultural world of
West Africa. Nevertheless, the introduction of Pidgin on such a scale into their
writing seems unequalled in other pidgin-speaking areas of the world. Several
explanations can be advanced:

(i)   Nigeria has such a large population that books will have a large print run
      and circulate widely—which is far from being the case in the South Sea
      Islands.
(ii) The anglicization of texts claiming to be pidgin is only possible because
      of a large educated élite at home in English. This does not exist in, for
      example, Cameroon or Vanuatu, where French speakers of the pidgin
      would find it difficult to understand the English words introduced.

It must be said that if, in these countries, official English/French bilingualism
is a major advantage for speaking Pidgin, it is a certain disavantage for its extension in the written form.

6. CONCLUSION

Literacy in pidgin vernaculars encounters too much prejudice and too many linguistic and technical problems to really develop. We have only to recall Fishman's

(1971) five criteria for a language to become a standard to realize that none of the English pidgins studied here fills the bill:

1. A certain vitality—i.e. used by quite a large segment of the population;
2. A certain history—i.e. links with a nationalist movement, an ideology, a glorious past, etc.;
3. A certain prestige among speakers and particularly members of the élite and the administration;
4. A certain degree of autonomy compared to the languages with which it coexists;
5. A certain level of language planning put into effect.

The sociolinguistic situations of the five countries reviewed here meet the first two criteria but the third is only partly met, the ambiguous attitudes towards pidgins having been one of the main points of this chapter. But the fourth and fifth points in particular are absent: autonomy in the face of English is wishful thinking, and language planning, never officially recognized, remains incomplete.

More than the future of these vernacular pidgins as written languages, it is their future as spoken codes distinct from English which is the main question. They are used in all walks of life, even in the most technical fields, by élites most often educated in English, and this extra-linguistic environment inevitably gives birth to various levels of language. Very anglicized new urban pidgins exist as well as the old rural pidgins. In the administration, jargons full of English words crop up in supposedly pidgin sentences which are losing more and more of their former structure.

In all Melanesian cities, next to a more or less considerable process of creolization according to the locality in question, the pidgins are being rapidly anglicized, leading to a post-pidgin (or, for a few, post-creole) continuum. In certain domains, the old pidgins are being replaced by pidgins which are so anglicized that they can be understood by any English-speaking newcomer, while the rural Pidgin-speakers cannot understand them. Such a trend is reinforced by English-medium education and the media and can only lead to a local, or even national, English so closely resembling the standard form that the problem of writing will no longer exist. The autonomy of the English pidgins will be more and more compromised as they come into contact with their source languages, even that of the basilectal varieties, making any literacy in these languages for ever impossible.

7

Motivations and Attitudes Influencing Vernacular Literacy: Four African Assessments

RALPH W. FASOLD

with contributions from R. A. Carr-Hill, J. Gerbault, and P. Ndukwe

I. INTRODUCTION

When the 1953 Unesco report was published, it was largely taken for granted that literacy was generally desirable; the central argument of the report was that initial literacy instruction in the mother tongue was the most efficient way to achieve it. As Weinstein (1987) points out, the Unesco report was written from a particular ideological point of view. He points out that most of the thirteen members of the committee had a long-standing interest in non-European languages and many had previously been advocates of minority languages in education and literacy. Weinstein is careful to note that there is nothing wrong with an orientation in favour of such ideals as the development of non-European languages or linguistic self-determination or the preservation of cultural and linguistic pluralism or the psychological and educational well-being of the individual child. The Unesco committee expressed a sincere and reasonable point of view that its members held consistently both before and after publication of the report. One should simply be aware that a certain unquestioned ideological framework is assumed in the report and much subsequent discussion. With some forty years of hindsight it is clear that the psycholinguistic efficiency factor assumed in the report is not the only force operating on the success or failure of vernacular literacy programmes; in fact, it seems not to be even a major one.

The motivations and attitudes of the proposed beneficiaries of vernacular literacy projects are crucial. Speakers of some vernaculars are very much opposed to their own languages being used in their children's education. The original Unesco committee, in fact, anticipated that a particular group might have this opinion. If so, the committee recommends that educators try to win the confidence of the people and convince them of the advantages of mother-tongue instruction. One means of persuasion was the institution of an experimental programme, which the committee, not doubting that such a programme would be successful, believed would convince the sceptical that vernacular-language education is sound policy (Unesco 1953: 54).

It turns out that such cases are far more common that the committee might have anticipated. The Old Order Amish Pennsylvania German groups located in various areas in the eastern USA and Canada constitute one striking example. The Old Order Amish are a highly conservative religious and sociocultural group descended from eighteenth-century immigrants from Germany and Switzerland to North America. Their home language, and the language used in religious services, is their variety of German, popularly called 'Pennsylvania Dutch'. Old Order Amish children attend parochial schools controlled by their own community, but the medium of instruction is invariably English. Furthermore, this fact seems not to have any ill effects on their achievement levels (Huffines 1980). The Hungarian minority in the east Austrian town of Oberwart studied by Susan Gal (1979: 162–4) made the same decision:

In the postwar years a Hungarian school was again established, this time unaffiliated with any church, but supported by the Austrian government's guarantee of minority rights. However, the school did not last long. By the 1955–56 school year there was no Hungarian first grade. By 1956–1957, the school was discontinued. And, most importantly, this was done on the orders of the bilingual community, which voted to close the school. Despite the Austrian government's official support, the bilinguals of Oberwart did not want their children to attend a Hungarian language school.

In this chapter we will present, in some detail, case studies from East and West Africa that illustrate that the motivations and attitudes, not only towards the language in which literacy instruction is provided, but towards the role of literacy itself, are far more complex than was previously anticipated.[1]

2. VERNACULAR LITERACY IN KENYA AND TANZANIA

The purpose of this section is to discuss the problems involved in assessing the functioning and effects of literacy programmes in developing countries and, in particular, on the difficulties involved in testing for literacy and its functionality. The national literacy programme in Kenya aims at mother-tongue literacy; that in Tanzania at lingua-franca literacy, in Kiswahili. These problems are of particular interest because of the large-scale surveys being instituted in several industrialized countries (see Centre for Educational Research and Innovation (1992)). The section is organized around the discussion of the findings of a project carried out under the auspices of the International Institute for Educational Planning (IIEP), the 'research branch' of Unesco. Two studies have been completed: one, funded by the International Development Research Centre (IDRC)

---

[1] Carr-Hill is the author of the section on Kenya and Tanzania, Gerbault presents the study of the Central African Republic (and Cameroon), and Ndukwe discusses the Nigerian case.

in Kenya; another, funded by the Swedish International Development Agency (SIDA), in Tanzania.

2.1. *Background*

It had been recognized for some time that the previous evaluation by Unesco of its functional literacy programme in the 1970s had not been very useful, either in its design or in its impact upon policy-makers. Whilst it was clear that the functional literacy programmes had not been as successful as had been hoped, the evaluation did not provide the basis for designing improvements. Many subsequent national evaluations have also failed to provide much useful data for policy purposes. In the Tanzanian context, apart from the national literacy testing organized by the Ministry of Education at regular intervals since 1976, there has been a substantial attempt to carry out an evaluation of the national literacy programme involving questionnaires administered to community leaders, learners, and teachers; neither the national testing programme nor the evaluation have provided information which can be directly used for policy-making (Kamwella 1985; Mpogolo 1985). Indeed, it is difficult to find research evidence anywhere, as distinct from rhetoric about the way adult literacy programmes operate or the results they produce (Izquierdo 1985).

2.2. *Literacy Strategy in Kenya and Tanzania*

The overall literacy strategies in Kenya and Tanzania have been very different: the programme in Kenya can be characterized as selective-intensive functional; in Tanzania, the emphasis was on a series of mass campaigns aimed at eradicating illiteracy in the medium term. A massive campaign to eliminate illiteracy in Tanzania was launched during the 1970s after the initial functional literacy Unesco pilot project around Lake Victoria (Nyerere 1969/70). The programme is conceived and directed with primers written centrally, although different ones are distributed according to the main type of economic activity in the area. In order to monitor achievements, a national literacy test has been held on a biennial or triennial basis since 1977, with the results shown in Table 7.1. The drop in enrolments in the first column of the table is ascribed to the gradual elimination of illiteracy as illustrated in the second column of the table.

This national test is an important national event and considerable effort is invested in preparation and mobilization for it. Anecdotal evidence suggested that many who sit the test have already completed several years of schooling and never been to a literacy class. Indeed, as we shall see, it appears that the announcement of the national test is often the crucial factor in setting up classes for at least the brief period in the run-up to the examination. Teachers are recruited, in principle, from among primary-school teachers in the village and receive a

TABLE 7.1. *National adult literacy rates, related to enrolment in literacy classes, Tanzania*

	Enrolment (m.)	Literacy rate (%)
1975	5.2	61
1977	5.8	73
1981	3.1	79
1983	2.3	85
1986	2.5	91

Note: Enrolment: numbers of illiterate adults enrolled in literacy classes. Literacy rate: national rate of adult literacy, i.e. the percentage of the adult population functionally literate as defined by passing the national literacy tests.

Source: Ministry of Education, Tanzania, Dept. of Adult Education.

minuscule 'honorarium' from the government (at the time of research, in 1989, this was around $US1 a month).

2.3. *Design of the Study*

Part of the problem of evaluation has been a lack of clarity as to what the effects of a literacy programme might be. In this project, we distinguish three kinds of effect:

(*a*) Have participants learnt what they were supposed to learn? To what extent do they master the 3Rs and the knowledge (about health, family planning, production, etc.) which constitutes the content of the literacy programme?

(*b*) Do participants actually *make use* of what they have learnt? Do they read, write, and calculate? Do they apply family-planning techniques or change their nutritional habits?

(*c*) What has been the *impact upon their daily lives*? Has the programme influenced the adult learners and their social environment in terms of income (through, say, increased productivity), improved health and nutritional habits, better housing, and social communication?

The objective of these studies was:

- to give a detailed description of the conditions under which the literacy programmes are functioning at grass-roots level by analysing in depth the characteristics of the literacy centres and the literacy environment in local communities;
- to find out who the literacy learners are, their general characteristics, home environment, and educational experience;

TABLE 7.2. *Locations in Kenya*

Location	District	Sector and type of economy
Starehe	Nairobi	Urban: tertiary sector
Isolo-Central	Isolo	Urban with rural hinterland: tertiary and pastoral
Kiirua	Meru	Rural: subsistence and cash crop
South Maragoli	Kakemega	Rural
Koru	Kisumu	Plantations and home subsistence

Source: Carron *et al.* (1989: ch. 3)

- to measure the levels of literacy and numeracy skills and the levels of functional knowledge and attitudes acquired by the participants;
- to evaluate the extent to which the learners are using the skills and knowledge acquired in their daily lives; and
- to identify some of the major factors that are influencing the acquisition and use of literacy skills and functional knowledge.

It can be seen that the studies were explicitly *not* designed to assess the impact of literacy upon the daily lives of participants (the third level of effect): this would have necessitated a complex and time-consuming longitudinal design, which would have required the mobilization of resources beyond our capacity. The methodological assumption behind the research design is that the real issues involved in the functioning and effects of a literacy programme can be best understood when the functioning of the programme and the possible effects upon individual participants are analysed within their local setting. For this reason a micro approach has been adopted, starting with a careful analysis of the local environment within which the literacy programme operates, so that variations in the results and interactions between variables can be interpreted on the basis of their meaning within their specific socio-economic context.

Communities were selected, representing contrasting developing contexts and living conditions, ranging from an urban zone to a remote rural area. This purposeful selection of areas and of all the literacy centres within each of them does not claim to be representative nationwide, but should allow for the analysis of variations in the functioning of the centres—and in the different results they have produced—according to the environments in which they are located. Tables 7.2 and 7.3 identify the locations in Kenya and Tanzania, respectively.

The research team was composed of national Kenyans and Tanzanians, with some advice on the methodology of questionnaire construction from the IIEP. The team members worked together in the suburban wards of Dar-es-Salaam and Nairobi, and then each member of the national research team spent a month

TABLE 7.3. *Locations in Tanzania*

Ward	District	Sector and type of economy
Buguruni	Dar es Salaam	Urban: tertiary sector
Mbweera	Hai	Long-established rural: diversified pastoral and plantation economy
Ugwachanya	Iringa Rural	Rural: subsistence, but with also some services provided to the Great North Road

Source: Carr-Hill *et al.* (1991: pt. II, chs. 4–7).

in each of the other locations both: (i) to prepare detailed community profiles, including information on the geographical features, population, economic activities, sociocultural characteristics, social services, school education, and the overall literacy environment in each community; and (ii) to hold focused group discussions and individual interviews with the administrative and political leaders and with groups of the learners. At the same time, they trained a small group of local teachers to administer an interview questionnaire to 100 previously identified recent literates, and organized a test of literacy and numeracy skills for the latter in both.

Obviously the most important issue for this book is to explain the methods used to assess literacy. In the Kenyan project, it was necessary to develop tests of literacy and numeracy *ab initio* with all the attendant opportunities for argument; in Tanzania we were comparatively fortunate in that the Ministry of Education in Tanzania, through its programme of biennial national literacy testing, had developed a particular style of testing for literacy and numeracy which we were able to copy.

The construction of tests for functional knowledge and for 'modern' attitudes and practices is, perforce, more arbitrary. Although a number of 'items of knowledge' were imparted in the primers used in the literacy programme, many of them were very commonplace in their context: it was therefore very difficult to ascribe their acquisition—or, more precisely, a correct response to a direct question—to the literacy programme. Nevertheless, it was felt that the items questioned had to be restricted to those which would have been learnt or otherwise absorbed during the literacy programme.

2.4. *Functionality*

As in many other adult literacy programmes, there is supposed to be a 'functional' theme to the programme in both countries whereby the literacy teaching should connect to the everyday activities of learners/participants. In both countries, this was taken to imply that primers should be written around daily economic activities, that there should be a project component, and, if possible, a local development official should be involved. This appeared to have been more successful in Kenya—partly, of course, because the programme was hardly functioning in Tanzania. Even so, only half the teachers in Kenya reported a recent guest lecturer and, whilst thirty-eight (60 per cent) of the surveyed centres in Kenya reported *project work*, thirty involved income generation for the participants themselves, and only eight were concerned with general community improvement; and in Tanzania projects were hardly mentioned. It is worth emphasizing that, given the system of centralized design and production in Tanzania, together with an erratic distribution network to the locations, there was bound to be little systematic relation between the primers and local economic activity. The fact that the primers were produced locally in Kenya obviously facilitated the incorporation of locally relevant materials; and the use of local languages also probably made them more accessible.

An important aspect of the organization of the programme was the creation of centre committees composed of representatives of the classes taking place at the centre. The process is seen as an important instrument to involve the learners in decision-making about the organization of the classes. In the four Tanzanian locations, less than half (twenty-one) of the fifty teachers interviewed mentioned the existence of a centre committee and only eleven reported that the committee had met during the last three months. Even in Kenya, where there was an active programme, seventeen of the sixty-one centres did not have a committee and eight of the remainder had not met during the previous three months.

It would be utopian to expect full pedagogical cross-fertilization between literacy learning, guest lectures, and project work, all being monitored by an active centre committee. Indeed, it is probably unrealistic to pace the learning of literacy to the requirements of a project. But the various components should be mutually supportive. Instead in some centres there was clearly a conflict in terms of time use, at least between learning to read and write and the project work, and there are dangers in overloading a literacy programme with project work and perhaps skill-training as well.

2.5. *Motivations and Aspirations of Participants*

In contrast to the classic rhetoric about wanting to participate in a developing society, the participants in these very different programmes in two countries gave rather more straightforward reasons for wanting to become literate (see Table 7.4). Indeed, even though the questions were standardized, the similarity between the patterns of responses is striking given the very different levels of economic development and stages of the literacy programmes in the two countries. The participants in these literacy programmes were more concerned with

TABLE 7.4. *Reasons given for attending literacy classes*

	Total responses	Percentage distribution of responses over:		
		Basic literacy and numeracy	Economic and functional	General and other
Kenya	498	65	17	18
Tanzania	875	63	15	22

Sources: Kenya: Carron *et al.* (1989: 132, table VII. 3); Tanzania: Carr-Hill *et al.* (1991: 249, table 12.6).

TABLE 7.5. *What participants claimed they would like to learn next*

	Total responses	Percentage distribution of responses over:				
		Kiswahili and/or English	Calculating	Writing	Functional skills	General and political
Kenya	519	50	28	12	10	0
Tanzania	573	20	8	0	43	29

Sources: Kenya: Carron *et al.* (1989: 138, table VII. 7); Tanzania: Carr-Hill *et al.* (1991: 250, table 12.8).

learning basic literacy and numeracy than with any possible functionality of the projects carried out in the literacy classes.

When asked what they would like to learn next, over 90 per cent of the Kenyan learners emphasized basic communication skills (reading, writing, or counting), whilst the Tanzanian participants were much more concerned with functional skills (see Table 7.5). These differences can probably be interpreted in terms of the salience of basic functional skills and of language to economic survival at the different levels of development of the two countries. For example, it could be argued that, in Tanzania, the issues of economic survival dominate, so that basic production skills to generate income at home are seen as the most important. In Kenya, success in market capitalism requires more advanced communication skills, so that a programme focusing on reading, writing, and arithmetic is most useful. A literacy programme is likely to be most effective at transmitting these communication skills, and, if this is what is useful to participants, then it is, correspondingly, likely to be more successful.

TABLE 7.6. *Comparison of percentages of learners achieving average or above-average passes in reading, writing, and numeracy*

	Reading	Writing	Numeracy	Overall[a]
Kenya	80	69	73	56
Tanzania	81	72	75	70

[a] Percentage of those taking the test who passed on all three tests (see Carr-Hill *et al.* 1991: 288–9).

Sources: Kenya: 1986: Carron *et al.* (1989: 190, graph X. 1); Tanzania: 1989: Carr-Hill *et al.* (1991: 289, table 14.1).

2.6. *Effects of the Programme*

The pass rates for the individual tests and overall are presented in Table 7.6. There are three major observations. First, the level and amount of literacy and numeracy imparted were low. Thus, in Kenya, only just over half reached the level where they were able to read and write simple sentences and perform the four basic arithmetical operations. Whilst a higher (70 per cent) pass rate was recorded in Tanzania, the tests were probably simpler. Thus, although the level in Tanzania was intended to be equivalent to that attained by Standard IV of primary-school pupils, a control group of pupils who were half-way through the Standard IV passed all the tests easily whilst even those among the learners who passed had difficulty with several of the questions: for example, less than 20 per cent of those who took the arithmetic test in Tanzania reached Level IV of the literacy programme, where the learner moves beyond mechanical operations to problem-solving. Moreover, at least in Kenya, not many completed the course, so that the proportion of those enrolled who were actually made literate was low. Thus, over the period 1980–6, the average enrolment per year was 2,358, but only 1,309 (56 per cent) were awarded certificates (although the test was not compulsory, it is likely that most of those who actually achieved literacy through the classes would also have taken the test).

Secondly, the extent to which the programme imparts 'functional' knowledge, attitudes, and practices is also doubtful. Whilst it is true that the literates always performed better than the illiterates in each test and in each location in both countries, the questions were so general—even though derived from the content of the primers—that the answers could have been obtained from almost anywhere. Indeed some of the questions used in the Kenyan survey seemed so obvious in this sense that they were dropped from the Tanzanian survey so the scores are not strictly comparable. With these caveats, a comparison of the overall scores suggests that learners in Kenya perform much better than those in Tanzania (see

TABLE 7.7. *Comparison of overall achievements of learners in response to questions testing functional knowledge, modern attitudes, and modern practices in behaviour*

	Knowledge questions		Attitudes questions		Behaviour questions	
	Pass level	%[a]	Pass level	%[a]	Pass level	%[a]
Kenya	6 or 7 out of seven	75	4 or 5 out of five	80	6, 7 or 8 out of 8	75
Tanzania	5 or 6 out of 6	33	5, 6 or 7 out of 7	39	5, 6 or 7 out of 7	21

[a] Percentage of candidates passing.

Sources: Kenya: Carron *et al.* (1989: 165, tables IX. 1; 167, table IX. 3; 171, table IX. 5); Tanzania: Carr-Hill *et al.* (1991: 276, fig. 13.8; 279, fig. 13.9; 180, fig. 13.10).

TABLE 7.8. *Comparison of answers to comparable questions testing knowledge, attitudes, and behaviour*

Questions on	Percentage of answers in	
	Kenya	Tanzania
'Which foods give energy?' (correct answers)	45	33
Family planning (modern answers)	82	49
'Fruits are more for children' (modern answers)	71	18
Use of latrines (modern answers)	94	46
'Do you eat fruits?' (modern answers)	99	30
'Do you use hybrid seeds?' (modern answers)	86	61

Sources: Kenya: Carron *et al.* (1989: 167, table IX. 2; 170, table IX. 4; 173, table IX. 6); Tanzania: Carr-Hill *et al.* (1991: 261, fig. 13.1; 267, table 13.1; 273, fig. 13.6).

Table 7.7), and this is confirmed when the responses to comparable data are compared (Table 7.8).

2.7. Conclusion

The principal results confirm the main original hypotheses that the effects of the literacy programme are strongly conditioned by the environment in which it operates (Carr-Hill *et al.* 1991). It is also clear that, whilst there are connections between performance on the tests and scores on indices of functional knowledge and of modern attitudes and practices, they are not close. Testing for literacy, and especially for functional literacy, is not therefore a simple task. Yet several national institutions in the developed world are launching into large-scale surveys with the presumption that adult literacy is closely connected to economic performance, without an adequate understanding of the subcultural variability in the importance and meanings of (functional) literacy. A little humility in respect of both cultural diversity and of work in the Third World of the kind reported here, would avoid many silly mistakes.

3. VERNACULAR LITERACY IN THE CENTRAL AFRICAN REPUBLIC

In this section we will continue to develop the argument that the development of vernacular literacy is very much dependent upon attitudes, overtly expressed or not, which are shaped by a wide range of societal variables interacting in specific national contexts. We will focus on the case of the Central African Republic (CAR). The points made will be highlighted by contrasting this case with the case of Cameroon, a neighbouring country, strikingly different from the CAR in a number of respects, where attitudes, however, play a comparable role.

Our reflection on the need to consider attitudes in the examination of the implementation of policies for the use of vernaculars in education has been triggered in part by the repeatedly observed failure—or absence—of such policies in a number of countries with varying profiles. For example, Ndukwe reports on conflicting opinions regarding literacy in the indigenous vernaculars of Nigeria. Other researchers have pointed to similar 'mixed' behaviours (e.g. towards literacy in Creole in the Caribbean). The case of the CAR seems an especially useful example to study, because the sociolinguistic context there is one that would seem particularly favourable to the development of vernacular literacy. In this country, there is a relatively stable type of societal bilingualism, with French, Sango, and a number of other local languages used in different domains.[2] Sango is the national language, and has been widely accepted by Central Africans as the expression of the national identity. There have been official statements of policy for the development of Sango, and the official orthography has been fixed by a government decree. Sango is not only the declared national language, it is also widely spoken all over the country, and especially in the urban areas. In Bangui, the capital city, it is used in the market, with friends, and on most informal occasions. It has become the first language learnt by the majority of children born there. For many years, the policy of the national radio has been to promote the

---

[2] Perhaps not the classical diglossia of Ferguson (1959), but the variation called 'double overlapping diglossia' in Fasold (1984).

development of Sango. The combination of such linguistic, psychological, and political variables might be expected to create a situation in which the use of the vernacular language in writing would develop smoothly. That it is not exactly the case suggests that there may be features in national sociolinguistic contexts, beyond those usually considered by linguists and language planners, that have to be taken into account.

Research conducted from 1984 to 1989 (Gerbault 1987, 1988, 1989, 1990; Gerbault and Wenezoui 1988) in Bangui has shown that Sango remains used mostly for spoken communication. Little reading is done in this language, and very little writing. All formal education is in French. The few experimental classes in Sango that were launched in the late 1970s have had no impact on the course given to education. Today the written production in Sango continues to be limited to religious materials. A few informal education booklets in Sango are also produced by Christian missions. A newspaper in Sango was created in 1974 and disappeared in 1981. The current (1994) daily newspaper is printed entirely in French. The official 'declared' policy, however, has been to extend the use of Sango to reading and writing. In 1984 both French and Sango were declared the languages of the school, and the official orthography of Sango was fixed. There was no follow-up action on these decrees, and no implementation of the policy took place. The office of the Direction de l'Éducation non Formelle et Permanente, whose literacy programmes for the provinces are in Sango, has a limited action, and is faced with the problem of lack of training of its personnel in the official spelling. In fact, the various orthographies available and the existing varieties of Sango are perceived as major problems by users of the written language.

Only one-third of the literate population interviewed in 1988 in Bangui declared that they wrote personal letters in Sango. Only 28 per cent of them were able to recognize the official orthography, and many were not even aware that an 'official' orthography existed. The majority of those who do write in Sango use one variety of religious spelling. A number of literate persons, however, show very positive attitudes towards the use of written Sango, the teaching of literacy in Sango, and the creation of a newspaper in Sango. As for illiterate persons, they feel no need to become literate. Literacy does not seem to be felt as a skill that it might be useful to acquire. Although the spread of formal education has had little effect on the spread of literacy in Sango, it had a definite influence upon the development of the language: school increases contacts between speakers of different Central African languages, thus reinforcing the need for a lingua franca —Sango. It also means more extensive learning of and contact with French. The mixing of French and Sango, which has resulted from increased contact, often referred to as 'Fransango', a variety very much in use among university students, is perceived negatively by all speakers (i.e. 'good' Sango should be free from French words).

More than ten years have elapsed since the publication of the first scientific dictionary of Sango (Bouquiaux *et al.* 1978). The spread of the new vocabulary, however, seems to be relatively slow. The National Committee for the Promotion of Sango was being organized at the end of 1988. Its objectives and status, clearly backed by the official declaration of language policy, were formally stated: to take concrete steps for harmonization and development of the language and of its uses. The Institute of Applied Linguistics (created in 1975) was to be the coordinating agency for all research and activities dealing with Sango. At the present time, however, the structure is still in the planning stage and no programme has been launched.

In the area of lexical development, as in the other areas of language, therefore, no action has been taken. The need for new Sango words is felt by a majority of persons. Spontaneous lexical creation is taking place, but there has been no general policy for spreading new terms. Central Africans in Bangui are generally aware that new vocabulary has been made available, but only a few of the new words are well known. The national radio has been the only official body with an internal language policy (training of translators, systematic use of French-free Sango, more uniform pronunciation, etc.) in agreement with the guidelines established by the higher political authorities.[3] (It should be noted that among the 700 persons interviewed in Bangui in 1988–9 for the Agence de Coopération Culturelle et Technique (ACCT) *Dynamique des Langues* survey, the desire for a standardized form of Sango and for the extension of its domains of use, including in formal education, was widely expressed.)

3.1. *Attitudes towards Literacy in Sango: The Interaction of Conflicting Forces*

The present state of development and standardization of Sango and of vernacular literacy in the CAR seems to reflect the association of conflicting forces. One can observe, on the one hand, that vernacular literacy has made little progress since official statements of policy, and, on the other hand, that progressive, 'spontaneous' normalization is taking place because the socio-psychological context calls for appropriation of Sango by the nation as a whole, and by city-dwellers in particular.

The actual place of literacy in social activities in this country is a variable whose importance should not be overlooked. Whilst school attendance has risen in recent years, and particularly since the time of the Unesco declaration, primary-school attendance still does not mean permanent literacy, and the social role of literacy has not really changed. Reading materials in Sango are scarce, and there is no need for the written media in traditional Central African modes of communication. In many parts of the country, and even in Bangui, the use of literacy is still reserved to a fraction of the population. As Savard and Vigneault (1975: 75) put it, 'it does not matter in which language you cannot read; illiteracy is

---

[3] Broadcasts in Sango occupy 65 per cent of the total broadcasting time.

omnilingual . . .'.[4] In Bangui and other cities, access to employment is not given by literacy in Sango—nor does any amount of school education, incidentally, guarantee employment; small jobs that can be secured often do not require reading or writing skills. Employment as a civil servant requires only oral competence in Sango, along with competence in spoken and written French.

It is clear that these social characteristics will have an impact on attitudes towards literacy in Sango. Sango is used nationwide in specific domains, but these domains are not those that have long been associated with literacy and/or formal education. The conceptual association is between writing and French, not between writing and Sango. Attitudes towards literacy only reflect established usage and social structure. The impact of societal contexts on attitudes can also be seen in the lack of commitment of local linguists and educators to the development of literacy in Sango. In the past twenty years, there have been in the CAR, as in other countries, meetings, decisions, and committees created, aiming at developing and standardizing Sango, at developing literacy in Sango, and at introducing the language in formal education. Programmes have collapsed because there has been no continued commitment to expressed objectives. When actual action was called for, no effort was made towards reaching the goal. In the CAR there exists no fully developed course for teaching reading, grammar, vocabulary, spelling, and so on in Sango. There is no fully developed course for teaching maths, or any science, at the primary level, and no teacher-training course for the teaching of the national language. The LEXIS project, an ACCT programme under which lexical development and an inventory of national languages was to be conducted in the CAR and in several other francophone countries of Africa, has not been completed. There is an obvious lack of determination on the part of project directors; individual initiatives are practically absent.

The lack of strong motivation on the part of national researchers may be viewed alongside the more or less conscious attitude of the upper or middle class, which are not willing to cut their own throat, as Carrington (1988a) put it, by changing anything in the system which brought them where they are. Thus there is no organized pressure for change from local linguists and educators, or other educated persons, upon the political authority. Decision-making at the upper level reflects attitudes which also have political and economic foundations. There is no implementation of officially stated policies, which, after all, appear as if they had been established, or 'dictated', by international agencies such as Unesco or 'CONFEMEN'. National institutions do not seem really concerned when it comes to taking action in their own country. A logical consequence of top-level inertia in such highly centralized administrative systems as the CAR is the maintenance of the status quo.

[4] One exception is to be found in the Department of Agriculture, where efforts are being made in two directions: developing Sango terms for the dissemination of oral information, and teaching reading to those involved in agriculture, enabling them to read technical information in order to improve their practical skills and production.

Another side of this political coin is that, in terms of funds for education, the CAR, like most other francophone countries of Africa, depends largely on the French government or other francophone funding agencies. Promoting *francophonie* has not at any time meant promoting national languages. Funds are allocated for developing and improving the teaching of French and literacy in French. As long as there is no national will to redistribute the functions of languages in education, the purpose of school education is to transmit knowledge through a language of wider communication, namely French, not to develop any kind of school bilingualism.

Contradictory pressures due to a variety of linguistic, social, socio-psychological, economic, and political factors can thus be identified. The argument here is that the dynamics of the development of vernacular literacy in such contexts has an important attitudinal component, and that attitudes can be explained by the interaction of those societal factors mentioned above. In the present state of affairs, however, slow changes do take place in the national language of the CAR, and this is mostly because of the continued activity of the spoken media—development, standardization, use of written Sango for transcription of broadcasts—which was achieved, it must be pointed out, through the strong personal commitment of a few men to make Sango the language of the radio. The changes are also due to increased language contacts among speakers of different varieties of Sango and to action in the domain of agriculture. Sango is being studied at the university, and this tends both to increase its prestige (an important factor in language development) and to accelerate its development. It is probably in the area of phonology that the standardization of Sango has made most progress. But the official orthography, with the current *laissez-faire* policy and with the restricted domains of use of written Sango, cannot be expected to spread in the immediate future.

3.2. *Conclusion*

In Cameroon, where a large number of local languages and the existence of several regional vehicular languages create a linguistic context which is quite different from the Central African context, the socio-psychological and political variables, however, are very similar. Local linguists and educators in Cameroon openly acknowledge general inertia and absence of personal commitment. Besides, in Cameroon, the fear that ethnic particularisms might endanger national unity remains strong among the governing class. Suggestions from language and education specialists have been made for introducing local languages in education (e.g. Tadadjeu *et al.* 1986), but no commitment to implementing a policy has been made, for reasons that are quite similar to those in the CAR. Although French and English in Cameroon play the role of lingua francas (a role played by Sango, along with French, in the CAR), the same reluctance to move forward and break the status quo can be observed in both countries.

As long as vernacular literacy has no place, either in the traditional social structure, or in the westernized social hierarchy, little prestige will be attached to the possession of that skill, and attitudes cannot be expected to change. Lewis's (1981: 262) comment on the importance of attitudes in the formulation of a policy seems quite appropriate here: 'In the long run, no policy will succeed which does not do one of three things: conform to the expressed attitudes of those involved, persuade those that express negative attitudes about the rightness of the policy, or seek to remove the causes of the disagreement.'

4. VERNACULAR LITERACY IN NIGERIA

Nigeria happens to be one of those African nations that are normally referred to as being committed to literacy (and education) in the mother tongue (see e.g. Jeffries 1967; Ansre 1975). During the colonial period language policies on the use of the vernacular swung from one extreme to the other depending on the recommendations of various commissions of enquiry, and varying from one region of the country to another. Post-independence (1960) policies have generally been favourable towards vernacular literacy. The most recent nationwide policy is contained in the document entitled *National Policy on Education* which first appeared in 1977 and was revised in 1981.

This commitment has been manifested to various degrees in language-related policies from the colonial times to the present. The size and linguistic complexity of the country notwithstanding, proponents of vernacular literacy would appear to have been vindicated, judging by the number of favourable programmes and policies that have been initiated in various parts of the country. All these should lead one to expect that solid progress should have been made, at least in terms of favourable attitudes towards vernacular literacy among the nation's populace —along with a corresponding move to de-emphasize or reduce the role of English in the nation's education system.

The impression one receives 'on the ground' is that this is not exactly the case. This section will focus closely on the situation in order to determine the nature of progress (whether real, ephemeral, or ambivalent) that appears to have been achieved. We will discuss below the more sophisticated initiatives that have been undertaken in connection with mother-tongue literacy in various parts of the country and will continue by trying to account for the somewhat ambivalent state of affairs that currently exists. Finally, we will discuss the actual effect of standardization efforts on adult literacy programmes.

4.1. *Some Initiatives for Mother-Tongue Literacy*

The most current national policy on language use in education (a revision of which was recently announced by the Minister of Education, sparking off a major nationwide controversy) contains a number of provisions with fairly obvious implications for vernacular literacy. The relevant portions of the document stipulate that (*a*) initial education (i.e. pre-primary and the first three years or so of primary) should be in the mother tongue or the 'language of the immediate community' (however that may be determined), (*b*) every Nigerian secondary-school student should offer as a subject of study one of the three major Nigerian languages and should have, as a core subject, the study of a Nigerian language and its associated literature. Official commitment to literacy in the indigenous vernaculars has been expressed in various policy statements since the early part of this century. Although it would be misleading to suggest that this policy provided the impetus for the initiation of all the programmes that will now be discussed, there is little doubt about its influence on the programme's subsequent development.

The oldest and probably best known of these programmes is the Six Year Yoruba Project (SYYP) developed in January 1970 by the Institute of Education of the University of Ife (later Obafemi Awolowo University), Ile-Ife. The experiment was intended to assess the effectiveness of teaching school subjects (namely, social and cultural studies, science, mathematics, Yoruba language arts, and English as a second language) in Yoruba, except English, which was to be taught by specialist teachers. As Babalola (1985: 10) reports:

> The children are divided into two groups, the experimental and the control. Both groups use the same text materials but in two different languages: Yoruba and English. Over 150 books (both Yoruba and English) have been written and mimeographed for the Project by a team comprising university teachers and professors, secondary school teachers and teacher-training college tutors or principals as well as some of those primary school teachers involved in teaching the project children.

Babalola goes on to claim that data obtained so far have strongly convinced the project leaders that the African child will learn better and develop his talents faster if he is taught in his mother tongue. By 1985, over 3,000 students have passed through the project and a good number have obtained masters' degrees in various disciplines. But all this notwithstanding, Babalola notes somewhat ruefully that other primary schools in Oyo State (i.e. where the university is located) are yet to go the Ife way, and this twenty years after the programme was embarked upon and despite its much acclaimed 'success'.

Not much information is available about the Primary Education Improvement Project (PEIP) started later at the Ahmadu Bello University, Zaria, in Kaduna State. But, like its Ife counterpart, it was intended to prove the efficacy of the use of the local vernaculars (in Kaduna and contiguous states) as the medium for initial literacy. The focus of the project was on the provision of materials in these languages and not experimentation on a grand scale, as in the Ife Project. It is, therefore, difficult to assess its achievement, particularly in the languages other than Hausa (of which more will be said below).

The Rivers Readers Project is another university-based project but financed by the Rivers State Government. The project leader and a good number of the more important participants are drawn from the University of Port-Harcourt in Rivers State. The aim of the project was to produce readers, teachers' notes, and supporting materials in all the languages of the state to enable children to attain some literacy in their own languages before going on to English. As Kay Williamson (the project leader) reported, first-year readers have been produced in over twenty languages, teachers' notes and orthography in almost as many languages. Unlike the SYYP and the PEIP, the Rivers Readers Project has not been precisely concerned with direct monitoring of the efficacy of their materials in the actual classroom situation. The same may be said of the activities of the Summer Institute of Linguistics through its Nigerian affiliate, the Nigerian Bible Translation Trust. The Trust has translated the whole Bible into at least four languages and the New Testament into about thirty languages. For these languages and some others the Trust has produced reading primers, literacy books, and selected portions of the Bible. The publications are now being used in the adult education classes organized by the churches which support the Trust and the primary schools run by them in various parts of the country.

The point of the above discussion is to provide a fair, but far from exhaustive, picture of the substantial amount of work that has been undertaken in vernacular literacy in Nigeria, particularly in the past two decades. Of the 400 or so languages available in the country, more than half have had some amount of literacy work done on them—and this without prejudice to the geographical distribution or statuses of the languages. It is true, of course, that a great deal more has been done on the major languages such as Hausa, Igbo, Yoruba, and Edo, in terms of production of materials, teacher-training schemes, and adult-education programmes.[5] This is hardly surprising, because of their size and importance and the competitiveness engendered by their potential as national, official languages.

However, it does not appear that the generality of Nigerians are persuaded, in spite of all this effort, of the intrinsic value of the mother tongue as medium of instruction for the initial—or any other—stage of literacy. The range and intensity (especially of passion) of the conflicting opinions expressed in various publications (especially newspapers and magazines) as a result of the announcement by the Minister of Education threw into bold relief the variegated attitudes to vernacular literacy to be found in the country. Interestingly, attitudes on both sides of the divide cut across all literate (in English) segments of society, high-level government officials (i.e. the policy-makers), educators, and media practitioners —to name a few of the professional groupings—and the non-literate grass-roots populace. These attitudes appear to point to the fact that there is a conceptual

---

[5] At the various tertiary institutions (particularly universities and colleges of education), various diploma and degree programmes have been developed in these languages.

disassociation between literacy and the vernaculars, a strong association having been historically determined between literacy and the official language, English.

Specific studies dealing with this situation are few and far between, but we will use Etim (1985), which contains results that seem to be generalizable to the rest of the country, as an illustrative study. This study was concerned with the attitude of primary-school teachers and headmasters towards the use of the mother tongue as the medium of instruction in their schools located in the multilingual Plateau State. Etim took account of such variables as the rural/urban dichotomy and the ethnic background of the teachers. The discovery was that, on a scale of preference, English was ranked higher than Hausa (the major lingua franca of the state), which in turn was ranked higher than the mother tongue for speakers of six of the state's languages: Angas, Ankwai, Berom, Eggon, Mwaghavul, and Tarok. This order of preference with regard to language choice (English, the local lingua franca, and mother tongue) for certain purposes has also been noted in Bendel State (Oke 1972). What makes the Plateau case interesting is that only teachers, the supposed point warriors in the battle for the enthronement of vernacular literacy, were involved. Etim explains the preference of English and Hausa over the mother tongue in these words: 'For both languages, materials to be used for instructional purposes are readily available. However, English was preferred over Hausa and the mother-tongue due to the fact that in the higher institutions, English is used and teachers in the primary schools have to prepare their pupils for this . . . one finds that teachers felt there would be cultural and social problems in the use of the local languages for education' (Etim 1985: 40).

4.2. *Reasons for the Ambivalence*

Etim did not specify the 'cultural and social problems' referred to, but some of them have been dealt with extensively in the literature (see Bamgbose 1976, 1985). These relate to the multiplicity of languages, the cosmopolitan nature of most urban centres, inherited colonial policies, insufficient number and inadequate preparation of teachers, reliance on expensive foreign models, and lack of (ideological) commitment on the part of government officials leading to a divergence between policy and practice. However, we would suggest that a deeper and more general explanation is required to account for the generally negative attitude, if not prejudice, towards mother-tongue literacy on the part of, not only teachers, but also the rural/urban élite, people of the grass roots, and even those one would have thought had been exposed to enough evidence relating to its benefits.

The point to note is the apparent disassociation between literacy and the vernaculars, similar to that we find in the CAR. It appears that, for many Nigerians, whatever reading and writing skills one may acquire in the vernacular, these should not be dignified by the term literacy. Except for certain parts of the country with a strong tradition of scholarship in Arabic, to describe somebody as literate is tacitly and automatically to link their literacy to English. For many of those who happen to have been persuaded of the usefulness of literacy in the vernacular, this is appreciated more as a patriotic gesture than for its educational value. For policy formulators, then, this dominant notion of English as the 'correct' or 'true' language of literacy has to be contended with in its various manifestations. It accounts for the 'barrier of communication' (Bamgbose 1985: 332) which exists between experts, researchers, and educators, on the one hand, and the decision-makers on the other, whereby the recommendations on vernacular literacy made by the former are not immediately obvious to the latter. It also accounts for the hypocritical attitude of the policy-maker who sends his children to English-medium private schools, whilst extolling the virtues of vernacular literacy which is to be found only in the public system. Finally, it also seems to inform the attitude of the newspaper correspondent who recently claimed that 'to experiment with our local languages as the media in which primary school pupils will be taught in their first two years is to court disaster' (Kalu 1990). It seems to be a measure of the ambivalent nature of the progress that has so far been made on vernacular literacy in Nigeria that such views would be expressed by highly educated and supposedly well-informed citizens.

4.3. *Standard Varieties and Adult Literacy in Nigeria*

A further example of the interaction of attitudes and planning for mother-tongue literacy comes to the fore when we examine how official standards fare in the practice of adult literacy programmes. Adult literacy theorists and practitioners appear to have encountered a little-expected problem—namely, that the existence of standard varieties for some particular languages could hinder rather than help the promotion of vernacular literacy in these languages. Illustrations will be taken from two language situations—namely, Hausa and Igbo, two fairly sizeable and well-known languages spoken in Nigeria.

The Kano variety of Hausa has long been acknowledged as the standard form. On paper this fact is uncontroversial and widely accepted. However, the reality is quite different in Sokoto and, possibly, Kebbi States of Nigeria. The varieties of Hausa spoken in these areas have a long tradition of writing in the Ajami (or Arabic) script, and are usually referred to as 'classical' by their exponents. This is because the varieties are, to a far greater extent than other Hausa varieties, saturated with loans from Classical Arabic in the form of words and constructions. Sokoto Hausa (Sakwatanci) is therefore regarded in these areas as a truer standard than the much-touted Kano variety. In practical terms, though, this attitude has had little effect on the use of the generally accepted orthography except on some spelling rules, and the vocabulary.

The case of Igbo is much more complicated. The accepted wisdom is that standard Igbo is 'Central' Igbo—that is, based on the varieties spoken in central (largely undefined) Igboland. Apart from the dialect issue, probably the most significant problem relates to the orthography. Whilst the varieties spoken in the central and northern areas have as many as forty to sixty consonant phonemes, the alphabet has only twenty-eight consonant letters and appears to be based on the Onitsha varieties in the western part of Igboland. The experience of the author (Ndukwe) with adult literacy programmes in the Nsukka (Northern Igbo) area is that the students have a scant regard for the standard forms and prefer to be taught using an orthography based on their local speech forms. This has necessitated the devising of primers significantly at variance with standard Igbo. The fact that much of the literature the students are likely to encounter after their literacy training would be in the standard form does not appear to make much difference.

The reasons behind these responses to the standard varieties are not too difficult to find. A significant factor is the attitude of the adult literacy instructors themselves, who are largely natives of the areas in question. From what one gathers in the course of interviewing them, they are not very enthusiastic about the standard varieties, which they see in the context of language politics as part of the attempt of the 'other' sections to dominate them. They are able to undermine the standard forms so readily because the general apathy towards vernacular literacy makes the monitoring of the linguistic aspects of adult literacy programmes certainly not a top priority for those who are supposed to be responsible.

5. GENERAL CONCLUSIONS

It might be of value to test both the explicit recommendations and the ideological orientation behind the Unesco (1953) report against more than four decades of experience in these African nations. Although it has been notoriously difficult either to establish or to refute the promised educational benefits of mother-tongue education by carefully controlled experimentation, there is something to be learnt from a somewhat less rigorous comparison of case studies such as we have here. We will examine these African experiences with respect to (*a*) the interpretation of the term 'mother tongue'; (*b*) the complex pattern of cultural and economic motivations; (*c*) the effect of demonstrated success as a means of persuasion; (*d*) problems of language standardization; and (*e*) hopeful signs.

5.1. *The Notion 'Mother Tongue'*

The 1953 report was very explicit on the definition of 'mother tongue' (see the discussion in Chapter 1 above). It was 'the language which a person acquires in early years and which normally becomes his natural instrument of thought and communication' (Unesco 1953: 46). However, in two of the four countries treated in detail (Kenya, Tanzania, the CAR, and Nigeria), the 'vernacular' in 'vernacular language education' is not necessarily the 'mother tongue' of the learners at all, but rather the national language. In Tanzania, the 'vernacular language' in question is Kiswahili, and in the CAR, it is Sango. Both nations have the advantage of a *double overlapping diglossia* (Fasold 1984: 44) sociolinguistic context, in which there is a single indigenous language between the imported European language and a number of local languages. In Kenya and Nigeria, there are three or four languages vying for this middle position. In Tanzania and the CAR, it is uncontroversial that, if there is to be any vernacular literacy at all, it will be in the national language. In Kenya and Nigeria, the vernaculars involved are more likely to be mother tongues in accord with the Unesco definition. Even in Nigeria, the language used might be the 'language of the immediate community' even if it is not the 'mother tongue'. It is also the case that a somewhat greater amount of literacy effort has been expended on the four major languages, Hausa, Igbo, Yoruba, and Edo.

Of course, the report considered the use of a lingua franca (such as Kiswahili or Sango) as the vehicle of vernacular literacy. But the committee seemed a bit sceptical of its use in initial education, unless '*nearly all of the children* have some knowledge of the lingua franca as well as of their mother tongue *before they come to school*' (Unesco 1953: 54; emphasis added). This criterion may actually be met, particularly in Bangui in the CAR, where children are beginning to learn Sango as their first language, and may be met in parts of Tanzania, with respect to Kiswahili, as well. Nevertheless, this pairing-off of the four countries shows fairly convincingly that the selection of a 'vernacular' is motivated by political considerations far more than the psycholinguistic efficiency motivation touted by the 1953 Unesco committee.

5.2. *Cultural and Economic Motivations*

It appears that the Unesco committee was not fully aware of the complexity of motivations that might influence people to accept vernacular literacy or not, or even to want literacy skills. Table 7.5 shows that there is a sharp difference between respondents in Kenya and Tanzania in what they wish to learn next. A large majority of Kenyans (over 90 per cent) said that they wanted language, calculating, or literacy skills; more than two-thirds of the Tanzanians, by contrast, wanted to obtain functional or general and political skills. This difference seems partially attributable to the differences in the economies of the two countries at the time. Skills with language and numbers would serve people in the Kenyan market capitalist economy, whilst, in Tanzania, issues of economic survival would lead people to want basic production skills. In cities in the CAR, access to employment is not given by literacy in Sango. Many jobs that are available do not require literacy at all, and civil service jobs require competence in spoken and written *French*, along with oral ability in Sango. Furthermore, there

is no need for written media in traditional Central African modes of communication, hence reading materials in Sango are scarce. These economic and cultural
considerations, not surprisingly, influence people to value literacy only to the
extent that they expect it will conform to and enhance life as they know it.

As for the middle classes and decision-makers, our overview of the CAR and
Nigeria makes it clear that, for many, there is little motivation to promote vernacular literacy when their own success has come as a result of acquiring literacy
in the imported European language. Add to this the concern that the necessity
for choosing among the multiplicity of languages in these countries—since not
all languages can be supported as vehicles of literacy—would tend to threaten
national unity, and the motivation for the national leadership to back vernacular
literacy is further eroded. This concern is particularly acute in Nigeria, Kenya, and
Cameroon, where the softening effect of a single accepted indigenous national
language is absent.

Despite the fact that English and French have been imported, the statuses and
functions they acquired were not swept away with independence. In the CAR,
the conceptual association is between writing and French, not between writing
and Sango, as we have seen. Similarly, in Nigeria, a strong association has been
established between literacy and English. In fact, even those Nigerians who have
been convinced of the value of vernacular language literacy see it more as an
expression of patriotism than for its educational value. It may be that attitudes
like these can contribute to an explanation for some of the limited success of the
literacy efforts that exist. At least in Kenya, a substantial drop-out rate meant
that the proportion of those enrolled in vernacular literacy programmes who
actually became literate was low. In the CAR, school attendance has risen,
especially since the time of the Unesco declaration, but primary-school attendance still does not guarantee lasting literacy; the social role of literacy in the
society does not inspire its retention. For many Central Africans, it seems that
literacy is not a skill that it would be useful to have.

5.3. *Successful Demonstrations as a Means of Persuasion*

Although the 1951 Unesco committee seemed sure that speakers from vernacular-
language speaking communities would be persuaded by demonstrations of
success in the acquisition of literacy when vernacular languages are used, the
experience in these African nations has not produced this result, at least not
consistently. Even when successful demonstrations are achieved, persuasion
does not always follow. Table 7.1 seems to show that, in Tanzania, the literacy
rate steadily increased between 1975 and 1986, with a corresponding reduction
in enrolment, apparently due to a reduction of need. However, it seems to us that
this apparent demonstration of success may not be all that it appears to be. It
may be that some test results come from people who have completed years of

schooling and are not the products of literacy classes, and that literacy classes may be set up for brief periods just before the national tests. Furthermore, the knowledge tested, although it was certainly available in the literacy materials, was also so commonplace in many cases that it is far from clear that a correct answer on the test had anything to do with what was learnt in the programme.

Even when the demonstrations seem valid, the persuasive effect does not always follow. A few experimental classes in Sango were initiated in the late 1970s but the results had no impact on the course of education in the CAR. Several successful demonstration projects, as we have shown, were conducted in Nigeria. In particular, the SYYP, carried out in the early 1970s, produced data that strongly supported claims of success. However, the results did not inspire the initiation of vernacular literacy programmes even in Oyo State, the site of the SYYP, let alone elsewhere. Given what we have learnt from the study of the four African nations, and the complexity of the economic, cultural, and political motivations surrounding vernacular literacy, perhaps this outcome is less surprising than it might have been forty years ago.

5.4. *Standardization*

It is generally accepted that a prerequisite for the use of a vernacular language in literacy is a certain level of standardization. Most often, the orthography is made standard, as are spelling rules, and one variety of the vernacular is selected to serve as the model for the standard language, followed by certain adjustments to some of its linguistic features. In fact, this has happened, at least for Sango in the CAR, and for Hausa and Igbo in Nigeria. The effectiveness of the standardization efforts, however, has not been complete. The official orthography that has been established for Sango is not insisted upon, and is not likely to spread in the immediate future. In fact, there are various orthographies available and the majority of those who write in Sango use one variety of religious spelling. A standard dialect has not been established effectively and the existing varieties of Sango are perceived as major problems by users of the written language. In Nigeria, although the Kano variety of Hausa is the acknowledged standard form, the reality is that Sokoto Hausa (Sakwatanci) is regarded in its own areas as a truer standard. It is seen as 'classical' because of its long tradition of having been written in the Ajami script and its wealth of loanwords from Arabic. The practical effect of this conflict in standards, though, seems to be minimal. In the case of Igbo, the official orthography allows for only twenty-eight consonants. In adult literacy programmes in the Northern Igbo area, students prefer to be taught using an orthography based on their local speech forms which have as many as forty to sixty consonant phonemes. Not only does the official orthography seem inadequate to them; they see it in a political light as an attempt by Igbo speakers from other regions to dominate them.

5.5. *Hopeful Signs*

In spite of the obstacles to vernacular literacy raised by the complexity of atti-tudes and motivations that were at best only dimly seen in 1953, there are certain facts in the overview of the four African nations that would be seen as encouraging by the Unesco committee. It is likely that the advances in literacy claimed by the programmes in Kenya and Tanzania are a bit overstated, but, on the other hand, it would be wrong to say that there has been no progress at all. It is no doubt true that many Kenyans and Tanzanians have learned to read and write through the media of indigenous African languages; perhaps some of them would not be literate at all if literacy had been available only in English.

There have been several examples of successful vernacular literacy programmes in Nigeria. In spite of the fact that they have been disappointing in their ability to inspire emulation, again, they brought literacy to their participants, with some going on to earn graduate degrees. Something similar can be said about Sango literacy in the CAR. There is some reading and writing conducted in Sango, even if literacy is fundamentally seen as connected to French. In Cameroon, too, some efforts continue at instituting programmes in vernacular literacy.

Perhaps the brightest sign of all is the promotion of Sango by the national radio in the CAR. It has a rather successful internal language policy in agree-ment with the guidelines established by the higher political authorities. If broad-cast media are destined to replace some of the functions of print-media literacy, and people learn to 'read television' and radio (Chapter 1), perhaps opportunities for a new 'vernacular literacy' will arise that the 1953 Unesco committee could not have foreseen.

8

Tradition, Trial, and Error: Standard and Vernacular Literacy in China, Hong Kong, Singapore, and Malaysia

ANNA KWAN-TERRY and K. K. LUKE

with contributions and help from Kamsiah Abdullah, Chia Shih Yar, J. Gibbons, Mary Li, Julia L. K. Seoh, S. C. Teo, S. P. Thinnappan, and P. Livesey

I. INTRODUCTION

Unity and diversity in time and space, in the meaning but perhaps even more so in the value and significance of literacy, both fascinate and promise to reward close study. In this chapter we attempt just such a study, if only in a small way. We restrict ourselves to East and South-East Asia, and within that region we make special reference only to those areas with which we are most familiar—that is, China, Hong Kong, Singapore, and Malaysia.

By 'tradition' in the title we mean to highlight one of the main themes of the chapter—namely, that we are consciously examining settings in which an element of tradition looms large. So large, in fact, that no discussion of education and literacy would make good sense without close reference to it. Thus the 'Great Tradition' of Chinese culture is partly manifested in the age-old practices of teaching, learning, and examination, all of which provide a backdrop to contemporary attempts at spreading literacy amongst the masses. By 'trial and error', we allude to officially sponsored initiatives in recent times in education and literacy, to changes and revisions, to realizations and new understanding.

A comparison of Malaysia, Singapore, and Hong Kong will allow us to address the question of how, in the context of standard and vernacular literacy and against the background of tradition, different past British colonies in this part of the world have coped with the British legacy, on the one hand, and with the new demands and challenges placed on them by national construction and modernization.

An added interest lies in the ways in which terms like 'national language', 'vernacular', and 'mother tongue' are defined and understood in these settings in the

Special thanks are due to Anthea Fraser Gupta for making available to us materials relevant to the subject, including her own as yet unpublished materials.

context of language planning and language education, as well as the use of less familiar designations like 'symbolic mother tongue' and 'provincial languages'.

For the reasons mentioned, the selection of situations here will, we believe, offer interesting opportunities for multiple comparisons and contrasts. We proceed along a country-by-country pathway because this allows us to set out first of all the most salient features in a national context and to establish certain crucial facts in each setting. As we do this, comments and cross references are made whenever appropriate. A discussion of similarities and contrasts is offered in the final section.

2. THE 'GREAT TRADITION' AND ITS MODERN ADAPTATION IN CHINA

2.1. *Literacy Past and Present*

Literacy as it is understood in China today differs in some ways from literacy as it was practised during a long period of time before the twentieth century. Traditionally, a literate person was first and foremost a classical scholar. The ability to read and write was associated with knowledge of the Confucian canon. It can even be said that reading and writing were regarded not primarily as an end in themselves, but as an instrument for, and a by-product of, studying classical texts.

Various terms have been used in English language books and articles written on the subject of public examinations and the civil service in traditional China: the literati, the gentry, the scholar-officials, the Mandarins. As terms intended for the group of *shi* or *shi-ren* in traditional Chinese society, each of the terms captures some of the senses and connotations of the Chinese term but at the same time misses other senses and connotations. No one term is therefore superior to all the others. Our own preference is for 'scholar-officials' because its meaning seems fairly transparent, and it does not have the social and cultural associations implied in 'the literati' or 'the gentry', which are foreign to the original word. The hyphenation in 'scholar-official' accurately expresses the close ties between the roles of scholar and government official in traditional China. 'Mandarin' is a neat term in so far as it doubles up as the label for the social group and the name of their language (the language of officialdom). Unfortunately it has acquired through many years of usage certain racial associations. For these reasons the term 'scholar-official' is used throughout this discussion, with the exception that 'the literati' is used occasionally in order to underscore the link between the *shi-ren*s and literacy.

The significance of literacy in traditional China was twofold. On the one hand, learning the classics was considered important for moral reasons. Through learning the wisdom of the sages one learns how to behave properly in the world. Hence the Confucian adage *zhi-shu shi-li* ('Study the classics; understand propriety'). On the other hand, there was always a pragmatic goal in learning to read and write: the pursuit of a career in the civil service. Literacy was the defining characteristic, and the exclusive property, of the class of scholar-officials (*shi* or *shi-ren*), a small but powerful élite who served the imperial court and helped rule the country. The four occupational groups recognized in traditional Chinese society—*shi* (scholar-officials), *nong* (peasants), *gong* (workers), and *shang* (merchants)—were ranked in that order on a social status scale, with the scholar-officials taking pride of place. With very few exceptions (of hereditary rights or appointments obtained through 'donations'), the only way to become a government official was to excel in the civil service examinations. And to excel in the examinations one had to learn the classics thoroughly. Years of hard work were put into practising the skills of reading and writing in the hope that in return one would succeed in the examinations and be appointed to the office of a *guan* (mandarin). This would be the ultimate honour and reward.[1] As a result, learning (*du-shu*, literally 'reading books') was greatly valued and respected. A well-known poem tells of how books bring fame and fortune—even beautiful girls!—and how any young man with an ambition was well advised to 'face the window and read [the classics]' (Miyazaki 1976: 17).

> To enrich your family, no need to buy good land;
> Books hold a thousand measures of grain.
> For an easy life, no need to build a mansion:
> In books are found houses of gold.
> Going out, be not vexed at absence of followers:
> In books, carriages and horses form a crowd.
> Marrying, be not vexed by lack of a good go-between;
> In books there are girls with faces of jade.
> A boy who wants to become a somebody
> Devotes himself to the classics, faces the window, and reads.

In spite of periodic variations and occasional shifts in emphasis, the essential character and substance of the civil service examinations had remained little changed throughout its 1,300 years of history, from their inception in the Sui Dynasty (581–618) until their abolition in 1906.[2] The aim of the examinations was to identify the most capable men of letters—or, to honour the Chinese writing system, 'men of characters'—for appointment to positions of authority at various levels of the government machinery; in other words, 'to employ the able and promote the worthy' (Purcell 1936: 15). The examinations were held at various

---

[1] 'In traditional China, government service was by far the most honourable and, in every sense, the most worthwhile occupation; and the [civil service] examinations played a large part in determining the composition of the elite, by moulding as well as selecting the men who operated the political system and dominated the society' (Miyazaki 1976: translator's introduction, p. 7).

[2] Purcell (1936) gives a good account of the history of the civil service examinations. Miyazaki (1976) explores their character and practice.

levels, and contained mainly essay-writing tasks in which the candidates were asked to demonstrate their familiarity with the prescribed texts and their ability to imitate their structures and styles.

Literacy in traditional China was thus perceived as a way of training one's moral character and, in addition to that—perhaps as a result of that—as a stepping stone for joining the class of scholar-officials. In the twentieth century, however, literacy, and for that matter education, has acquired rather different associations. The concepts of education and literacy have become virtually synonymous with mass education and mass literacy. Learning the Chinese characters is no longer directed towards reading Confucius and Mencius. Reading and writing have become something of an end in themselves; and education, a citizen's right.

However, in spite of the differences in the meaning and significance of literacy in traditional and modern China, two important similarities remain. Firstly, the civil service continues to be the most sought-after career, dominated by the intellectuals. The only difference, as far as the People's Republic is concerned, is that the link between scholars and officials is now mediated through the Communist Party. Millions have become literate in the last forty years, but only a handful have made it into the Party, and from there into public service. In more ways than one, the cadre (*ganbu*) is the modern People's Republic of China (PRC) equivalent of the traditional mandarin (*guan*). Mao Zedong, Deng Xiaoping, and most of the well-known political leaders of the People's Republic of China (PRC) are intellectuals. Mao was famous for his poems and songs written in the classical *Wenyan* style. General Chen Yi was known for his talents in, and love for, traditional forms of art. To this day, it is customary for political leaders to give their blessing to new projects and ventures by writing congratulatory remarks in traditional calligraphy.

A second feature of similarity is that literacy now, as before, is strongly associated with moral—and often moralistic—imperatives. Learning to become literate is inextricably tied up with learning the rules of correct social behaviour. For example, the view has been expressed in official publications that 'a positive attitude towards birth control'[3] cannot be 'successfully instilled' into the minds of uncultivated peasants until they become literate: 'family planning has met more resistance in rural areas where illiterate people are concentrated than in urban areas. An intellectual young couple seems to have one child voluntarily, while uncultivated parents are inclined to be reluctant' (Li Haibo 1989). The equation here between literacy and sensible, correct behaviour is quite remarkable. In the same vein, literacy campaigns have been described as 'a war against ignorance and backwardness' (ibid. 4). The Chinese word for illiteracy is *wen-meng*, literally 'text-blind'. A non-literate person is then someone who is 'blind' to a text,

[3] It was reported (*Beijing Review* 1990a) that Jianyang county of Fujian Province had been awarded the title 'An Advanced County in Implementing the Nation's Family Planning Programme' for its success in eliminating illiteracy, and instilling 'a positive attitude towards birth control'.

which in one sense is perhaps a fair description. But the meaning of the word goes much further than that. It has all the negative connotations of the word *illiterate* in English, and more. The Chinese word suggests limitations in comprehension and understanding (if not intelligence), and, by being likened to the loss of sight, it signals an inability perhaps not only to see, but to see reason.

2.2. *Vernacular Literacy, 1911–1949*

By far the most significant event culturally and intellectually in modern China was the May Fourth Movement. Led by a group of progressive staff and students of Peking University, thousands of college students gathered at Tiananmen Square on 4 May 1919, to protest against Japan's annexation of Shandong by means of the Versailles treaty. The political protest soon took a cultural and linguistic turn. Calls were made for reforms aimed at revitalizing the country and making it fit to survive in the modern world.[4] Part of this massive, nationwide campaign was called the Vernacular Language Movement, or 'Plain Language Campaign' (*Baihua-wen Yundong*), a major initiative to reform the written language in anticipation of mass literacy. Precursors of language reform went back many years before 1919, but it was in the context of May Fourth that literacy in the vernacular was first explicitly and effectively articulated. The aim of the Vernacular Language Movement was to replace Wenyan, the classical literary language, with Baihua, the written vernacular. According to the arguments advanced in favour of the vernacular, Baihua was 'the language of the man on the street', and Wenyan the language of the élite. In line with the nationalistic and romantic spirit of the period, it was advocated to replace the 'dead' classical language with one that was 'alive' and belonged to the ordinary people.

In spite of its rhetoric, however, the Vernacular Language Movement was in a sense an argument about literary styles. While it is true that the written vernacular is vastly better suited as a vehicle for mass education and mass literacy, Baihua, which according to the reformers has a respectable history stretching all the way back to at least the Tang (618–907) and Song (960–1279) Dynasties (see Norman 1988: 111–12), had never really been 'the language of the people'. If anything it was an alternative style of writing for unofficial and non-serious purposes (e.g. popular literature). However simple it might have looked in comparison with Wenyan, Baihua was itself a literary language, and as such was available only to the literate élite.

The challenge to the centrality and sole legitimacy of the classical style did cause considerable controversy, with some conservatives making a desperate attempt to preserve the status quo, but to no avail. In the end it did not take long for Baihua to come out as the clear winner. In a series of directives in the 1920s

---

[4] For an account of the *Baihua-wen Yundong* and the rise and development of modern standard Chinese, see Norman (1988: ch. 6). See also Spence (1990: 310–18) for an account of the May Fourth Movement.

and 1930s, the educational authorities legitimized the vernacular style and promoted its use in education. Meanwhile many literary journals came into being
with scholars and writers producing 'New Literature' in the vernacular. With
Wenyan rapidly receding into the background, being no longer the sole criterion
for literacy, Baihua was looked upon as the language of the modern nation and
the language of the masses. The meaning and significance of 'literacy' have as
a result of the Vernacular Language Movement undergone a fundamental change
in character, the link with the classical tradition permanently severed.

But although the movement was such a success, it is far from the case that, as
a result of the adoption of the vernacular style, anyone can now put down their
thoughts on paper in the same way that they would express them in colloquial
speech. The slogan *wo shou xie wo kou*, literally 'my hand writes my mouth'
(i.e. 'write as you speak'), remains as much a goal in the far distance as it was
when it was first propounded in the nineteenth century. For one thing, the written language did not transform itself overnight from a 'classical style' to a mutually exclusive 'vernacular style'. Many essays written in the 1920s in support of
the vernacular movement were themselves written in the classical style, or else
contained a significant classical element. Even today, some seventy-five years
after the movement, it is quite common to find classical words and phrases in
many forms of writing. 'Modern *Baihua* still contains a relatively strong *Wenyan*
element; attempts to purge the modern written language of its literary components
have not been entirely successful; although at the present time *Wenyan* influence
on *Baihua* seems to be gradually diminishing, current *Baihua* is still by no means
identical to the spoken standard' (Norman 1988: 136). In general, the more formal
the situation, the greater the classical presence. This is further complicated by
the fact that important differences exist in the norms prevalent in the PRC
and Taiwan, and to some extent Hong Kong. On the whole, writing in the PRC
tends to be based more closely on speech (Putonghua), but not so in Taiwan and
Hong Kong, where tradition still looms large. This is hardly surprising given the
length of time (over 2,000 years) during which Wenyan dominated every aspect
of public life, and the sheer volume of literature written in it. The literary tradition is there, and it cannot simply be wished away.

Another reason why nothing like 'full-fledged vernacularization' has come
about—in so far as this still remains a goal—is the immense diversity in speech.
Across the country numerous dialects and sub-dialects are spoken, not all mutually intelligible. From the point of view of helping to unite a vast country, there
is a certain logic in the use of a logographic script. A non-phonetic script is in
fact better suited than a phonetic one in facilitating inter-provincial communication. Precisely because it is non-phonetic, it can have an existence independent
of the phonetic systems of the individual dialects. If the written vernacular is to
serve its function of inter-provincial communication well, then like Wenyan it
too must rely on the logographic script and remain to some extent pan-dialectal.
In the past this was not a problem as the classical style was not based on any

one particular spoken variety. But when the principle of a written vernacular was adopted it became painfully apparent that a variety of spoken Chinese would have to be selected to provide the basis for the written language. Norman (1988: 184) recognizes three major dialect groups (Northern, Central, and Southern) and eleven subdivisions (Northern Mandarin, North-West Mandarin, Southern Mandarin, South-West Mandarin, Wu, Min, Kejia, Yue, Huizhou, Xiang, Gan). In terms of the linguistic systems most of the subdivisions (except the four kinds of Mandarin) are mutually unintelligible and sufficiently diverse to be regarded as different languages (of the same family). Yet further differences and variation are found within each subdivision. For example, within the Min subdivision, Northern Min and Southern Min are considerably different. Fujian, where numerous Min dialects are spoken, is known as 'the province of a hundred dialects' (Moser 1985: 165). And the dialect of Amoy (Xiamen), a variety of Southern Min, is said to be unintelligible to anyone living more than a hundred miles away in any direction (Ramsey 1987: 21–2). Clearly, whichever variety was chosen, not everyone would speak it as their mother tongue. The opposition between Wenyan as the language of the élite and Baihua as the language of the people may well have an intuitive appeal, even some validity, but when one actually gets down to defining what the vernacular is, it soon becomes clear that there is no real alternative to defining 'the people's language' in terms of *some* people's language. One possible solution might have been to devise an artificial variety that is in principle more or less equidistant from the major dialect groups, and something along these lines has been attempted (e.g. Chao Yuen-ren's unified reading pronunciation). But nothing much came of it because of its impracticalities (no one could speak or teach it). Indeed even more radical possibilities have been suggested, e.g. give up the Chinese languages altogether and replace all with Esperanto. But no such solution could get off the ground.

From the very beginning of the Republican era, efforts were made to standardize a common tongue for the nation as a whole, and to use it as a vehicle for mass literacy. A Conference on Unification of Pronunciation was held as early as 1913. Unfortunately this only led to bitter arguments between the delegates from the North and the South, with the latter finally walking out of the conference. Thereupon the other participants adopted a Mandarin-based (northern) pronunciation as the national standard. But because of the difficulty of the task and the strife between the north and the south, for many years after the conference little progress had actually been made in teaching the standard in the schools. It took almost twenty years before another major step was taken in that direction. A 'Vocabulary for Everyday Use' (*Guoyin Zhangyong Zihui*) was published by the National Language Unification Commission in 1932, providing an authoritative manual of reference.[5]

---

[5] See Ramsey (1987: 3–18) for an account of early efforts at language standardization in modern China. Jernudd (1986) is a special issue of the *International Journal of the Sociology of Language* devoted to Chinese language planning.

2.3. *Language Reform and Literacy Campaigns since 1949*

The PRC (People's Republic of China) government has attached great importance, at least in principle, to education and literacy.[6] Mao's vision of a new
China was one in which workers and peasants could contribute fully to building
a nation with a new culture. As a step in that direction, the 'cultural level' of
the masses must first be raised. In a country where 80 per cent of the population
were hardly able to read or write, one of the first tasks for the new government
was to provide universal education.[7]

The trend for language reform and vernacularization was firmly in place by
1949. When the Communist Party took over, it carried forward some of the projects already in progress. It was strongly committed to promoting a national
spoken standard, tackling the problem of illiteracy, and working towards the
goal of universal education. But in addition to these well-established objectives,
new or at least renewed initiatives were introduced, which stemmed from the
assumption that there was something fundamentally wrong about the Chinese
language itself, and that it needed an extensive overhaul before it could fulfil the
demands made on it by a new nation with a great deal of catching up to do. Thus
the PRC government, in a determined attempt to modernize and strengthen the
nation, and with a great sense of urgency brought to bear on the task, saw language reform, perhaps more than ever before, as a key to success for its programme of national construction. The complexity and difficulty of the traditional
writing system was singled out as the greatest hindrance to universal education
and mass literacy. To this end, a Committee for Research on Language Reform
was established in 1951 'to make a selection of the commonly used characters
and simplified characters, and for the adoption of a phonetic system, as a preparatory step for developing the literacy campaign among workers and peasants'
(NCNA 1951).

'Language reform' is not strictly speaking an accurate rendering of the original Chinese term *wenzi gaige*, which literally means 'script reform' (DeFrancis
1984: 223; see also DeFrancis 1950). Indeed of the four main aspects of China's
programme for language reform, three address the written language. The four
aspects are: (1) reduction and simplification of Chinese characters; (2) popularization of Putonghua; (3) introduction of Hanyu Pinyin (Alphabetization); and
(4) vernacularization (see Livesey 1986).

Reduction and Simplification of Chinese Characters
Reduction concerns the total number of characters, and simplification the number
of strokes to each character (i.e. its actual shape). Reduction amounts to cutting

---

[6] This section deals mainly with the PRC. For references on the situation in Taiwan, see Tse
(1986).
[7] In what was to become the first Constitution of the PRC, the country was promised universal
education: 'In order to meet the widespread need of revolutionary work and national construction
work, universal education shall be carried out . . .' (Common Program of the Chinese People's
Political Consultative Conference (Sept. 1949), Article 47).

down on multiple graphs for the same word. Simplification is based largely on existing conventions. Thus, the character for 'a few' (幾), whose original form has twelve strokes, has for hundreds of years had an alternative, simplified, rendering in two strokes (几). This latter character has become to some extent conventionalized through constant use. This simplified form is then adopted as the standard, replacing the original character, and listed in dictionaries. Such conventions are sometimes extended to whole sets of graphs containing that graph as a component part. Thus, the characters for 'opportunity' (機) and 'hunger' (饑), both of which contain 'a few' (幾) as a phonetic (that part of the character which gives some indication of the sound of the word) are now rendered as (机) and (饥). This particular extension, and others like it, have produced simplifications that most have found acceptable. But occasionally the concern to reduce the number of strokes gets on top of good sense. The result is radical simplifications not acceptable to the majority. Thus, while the character 'not' (沒) occurs frequently in texts and is one of the best-known characters, simplifying it to (殳) results in a form whose relationship to the original is not obvious to most people, and therefore unacceptable to them.

The first scheme was announced in 1956. It consisted of 515 simplified graphs and 54 radicals. The scheme was extended in 1964 to include another 1,754 characters. Most of these have been accepted within the country. A second scheme came out in 1977, consisting of 853 simplified characters, but this time the scheme was judged by most people as having gone too far. Neither scheme is adopted, officially or otherwise, in Taiwan or Hong Kong. Both are accepted in Singapore, through government decree. As for overseas Chinese communities, the traditional characters are still most commonly used, but the simplified characters have a following particularly amongst those who are sympathetic to the PRC government.

Popularization of Putonghua

As mentioned earlier, the aim since the 1910s has been to standardize and promote a 'common tongue'. Prior to 1949, the standard was known as *Guoyu*, 'National Speech', and it has continued to be referred to by this name in Taiwan and Hong Kong up to the present. In mainland China, however, the designation of the standard has since the 1950s been changed to 'Common Speech' (*Putonghua*), perhaps to underscore the ideology of 'people power' and equality amongst the ethnic groups. For all practical purposes Guoyu and Putonghua are much the same thing. In fact, the speech of educated speakers in Beijing and in Taipei are not only mutually intelligible, but highly similar.

Introduction of Alphabetization

Using roman letters to represent Chinese speech goes back at least to the seventeenth century, when missionaries used phonetic scripts of their own making for teaching and learning Chinese and to help in their work. Full alphabetization was not seriously pursued until the 1930s when a movement called Latinxua, which originated in the USSR, was adopted and promoted mostly by members of the Chinese Communist Party. It did not gain widespread support, although some prominent figures such as the writer Lu Xun were sympathetic to it (see Norman 1988: 257–63). Mao himself also expressed some sympathy. He said in 1951: 'The written language of our country must be reformed and oriented to the use of a phonetic alphabet as is common with the world's other written languages' (quoted in Wen Hua 1973).

Nevertheless, experience has shown that neither Latinxua itself nor any other form of romanization can gain much support, or have much chance of success, in spite of occasional rhetoric about radical reforms. Full alphabetization has always had a (small) following. For example, some articles were published in 1973 which called for the full alphabetization of the language: 'While engaging in the cause of socialist revolution and construction, the masses are eager to master the written language as quickly as possible so as to study Marxism-Leninism-Maozedong thought and obtain cultural and scientific knowledge. But the complicated and difficult characters are an obstacle to their efforts. Hence the necessity to reform the written language' (Wen Hua 1973, in Hu and Seifman 1976: 291). The author then goes on to describe the various steps necessary to bring about full alphabetization. According to this view, the other aspects of language reform—character reduction and simplification and the teaching of Putonghua—are essentially only means towards an end, the end being the replacement of the Chinese characters (in some distant future) by the phonetic system. The advantages of a roman script like Pinyin may at first seem obvious. It can be learned significantly faster and much more easily than the traditional logographic script. And if Putonghua is made the language of education of the masses everywhere in China, then all speakers ought to be able to learn to read and write in Pinyin. The disadvantages of Chinese characters may seem equally apparent. Not only are they harder to learn, they are also harder to retain and recall from memory. Even well-educated people would from time to time make mistakes in writing the characters. And it is not uncommon for people who are out of practice temporarily to forget the correct combination of strokes necessary to render particular characters. And yet, in spite of these advantages of roman letters over the traditional characters, many Chinese people have yet to be convinced that abandoning the age-old writing system is either necessary or desirable. For one thing, the traditional association between mastering the logographic script and being an educated person is exceedingly strong. To be an educated and a cultured person is to know the characters. For many people a roman script is so obviously 'foreign' in appearance as to make it an unacceptable candidate for a symbol of learning. But there are real problems too in replacing the traditional script. Whole libraries and archives are filled with books and manuscripts written in characters, but very little is available in Pinyin. There is, therefore, little motivation to learn romanization as a substitute for the characters. No change is likely to be even conceivable unless a lot more good writing is available in Pinyin, and a lot more of the books written in the old script in the last 2,000 years are reprinted in the new roman script. This reprinting is itself an enormous undertaking. But since most of the texts were written in Wenyan, the classical language, they would first have to be translated into modern Chinese before they could be transcribed, which is an even more daunting task. It is true that not all classical texts need be translated into the modern language, and not every person wants or cares to study them. Still, because of the central place this literature occupies in Chinese history and culture, and because of the presence of classical elements in the modern language, a substantial proportion may need to undergo such an expensive and time-consuming process.

On balance, it now appears that the shortcomings of the logographic script are outweighed by its advantages. Chinese characters have been in use for centuries and have proved to be a successful means of inter-dialectal and inter-provincial communication. This is so precisely because the traditional writing system is non-phonetic. The same character can be read aloud in different ways depending on the sound system of one's dialect. To spell a word in Pinyin, however, one will need not only to learn Putonghua, but also to have native-like command of its sound system, on which Pinyin is based. For example, the Mandarin syllables *si* (whose initial consonant is a dental fricative), *shi* (a retroflex fricative), and *xi* (a palatal fricative) would all be rendered as *si* by a speaker whose first language is Cantonese. He makes no distinction between these three fricatives: they are all alveolar in his dialect. On top of numerous differences in pronunciation there are many morphological and syntactic differences. Thus, the roman script does not offer a real alternative to the characters, since half of the country does not speak Mandarin as a first language. In terms of the north–south divide, the southern half of the country is non-Mandarin speaking. In terms of actual numbers, the non-Mandarin speaking area makes up about one-third of the total population. And since inter-dialectal and inter-provincial communication provides the basis for national unity, it should come as no surprise that early fervour for complete alphabetization was short-lived.

Vernacularization of the Written Language

This fourth aspect should perhaps be described as 'further vernacularization', since, as we have seen, vernacularization, or at least the first phase of the process, began some seventy-five years ago. The current concern is to move the norms of the written language further in the direction of colloquial speech. At the moment, a plainer style based more closely on Putonghua is found in the PRC, but a greater classical element is retained in writing in Taiwan and Hong Kong.

As we said, the language-reform measures are carried out in the service of universal education, and to facilitate mass literacy. The PRC government has often prided itself, and not without justification, on the achievements made in literacy.

According to official figures, the country's literacy rate has improved dramatically over the last forty years: 'In the last four decades, China has wiped out illiteracy for some 165 million people, reducing the 80 per cent illiteracy rate of the early post-liberation years to a current level [as at 1990] of 20.6 per cent' (*Beijing Review* 1990: 18).

'Literacy, as defined by the Chinese Communist Party Central Committee (and State Council) in 1956, required peasants to be able to recognize some 1,500 Chinese characters, as well as to perform simple calculations on an abacus, write informal notes, keep account books, and read "easy to understand popular newspapers and journals"'. Officially, for 12-year-olds and above, knowledge of 1,500 characters constitutes literacy. Anyone in command of between 500 and 1,500 characters is classified as 'semi-literate', while anyone who knows fewer than 500 characters is deemed illiterate (Woodside 1992: 23–4).

Initial euphoria in the early days of the PRC manifested itself in more ways than one, and literacy work was one of them. Official announcements then would have people believe that it was only a matter of a few years before illiteracy was completely eradicated. In a directive issued in 1956, the view was expressed that universal literacy could be achieved in five to seven years' time, i.e. by 1963 at the latest. 'All places are required to eliminate illiteracy basically in 5 or 7 years' time in accordance with their conditions' ('Decision of the Chinese Communist Party Central Committee and State Council concerning the elimination of illiteracy', NCNA, Beijing, 30 Mar. 1956).[8] As it turned out, the resilience of the problem was seriously underestimated. The size of the population means that even the slightest percentage growth results in huge numbers, so that, as some people become literate, others in need of education take their places. The minority nationalities and the countryside were constantly referred to as areas where literacy work was particularly arduous. Thus, by 1980, in spite of the considerable progress made, 220 million remained illiterate, 'of which 210 million are in the countryside, and 70 per cent of the total are women' (*Beijing Review* 1989: 4). In 1990, the International Year of Literacy, yet another anti-illiteracy campaign was launched 'to eliminate illiteracy among the 71 million youth and adults between the age of 15–40 and eliminate illiteracy and semi-illiteracy among people 41 or older by 2000' (*Beijing Review* 1989: 18). A report in the same year based on the Population Census of 1990 suggests that the overall illiteracy rate has come down again since 1980, although the absolute numbers are still forbidding— 180 million (*Beijing Review* 1990b: 18). Whether this latest target can be met remains to be seen, although previous experience should make one sober about the scale and difficulty of the task.

Since the 1980s the PRC government has been strongly emphasizing economic development and market reforms. As a result, literacy is even more than before portrayed in official documents in terms of its contribution to modernization and

---

[8] Translated and reproduced in Hu and Seifman (1976: 74–7).

economic progress. At a personal level, literacy programmes are increasingly presented as a key to securing financial gains for the individual. In an article entitled 'The anti-illiteracy campaign goes on', it is said that 'the need to become literate in order to get rich is now recognized by the majority of Chinese farmers and is the most remarkable feature of the current campaign to eliminate illiteracy' (*Beijing Review* 1990a: 20). In the same article, the story is told of how Farmer Hu at the age of 52 learned to read 600 characters and as a result learned how to grow plums and 'earned about 10,000 yuan' (ibid.).

The question is: even if Farmer Hu did learn to grow plums through the 600 characters and not through some other sources of knowledge, how many Farmer Hus can there be? Learning to become literate in the Chinese script is no mean task. It takes time, and it takes time away from production. Short of coercion, people (particularly in the rural areas) have to be convinced of the worth—and under the present circumstances the economic worth—of the time and effort invested in the enterprise. While Farmer Hu may well be very sensible, evidence is yet to be found to suggest that many farmers follow his example. They may well be persuaded to work longer hours or take up part-time work endeavours to achieve a more immediate financial reward.

Will drop-out rates in schools increase as the present economic boom continues? Will more and more children in the rural areas be tempted to leave school early to capitalize on job opportunities created by the boom? Will more and more young people leave the country to find opportunities in the cities, perhaps at the expense of disrupting their education? Will urbanization itself bring a greater motivation for literacy, or not? Questions like these are intriguing and crucial to further literacy work throughout the country.

2.4. *Vernacular Literacy for Women, Rural Communities, and Minority Nationalities*

Three particular groups in society have been identified as having the lowest literacy rates, and therefore needing the most attention. They are: women, people in rural areas, and minority groups. All three groups are socially disadvantaged, but the last two are further disadvantaged as a result of their languages.

Women

Prejudice against women was pervasive in traditional China. The practice of foot-binding is but a particularly inglorious example of such discrimination. Not only were women given lower status in all aspects of social life; they were made economically dependent on men by being barred from education and public office, and by being denied all rights of inheritance. Literacy, the key to knowledge and self-esteem, was kept away from them. A widely held 'moral imperative' identified virtue in women with ignorance and mediocrity: 'The virtuous woman is one who is good at nothing.'

In spite of government incentives in this century to provide education for all regardless of gender, traditional attitudes die hard. Even now, sons are much more keenly sought than daughters. They also tend to be given the best opportunities, educational and otherwise. While it is true that basic literacy is now available to both boys and girls, nevertheless higher education, especially in the field of science and technology, is still felt to be the proper province of men. But, thanks to literacy and education, these old ideas are giving way to new ones. Attitudes do seem to be changing, and changing for the better.

Rural Communities

As a rule, education in rural areas is a much more difficult task than in the cities, at least from the point of view of human and other resources. It is no different in the case of China. In fact, such problems are if anything likely to be more pronounced in China because of the size of the country and the inaccessibility of mountainous areas. The list of problems gets longer when the rural community also happens to be in a non-Mandarin dialect region. Children who do not speak a Mandarin dialect as their 'mother tongue' have an extra hurdle to cross: they must first learn to speak Putonghua.

One of the biggest problems in a non-Mandarin-speaking rural area is that teachers cannot always be found who can speak and teach Mandarin. In some areas it is a lucky chance to find someone who can speak the provincial standard, which may be quite different from the local dialect, let alone a teacher who speaks the national standard. In non-Mandarin speaking urban areas—for example, Shanghai (Wu-speaking) and Guangzhou (Yue-speaking)—at least, suitable teachers are more readily available. As a result, it is not uncommon in the more remote and ill-equipped regions for a local variety of some dialect to be used initially as the teaching medium.

Between seven and nine major dialect groups are usually recognized in China. The biggest and most homogenous (relative to the other groups) is the Mandarin group. The other groups are smaller relative to Mandarin, but in terms of absolute numbers of speakers they run into millions (see Table 8.1).

Numerically about one-third of the country's (Han) population speak a dialect other than Mandarin. As is well known, these 'dialects' are mutually unintelligible and differ one from another greatly in their phonology, vocabulary, and syntax. Linguistically, they are more like separate languages, as French, Italian, and Spanish are separate languages. But there is a crucial difference: the Chinese 'languages' are called 'dialects' because for centuries they have had a special relationship through the writing system, which is by and large accessible from the different vantage-points of the individual dialects. Certainly, there are special dialectal features in the writing of different dialect regions, but these tend to be extensions built on the basis of the master set of common characters. Given the Chinese tradition, literacy *in* the vernaculars, as far as the Han dialects are concerned, is therefore something of a contradiction in terms. Paradoxically,

TABLE 8.1. *The major dialect groups and speakers*

Major dialect groups	Number of speakers (m.)
Mandarin	622
Yue (Cantonese)	55
Wu	85
Xiang	50
Gan	25
Minnan (Southern Min)	40
Minbei (Northern Min)	12
Huizhou (Wannan)	4
Hakka	40
TOTAL	933

Note: The estimates are based on statistics available in the early 1980s.

Source: Moser (1985: 4).

vernacular literacy can only come *after* standard literacy; and standard literacy is learned *through* the vernaculars. Once again, the key to this is the logographic, non-phonetic, nature of the script.

If one could conceive of a situation in which all the dialects had given way to a single spoken language, then of course it would be possible to adopt alphabetic writing in place of the age-old script. But then this is purely hypothetical. While radical views have been expressed according to which the dialects have only put up barriers to a unified spoken language and therefore hindered full alphabetization,[9] the considered view today is that the dialects are here to stay. Little is made of planning for their dissolution, and alphabetization is firmly contained in an auxiliary role.

Minority Nationalities

The last group of people often cited in official reports as needing extra help are the ethnic minorities. So far, fifty-five ethnic minority groups are officially recognized in China. Others have applied for recognition but have not yet been granted that status. Still others may request to be listed in future. The 1990 census shows that of a total population of some 1.1 billion, 91.96 per cent are ethnic

---

[9] An example of this extreme view is the following: 'With a vast expanse of territory, China has a great diversity of local dialects. Such a state of affairs adversely affects the political, economic, and cultural life of our people and makes for difficulties in alphabetizing our written language', *Peking Review*, 32 (10 Aug. 1973), 11–13. Translated and reproduced in Hu and Seifman (1976: 291–4).

Han, 8.04 per cent are minorities (*Beijing Review* 1990b).[10] Some of the larger minority groups include the Zhuangs (13.3 million), the Huis (i.e. Muslims; 7.2 million), the Uygurs (5.9 million), the Yis (5.4 million), the Miaos (5 million), the Manchus (4.3 million), the Tibetans (3.8 million), and the Mongolians (3.4 million) (see Ramsey 1987: 164–5; Heberer 1989: 11).

The qualification must always be made that it is very hard to generalize about the minorities in China, because one group may be vastly different from another. This is especially true in the case of the north–south division. The northern groups—Huns, Turks, and Mongolians—are nomadic peoples and traders. Those in the south—Tais, Zhuangs, and others—are mostly traditionally farmers. In spite of the great diversity, and with some notable exceptions,[11] literacy rates amongst many minority groups are significantly lower than among the Hans.[12] Linguistically the gap between the minority languages and Han Chinese is much greater than the 'internal' differences between the Han dialects.

Little was known about the ethnolinguistic characteristics of the minority peoples until the 1950s and 1960s, when centrally-funded ethnographic work began to be done seriously, mostly by researchers of the National Minorities Institutes. Officially, before the Cultural Revolution, the minority nationalities enjoyed political autonomy, and they had 'the freedom to use their own spoken and written languages'.[13] As far as primary education is concerned, government policy allowed (but did not guarantee) the use of minority languages. According to Ramsey (1987: 160):

> The medium of education in elementary school is the minority language for the first three years, and it is taught as a subject through middle school. In minority areas, such things as newspapers, books, and magazines are often published in the local languages, and in Peking the Nationalities Publishing House (*Minzu Chubanshe*) regularly issues books in the five major minority languages: Tibetan, Mongolian, Uighur, Zhuang, and Korean. Similarly, local radio stations broadcast in minority languages as well as in Chinese, and the Central Broadcasting System in Peking puts together programming in the major minority languages.

Efforts were also made to include, as part of the research done amongst the minority groups, work on devising writing systems (romanization) for those who had none of their own, although this was not done in every case. This would

---

[10] According to the previous census (1982), there were 67 million non-Han people in fifty-five nationalities, making up about 6.7 per cent of the total population. According to a random sample census in 1987, the ethnic minorities accounted for 8 per cent (about 80 million people) of the total population (Heberer 1989: 16–17). It seems therefore that the proportion of ethnic minorities has been on the increase.

[11] According to Postiglione (1992: 315), at least fifteen minority groups have literacy rates higher than that of the population as a whole. The most prominent example is the Koreans, who are 90 per cent literate.

[12] The proportion of people who are semi-literate and illiterate amongst the minorities is 1.25 times that of the Han nationality. See Postiglione (1992: 316, table 12.2).

[13] Constitution of the PRC, adopted in 1954, Article 4. See *Peking Review*, 24 Jan. 1975, 4.

have been a great help in providing primary education in the vernacular languages of the minorities. Unfortunately, whatever freedom they had up until the mid-1960s was taken away from them during the Cultural Revolution. Minorities lost the autonomy guaranteed in the Constitution. Their 'languages, scripts, customs, and manners were condemned as backward, and an attempt was made to abolish them officially' (Heberer 1989: 25). Heberer (ibid. 25–9) details the many 'prohibitions and indignities' committed during this period:

Of the written scripts, only five were allowed (Mongolian, Tibetan, Uighur, Kazak, and Korean), but even their use was restricted. Only Chinese was to be spoken at meetings, and in many places it was a 'misdemeanor' to use one's native language.

Almost all schools and colleges for minorities were disbanded . . . In many minority regions only Han [Chinese]—and no local language—was the language of instruction in the schools. The number of individuals belonging to minorities who could attend college dropped, and the illiteracy rate increased.

Minority songs, dance, films, folk songs, operas, and the like were called 'feudal, capitalist, revisionist, poisonous weeds' . . . As for literature, no minority writer dared write anything during the Cultural Revolution; most writers were persecuted and their writings banned.

During this period, a policy of subjugation and forced assimilation was adopted towards the minorities. As a result, education came to a standstill; developments in the minority languages and scripts suffered major set-backs; earlier efforts in literacy training were all but wasted. But most of all, what trust the minority nationalities might have had in the government was lost. The relationship between the central administration and the minorities reached a record low.

Attempts have been made since the 1980s to 'correct the errors', but the scale of the malice and destruction inflicted upon the minorities means that the wounds will not be easy to heal. Nevertheless, the minorities' right 'to use and develop their own spoken and written languages, and to preserve or reform their own ways and customs',[14] which was repealed in 1975, was reinstated in the 1982 Constitution. A special law was passed in 1984 to stress once again the importance attached to the autonomy, the freedoms, and the rights of the minorities.

Autonomous organs of the national autonomous areas should independently develop education for nationalities, wipe out illiteracy, run various kinds of schools, popularize primary education, develop secondary education, and run teachers' training schools for nationalities, vocational schools for nationalities, and institutes for nationalities in order to train specialized personnel of minority nationalities.[15]

In schools which mainly recruit students of minority nationalities, both textbooks and instruction should whenever possible be in those languages. Primary-school students of higher grades and secondary-school students should learn

---

[14] Constitution of the PRC, adopted on 4 Dec. 1982, Article 4. See *Beijing Review*, 52 (27 Dec. 1982), 10–29.

[15] The Law on Regional Autonomy for Minority Nationalities of the PRC, adopted 31 May 1984, Article 37. Translation in Hu and Seifman (1987: 177–9).

Chinese. Putonghua, which is commonly used throughout the country, should be popularized among them.

Unfortunately, even before the effects of these new measures can be properly assessed, another major political event has taken place which may once again throw the work of rehabilitation and reconstruction into disarray. The democracy movement which culminated in 'the Tiananmen incident' of 4 June 1989 has apparently led once again to revisions of policy in the direction of tighter control over the country as a whole, and over the minorities in particular. Tension seems to be building up again beneath the surface calm. Confrontations in Tibet with the police and peasant unrest in Sichuan are just two examples that have come to the world's attention. In Tibet, demonstrations and calls for independence were met with police force, resulting in the death of a number of Tibetans and many injuries. In Renshou county, Sichuan, peasants protesting against unreasonable taxation had a series of confrontations with the police and the armed forces, resulting in major violence. Both events happened in June 1993. As far as education and literacy are concerned, there has apparently been 'a renewed call for Chinese to be the main medium of instruction' (Postiglione 1992: 328). What will come out of these changes remains to be seen. But it may not be unfair to say that, whilst considerable work has been done in assisting and promoting literacy in the vernacular amongst the minority groups, the real progress which would have brought long-term benefits to the communities concerned must be assessed against the frequent disruptions and periodic setbacks of the last thirty years.

3. LITERACY THROUGH THE VERNACULAR: THE 'LITTLE TRADITION' OF HONG KONG

3.1. *The Three Traditions*

The character of education in Hong Kong is shaped by three main contributing factors: the Chinese tradition, the Yue tradition, and the British tradition.

Much of what was said in the first part of the previous section about traditional learning and modern education in China applies in the case of Hong Kong. Indeed it is in the context of this 'Great Tradition' that the 'Little Tradition' of the Yue (Cantonese) people is best understood.[16] But the picture would not be complete without mentioning some additional historical facts. Hong Kong as we know it in 1996 is made up essentially of migrants and refugees and subsequent generations of those who have settled in the territory.[17] There was hardly

---

[16] The terms 'the Great Tradition' and 'the Little Tradition' are used in this context in Moser (1985). We find them useful in introducing the particular situation of Hong Kong.

[17] As at 1991, 35 per cent of the total population are migrants from China. Clearly 60 per cent were locally born, and a substantial proportion of these are second or third generations of migrants originally from the southern parts of China.

TABLE 8.2. *'Reading pronunciation' and 'colloquial pronunciation' in Cantonese*

Character	Reading pronunciation	Colloquial pronunciation
'green/blue'	cing1	ceng1
'name'	ming4	meng2
'level/good/proper'	zing3	zeng3
'live'	sang1	saang1
'compete'	zang1	zaang1
'carp'	zik1	zak1
'zinc'	sik3	sek3
'kitchen'	coei4	cyu4
'skeleton'	hoi4	haai4
'hit' (on the face)	gwok3	gwaak3
'wipe'	mut3	maat3
'break'	dyun6	tyun5

Note: The romanization of Cantonese adopted here is based on the scheme recommended by the Linguistic Society of Hong Kong in 1993. The consonants *c* and *z* correspond to *ch* and *j* respectively in the Yale system. 1 to 6 are the tone numbers.

a community to speak of when Hong Kong was ceded to Britain in 1842. The astonishing growth in population[18] since then is a result mainly of people migrating and fleeing in large numbers in the course of the last 150 years from various parts of China, but particularly South China and the Lingnan (Guangdong) region. As a result, life in Hong Kong has an unmistakable flavour of Yue (Cantonese) culture.

Apart from customs, folk religion, music, and vernacular literature, two elements of the Yue tradition must be mentioned which are of special relevance to the question of language and literacy. First, there is a long and respectable tradition of teaching and learning the Chinese script *through* Cantonese. Not only is it possible to recite a classical text or a *Baihua* passage in Cantonese; for the monolingual learner in a Yue-speaking region there is no alternative way of learning the pronunciation and the meaning of the Chinese characters. As a result, a gap has developed between colloquial speech and a reading style, so that some characters have both a 'colloquial pronunciation' and a 'reading pronunciation'.

The second feature of the Yue tradition is that it has many dialect words of its own, some of which are represented in a special way in writing—that is, in the form of 'dialect characters'. These are designed on the basis of the standard

---

[18] From a tiny settlement of no more than 5,000 in 1841, the population has grown to 5.6 million in 1991. The latter figure comes from the 1991 Population Census.

character set, but are unintelligible to speakers of other dialects. They are relatively few in number—many dialect words simply do not have a common written representation—but some are high-frequency words—for example, the third person singular pronoun *keui5* 'he/she', the plural suffix (to personal pronouns) *dei6*, and numerous sentence particles which occur frequently in speech.

Apart from the Great Tradition of China and the Little Tradition of Yue, a third factor in shaping education in Hong Kong has been the British presence. In particular, the importance traditionally attached to education in the UK and the link between a good education and a career in the civil service have helped strengthen even more the extent to which literacy and learning are valued and respected in the society.

3.2. *Vernacular Education and Literacy through the Vernacular*

According to the 1991 Population Census (Hong Kong Census and Statistics Department 1992: 43), Cantonese is by far the most common language of Hong Kong; 89 per cent of the population speak it at home, and call it their 'usual language'; another 7 per cent claim to speak it as their second language. English is the home language of only 2 per cent of the population, but another 29 per cent say they can speak it. In comparison, Putonghua is spoken by only 18 per cent of the population.

The relationship between these three languages, and the many dialects spoken in Hong Kong, can be represented in terms of a three-tier structure.[19] Picture Cantonese, the 'provincial language', as the middle layer, the core, in such a structure. One tier up are two languages: Putonghua, the national standard, and English, the official language, the language of higher education, business, and international communication. One tier down are numerous dialects (mutually unintelligible with Cantonese, e.g. Hokkien, Hakka, Chiuchow, Shanghainese) and sub-dialects (of Cantonese and the other dialects). Of the non-Cantonese dialects, numerically the most prominent are Hokkien and Hakka, each having about 100,000 native speakers.

Given this language situation, the question whether Cantonese is a vernacular becomes very interesting. In one sense it *is* a vernacular, *vis-à-vis* English and Standard Chinese, the two languages on the top tier. In another sense, Cantonese occupies a higher level in the hierarchy than the other dialects. This can be seen in the stigma attached to speakers of dialects other than standard Cantonese. Imitations in the mass media of non-Cantonese speakers speaking their own dialects or speaking Cantonese with an accent provide a constant source of 'humour'

---

[19] We find Fasold's suggestion of the three levels of 'world languages', 'national languages', and 'small-group languages' very useful. In the case of China, it may work even better if we add another level, provincial languages, between the 'national' and the 'small-group' languages (Fasold 1984: ch. II).

for the Cantonese audience. *Vis-à-vis* these dialects and sub-dialects, Cantonese is the provincial language and is higher in status. In *this* sense then the dialects and sub-dialects might be identified as the 'real vernaculars'. If that is the case, should literacy be provided in, say, Hakka or Hokkien? There is hardly any demand for it.

In practice, primary education in Hong Kong has always been in Cantonese. On the one hand, opportunities in education and basic literacy in the second half of the nineteenth century were made available as a result of the work of the missionaries, who were naturally more concerned to spread the Christian faith through the vernacular than propagate a colonial English education. But even the colonial government was not too keen on promoting English education in Hong Kong, or to be involved directly in running any kind of primary education for that matter. More important, the kind of colonial policy in education as spelt out in the Macaulay Minutes of 1835[20] in the context of India was not in evidence in the case of Hong Kong (Ng 1984: 29; see also Sweeting 1990). The British have from the very beginning been keenly aware of the proximity of China and the influence of the Chinese tradition. The Colonial Office did not on the whole dictate to the Governor of Hong Kong, but allowed him to depart from colonial policy whenever necessary to take into account local customs and practices. For example, polygamy was permitted until 1972. Capital punishment was not abolished until 1991. While it is illegal to gamble in public places, action is hardly ever taken against mahjong-playing in Chinese restaurants.

When it comes to primary education, the government's policy in the early period was to play an auxiliary role by providing financial support, but to leave the actual running of the village schools to the missionaries. In the modern period, the policy continues to be to give churches and other charitable organizations the land they need to build schools and to offer grants-in-aid for their operation and maintenance. In spite of developments since the 1840s, primary education has remained to this day essentially Cantonese-based.

The policy of leaving vernacular education in the hands of the missionaries was criticized in the Burney Report in 1935 as an abnegation of responsibility. As a result, the government began to play a more active role in providing primary education, although the churches and many non-governmental organizations continue to expand this service. Extra momentum has gathered particularly since the mid-1970s, during a period of rapid economic growth. Universal primary education became a distinct possibility. It was decided in 1971 to provide all children with six years of primary education in Cantonese.

In 1979 free education was extended into the first three years of secondary schools. A hitherto unexpected problem came about as a result of this policy.

[20] The Macaulay Minutes advocated the substitution of Western culture for the Indians, aiming to create a class of persons who would be 'Indian in blood and colour, but English in tastes, in opinions, in morals, and in intellect' (Ng 1984: 29). Ng's work offers a very useful account of early public education in Hong Kong.

Most secondary schools had up to that point been teaching through the medium of English. This was just about manageable, because the weakest students would have been 'screened' out of the system by the time they finished primary school. But as free education became available for another three years, almost overnight secondary schools found themselves having to teach students from a much wider range of abilities, and much more varied in their proficiency in English. And yet most parents continue to expect schools to teach their children in English. Schools are therefore faced with a dilemma: should they continue to try to teach in English to satisfy the parents' demands, or should they begin to teach in Cantonese in view of the change in the students' profile? Opinions differ as to whether the universalization of basic education justifies a reassessment of the first three years of secondary education, and whether this part of the government's package should also be provided in the vernacular (see Lord and Cheng 1987; Luke 1992).

3.3. *Opting out of Vernacular Education*

Ironically, in spite of the new provision of nine years' free education and literacy in Chinese through the vernacular, the demand is growing for English-medium education at the pre-school and primary levels as 1997 approaches.[21] More and more parents now opt for privately run 'international schools' which teach in English, although only a tiny minority can afford it. Being in great demand, the dozen or so international schools and kindergartens all require applicants to pay a 'debenture' to gain admission. One of the most sought after of these international schools, for example, charges a debenture of HK$100,000 (about US$13,000) before a child's name is even put on the waiting list.

A steady economic growth and good career opportunities in recent years mean that many young couples prefer to work full-time during the day, leaving the children in the care of live-in domestic helpers, mostly from the Philippines.[22] Most Filipino helpers do not speak Cantonese, but do speak some English. As a result, many children today grow up speaking Cantonese and English at home. Another trend has been that, as a result of economic recessions in most Western countries, many people who had emigrated overseas in the last ten years are now returning to Hong Kong. But their children have become used to English-medium education in Australia, Canada, or the USA. In response to this significant growth in demand, more and more privately run English-medium schools have come into being, the Singapore International School and the Canadian International School being two recent examples. Even the Hong Kong government is planning to build some English-medium schools as an incentive to lure emigrants back from overseas and as a measure to curb the feared 'brain drain'.

[21] According to the Chinese–British Joint Declaration signed in December 1984, Hong Kong will revert to China on 1 July 1997 as a Special Administrative Region. The existing capitalist social and economic systems will remain unchanged for another fifty years.

[22] By 1993 there were some 90,000 Filipinos working as domestic helpers in Hong Kong.

It is perhaps ironical that, even though vernacular education is available free, more and more people are finding ways of opting out of the system because of the value of English. There is some concern that the 'state system' is being undermined by this private, privileged subsystem. It may well be that a split will inevitably be created as a result of the expanding private sector, access to which is based on wealth. It is clear that the need is for literacy to be provided in both languages, i.e. a bilingual system. To what extent this is possible on a large scale and to what extent it will work in practice and succeed in real terms[23] remains an open question. The Singapore experience seems to suggest that at the end of the day only one of the languages will prevail.

4. 'MOTHER TONGUE' REDEFINED: THE SINGAPORE EXPERIENCE

4.1. *Traditional Languages*

The population in Singapore is made up largely of people from three ethnic groups, Chinese (78 per cent), Malays (14 per cent), and Indians (7 per cent) (Department of Statistics 1991*b*: 12). Table 8.3 below, based on the Census of Population in 1980 and 1990, gives a breakdown of the predominant household language by ethnicity. As the predominant household language is defined as 'the language or dialect that is used most frequently among family members' (Lau 1993: 5), it is likely to be the mother tongue of young Singaporean children, although, as will be shown later, it is not always easy to identify a Singaporean child's mother tongue.

The ethnic Chinese came originally from southern China; so traditionally, up to around 1980, the southern Chinese languages or dialects—Hokkien, Teochew (Chiuchow), Cantonese, Khek (Hakka), and Hainanese among others—were the mother tongues of a large proportion (76.2 per cent in 1980) of the Chinese children in Singapore.

The ethnic Indians came from different parts of India. The mother tongues of the Indian children in Singapore included Telegu, Malayalam, Kannada, and Tamil under the Dravidian group, and Hindi, Gujarati, Punjabi, Bengali, and Urdu under the Indo-Aryan group. Of these, Tamil, the official Indian language in Singapore, was the most widely used (52.2 per cent of Indian households claimed to use it in 1980). The use of the other Indian languages, included under 'others', was substantially lower (14.9 per cent in 1980).

As for the ethnic Malays, the picture was very different. The language used in the home was almost exclusively Malay (96.7 per cent in 1980).

English as the mother tongue was confined largely to the English-educated

[23] 'Real success' in the context of Hong Kong must mean at least the ability—and the habit, in so far as reading is done at all—to read newspapers and magazines in both languages.

TABLE 8.3. *Resident private households by ethnic group of head of household and predominant household language spoken, 1980 and 1990 (%)*

Predominant household language	1980	1990
Chinese households	100.0	100.0
English	10.2	21.4
Mandarin	13.1	30.0
Chinese dialects	76.2	48.2
others	0.5	0.4
Malay households	100.0	100.0
English	2.3	5.7
Malay	96.7	94.1
others	1.0	0.2
Indian households	100.0	100.0
English	24.3	34.3
Malay	8.6	14.1
Tamil	52.2	43.5
others	14.9	8.1
All households (all groups)	100.0	100.0
English	11.6	20.8
Mandarin	10.2	23.7
Chinese dialects	59.5	38.2
Malay	13.9	13.6
Tamil	3.1	3.0
others	1.7	0.7

Source: Lau (1993: 6).

Chinese and Indians and, in 1980, 10.2 per cent and 24.3 per cent respectively claimed to use it as the predominant household language.

4.2. *Language Shift in the Home*

A comparison of the census of population data of 1980 and 1990 (see Table 8.3 above) also shows that, taking all racial groups together, there was a significant increase in the use of English in the home, from 11.6 per cent to 20.8 per cent. Among the Chinese, there was a significant increase in the use of Mandarin (from 13.1 per cent in 1980 to 30.0 per cent in 1990) and English (from 10.2 per cent to 21.4 per cent) at the expense of the Chinese dialects, which fell from 76.2 per cent to 48.2 per cent. In Malay households, the use of Malay yielded in a small degree (from 96.7 per cent in 1980 to 94.1 per cent in 1990) to

TABLE 8.4. *Languages most frequently spoken at home for Primary 1 (entry class) Chinese pupils (%)*

Year	Dialect	Mandarin	English	Others
1980	64.4	25.9	9.3	0.3
1984	26.9	58.7	13.9	0.4
1989	7.2	69.1	23.3	0.4

Source: *Business Times*, 4 Oct. 1989, p. 2.

English. In Indian households, the gain in the use of English (from 24.3 per cent in 1980 to 34.3 per cent in 1990) and Malay (from 8.6 per cent to 14.1 per cent) was made at the expense of Tamil and other Indian languages. If this trend towards increased use of English (among all ethnic groups) and Mandarin (among the ethnic Chinese) continues—and certainly it is the government's policy to encourage this—then it is possible that in another twenty to thirty years there will be very few Chinese children who will have the Chinese dialects, or Indian children who will have the Indian languages other than Tamil, as their home languages. Most Chinese children are likely to speak either English or Mandarin Chinese, most Malay children are likely to speak Malay, and more Indian children are likely to speak English, Malay, or Tamil.

This change in the predominant household-language situation corresponds to a similar change in other domains of use, as shown in other, smaller-scale studies. The Chinese newspaper in Singapore, *Lianhe Bao*, conducted a study on the use of the Chinese languages in different types of food outlets and shops and noted a shift towards Mandarin at the expense of the Chinese dialects (*Straits Times*, 5 Oct. 1989). The most noticeable shift is that in the most frequently spoken language at home for Primary 1 (i.e. entry class) Chinese pupils that took place between 1980 and 1989 (see Table 8.4).

In 1989, the vast majority (92.4 per cent) of Chinese pupils claimed either English or Mandarin as the language most frequently used in the home. Naturally, the figures are likely to be inflated in that these are the preferred or endorsed languages of the government, but there is no denying that English and Mandarin Chinese are clearly gaining ground in the home, as reflected in other independent studies. Kwan-Terry noted in a study that many Singapore parents choose to speak either English or Mandarin with their children in an attempt to introduce them early to their school language (Kwan-Terry 1989). The introduction of the school languages into the home is also noted by Gupta (1994*b*).

With the Indians, the general consensus is that the Indian languages other than Tamil are gradually dying out, replaced in the home by either English or Malay. The position of Tamil is more stable. A recent study among primary Tamil schoolchildren in Singapore shows that Tamils are able to maintain their language in the domains of family, prayers, entertainment, neighbours, and kin (the use of Tamil in these domains ranges from 65 per cent to 72 per cent). However, the shift towards the use of English is striking in the domains of friends, reading, and school (here the use of Tamil is only between 27 per cent and 40 per cent). This suggests that, while spoken Tamil is not threatened, being maintained through the family, kin, and neighbours as well as religion, literacy in the language is threatened, as reading in Tamil is found in only 33 per cent of the cases studied (Ramiah 1991: 51–2). The Malays stand out in that they remain very faithful to their language: it is a marker of their ethnic affiliation as well as their religion.

4.3. *Reasons for the Shift*

A main reason for the shift to English, noted particularly among the Chinese and the Indians, is the high economic value and social prestige of the language in Singapore, it being the language of international commerce, science, and technology (Llamzon 1977; Kuo 1980). Another related reason is the switch to English-medium education that took place between the 1950s and the 1970s (Kwan-Terry and Kwan-Terry 1993), which means that more and more people have had English-medium education and are in a position to speak English in the home. The government's promotion of English, for political as well as for economic reasons, no doubt has had its effects too.

What then accounts for the dramatic increase in the use of Mandarin? In 1979 the Singapore government launched its 'Speak Mandarin Campaign' when it strongly advocated the use of Mandarin for all ethnic Chinese to replace the dialects. The rationale at that time was largely educational. The government was concerned about the poor command of English and the low level of literacy in Chinese among the younger generation Chinese. It argued that, through replacing the Chinese dialects in the home by Mandarin (a school language and the language on which written Chinese is based), Chinese children would have fewer languages to contend with and would therefore develop a better control of both English and written Chinese. As the government enjoys much credibility with its people, and since the rationale behind its promotion of Mandarin supports parents' desire for educational success for their children, the Speak Mandarin Campaign has met with remarkable success.

The campaign has been kept up since its inception, but in recent years it has taken on a second mission. Speaking Mandarin, and, perhaps more importantly, developing literacy in Modern Standard Chinese (MSC), are increasingly being seen by the government as important ways to maintain Chinese cultural values. Goh Chok Tong, the Prime Minister of Singapore, spoke in 1981 about the need to 'preserve the fine traditional culture, values and moral concepts of ethnic Chinese' (*Straits Times*, 4 Oct. 1989). The emphasis on learning Chinese as a way to maintain Chinese cultural values has been brought more and more into focus with the years (Kwan-Terry 1993; Kwan-Terry and Kwan-Terry 1993).

The low status of the Chinese dialects no doubt also contributes to the shift away from them. Since Chinese-medium education is based on Mandarin, the use of the dialects is viewed as a sign of lack of education and refinement. Moreover, since 1985, when the government introduced the slogan 'Mandarin is Chinese', implying that it is the ability to speak Mandarin, and not the dialects, which defines one's ethnic affiliation, the Chinese dialects as a marker of Chinese identity have been seriously threatened. This is confirmed in a study looking into language and identity among first-year Chinese undergraduates in Singapore (Wee 1990: 62).

4.4. *'Mother Tongue' Redefined*

In Singapore, many children speak more than one mother tongue. This is because many Singapore women take up jobs outside the home, thus leaving their young children to the care of either their grandparents or a maid in the day. The grandparents are likely to speak in either a Chinese dialect or an Indian language or Malay, and the maid is likely to speak some form of English. The parents, on the other hand, may communicate with their offspring in one or more of several languages—English, Mandarin, a Chinese dialect, an Indian language, Malay—depending to some extent on their command of the languages. Many parents opt to use one of the school languages with their children in the hope of giving them an early start in a language that they will later need in school (Kwan-Terry 1989). It has also been found that very often older siblings bring home a school language and use it with their younger siblings, and this adds to the likelihood of young children speaking a school language before attending school (Kwan-Terry 1989). Thus it is common for Singapore children to be able to speak two or more languages by the time they start schooling.

Tay, in her study of the languages spoken by young Singapore children (based on reports from university students recalling their childhood language use) before the age of 6, concludes that a Singapore child may speak 1–6 languages, with 2–3 languages the norm (Tay 1984: 178). The languages they spoke—in cases where they spoke two languages—were likely to be a Chinese dialect + English; a Chinese dialect + Mandarin; English + Malay; English + an Indian language, or English + Mandarin.

Another study, done more recently and based on direct observation as well as reports from parents and teachers, also points in the same direction. The study was conducted in an education centre in a typical government housing estate, and the subjects were on the whole representative of Singapore children. When 220 of the parents of these children were asked the number of languages spoken at home, four claimed to use only one language, ten claimed three languages or more, and the rest claimed two languages, either English and Mandarin or English and Malay. The teachers estimated that about half of the children knew English and over three-quarters knew Mandarin, while only a handful of them knew neither English nor Mandarin (Gupta 1994*b*: 170).

Whereas Unesco (1953) recommends the adoption of the mother tongue in the initial years of education to bridge the gap between the home and the school, Singapore parents have anticipated the gap and tried to bridge it by changing their home language. Unesco (1953), in recognizing the educational and psychological benefits of using the mother tongue in initial teaching, has failed to recognize the social, economic, and political factors which play a role in determining the linguistic scene in a country.

4.5. *The 'Mother Tongue' in Education*

From the above, it would seem that the adoption of the traditional home languages —namely, Chinese dialects such as Hokkien and Teochew (Chiuchow) and Indian languages such as Telegu, Malayalam, Hindi, Urdu, etc.,—as the medium of teaching in early education is problematic, to say the least. A major problem is their low economic value and low social prestige. Then too, the government's active steps in encouraging the use of the 'symbolic mother tongue', one for each of the three major racial groups—Mandarin for the Chinese, Tamil for the Indians, and Malay for the Malays—for the purpose of promoting communal identity and Asian cultural values, as well as education, has helped weaken the position of the traditional languages further. It must be remembered that, in Singapore, the government carries great credibility with its people and thus its views (some fiscal policies excepted) carry much weight. On the encouragement of the government, some Singaporean parents, as was pointed out, turn to using the official or school languages in the home, if not for other reasons, then at least for the sake of their children's education. Among the Chinese, the general recognition that Mandarin is the national language in China, the common language among all Chinese, also contributes to the interest in learning the language. Added to this is the problem of the large number of languages in a very small population, making the adoption of selected traditional mother tongues as the medium of education a great administrative convenience. Moreover, not only are the major traditional mother tongues fast changing, but, as the study by Gupta (1994*b*) shows, most children go to nursery, kindergarten, or school with enough English or Mandarin. This means that the Unesco concern—the gap between the home and the school in terms of language—is not a primary concern in Singapore.

4.6. *Varieties of English in Singapore*

English is now the main medium of instruction in Singapore schools. What variety of English is most widely used in Singapore and is this the variety children are encouraged to develop in the schools?

Three varieties of English are used in Singapore. They are the standard variety used in formal situations, the colloquial variety used in informal situations, and finally a variety, if it can be called a variety, spoken by those who are not proficient in the language. The term Singlish has often been used indiscriminately to refer to both the second and the third varieties. However, it is important to realize that the colloquial variety has its own set of rules. Gupta, among others, has pointed out that nearly 'all Singaporeans who are proficient in English choose to speak SCE (Singapore Colloquial English) in certain social settings, and Standard English in others. They do this to express their relationship to the situation and to their interlocutors' (Gupta 1994a: 16). For example, among university students, the variety that is expected at tutorials would be the standard variety, but once the students leave the tutorial room, to talk casually among themselves, the use of the standard variety would seem unnatural and unfriendly, and would be looked upon askance by others. While with very few exceptions speakers of the standard variety are able to switch at will between the standard variety and SCE, it is less certain if all speakers of the colloquial variety are similarly able to switch upwards to the standard variety. Again no research has been done in this respect. However, it is highly likely that there may be in Singapore a substantial number of people who have developed, through their education (with limited exposure to standard English) and/or the wide use of SCE in Singapore, a good command of the colloquial variety, but who, on account of their limited exposure to the standard variety, have not had the opportunity to develop ability in this higher variety. The variety that is most widely used in Singapore is undoubtedly the colloquial variety (SCE), which differs substantially from the standard varieties (spoken and written). This means that when children speaking this colloquial variety start attending school and learning Singapore standard English, certain adjustments have to be made and interference from the colloquial variety is bound to occur.

4.7. *Bilingual Literacy and Cultural Values*

The Singapore government is aware that English is important for political as well as for economic reasons, but while it promotes education in English, it has also taken pains to promote the so-called ethnic languages—(Mandarin) Chinese, Malay, and Tamil—through its bilingual policy. In the early years of nation-building, government emphasis was largely on English, as it was a neutral language and one vital for the country's economic well-being, and the development of the ethnic languages among the people took only second place. However, now that Singaporeans have developed a strong sense of national identity and the country is set on a firm footing in terms of economic development, the role of the ethnic languages in the maintenance of cultural values comes to the fore. As early as 1956 it was made clear in a report by the All Party Committee of which Lee Kuan Yew was a member that all the local ethnic languages and cultures have an important role in contributing towards the development of a Singapore national identity and culture (Singapore Legislative Assembly 1956:

4). The promotion of ethnic languages has taken centre stage especially since the 1980s when the government realized that Singaporeans were becoming more and more westernized, so much so that there was a danger of their losing their cultural roots and values. The position of the government was clearly stated:

> Western ideals emphasize the rights and privileges of the individual over the group, and particularly over the state . . . Oriental societies believe in individuals fulfilling themselves through the greater identity of the group . . . This emphasis on other-directed values —communitarian values—on duties above rights—is one of the distinguishing features of the NICs (newly industrialized countries), and in the view of many sociologists, a key factor in their success . . . every society contains strands of both communitarianism and individual drives. Every society must find its own balance between the two. (*Straits Times*, 12 Jan. 1989)

It can be argued that it is the Confucian tradition of respect for authority and discipline that is behind, first, the cooperation that the government has been able to get from its people, and, secondly, the disciplined workforce that Singapore boasts of. After all, a strong government well supported by its people and a disciplined workforce have helped to make Singapore an economic success. Thus it is reasonable to interpret the Singapore government's promotion of Chinese cultural values in political and economic terms.

In the transmission of cultural values, the written language plays an important role, the Singapore government advocates. Spoken Mandarin Chinese, so says Ong Teng Cheong, Singapore's Second Deputy Prime Minister, is 'insufficient for the appreciation of Chinese cultural values and traditional values, for which a knowledge of written Chinese (is) necessary' (*Straits Times*, 31 Oct. 1988). It is to ensure the continuance of Chinese cultural values that the government is anxiously promoting literacy in Chinese among its Chinese population.

4.8. *The Problem of Learning Written Chinese in Singapore*

Unfortunately the task of developing literacy in Chinese up to a level necessary for the inculcation and maintenance of Chinese cultural values is not an easy one. Studies have shown that very few children read story books in Chinese on their own (Kwan-Terry 1989) and that many students read the Chinese newspaper merely as a way to help them pass examinations in Chinese. Once the need to pass examinations in the language is no longer there, many stop reading Chinese newspapers. Those who continue read only the entertainment sections (Ng 1986). A survey conducted at one of the polytechnics in Singapore (*Straits Times*, 20 June 1992) also shows that, while the younger generation of Chinese Singaporeans prefer to speak Chinese among themselves, and watch Chinese television programmes, they read English more readily than Chinese. The survey did not cover writing; if it had, it would have shown an even stronger preference for writing English. In other words, students in Singapore learn written Chinese merely to satisfy education requirements, to pass examinations in the language; the written language is not a part of the life of the younger generation of Chinese and does little to inculcate Chinese cultural values.

One of the reasons for this is that the education system is not geared towards producing balanced bilinguals. The medium of teaching in schools and institutes of higher learning is English, where the students learn mostly in English and sit for examinations in English, except for the second-language papers. The second language—Chinese, Malay, or Tamil—is taught as a subject, and a pass in the second language in public examinations is necessary for a student to move up the educational ladder.

One might expect that constant exposure to and use of Mandarin Chinese outside the classroom would compensate for the fewer hours allocated to Chinese in the school timetable. However, the optimum conditions for reinforcement of writing and reading by exposure to spoken output are a strong phoneme–grapheme correspondence, and a minimum of difference between the spoken and written language. Neither condition is met by the logographic nature of written Chinese.

Thus, reaching a given standard in writing Chinese will take longer (and defeat more learners) than reaching an equivalent standard in even such an imperfect phonographic script as English. Since in the Singapore education system the time spent operating in written English is far greater than the time spent operating in written Chinese, it is obvious that writing in English is going to be easier for most people than writing in Chinese. In reading, the problems are less acute, but it is true that, by O levels (aged 16), most Singapore secondary pupils will find it difficult to read authentic Chinese. Many have not reached the threshold at which they can read for pleasure, whereas in English they are more advanced. A vicious circle thus ensues: it takes a much longer time for children to reach the critical level when they can read something in Chinese without aid and with pleasure and thus it is natural that most primary-school children do not form the habit of reading in Chinese, as the survey by Kwan-Terry (1989) shows. Moreover, compared to story books in English, those in Chinese seem to be uninteresting: children complain that Chinese stories are boring because they all aim at teaching a moral lesson. Even the packaging of Chinese books presents a problem compared with English books: English books come in glossy, colourful covers with equally attractive illustrations, but Chinese story books come in low quality paper, and the illustrations, if there are any, are not coloured. These features are bound to affect children in selecting books to read, and the less they read in Chinese, the slower their development in the language. Furthermore, once students have passed the second-language paper in Chinese at O level (which is a requirement under the education system), they go on to study almost exclusively in English. Not being able to read stimulating material in Chinese, they read little in that language—and write less if at all—so that their literacy level declines.

Besides the learning problem described above, the learning of written Chinese is also hampered by a motivational problem. Chinese has a low social and economic value, at least up to the present; moreover, written Chinese is not widely used or much needed in Singapore today.

It has been claimed that a person's value system is formed early in life, and, if reading of books, particularly the pleasurable reading of books, is an important way of inculcating values, then it would seem that, for primary-school children, written Chinese has not contributed much to the development of their value system. Then too, while year after year students pass examinations in Chinese, one wonders to what extent their ability in written Chinese—as reflected in the O- and A-level passes that students have obtained—has helped to inculcate Chinese cultural values in them. To attain this goal, written Chinese has to be made a part of the life of Singapore children. Yet how can this be done? This seems to be the crucial question.

4.9. *Alternatives to Present Policy*

What are the goals of bilingual education in Singapore and to what extent have these goals been met? The goal in learning English, for the majority of people, is functional literacy. Singaporeans need to use English to handle their jobs at different levels. What is the average Singaporean's level of literacy in English? Is this level of attainment adequate for the purpose described? In 1990 (with English as the medium of education), 96.8 per cent of children between the ages of 6 and 16 were students, up from 90 per cent in 1980 (Lau 1993: 9). Furthermore, the level of education received is also rising. The 1990 census shows that, among those aged 25–29 years, 20 per cent had at least an upper secondary qualification as against 16 per cent for the 30–39 age group and 12 per cent for the 40–49 age group (Lau 1993: 12). Thus the English literacy level of Singaporeans, as well as their level of education, has been rising to match the needs of industry and trade. Singaporean workers are generally highly rated in terms of efficiency and productivity.

But how about attainment in the Asian languages, particularly in written Chinese? The government's goal is to raise the Chinese-language literacy level amongst the Chinese sector of its population so as to ensure the inculcation and maintenance of traditional Chinese cultural values. It still has a long way to go before the government can claim success in this aspiration. If the present education is less than satisfactory in terms of the inculcation and maintenance of cultural values, then what are the alternatives?

To what extent is education in the 'symbolic mother tongue'—English, Mandarin Chinese, Malay, or Tamil—at the primary-school level with a gradual move to education in the English medium at the secondary school a viable alternative? This may have the advantage of ensuring a reasonable command of written Chinese among those who begin their education in this medium and it is no doubt in line with the Unesco (1953) recommendation of early education in the 'mother tongue', but such a move is not a likely solution for several reasons. First, the most important language in Singapore from the economic point of view is still English, and that is the language parents in Singapore want their children to be strong in to ensure good career prospects. A change in education policy requiring children who do not speak English at home to begin education in Chinese, Malay, or Tamil, but not in English, will mean a drop in the children's command of English, and this is likely to result in widening the income gap between the English-speaking and the non-English-speaking, leading eventually to further social stratification. Furthermore, as the Hong Kong experience shows, switching then to English-medium education at the secondary level is likely to lead to a high drop-out rate at the point of switch. Although it can be argued that, in the case of Singapore, because of the strong social support for English, the switch is likely to be easier than in the case of Hong Kong, one cannot ignore altogether the likelihood of the damaging effect the switch has on at least some of the less linguistically adept children. These two possible consequences are definitely not acceptable to Singapore parents, who are all aspiring to a better future for their children through education.

If early mother-tongue (symbolic mother tongue) education is not a desirable alternative, what then? An alternative that may not be completely satisfactory but which nevertheless is likely to lead to an improvement over the existing situation is the provision of language immersion. In the early 1980s, in its attempt to upgrade the Chinese-language command of the younger generation, the government set up some secondary schools where the students could take Chinese at the first-language level (a level that is higher than the second-language level). These schools have proved to be very successful and students now vie for places in them. This scheme was later extended to the primary schools and now there are primary schools where Chinese is taught at the first-language level. Many children from English-speaking homes seek places in these schools. The predominantly English-speaking parents are of the view that early immersion in Chinese will help their children overcome the problem of learning written Chinese, a problem that is now faced by many older children with an English-speaking background who have followed the national stream of education (with English used as the main medium and Chinese taught at the second-language level). Realization of the problem has resulted in many English-speaking parents sending their children to primary schools with a heavy Chinese bias, in an attempt to immerse them in the language early. This measure seems to have positive effects. Indeed a parallel trait has been noted of parents of Chinese-speaking homes (both dialect-speaking and Mandarin-speaking) who tend to send their children to the regular schools which do not have this Chinese bias. Moreover, many of these parents also employ private tutors for their children to help them with their English, because this is the language they are expected to be weak in. A logical conclusion to this, then, is the provision of early education in the language with which the children are likely to have problems. This means early English-medium education for those who speak an ethnic language in the home and ethnic-language education for those who speak English in the home.

While this strategy may not entirely solve the problem of inculcating and maintaining Chinese cultural values, at least it will help to raise the level of command of written Chinese of children from largely English-speaking homes. This will help to develop their control of the vocabulary of written Chinese important for the ability to read in the language, for it is only when children have breached a critical level of command of the Chinese vocabulary that they can read Chinese with pleasure and thereby assimilate Chinese cultural values. If such a step is complemented with efforts at making available suitable and appealing books for children, then, in view of the growing importance of China, and therefore the growing economic value of the Chinese language, there is no reason why positive effects cannot be achieved. Moreover, it is possible that such a change may have secondary effects. Since these children are from the advantaged families who hold much of the economic power in Singapore, a rise in their level of command in Chinese may also help to raise the social status of Chinese, especially when this is accompanied by the increasing importance of China as a trading partner.

Could the same be said of introducing education in Tamil and in Malay? The need to inculcate and maintain Malay cultural values is less urgent in Singapore. Malay cultural values are very much alive partly because of the proximity of Malaysia and partly because Islam is a powerful means of ensuring the preservation of the language and its culture. The need to preserve Tamil or Indian languages and culture, on the other hand, is seen as urgent, as there is a gradual drop in the use of both Tamil and other Indian languages in the home, according to the 1990 Census of Population (Department of Statistics 1991: 18), although apparently there is no drop in the official literacy rate. To what extent this reported level of literacy is a reflection that the Indian languages are alive and well needs to be looked at. As in the case of Chinese, the literacy rate could be superficial, referring to children having taken the language subject at school, rather than reflecting a real ability to use the language.

5. 'ONE NATION, ONE LANGUAGE': MALAYSIA IN INDEPENDENCE

5.1. *Ethnic Composition and Languages*

Like Singapore, Malaysia is multiracial. It has a total population of 16.9 million, of whom 60 per cent are Malays or Aborigines, 31 per cent Chinese, and 8 per cent Indians, Pakistani, and Bangladeshi (*The Economist Atlas* 1991: 241).

The home languages of the people of Malaysia are very varied. The Malays use some variety of the Malay language which can be classified into four major dialect groups: the north-western group (Kedah-Perlis-Penang dialect); the north-eastern group (Kelantan dialect); the eastern group (Trengganu dialect); the southern group (Johor-Malacca-Pahang-Selangor-Perak dialect) (Omar 1982: 175).

The standardized national language, Bahasa Malaysia, is based on the educated usage of the southern group. Varieties of Malay differ from each other (and from Bahasa Malaysia) mostly in terms of phonology and lexis, and are fairly similar in syntax and morphology. It can be said that, generally, the 'sub-varieties' and the standard varieties are mutually intelligible. This applies also to the varieties spoken in East Malaysia—namely, Sabah and Sarawak.

The Chinese in Malaysia, like those in Singapore, are mainly from the southern parts of China. The dialect groups of the Chinese are, according to the latest available data—the 1970 Population and Housing Census of Malaysia—Hokkien (34.2 per cent), Khek (Hakka) (22.1 per cent), Cantonese (19.8 per cent), Teochew (Chiuchow) (12.4 per cent), and Hainanese (4.7 per cent), among other minority dialects (Chander 1972: 24). A substantial proportion of the people from these dialect groups speak their own dialects in the home, with a small proportion, the English-educated, speaking English as their mother tongue. In Sarawak and Sabah, generally the same Chinese varieties are used, except that Foochow (Fuzhou), a Min dialect, is quite widely spoken in Sarawak (Ismail and Omar 1973: 57).

The Indians in Peninsular Malaysia come from various language communities, speaking Tamil, Telegu, Malayalam, and Punjabi, with Tamils forming 80.9 per cent of the total Indian population (Ismail and Omar 1973: 54). A proportion of these have had English-medium education and speak English as their mother tongue, while others speak their regional languages. The number of Indians in Sarawak and Sabah is very small.

The aborigines in Peninsular Malaysia, mainly the Orang Aslis, form only about 1.5 per cent of the total population there. In Sarawak, the percentage of aborigines is much higher, with Dayaks forming 39.6 per cent and other natives another 10.6 per cent. In Sabah, the Kadazans form 28.2 per cent and other natives another 35.9 per cent (Ismail and Omar 1973: 53–6). In addition, there are also other minor languages spoken in Malaysia, including Thai and Creole Portuguese. Thus Malaysia is culturally and linguistically heterogeneous.

5.2. *The Colonial Period*

Before the independence of Malaysia in 1957, education was available in four languages: English, Malay, Chinese, and Tamil (education was also available in Telegu and Punjabi, although on a very small scale). There was a clear correlation between the ethnic background of the schoolchildren and the language medium of the schools they went to. A 1967–8 study shows that most Malays attended Malay-medium schools (89 per cent), most Chinese Chinese-medium schools (85 per cent), and most Indians Tamil-medium schools (67 per cent). The English-medium schools, on the other hand, cut across racial boundaries, and 28.3 per cent of the pupils were Indians, 14.3 per cent Chinese, 8.6 per cent Malays, and 48.8 per cent pupils of other origin. Considering the small number of Indians in Malaysia, they were significantly over-represented in the English-medium schools, while the Malays, being the largest group, were very much under-represented.

English-medium education, available from primary to tertiary, was promoted by the colonial government for reasons of administration and trade. Education in English provided the best job opportunities. It was the most sought after, and those who received education in English formed an élite group. Furthermore, pupils from these schools were mostly from economically and socially advantaged homes: the parents were keenly aware of the benefits of education and this attitude certainly had its effects on their children and their educational performance. But English-medium schools were found only in urban areas, and, because the urban areas were populated largely by the Chinese and the Indians, the Malays, who were mostly rural dwellers, were very much left out from this privileged group (Omar 1979: 15). Some of the Chinese and Indian pupils in the English-medium schools spoke English in the home: to them, therefore, education *was* in the mother tongue. This, however, was not true of all the pupils in these schools. The success of the children in this stream of education was due, not so much to whether the medium of instruction was their mother tongue, but to their socio-economic background, which directly or indirectly affected their attitude to education and their ability to climb up the education ladder.

The colonial government also supported education in Malay, taking the view that it was its duty to safeguard the language of the Malays. However, the government provided education in Malay only up to the primary level, for it argued that most Malays would go back to work in the plantations or follow traditional Malay trades. Partly because of the lack of opportunities for Malay-medium education at higher levels, and particularly because most Malays, especially those in the rural areas, were not very interested in the pursuit of education, many Malays ended up with menial jobs, working in smallholding rubber plantations and traditional Malay crafts; many were subsistence farmers (Omar 1979: 15).

Education in the Tamil medium was generally in a poor state and was available only at the primary level. The schools were located in rubber estates, set up for the children of Indian plantation workers. Absenteeism was high, and so was the drop-out rate. 'For every hundred pupils in Standard I [i.e. Grade or Year 1 of primary school], there were twenty in Standard IV, fifteen in Standard V and eleven in Standard VI' (Omar 1979: 17–18).

Although six years of primary education in the mother tongue were available to Malays and Tamils, few of these children in fact completed primary education for social reasons: they came from poor homes without much educational background.

Education in the Chinese medium was funded mainly by various Chinese communities rather than by the British government. It was available for twelve years, taking students to the end of secondary education. Before 1920, the spoken language in the classroom was a Chinese dialect—e.g. Hokkien, Khek (Hakka), Cantonese, etc.—depending on whether it was a Hokkien, Khek, Cantonese, etc. community which was supporting the school. The written norm, however, was not dialect based, but the common written norm used throughout China. In other words, education in Chinese, up to the 1920s, was in the mother tongue as far as the spoken language was concerned, for in most cases Hokkien-speaking pupils would go to Hokkien schools, Cantonese-speaking pupils to Cantonese schools, and so on. Since the May Fourth Movement in China, Mandarin Chinese has been used in place of the dialects in the classroom. Thus the Chinese-medium schools ceased to be divided into Hokkien schools, Khek (Hakka) schools, Cantonese schools, etc.: all became Mandarin-medium schools. This change meant that, for most Chinese children, starting school also meant starting a new language, Mandarin Chinese, which was not generally used in the home. Mandarin Chinese is close to the southern Chinese dialects, the home languages of the pupils, in respect of lexis, morphology, and syntax, but very different from the dialects in respect of phonology, so much so that most of these dialects and Mandarin are not mutually intelligible. However, what is of note is the fact that, whether before or after 1920, and whether or not the pupil's mother tongue—Hokkien, Khek (Hakka), Cantonese, etc.—was used in the classroom, the number of children who went beyond the primary level of education was low, and the number of those who completed secondary school was even lower (Omar 1979: 19). The high drop-out rate suggests that the use of the mother tongue was not the only factor affecting success in education. Social factors such as the attitude of the parents towards education, their economic and educational background, and the educational support in the home all played a vital role in determining a child's success in education.

5.3. *Language Education Policy in Independent Malaysia*

With independence, Bahasa Malaysia became the national language. In the early years of independence, education continued to be offered in Malay (Bahasa Malaysia), English, Mandarin Chinese, and Tamil at the primary level. However, at the secondary level, the government supported education only in Bahasa Malaysia and English, the former because it is the national language and the latter for its economic value.

It is felt that Malay-medium education for all, at least from the secondary level onwards, is desirable, because Malay (Bahasa Malaysia) is the national language and because education in this medium will help towards national identity and the assimilation of all the racial groups in the country. The slogan is: one nation, one language, one culture. It is argued that education in different ethnic languages would lead towards segregation of the racial groups because it would socialize the child to a Malay, or a Chinese, or an Indian world-view which would be relevant to the maintenance of the cultural identity of each group, but increasingly incongruous in the rapidly changing political, social, and economic conditions of a newly independent country (Chai 1977: 26). Thus a main reason for using Bahasia Malaysia in the education system is for nation-building and national identity.

In the early years of independence, English, too, was given recognition for economic and educational reasons: it was important for employment purposes as well as for tertiary education, the latter because there were not enough Malay reading materials for tertiary education. Thus education in English was made available. However, English-medium education in Malaysia was short-lived, because those in the Malay-medium schools and in certain states of Malaysia where English-medium schools were not easily available felt that they were deprived of the advantages enjoyed by those in the English-medium schools. Various Malay groups therefore agitated for the enforcement of the Malay language policy—the 1961 Education Act—making Malay the only medium of education in Malaysia. As a result, in 1970, the decision was made that all English-medium schools were to be converted gradually to Malay-medium schools, a process which would be completed by 1983 or 1984. Chinese-medium and Tamil-medium (or Punjabi-medium or Telegu-medium) education, on the other hand, continued to be supported by the government, although only at the primary-school level. At the secondary-school level, only Malay-medium schools were supported by the government. The motivation behind this move was political: to remove the advantage enjoyed by the English-educated, who were mostly Chinese and Indian, and to give the Malays an edge over the other groups by making their language the main medium of education.

Thus the new education system that has been in force since 1970 provides for two types of school at the primary level: the national schools and the national-type schools (described below). The national schools use Bahasa Malaysia, and English is a compulsory subject. There is also provision for the teaching of an ethnic language (in most cases the ethnic language of the pupils) where the number of pupils warrants it (e.g. Chinese, Tamil, Thai, Iban).

These national schools are attended by almost all the Malays, the vast majority of the Indians, and a small proportion of the Chinese. Most Indian parents send their children to the national schools because Indian parents are aware of the lack of economic value of Tamil in Malaysia and the advantages, on the other hand, of learning Bahasa Malaysia. As for the Chinese, according to a report in the *Straits Times* (26 Oct. 1987), 86 per cent of Chinese parents send their children to Chinese-medium primary schools, thus leaving only slightly over 10 per cent of Chinese primary-school children going to the national schools. Those Chinese parents who choose to put their children in a national school do so in order that their children can go directly from the primary school to the secondary school without having to spend one year attending 'remove' classes. The 'remove' classes are a kind of crash course in Bahasa Malaysia to prepare

TABLE 8.5. *Enrolment of ethnic Chinese pupils into Standard 1 of primary school, 1967–1982*

Year	Education				Total
	Malay-medium	English-medium	Chinese-medium	Tamil-medium	
1967	197	21,894	67,448	5	89,544
1968	235	22,108	70,521	1	92,883
1969	229	21,267	71,838	8	93,342
1970	16,425	—	76,457	1	92,883
1971	14,468	—	79,362	1	93,831
1975	14,108	—	83,123	2	97,233
1980	11,334	—	82,299	6	93,639
1982	11,126	—	79,645	6	90,777

Source: Gaudart (1985: 142).

children from non-Malay-medium primary schools for Malay-medium education at the secondary school.

The national-type schools are those where the principal medium of instruction is either Mandarin Chinese or Tamil (in a small number of cases, Telegu or Punjabi is used). In these national-type schools, Bahasa Malaysia and English are compulsory subjects. What proportion of the Chinese children go to Chinese-medium schools and what proportion go to the other schools? Table 8.5 gives the statistics for 1967–82.

It can be seen from the table that, with the closing-down of English-medium primary schools, about a quarter of the students went to the Chinese-medium schools and the rest to the Malay-medium schools (Gaudart 1985: 142). For a picture of the more recent situation, the report in the *Straits Times* (26 Oct. 1987) points out that about 86 per cent of Malaysian Chinese parents send their children to the country's 1,290 Chinese primary schools where the medium of instruction is Mandarin, the symbolic mother tongue of the Chinese, although the real mother tongue or home language of these children is not Mandarin but a dialect: Cantonese, Teochew (Chiuchow), Khek (Hakka), and so on.

The Tamil, Telegu, and Punjabi primary schools, mainly in the plantations in rural areas, are attended by children from Tamil-, Telegu-, and Punjabi-speaking homes. Very often the parents send their children to these schools because there are no national schools in the vicinity. Their choice, where there is a choice, is the national schools rather than the Tamil, Telegu, or Punjabi schools, because these Indian languages have little economic value in the country. Moreover,

interestingly, Tamil pupils find written Bahasa Malaysia easier to learn than written Tamil, in spite of the fact that they speak Tamil at home.

As for education in the aboriginal languages, there is no record of any such
school. Indeed, there is little economic and social motivation for learning these
languages. Nik Safiah Karim points out in her 1981 study that there is as yet no
script for any of the Orang Asli languages, except for those improvised by the
broadcasters of Semai and Temiar (Orang Asli languages) on Radio Malaysia
(Gaudart 1985: 78).

At the secondary school level, all government-supported schools are in the
Malay medium, with English taught as a second language. Although a pass in
English is not obligatory in obtaining a secondary school certificate, the importance given to English is subtly recognized in the fact that, for promotion from
the Lower Secondary to the Upper Secondary, a pass in English is required. Furthermore, in order to be admitted into the much sought-after residential schools
or other élite schools in Malaysia, an A grade in English is expected (Gaudart
1985: 381). Of the Chinese children who go to a Chinese primary school, about
90 per cent continue their secondary education in the national schools where
Malay is the medium used (*Straits Times*, 26 Oct. 1987). However, there are
in Malaysia a number of private Chinese-medium secondary schools. In these
schools, Bahasa Malaysia and/or English are taught as second languages. Places
in these schools are very much sought after and only the best students obtain them.

At the tertiary level, the government-supported universities use Bahasa Malaysia as the medium of instruction. There is a quota system for the admission of
students into these universities and the places given to the Chinese and Indian
students are limited. There are also a number of American universities operating
in Malaysia where the students receive the first two years of their university
education in Malaysia, before going on to the mother university in America to
complete their degree. However, the cost of sending children to these institutions
is high, and only the well-to-do are able to afford it. In this connection, it should
be noted that the government of Malaysia spends a substantial sum of money
each year sending Malay children to England for their secondary and tertiary
education. This is also true of the Malay royal houses, many of whom send their
children to England for their education.

Given the linguistic background of the children and the kind of education
system operating in Malaysia, what is the performance of children in the schools?
To what extent is the use of the mother tongue in education a positive influence on educational development? What are the other factors that affect the
promotion and spread of education? As statistics on language, literacy, and educational trends in Malaysia in relation to people of different ages and origins are
either outdated, unavailable, or deemed 'sensitive', what can be given here are
just patches of information which do not yield a comprehensive picture. However, several prominent features of the education system are apparent. First, a
main determinant of success in education in Malaysia is the location of the

TABLE 8.6. *SRP and SPM results in Bahasa Malaysia and English (%)*

	SRP		SPM	
	Bahasa Malaysia (1983)	English (1983)	Bahasa Malaysia (1984)	English (1982)
Selangor	78.74	60.03	82.34	53.03
Kelantan	40.00	40.00	16.45	16.45

Note: SRP is a public examination held at the end of the third year of secondary education; SPM is a public examination held at the end of the fifth year of secondary education and is equivalent to the GCSE examination in England and Wales.

Source: Gaudart (1985: 319).

school in terms of the rural–urban dichotomy. This seems to override considerations of whether or not the mother tongue is used as the medium of instruction. This conclusion is supported by a comparison of public-examination results in Bahasa Malaysia and English from an urban and a rural state (see Table 8.6).

Selangor is a largely urban state where Kuala Lumpur, the capital, is situated. Kelantan, on the other hand, is a rural state in the north-eastern part of Malaysia. The statistics in Table 8.6 show that the urban state of Selangor performs consistently better, both in Bahasa Malaysia and in English, than Kelantan, which is comparatively less urbanized. Performance in Bahasa Malaysia and English can be taken as a measure of general educational performance, because a pass in Bahasa Malaysia in the public examination is mandatory for moving up to the next stage of education. Similarly, a credit (very often an A grade) in English is necessary in order to be accepted into the élite residential schools or universities. Even within an urban state like Selangor, there is considerable difference in the pupils' language ability, varying according to the area the school serves and the background of pupils in the school (Gaudart 1985: 320–1).

Several factors account for the superior performance of pupils in urban schools compared to those in rural ones. Urban children, because of better facilities in the schools, greater availability of trained educational personnel, greater exposure to the mass media, and generally higher socio-economic background, tend to outperform markedly children from rural areas. Children in rural areas are hampered in several ways. A major problem is the shortage of trained teachers. Even when trained teachers are sent to rural areas, they find it difficult to adapt to the rural environment and the local culture (Gaudart 1985: 365). Another problem is that of attitude or motivation. Many parents in rural areas are themselves uneducated and do not aspire to a high level of education for their children. Few of them see higher education as a way to better their children's lives. The problems of education in rural areas hold true for schools of each language medium. The poor performance of Malay pupils in rural areas is a cause of grave concern (Gaudart 1985: 62). The problems exist among Chinese-medium schools and are reflected in a Malaysian Ministry of Education study which shows that, in the 1991 Primary Six Assessment Examination, out of 349 rural Chinese-medium primary schools, there were fifty-eight schools with fewer than 10 per cent, and eleven schools with 0 per cent, passes in Bahasa Malaysia (*Straits Times*, 11 May 1993). The problems certainly exist in the Tamil schools, where 'the culture of poverty' of the home, combined with poor physical facilities in the schools, produces a 'hopeless educational condition'.[24] Part of the problem of rural education is the problem of teaching Bahasa Malaysia. This afflicts not only rural schools but also, to a lesser extent, urban schools. The shortage of trained teachers to teach the language and teachers competent enough in Bahasa Malaysia to teach other subjects in the language are two main reasons (Gaudart 1985: 63). Besides, Bahasa Malaysia has not yet been fully standardized. This, and the lack of adequate and suitable materials in the language, render the learning of the written language a problem even for Malay-speaking children (Karim 1981: 50–4).

Those who fare best in the Malaysian system are children from English-speaking families, although the education they receive is not in their mother tongue, English. Apart from being advantaged by belonging to the higher socio-economic group which provides strong home support for education, these children are linguistically advantaged. They will probably be bilingual in English and Bahasa Malaysia. Bahasa Malaysia is the language used in their education from the secondary school onwards and it is the language they are surrounded by. Their home-language background provides them with a firm grounding in English, and the language is taught as a second language in all schools. Then, too, their command of English is reinforced by the mass media—English television shows, English movies, English-language newspapers, and other reading materials. Motivation in learning English is also provided by the fact that English is a requirement for many high-paid jobs. A small number of children from English-speaking homes may become trilingual in Bahasa Malaysia, English, and Chinese or Tamil (Chai 1977: 48).

From the above, it can be seen that whether or not the mother tongue is used as the medium of instruction is not a chief determinant in the success of education of Malaysian children. More important are a host of practical, political, social, and economic factors. As Chai (1977: 33) points out, 'Educational outcomes will continue to depend, in large part, upon the quality of teachers, the environment of the home of the child, and the quality of textbooks and other learning materials.'

---

[24] The phrases come from T. Marimuthu, as quoted in Gaudart (1985: 76).

6. DISCUSSION

In spite of its apparent simplicity and intuitive appeal, the notion of 'vernacular education' turns out to be far harder in practice to pin down than it seemed in 1953. On the face of it, it ought to be possible to identify a vernacular language by defining it, as the original Unesco document did, as 'the language which a person acquires in early years and which normally becomes his natural instrument of thought and communication' (Unesco 1953: 46).

The Unesco report identified and discussed a whole range of known and foreseeable problems in implementing vernacular education, from the availability of writing systems and resource limitations to cultural and psychological resistance. The general call for vernacular education was to that extent qualified. But the notion itself was never in doubt.

Our review of the four situations in this chapter suggests two kinds of problem when the terms 'vernacular language' and 'mother tongue' are applied in particular settings. Firstly, it turns out that some people in some societies may acquire in early years not one but many languages. Indeed, it may be the norm in some societies for bilingualism to begin very early. Thus, studies have shown that most children in Singapore are now growing up speaking two (or more) languages. To some extent but on a smaller scale, something similar is happening in Hong Kong. It would not be a simple matter to say what for these children should count as vernacular education.

The second problem is that, in practice, vernacular languages are almost always identified relative to some other languages which are standard, dominant, or more powerful. It is true that the Unesco report anticipated this, but the actual contrasts found often turn out to be multiple-level and complex rather than simple dichotomies. Thus, in contrast to Wenyan in traditional China, a style of writing more closely based on spoken norms was vernacular. But the spoken norms on which Baihua is based may bear little resemblance to a person's mother tongue, if he or she speaks a 'dialect'. In the provinces, it is not unreasonable to regard the provincial standards as vernaculars, in relation to the national standard, although we know that, a further level down, numerous local forms of speech are used which may depart from the provincial standards in significant ways. At the end of the day, what typically happens, if anything, is that a nation would, for purposes of education, settle on a language somewhere in between the 'real vernaculars' (according to the strictest possible definition) and the dominant language, and identify it as the vernacular.

This is true not only where the dominant language in question is more powerful politically or economically, but also where the language serves wider functions. We have seen how, in the case of Hong Kong, Cantonese can be regarded as the dominant language *vis-à-vis* other Chinese dialects spoken within its borders, but it is not dominant politically or economically. Apart from the sheer number of speakers, Cantonese also works like a provincial language by performing many public and cultural functions. It is the vehicle of a small literary tradition, the language of various art forms such as songs and operas, and for hundreds of years a language of education. Nowadays it is being used increasingly for such 'high' functions as delivering public speeches, addressing the Legislature, giving university lectures, and reading the news on television.

The relativity of definition also means that a language can be presented as a 'vernacular' *vis-à-vis* another language—for example, a colonial language— but the contrast at that level may well mask contrasts at some other level. Thus, in Malaysia, a great deal is said and done about replacing English with Malay in education, but little is known, and still less action taken, about the many aboriginal languages in Malaysia. This is not to say that provisions *ought to be* made, or even that the people concerned would themselves want or prefer to have that provision, but simply that the idea of vernacular education, when used uncritically, could obscure rather than clarify the reality of a situation.

An extreme case where this relativity is stretched to its limits is the notion of 'symbolic mother tongues' in Singapore, and the striking phenomenon of 'language planning' in the private domain of the home. It has been said that in Singapore, as a result of the government's promotion of English-medium education, and the officially-run 'Speak Mandarin Campaign', language shift has been taking place at a remarkable rate in the home domain from the local languages in the direction of English and Mandarin (Huayu). At least such is the situation as far as one can tell from the last census (although census figures may be very misleading).[25] Official policy is to designate four languages as 'symbolic mother tongues'. One of these is then assigned to each person in accordance with family background and racial characteristics, as 'mother tongue'.

This unusual reinterpretation was evidently not anticipated in the Unesco report, and there is no reason why it should have been. In response to government policy families are apparently 'planning' their home languages both to fit official definitions and to prepare their children better for the schools. To the extent that available statistics represent some semblance of the real situation, some Chinese families would seem to be abandoning their home dialects in favour of Mandarin, their symbolic mother tongue. At least this is what they say they are doing. At the same time, English is spoken very early on, in preparation for the children's education. For quite different reasons middle-class families in Hong Kong are also increasingly turning to English and bilingualism within the family. In the case of Singapore, primary education is simply not available in the dialects.

---

[25] With the possible exception of Hong Kong, relevant statistics are rather hard to come by, and when available, cannot always be taken at their face value. Little reliable information is found about the dialect regions and minority nationalities in China, or the ethnic Chinese or aborigines in Malaysia. Statistics *are* available in Singapore, but because the government both makes the policies and studies their implementation in practice, one cannot always be sure how reliable the responses to official surveys are.

Tradition, Trial, and Error 315

In Hong Kong some parents are opting out of the vernacular system in favour of English-medium education, perceived to be superior in quality and a surer way of securing better prospects for the children.

As far as the British legacy is concerned, there cannot be two more radically different cases than Singapore and Malaysia in coming to terms with their colonial past, particularly in matters of language and education. Malaysia has moved hastily to remove English and to put Malay in its place. Singapore, on the other hand, has done its utmost to capitalize on the legacy, so much so that not only is English firmly established as the language of the administration and education, but it is also, as we have seen, apparently fast becoming a home language.

In this regard, Hong Kong may stand to gain from reviewing the Malaysian and Singaporean experience. Although Hong Kong is still a British colony until 1997, the process of coming to grips with the British legacy has already begun, not least because, in this most unusual case, a date has been set by international treaty for the change of sovereignty. As far as language and education are concerned, Hong Kong may well steer a cautious middle course. Primary education has been in Cantonese and there is no reason why it should not remain that way. It is only natural that the demand for English and Putonghua will continue to grow. A 'trilingual' system is evolving with English, Putonghua, and Cantonese making up the three sides of the triangle.

Our review suggests that, while there are some common features and continuities, literacy does not have a constant meaning or significance across time and space. It is very much a feature of the modern condition that emphasis is put on the masses and the underprivileged and their rights, and in this light one can perhaps better appreciate the way in which a concern for universal education and vernacular literacy culminated in a Unesco report published in the middle of the twentieth century, Unesco being obviously an altruistic and international organization. As the world's nations continue to develop socially and economically, some regions are bound to stand out as being more industrialized and technologically more advanced, and, particularly in metropolitan areas, our understanding of literacy may undergo yet another transformation. Even now, there are calls for 'musical literacy' and 'computer literacy'. We will no longer be satisfied with basic literacy. We will want 'higher literacy'. And soon it will not be too much to ask for bilingual literacy.

Conclusion

ANDRÉE TABOURET-KELLER

This final chapter has the following aims:

- to underline aspects which differentiate our book from the 1953 Unesco monograph, arising from the personal involvement of all our contributors in the problems of literacy in the intervening forty years, and their collaborative effort in discussing them together;
- to emphasize the important political, economic, and social changes which have taken place during these forty years and the fact that we stand on the threshold of major technological and economic changes which are likely to have a profound effect on the future of education;
- to draw out from the foregoing chapters a coherent cognitive framework for the future discussion of vernacular literacy;
- to develop further some demographic and economic issues adumbrated earlier: in particular, the enhanced role that women may play in various societies in the future; the growing youth of the global population; and the potential shift of international economic development to the countries of the Pacific Basin.

Finally, we return to a reconsideration of some theoretical questions which the social upheavals of the last forty years have thrown into fresh relief.

I. OBSERVATIONS FROM THE FIELD, INSIDE VIEWS AND COLLABORATIVE WORK

Our book owes its qualities first of all to the fact that it stems from the collaboration of the participants in the four biennial Workshops of the IGLSVL. We have drawn on the personal observations and direct field experience of each member of IGLSVL, often in their own community, shared and discussed in our sessions. It is a book of first-hand experience, of concern for and thought about the values of vernacular literacy, its difficulties and its advantages. Our inside view contrasts with that of most official reports from international institutions such as UN or Unesco, or with humanitarian reports from religious or aid foundations or other sources. We have tried to base our work on in-depth reports and to look at literacy from a viewpoint other than a Western one.

The multifaceted studies contained in this book illustrate a large number of the factors involved in realizing or failing to realize the aims of vernacular literacy: historical, political, economic, social, psychological, pedagogical, technical. Not only are these factors numerous but they are highly intricate and differ in their respective weight according to the different situations. One of the challenges in our enterprise was to include every observation, even if it was not easy to deal with because it did not enter a general picture or because we did not know if it was possible to analyse it into discernible factors. A complementary difficulty was to respect the complexity and *sui generis* quality of each situation, to analyse it in order to extricate possible factors involved and, at last, to try to achieve some rational overall picture or to formulate afresh old questions and some new ones.

The 1953 Unesco monograph on Fundamental Education *The Use of Vernacular Languages in Education* was a milestone, the datum point which allowed us to contrast our experiences with the type of analysis in its seven case studies, and with the recommendations and conclusions reached by the fourteen specialists (plus two Unesco observers) after a three-week working session in December 1951 (see Chapter 1). That work has remained of major importance: vernacular literacy has since been on the agendas of international public agencies, has been sponsored by them, and has hence become a concern internationally shared; governments have also been made aware of literacy issues, in their own country and elsewhere.

2. CHANGES IN THE SECOND HALF OF OUR CENTURY

The period we cover, from the beginning of the 1950s to the beginning of the 1990s, corresponds with that labelled by Eric Hobsbawm (1994) as 'The Golden Age', from the end of the 1950s to the end of the 1970s, and as 'The Crisis Decade', from then until the 1990s. When the 1953 Unesco monograph was published, a social revolution was beginning:

almost as dramatic as the decline and fall of the peasantry, and much more universal, was the rise of the occupations which required higher education. Universal primary education, i.e. basic literacy, was indeed the aspiration of virtually all governments, so much so that by the late 1980s only the most honest or helpless states admitted to having as many as half their population illiterate, and only ten—all except Afghanistan being in Africa— were prepared to concede that less than 20 per cent of their population could read and write. (Hobsbawm 1994: 295)

But, as we must now note, and as our contributors have noted from their experiences, declared aspirations are one thing; an effective will to action quite another.

2.1. *Decolonization, Political Independence, and Literacy*

'Decolonization' has meant different things, historically, and in different parts of the world, just as colonization did; and the residual problems of decolonization remain powerfully with us though in different manifestations in the former empires of China, the USSR, the Arab countries, the European countries, and the Americas. The decolonization process gave rise to the emergence of social factors which had been oppressed or suppressed before; in particular the extension of democracy meant that the targets in the lives of most people became economic in the sense of a demand for cash and for the possibility to enter and to participate in the world of consumers of industrial goods. These targets were described and thought of as demanding literacy. But it is still very difficult to assess what exactly was needed: whether literacy, or vernacular literacy; by whom and for whom; whether by governments, or by the producers and business people who wanted to sell industrial goods which were difficult to use without a certain amount of reading, deciphering, or picture-reading skills, or by all those who were at that time not literate; by all of these or only a certain number of them? These were a huge and heterogeneous set within which the awareness of a need and the expression of a want for literacy was very unevenly distributed (see Chapter 2), even more so for vernacular literacy. Not only had literacy campaigns to be launched with external help but Unesco implementation of vernacular literacy was often the concern of Unesco intellectuals, defining and sometimes organizing 'communities' from outside.

The meanings of 'literacy', including 'vernacular literacy', have, as the Introduction has stressed, varied widely. Most of the Third World has differed from most of Europe. Hobsbawm (1994: 202) stresses that 'the history of the makers of the Third World transformations in this century is the history of elite minorities, and sometimes relatively minute ones, for—quite apart from the advance of the institutions of democratic politics almost everywhere—only a tiny stratum possessed the required knowledge, education or even elementary literacy'. But this has changed. Many members of IGLSVL have testified to the critical phases through which decolonizing or newly 'liberated' countries are passing, experiencing the tensions between 'nationism' imposed by a desire to maintain more inclusive political frontiers, 'nationalism' based on ethnicity, and the internationalism of economic forces—each of these having linguistic implications. In any case, anybody wishing to be active in national government and in international institutions needs to be literate not only in the common language of the region, which is not necessarily that of their community, but also in one of the small number of international languages, or at least in the regional lingua francas which since independence have tended to be developed into 'national' languages, like Swahili or Bahasa Malaysia or Bahasa Indonesia (see Chapter 1).

2.2. *Developed Countries and Literacy*

During the Golden Age, the vernacular literacy problem was considered primarily a Third World problem, whereas now, in the 'Crisis Decade', it has become a problem in 'developed' countries also, in at least three sectors: (1) the integration of immigrants and the schooling of their children (see Chapter 5), (2) the increase of illiteracy, and (3) the increase of the number of people who relapse into a bare functional literacy or complete illiteracy.

Take two examples. First, in France, in 1985, 6 per cent of French-born citizens were functionally illiterate; but in 1992, according to a Ministry of Defence report on the reading abilities of French army conscripts aged 18 to 22 (military service was obligatory in France), 9 per cent could read only a very simple sentence, and 10 per cent more could not manage a simple seventy-word text at normal speaking speed. Secondly, at the beginning of the 1990s, in the Province of New Brunswick (Canada), 27 per cent of the adult population were recorded as illiterate.

Various reasons are advanced for such developments. That most often mentioned is increasing social marginalization in cities, linked to unemployment, alongside falling standards in the public education system. But a recent survey in Germany, on adult illiteracy and economic productivity, showed that functional literacy—as defined above—must be measured not in terms of these falling standards, but of the ever-increasing level of literacy expected by employers in modern industry (Mitter and Schäfer 1994). The illiteracy phenomenon in Canada, however, responds to a very different analysis, since part of the population of New Brunswick belongs to the Acadian French minority. 'Minority illiteracy', seen as a worldwide phenomenon, means that belonging to a linguistic minority —even if taught basic literacy in the minority vernacular—may lead to functional illiteracy in both that and the official language (see also Chapters 5 and 6). In the case of Nigeria (see Chapter 7), Ndukwe advances the useful concept of the 'dissociation' of the vernacular languages from literacy: they are not thought of as languages in which it is possible to be literate. (Similar comments have been made in respect of West Indian creoles: the concept of 'correctness in a language' associated with written language is alien to how creoles are perceived; as Charpentier illustrates in Chapter 6, the same is true concerning pidgin languages.)

The period covered by the experience of the members of IGLSVL is very short compared with the long history of literacy but it is our time and the one for which we feel that we must take some responsibility, certainly as linguists, as Gardner-Chloros stresses at the end of Chapter 5. We have had no experience of a society completely detached from literacy to use as a datum point: among those studied, there is none without either a tradition of literacy in some of its parts, or, at least, contact with other literate societies. We had to place each case within its historical context in these respects. Moreover, the world's literacy is a fully dynamic situation constantly dependent on world language problems of which literacy is one part. For example, the computer software programme, *Windows 1995*, by Microsoft, which has just (August 1995) flooded the world market, attempts to detach computer use to some extent from a dependence on international literacy, through the use of such graphics as *emoticons* or *smileys* (Barlas 1994).

3. CONSTRUCTIVE PROPOSITIONS FOR A COHERENT FRAMEWORK FOR DISCUSSION

We will not repeat the discussion or conclusion to each of the chapters but we will draw on them to try to formulate some conclusions now of general application.

Seen from an orbiting satellite, the picture of literacy would be different from that as seen from a country, town, or village. The general introduction gives a sort of satellite image: dismal facts tell us that the overall result of all the efforts made over the years to develop literacy do not amount to a lasting success story. Most of the information given in Chapter 1 confirms this: statistics show the horrors of the global situation, case studies reveal the complexities within each case, ranging from a lack of political interest and will or a lack of incentive among the illiterates to excessive investment in literacy pursued as an instrument and symbol of an ethnic and nationalistic cause.

3.1. *A Cognitive Frame for the Discussion of Vernacular Literacy*

In order not only to describe and to analyse cases of vernacular literacy but also to make sure that what we say will make sense, we must try to have a cognitive frame for our critical and possibly constructive thinking. We must apprehend cognitive processes (such as distinguishing, opposing, categorizing, classifying), not as coming to us out of the blue, but as the result of constructed discourse, and as dependent on the use of relevant cognitive tools. These are basically linguistic and we do know that nothing is purely linguistic, or purely formal; as soon as uttered, or used, linguistic matter, lexicon, syntax, etc., gets coated with symbolic, historical, and social functions. The achievement of a pure and transparent cognitive frame remains an unattainable ideal.

Inaccuracy of Terms and Notions and the Need for Case Definitions

One shared response in our group to the 1953 Unesco monograph is the sense of the inaccuracy of its terminology and the vagueness of some of its notions. We had neither 'non-literate' situations to deal with, nor new words to use. Terms such as 'literate' and 'literacy', 'vernacular', 'oral literature', 'mother tongue', 'language' are notions, some with long traditions, and all with very varied and complex contexts of use. Their use incorporates all kinds of beliefs, too often not explicitly expressed. Hence the necessity to discuss and to evaluate them now and to refuse to take the easy way out—which is to label complex phenomena as 'natural' when it is our responsibility to assess and understand their cultural complexity and diversity.

We have reconsidered definitions and notions in the light of our field observations. This has led to fresh insights, in particular about 'mother tongue', 'vernacular', and 'literacy'.

As noted in the Introduction, we have reservations about the use of 'mother tongue': its metaphorical dimension makes it more apt for ideological manipulation than for scientific use (Tabouret-Keller and Le Page 1986). Article 3 of the Turkish Law, no. 2932 of 19 October 1983, states that 'The mother-tongue of the citizen of Turkey is Turkish' when an important part of the population is using Kurdish (Akin, forthcoming). We wish to distinguish the 'language of the home', or 'family language' or 'languages', from that of the mother or the father, or some other guardian. 'Mother tongue' demands precise *case definitions*, as, for example, in the case of the 'symbolic mother tongues' in Singapore (Chapter 8).

We need 'case definitions' also for some other terms, 'vernacular' and 'literacy' in particular. We observe repeatedly that 'vernacular' is a relative concept with meanings changing in time but also in space according to different geographical areas—as shown in Part Two of the book, from contrasting situations in Africa and Asia (Chapters 7 and 8)—under the pressure of political and economic factors—as shown again in Chapter 1, but also in Chapter 8, where four Asian countries in various stages of development (China, Hong Kong, Singapore, and Malaysia) are contrasted. Nor does literacy have a constant meaning or significance: this again is illustrated in Chapters 4 (on the pedagogical aspects of literacy), 5 (on literacy in the new minorities settings in Europe), and 8 (on tradition, trial, and errors in the four above-mentioned countries).

The Literacy–Illiteracy Continuum

Our observations here converge in the need to replace a full dichotomy between 'literacy' and 'illiteracy' with the notion of a continuum of levels of literacy. We must distinguish two dimensions in this continuum—that from non-literacy to literacy being distinct from that from literacy to non-literacy. The first is illustrated by countries where literacy replaces to some extent a more or less purely oral tradition; the second, by developed countries in which public and private education had, mainly from the end of the nineteenth century, brought about a fairly general literacy but where now, usually for economic reasons, a level of illiteracy is appearing.

In the first case, non-literate societies coexist with literate societies, or, within the same society, non-literate groups coexist with literate groups—as in most European countries before the nineteenth century. In the second case—as today in most European countries—illiteracy seems to have spread like an illness in societies whose pride has been a century or more of development towards the ideal of a fully literate community. Today the ideal is threatened for two very different reasons: first, widespread unemployment among the younger generation has devalued literacy and maintenance of their acquired literacy and undermined belief in the values of literacy; and, secondly, the new electronic media seem to give access to vast amounts of information with a limited amount of literacy, or even none.

Vernacular Behaviour and Vernacular Literacy

We have attempted to distinguish the use of vernacular speech from vernacular literacy, to see how far they overlap and are complementary, and to analyse developments in both literacy and illiteracy in such a frame.

In many of our case studies, the written 'vernacular' in a literacy campaign is different from the spoken vernacular of at least some part of the population. We have to deal with situations more or less diglossic or bilingual. In a number of cases, in particular in Europe (Chapter 5) and in pidgin situations (Chapter 6), bilingual literacy appears to be a positive solution though with inherent difficulties, as we will see below.

3.2. Reality Factors in Literacy Politics and Programmes

We need relevant cognitive tools, but, indispensable as they are, they will not suffice if we do not consider the political and social realities which constrain their efficiency.

Large-Scale or Small-Scale Approaches?

Many of our examples of literacy campaigns after 1953, if not all of them, have shown the great difficulties encountered in large-scale approaches. States are more or less highly centralized, and make decisions about literacy centrally; but the implementation of these decisions must be local. The difficulties arise from the lack of differentiation between general large-scale programmes, centrally or regionally implemented, and their local applications (see Chapter 4). Today, the definition of the appropriate level for taking responsibility is a general political problem, in our case not only for decisions concerning the way in which money should be spent locally, but also for the teaching methods that should be implemented locally.

Here we encounter an idea discussed by Brian Street, 'What is meant by local literacy?' (in Barton 1994). We must recognize the possibility of multiple literacies, not only local- as opposed to government-sponsored literacy but also literacies based on coexistent languages and writing systems, invented local literacies, and vernacular literacies—these last two possibly in existence even if the formal school literacy is absent or scarce. Our experience testifies that, in any given time and place, multiple literacies can coexist. The case-study approach we recommend, therefore, must allow us to contrast various levels of the realization of literacy and to assess their relative importance in a more general picture. Questions linked with the definition of the relevant level to be chosen for a decision are of prime social and political importance today, and decisions concerning literacy are a relevant example.

The Economics of Literacy

Cost-benefit analyses of language planning and literacy programmes have hardly yet begun. In order to identify benefits, Grin (1994) elaborates a complex model, which distinguishes between the political, the economic, the cultural, and the psychological values attaching to a language. He distinguishes (1) its immediate use in the production of goods and services, (2) its use as a secondary factor facilitating activities other than language itself (that is, all activities less those already considered under (1)), and (3) its values in existing as an option whose survival one may favour for reasons of social or psychological satisfaction. Such a model might be used also in a cost-benefit analysis of literacy, but we are far from having the data necessary to implement it, and almost as far from knowing if these are the pertinent distinctions in our case.

Youth, Development, and Employment

The nature of functional literacy is changing in relation to the worldwide problem of employment for youth, when more than half of the global population (5.5 billion) are under 25 years of age.

At the end of Chapter 1 Le Page stresses two nascent developments which are likely to have profound political and economic implications for the future of mass literacy. One is the shift of industrial and hence political power to the countries of the Pacific Basin, the other 'the development of women's movements in many countries, but in particular in India and other countries of South and South-East Asia and Latin America'; we shall deal with these further on.

The countries of the Pacific Basin are not uniformly developed in respect to literacy—highly developed in Japan, Hong Kong, Singapore, and North America (though not in Mexico), little developed in China and Indonesia, for example; but these are very populous countries most with increasing rates of economic activity and development, and of concomitant political importance (many examples are given in our book, but see in particular Chapter 8). We have to question here the precise weight to be attached to literacy in relation to a series of other factors, such as a huge labour force with a long traditional ethos of hard and harsh work; for example, the new harbour development north of Beijing still uses a workforce of hundreds of women carrying baskets of stones; such sights are commonplace generally in China, in the Indonesian archipelago, and in India. We know also that, whereas in the European Industrial Revolution technological advances created employment, today on balance they create unemployment.

Thus, not only is industrial development shifting from the West to the East, and particularly to the Pacific Basin, but the activities covered by the terms 'industry', 'industrial development', and 'development' are changing rapidly. Whereas in the Industrial Revolution in Europe, technological advances meant increasing profit and increasing job opportunities, today they still mean increasing profit but no longer an increase of job opportunities. Labour skills tend to depend on something more than the limited functional ability to read and to write: numeracy has become more important; however, this, in turn, may involve calculating machines. At the same time, the unskilled and largely unemployed labour force to which in many countries a high proportion of young people belong may have a very low level of functional literacy without any motivation for reading and even less for writing.

Women: Strengths and Weaknesses

Slightly more than half of the five billion world population (51 per cent) are women. The 1995 Fourth World Conference on Women, in Beijing, discussed the many inequalities affecting them in education, health, employment, political power, poverty, and violence. Of 1,000,000,000 people living in 'poverty', 65 per cent are women (Aulagnon 1995); at the same time, 66 per cent of the 1,000,000,000 illiterates worldwide are women, mainly from rural areas. Of course, we do not have the information to correlate these two statistics, but something more than coincidence might be involved. There has been progress in getting girls to school (in 1960, 65 girls attending for every 100 boys, today 85), but only 34 per cent of the recorded world labour force are women—meaning not that women do not work but that their work is not officially recognized, is not recorded as 'labour', or that it is practised in informal sectors. It was observed that between 1975 and 1993 the proportion of members of legislative bodies worldwide who were women decreased from 12.5 per cent to 10.1 per cent; it was also observed, however, that the proportion in the parliaments was higher in the developing than in the developed countries.

To assess the importance of women in the evolution of vernacular literacy, and literacy in general, raises complex questions. Two examples may help. In France, a highly literate country, women make up 53 per cent of the electorate, 40 per cent of the active population, and generate 40 per cent of the household incomes. But France is next to last in the EU league table for the proportion of women in parliament (the last being Greece): 6.1 per cent in the National Assembly, 4.8 per cent in the Senate. The second example comes from a suburb of Dakar (Senegal) where women formed a group to learn basic literacy. They used a public scrivener to ask all the embassies in Dakar for help; only the Dutch replied, prepared to help as long as the chosen language was Wolof. The women held their classes and achieved some level of literacy. When asked some time later by a fieldworker colleague (Caroline Juillard, p.c.) why they had made this effort, they replied that they did not merely want to be able to read and to write; they wanted above all to be able to count, to calculate, and to keep an eye on their husbands' finances. Reading and writing were in fact a secondary aim, but they had to make it their primary aim in public.

This second example seems to point to the idea of a threshold. Above it, easier circumstances for women favour their education; beneath it, at the level of poverty and daily worries about survival, they are prisoners of illiteracy, particularly in a rural environment but also in the case of women who are urban immigrants confined to their houses or to ghetto-like urban communities. These conditions are common among the wives of immigrant workers in the cities not only of Africa, Asia, and South America but also of Europe.

Correlations are not explanations. It must be made clear that high birth rates, or high prostitution rates, do not stem from high rates of illiteracy among women, though the latter contribute to the maintenance of the former. More generally, social marginality is a cause more than a consequence of illiteracy; literacy is likely to develop in association with other improvements. Worldwide economic marginality of the Third World countries will not be reduced simply by implementing literacy programmes, although literacy may well be a factor of change, locally or regionally, in hygiene, the birth rate, and so on. We must guard against overemphasizing the importance of literacy alone.

3.3. *Theoretical Questions*

The Importance of the Written Representation of Speech

In Chapter 3, Baker has set the development of ways of writing vernacular in historical perspective. Certainly, at the end of the nineteenth century and until very recently, widespread command of the written medium was seen as paramount for development and for the institutional life of societies, mainly through their bureaucratic systems. But there is in theory no reason why other forms of the representation of speech should not prevail. In the Middle Ages a tiny élite was literate, a clerisy who served government when their rulers were often themselves illiterate. The function of the written word was predominantly in religion and politics. For the non-literate masses instruction from the pulpit was vividly supplemented by representation of scripture on the walls of churches and in their windows by pictorial images.

Today we are no longer sure that the importance of the written word for the machinery of states and governments corresponds to the importance of the written word in the everyday life of most people. It seems rather that a certain dissociation affects the ever-increasing importance of written documents for public affairs—this itself may change in the near future—compared with the decreasing importance of writing in the day-to-day life of many who rely instead on the pictorial media.

Problems of Bilingual Literacy

In theory, bilingual literacy should not give rise to difficult problems; in practice, its implementation does. They can be summed up under three headings: (1) the fact that to define bilingual literacy, one needs to define languages as distinct entities and that such definitions are constrained not only by linguistic theory but also by territorial and demographic history, and more generally by political situations; (2) the political and economic values attached to a language, and the frequent nationalistic exploitation of these; and (3) the view many people still have of bilingualism as psychologically harmful, in particular for children. All these factors are illustrated in a study of the linguistic situation in the Russian Federation (Solntsev *et al.* 1992). The authors stress the impact which linguistic legislation in other countries, in particular in Quebec, has had on new linguistic legislation in the Federation. As early as 1990, the Quebec legislation inspired that of the former Republic of Estonia, which is based on the following assertions, in this order: first, that bilingualism has harmful psychological consequences; second, that only a language which fulfils all the social functions of a language over a given territory shall be recognized as a viable language in this territory; and, third, that, over a given territory, an absolute priority shall be given to only one language.

A very different example stems from recent developments in the San Francisco public schools system (Pyle 1995). The Bilingual Law of California was passed in 1976. The proportions of bilingual Chinese–English and Spanish–English children had increased in recent decades; bilingual schools were therefore established locally and used by a population, including more or less bilingual children from immigrant families and monolingual Anglophone children, mainly from the Black American population. The law required that at least one-quarter of the children in each class should be anglophones. Because of a series of disparate and not easily verifiable claims—for example, by the anglophone parents that their children were not making such good progress as those in monolingual schools, and by the immigrant parents that their children were frightened of the Blacks, and so on—the San Fransisco school authority decided to have separate classes for monolinguals and for bilinguals, at least until the latter reached the same linguistic and educational level as the former. The separation is also often justified by the need for the anglophones to begin their education in their mother tongue, but this is not urged also on behalf of the children who speak other languages.

No Universals for Literacy

Is there any general picture for literacy? Should we not expect one to have taken shape after all the work which has been done?

In *Cross Cultural Approaches to Literacy* (1993), a collection of papers exploring various literacy practices in some non-Western cultures, and in certain school settings, the editor Brian V. Street argues that we need 'bold theoretical models' and 'new theoretical approaches to literacy', including 'universals of literacy studies' (Street 1993: 5–17).

Our experience leads to caution. We will not offer any 'bold theoretical models' for vernacular literacy nor do we offer a hypothesis pointing in the direction of 'universals of literacy'. On the contrary, we stress two sets of observations. First, the mere statistical description of vernacular literacy results are not self-explanatory and cannot be so, if only for epistemological reasons, statistics being results and not causes. Second, vernacular literacy cannot and must not be separated from the situation in which it develops; in every known case it seems linked to the chief factors influencing any social situation, mainly historical and economic, although most of our cases seem to point to the dominant weight of economic factors (see conclusions of Chapter 1) and to worldwide economic inequalities which seem at present difficult to reform. Generally speaking, literacy is not autonomous: as a dependent variable it cannot give rise to universals; nor—more fundamentally—can it do so, because of individual behaviour, social constraints, or motivations, and of the politics of education. We would rather suggest as a working hypothesis the notion of a mathematical resultant of the main vectors we have just mentioned, if it were feasible to assign numerical values to these.

Literacy and Society

We see reading, vernacular literacy, and more generally, literacy, not as a technical but as a social act. To whatever extent it may be possible for advances to be made in democracy, health, hygiene, employment, and education independently of general advances in literacy, to that extent literacy itself will have the best chance to develop.

Certainly illiteracy is an obstacle to an informed participation in the decisions taken at all levels in contemporary societies, and for the one who is unable to read a newspaper or a political programme, the exercise of political right is in practice without a foundation. But neither illiteracy nor literacy can protect against the extremes of fundamentalism and nationalism. Concerned as we are with the spread of literacy, we cannot avoid being concerned with what is being spread by literacy. The most favourable circumstance for the mass of ordinary people to become literate, either in the vernacular or in some standard language, would be the genuine utility of such literacy for those aspects of social and political life with which they are concerned.

Excerpt from OXFAM (1993: 2–4)

Women have been at the epicentre of the social crisis caused by Africa's economic decline. With their multiple roles in production, motherhood and in household labour, African women commonly work between 16 and 18 hours daily. This excessive work burden is one of the major reasons for their poor health status—and the demands on their time are increasing. Falling household incomes have forced women to work longer hours, often taking on two or more occupations; to allocate additional time and energy in finding cheap foods and gathering fuelwood (as kerosene becomes too costly); and to spend more time and money tending sick children. Meeting these demands has forced women to sacrifice the only two resources available: their sleep and already virtually non-existent leisure time. Women's employment conditions have also deteriorated. Already less likely than men to be employed in formal sector employment, women are more than twice as likely to be laid-off. This has a negative impact on their ability to care for themselves and their children. The growing informal sector has provided a cushion of sorts, as women try to meet family survival needs. But work in the informal sector produces low returns for long hours, and is often undertaken in unsafe and insanitary conditions, with attendant implications for women's health.

Health and Education

Pressure on governments to cut back on social expenditure, such as schools, hospitals, and housing, has compounded the plight of the poor. By 1990, two-thirds of African governments were spending less on health in *per capita* terms than in 1980. Infrastructure for health care has visibly deteriorated as a result, especially in rural areas. Budget pressure has also prompted governments to recoup costs by increasing charges—or 'user fees'—for health and education services. Both the World Bank and the IMF have backed this approach on the grounds of efficiency, but the effect has been to put many services beyond the means of the poorest groups. In countries such as Ghana and Nigeria, the indiscriminate or poorly-targeted introduction of user fees caused a contraction in demand for services, especially preventative services such as immunisation and ante-natal care.

Reduced access to already inadequate health provision would have dire consequences at any time. In the midst of a recession, where the brunt of costs is falling on the poor, it has been a prescription for catastrophe. In the Zambian capital of Lusaka, epidemics of diseases such as cholera and typhoid, conditions that were not life-threatening on a large scale a decade ago, are claiming an increasing number of lives. Malaria, once subdued, is returning as a major hazard. In West Africa diseases such as yellow fever, which had been almost eradicated, are gaining ground again. And the incidence of potentially fatal respiratory and diarrhoeal infection among infants is increasing across the region.

TABLE AI. *Poverty in the developing world, 1985–2000*

Region	Percentage of population below the poverty line			Number of poor (m.)		
	1985	1990	2000	1985	1990	2000
All developing countries	30.5	29.7	24.1	1,051	1,133	1,107
South Asia	51.8	49.0	36.9	532	562	511
East Asia	13.2	11.3	4.2	182	169	73
Sub-Saharan Africa	47.6	47.8	49.7	184	216	304
Middle East & North Africa	30.6	33.1	30.6	60	73	89
Eastern Europe	7.1	7.1	5.8	5	5	4
Latin America & the Caribbean	22.4	25.5	24.9	87	108	126

Source: World Bank (1992).

The minds as well as the bodies of Africa's children have suffered from the region's economic decline. Rising costs of education, declining standards, and pressures on children to earn income have reversed what was a steady improvement in school enrolment. Primary-school enrolment rates, which rose rapidly in the 1970s, fell from a regional average of 78 per cent to 68 per cent in the 1980s; and less than a third of children now attend secondary school. This is in a region where only around two out of every three men, and one out of every three women, are literate. The education of young girls has been particularly vulnerable to economic pressures, since families with limited financial resources tend to withdraw their daughters from school rather than their sons. The overall result is a twin process of disempowerment. Africa's women are being disempowered and their low status reinforced by increasingly inadequate education; and Africa is being disempowered as the educational gap between itself and other parts of the world widens.

These pressures on health and education expenditure have serious long-term consequences for Africa because educated, healthy people are essential for achieving social and economic development. This should be readily evident to governments in the industrial countries, which recognise that investment in health and education is essential, not only for moral reasons, but to provide the foundations for economic growth and future prosperity. It is also evident to local communities in Africa, who are seeking to maintain health and education services through local initiatives.

Prospects for the Future

Grim as the experience of the 1980s was, things are getting steadily worse. On current trends, more than nine million people will fall below the poverty line each year for the rest of the decade, making Africa the only developing region in which the proportion of the population in poverty rises. (See Table AI.) As a result of these trends, Africa has the further tragic distinction of being the only region in which child welfare is set to deteriorate. The United Nations Children's Fund (UNICEF) estimates that by the year 2000

African children will account for 39 per cent of infant deaths worldwide—compared with 29 per cent in the mid-1980s.

Averting this deterioration in human welfare depends critically on economic recovery. Rapid population growth rates mean that the region's economies need to expand by over 3 per cent a year, simply to keep incomes constant. This has prompted some to argue that Africa's development crisis is, essentially, a 'population problem'—and that reduced population growth is the key to Africa's recovery. Oxfam regards this view as simplistic. In many countries, rapid population increase does contribute to a cycle of low growth and poverty. But the linkages between population, poverty and economic growth are complex. At one level, rapid population growth is itself a symptom of poverty. For example, high infant mortality rates and the prospect of insecurity in old age encourage people to have larger families. This is why rising living standards are usually accompanied by a slowdown in population growth. There is an even more powerful correlation between improvement in the status of women and reduced birth rates. Access to education, effective family-planning services, the provision of employment opportunities beyond childbearing, and the right of women to decide for themselves how many children they will have and when, are particularly important determinants of population growth rates.

Sustained economic growth is essential if the link between population increase and poverty in Africa is to be broken. Some indication of the scale of growth required was provided by the World Bank in a 1990 report, *Sub-Saharan Africa: From Crisis to Sustainable Growth*. This estimated that a growth rate of between 4 per cent and 5 per cent would be needed for the rest of the decade to provide for a modest improvement in income, employment, and nutrition. Without recovery on this scale, Africa will become increasingly unable to feed and clothe its people, to educate a school-age population rising by over 4 million annually, and to provide jobs for a labour force which is set to double in size over the next 30 years. With unemployment already affecting 100 million people (four times as many as in 1979), the implications for human welfare of continued economic stagnation are obvious.

Unfortunately, the World Bank's 1990 target now appears wildly optimistic. During the first two years of the 1990s, growth for the region (excluding Nigeria) was under 2 per cent, so that average incomes continued to fall. Agricultural and industrial production levels have expanded at less than half the target rate set by the World Bank, and investment levels, one of the main determinants of recovery, have not recovered. These are now hovering around 16 per cent of Gross Domestic Product (GDP)—a quarter lower than in 1980 and well below the 25 per cent level which the World Bank estimated was needed to sustain recovery.

More recent projections of Africa's economic prospects (in the World Bank's 1992 *World Development Report*) suggest that the rate of growth of *per capita* income in sub-Saharan Africa is unlikely to exceed 0.3 per cent a year for the rest of the century. This is well below the anticipated increase in other developing regions, and in the North (Table A2), and it would be entirely inadequate for a sustained assault on poverty. In reality, however, even this modest target is likely to prove unduly optimistic, since it is based on the dubious assumption that growth in the industrial world will recover to average over 3 per cent a year; and the almost certainly flawed assumption that prices for Africa's commodity exports will not worsen. Against this background the prognosis is for a future of continued economic decline, with inevitable implications for the welfare of poor people.

TABLE A2. *Growth of real per capita income in industrial and developing countries, 1980–2000 (average annual percentage change)*

Country Group	1980–1990	1990	1991	1990–2000[a]
High-income countries	2.4	2.1	0.7	2.1
Developing countries	1.2	−0.2	−0.2	2.9
Sub-Saharan Africa	−0.9	−2.0	−1.0	0.3
Asia and the Pacific	5.1	3.9	4.2	4.8
East Asia	6.3	4.6	5.6	5.7
South Asia	3.1	2.6	1.5	3.1
Middle East & North Africa	−2.5	−1.9	−4.6	1.6
Latin America & the Caribbean	−0.5	−2.4	−0.6	2.2

[a] Figures in the last column are a projection.

Source: World Bank (1992).

List of Contributors

Dr Rama Kant Agnihotri
Dept. of Linguistics
University of Delhi
Delhi 110 007
India

Jeff Allen
Société Internationale de Linguistique
(SIL)
1 rue d'Orgemont
93800 Epinay-sur-Seine
France

Dr D. Al-Emadi
Dept. of English
University of Qatar
PO Box 2713
Qatar
Arabian Gulf

Dr Lalit M. Bahuguna
C2D/68B Janakpuri
New Delhi-110058
India

Dr Philip Baker
137 Queen Alexandra Mansions
Judd Street
London WC1H 9DL
England

Dr David Barton
Linguistics Department
University of Lancaster
Lancaster LA1 4YT
England

The late Dr Adrian Battye
Dept. of Language and Linguistic Science
University of York
Heslington
York YO1 5DD
England

Dr Jennifer Bayer
Central Institute of Indian Languages
Manasagangotri
Mysore 570006
India

Professor Tove Bull
School of Languages and Literature
University of Tromsø
N-9037 Tromsø
Norway

Dr J.-P. Caprile
9 avenue Claude-Vellefaux
75010 Paris
France

Professor R. A. Carr-Hill
Education and International Development
Institute of Education
University of London
20 Bedford Way
London WC1H 0AL
England

Dr Lawrence Carrington
Faculty of Education
University of the West Indies
St Augustine
Trinidad
West Indies

Professor J.-M. Charpentier
Gragnague
Route de Beaupuy
31380 Montastruc la Conseillère
France

Dr Teresa Chisanga
Department of English
University of Transkei
PB X 1
Umtata
RSA

Mr Amitav Choudhry
Indian Statistical Unit
208 Barrackpore Trunk Road
Calcutta 700 035
India

Dr Pauline Christie
Dept. of Language and Linguistics
University of the West Indies
Mona, Kingston 7
Jamaica
West Indies

Dr C. Cooper
Department of English Literature
University of the West Indies
Mona, Kingston 7
Jamaica
West Indies

Dr A. Coveney
Faculty of Languages and European
    Studies
University of the West of England
Frenchay Campus
Coldharbour Lane
Bristol BS16 1QY
England

Nigel Crawhall
National Language Project
PO Box 378
Salt River 7924
South Africa

Martine Dechamps-Wenezoui
5 rue de Petit Fay
79190 Yoetot
France

Professor N. Denison
Am Foehrengrund 12
A-8043 Graz
Austria

Dr H. Devonish
Dept. of Language and Linguistics
University of the West Indies
Mona, Kingston 7
Jamaica
West Indies

Dr Marcel Diki-Kidiri
CNRS-LLACAN
4ter Route des Gardes
92190 Meudon
France

Professor Dr N. Dittmar
Freie Universität Berlin
Fachbereich Germanistik
Habelschwerdter Allee 45
14195 Berlin
Germany

Professor R. W. Fasold
Department of Linguistics
Georgetown University
Washington DC 20057–1068
USA

Dr P. Gardner-Chloros
Department of Applied Linguistics
Birkbeck College
43 Gordon Square
London WC1H 0PD
England

Dr J. Gerbault
La Bourdigolle
33240 Verac
France

Professor J. N. Green
Department of Modern Languages
University of Bradford
Bradford BD7 1DP
England

Professor Brian Harlech-Jones
PO Box 6406
Ausspannplatz
Windhoek
Namibia

Dr Abdullah bin Hassan
School of Humanities
Science University of Malaysia
11800 Minden
Penang
Malaysia

Mrs M.-A. Hintze
Dept. of French Language and Literature
The University of Leeds
Leeds LS2 9JT
England

Dr C. Juillard
116 rue St Dominique
75007 Paris
France

Dr A. L. Khanna
Rajdhani College
University of Delhi
Delhi 15
India

Professor Ruth King
Dept. of Languages, Literatures, and
   Linguistics
York University
4700 Keele Street
North York, Ontario
Canada M3J 1P3

Professor A. Kwan-Terry
Nanyang Technological University
Nanyang Avenue
Singapore 2263

Professor R. B. Le Page
Dept. of Language and Linguistic
   Science
University of York
Heslington
York YO1 5DD
England

Mr P. Livesey
Dept. of Cultural Studies
University of Central Lancashire
Preston PR1 2HE
England

Professor Dr G. Lüdi
Direktor, Romanisches Seminar
Universität Basel
Stapfelberg 7
Ch—4051 Basel
Switzerland

Dr K.-K. Luke
Dept. of English
The University of Hong Kong
Pokfulam Road
Hong Kong

Professors L. and J. Milroy
Program in Linguistics
1076 Frieze Building
University of Michigan
Ann Arbor, Michigan 48109
USA

Professor K. G. Mkanganwi
Dept. of Linguistics
University of Zimbabwe
PO Box MP 167
Mount Pleasant
Harare
Zimbabwe

Professor P. Mühlhäusler
Dept. of Linguistics
University of Adelaide
Adelaide 5005
Australia

Dr Hermas Mwansoko
Institute of Swahili Research
University of Dar es Salaam
PO Box 35110
Dar es Salaam
Tanzania

Dr P. Ndukwe
Dept. of Linguistics and Nigerian
   Languages
University of Nigeria
Nsukka
Nigeria

Hubisi Nwenmely
23 Lister House
Lomas Street
London E1 5BG
England

Dr A. E. Odumuh
Dept. of English and Literary
   Studies
University of Abuja
PMB 117, Abuja
Nigeria

Rebecca Pang
456 7/F On Cheong Building
Nathan Road
Yaumatei KLN
Hong Kong

Mme M.-L. Pradelles-Monod
Section de Psychologie
Université Louis Pasteur
12 rue Goethe
67000 Strasbourg
France

Ms C. Pyle
2 St Mark's Road
Henley on Thames
Oxfordshire
England

Dr Ben Rampton
Thames Valley University
18–22 Bond Street
London W5 5AA
England

Mr Euan Reid
Culture, Communication and Societies
Institute of Education
20 Bedford Way
London WC1H 0AL
England

Professor S. Romaine
Merton College
Oxford OX1 4JD
England

Dr C. V. J. Russ
Dept. of Language and Linguistic
   Science
University of York
Heslington
York YO1 5DD
England

Dr J. Russell
Dept. of Language and Linguistic
   Science
University of York
Heslington
York YO1 5DD
England

Professor W. J. Samarin
Dept. of Anthropology
University of Toronto
Toronto
Ontario M5S 1A1
Canada

Mrs Yuko Shirakawa-Chia
Block 602, No. 09–14
Clementi West Street 1
Singapore 0512

Mr N. Shrimpton
Dept. of English
Umeå University
S-901 87 Umeå
Sweden

Mr S. K. Sinha
6C Mecklenburgh Street
London WC1N 2AH
England

Dr I. Smith
Dept. of Languages, Literatures, and
  Linguistics
York University
4700 Keele Street,
North York, Ontario
Canada M3J 1P3

Professor E. Zuanelli Sonino
Seminario di Linguistica e di Didattica
  delle Lingue
Università degli Studi di Venezia
Venice
Italy

Professor Michael Stubbs
FB2 Anglistik
Universität Trier
D-54286 Trier
Germany

Professor A. Tabouret-Keller
8 rue des Arquebusiers
Strasbourg 67000
France

Ms I. Tasker
79 Hope Street
White Gum Valley
6162 W. Australia

Mrs S. C. Teo
8 Alexandra Avenue
Croydon
New South Wales 2132
Australia

Dr L. Todd
School of English
University of Leeds
Leeds LS2 9JT
England

Professor E. Tonkin
Dept. of Social Anthropology
The Queen's University
Belfast BT7 1NN
N. Ireland

Graham H. Turner
Department of Educational Studies
University of Central Lancashire
Preston, PR1 2HE
England

Professor A. Valdman
Creole Institute
Ballantine Hall 602
Indiana University
Bloomington, IN 47405
USA

Dr G. Varro
64 Bld Diderot
Paris 75012
France

Mr M. Verma
Dept. of Language and Linguistic Science
University of York
Heslington
York YO1 5DD
England

Professoressa J. M. Vincent-Marrelli
Istituto Universitario Orientale (DSLLO)
Largo S. Giovanni Maggiore
Naples 80134, Italy

Dr William H. Walcott
Settlement and Immigration
Language Instruction to New Canadians
49 Kennedy Road South
Units 3 & 4, Brampton
Ontario, Canada
L6W 4P4

Dr A. Warner
Dept. of Language and Linguistic Science
University of York
Heslington
York YO1 5DD
England

Ms J. Warwick
c/o Dept. of Language and Linguistic
   Science
University of York
Heslington
York YO1 5DD
England

Professor K. Williamson
Dept. of Linguistics
University of Port Harcourt
PMB 5323, Port Harcourt
Rivers State, Nigeria
W. Africa

Dr A. Wray
Fedw Barn
Devauden
Chepstow
Gwent
NP6 6PH

References

Abdulaziz, M. H. (1971), 'Tanzania's National Language Policy and the Rise of Swahili Political Culture', in W. H. Whiteley (ed.), *Language Use and Social Change* (Oxford).

Abercrombie, D. (1967), *Elements of General Phonetics* (Edinburgh).

Abstracts (1986), (1988), (1990): R. B. Le Page (ed.), *Abstracts and Transcriptions of the Discussions of the IGLSVL (International Group for the Study of Language Standardization and the Vernacularization of Literacy) Workshops at York* (Department of Language and Linguistic Science, University of York, York YO1 5DD, England).

Achebe, Chinua (1960), *No Longer at Ease* (London).

—— (1966), *A Man of the People* (London).

—— (1972), *Girls at War and Other Stories* (London).

Adams, M. (1990), *Beginning to Read: Thinking and Learning about Print* (Cambridge, Mass.).

Agnihotri, R. K. (1987), *Crisis of Identity: The Sikhs in England* (New Delhi).

—— (1994), 'Campaign-Based Literacy Programmes: The Case of the Ambedkar Nagar Experiment', in *Language and Education*, 1–10.

—— and Khanna, A. L. (1992a), 'Interaction between the Spoken and Written Forms of Hindi', paper presented at the fourth international IGLSVL workshop, Sèvres, France, 10–13 Apr.

—— —— (1992b), 'Total Literacy in Delhi: The Ambedkar Nagar Experiment' (mimeo).

—— ——, Verma, M. K., and Choudry, A. (1991), 'Social, Political and Economic Factors in Literacy in India', (mimeo).

Aguado Candanedo, D. (1988), 'La segunda generacion de Castellanohablantes y sus Actitudes Lacia el Euskera', in Congreso (1988), ii. 275–81.

Akin, Salih (forthcoming), 'Désignation d'une langue innommable dans un texte de loi', in Andrée Tabouret-Keller (ed.) *Le Nom des langues*.

Allen, C. G. B. (1893), *Ivan Greet's Masterpiece* (London).

Anciaux, R., and Baucy, D. (1993), *Langues, cultures et interculture: Une expérience pilote d'éducation interculturelle dans l'enseignement secondaire*, i (Brussels).

Annamalai, E. (1979), 'Symbolization of Alphabet for an Unwritten Language', in G. S. Rao (ed.), *Literacy Methodology* (Mysore), 117–28.

Ansre, G. (1975), 'Four Rationalisations for Maintaining European Languages in Africa', *African Languages* (London), 5/2: 10–17.

Archer, David, and Costello, Patrick (1990), *Literacy and Power: The Latin American Battleground* (London).

Argüeso, M. A. (1988), 'Factores sociolingüisticos en la Adguisicion del Euskera en el Pais Vasco', in Congreso (1988), ii. 205–10.

Arnove, Robert F. (1987), 'The 1980 Nicaraguan National Literacy Campaign', in Arnove and Graff (1987), 269–92.

—— and Graff, Harvey J. (1987) (eds.), *National Literacy Campaigns: Historical and Comparative Perspectives* (London).

Asher, R. E. (1994) (ed.), *The Encyclopaedia of Languages and Linguistics* (Oxford).

Auer, J. C. P. (1994), 'Broken Discourses: East German Everyday Rhetoric after the "Unification"', paper given at Sociolinguistics Symposium 10, Lancaster University, 23–5 Mar.

—— and Di Luzio, A. (1982), 'The Development of Italian-German Alternation among Italian Migrant Children in Germany' (Projekt: Muttersprache italienischer Gastarbeiterkinder, University of Konstanz).

Aulagnon, M. (1995), 'Menaces sur le droit des femmes', *Le Monde. Dossiers et documents*, 236 (Oct.), p. IV.

Ayestaran, Sabino, *et al.* (1986), *Psicosociologia del adolescente vasco* (Vitoria-Gasteiz).

Babalola, A. (1985), 'West African Languages in Education: The Literacy Dimension', in Williamson (1985), 3–21.

Bailey, Beryl Loftman (1966), *Jamaican Creole Syntax: A Transformational Approach* (Cambridge).

Baissac, C. (1880), *Étude sur le patois créole mauricien* (Nancy).

—— (1888), *Le Folk-lore de l'île-Maurice (texte créole et traduction française)* (Paris).

Baker, Philip (1988), 'The Major Languages of Mauritius and their Domains', in *Abstracts* (1988), 39–45.

—— (1991), 'Writing the Wronged', *Journal of Pidgin and Creole Languages* (Amsterdam), 6: 107–22.

—— (forthcoming), 'The Potential for the Development of Arabic-Based and Other Contact Languages along the Maritime Trade Routes between the Middle East and China, from the Start of the Christian Era', in P. Mühlhäusler, D. Tryon, and S. A. Wurm (eds.), *Atlas of Languages for Intercultural Communication in the Pacific*.

Bamgbose, Ayo (1965), *Yoruba Orthography* (Ibadan).

—— (1985), 'Barriers to Effective Education in West African Languages', in Williamson (1985), 22–38.

—— (1991), *Language and the Nation: The Language Question in Sub-Saharan Africa* (Edinburgh).

—— (1976) (ed.), *Mother-Tongue Education: The West African Experience* (London).

Barbag-Stoll, Anna (1983), *Social and Linguistic History of Nigerian Pidgin English as Spoken by the Yoruba with Special Reference to the English-Derived Lexicon* (Tübingen).

Barlas, Chris (1994), 'The End of the Word is Nigh', *Sunday Times (London)*, 4 Dec., p. 10.

Barreteau, D., and Dieu, M. (1991), 'Linguistique et développement rizicole dans le nord du Cameroun', *Cahiers ORSTOM, série Sciences Humaines* (Lisbon), 27/3–4: 367–87.

Barros, Marcellino Márques de. (1885), 'Notas sobre as linguas e dialectos da Guiné, e uma collecção de 30 poesias crioulas', *Jornal das Colónias*, 23 June.

Barton, David (1990), 'New Views of Literacy in Industrialised Countries' in *Abstracts* (1990), 80–4.

—— (1992), 'Understanding and Promoting Adult Literacy', in L. Verhoeven (ed.), *Functional Literacy* (Amsterdam), 1–18.

—— (1994), *Sustaining Local Literacies* (Clevedon).

Bassam-Tahhan (1989), 'L'Arabe ne doit pas être considéré comme langue religieuse', (interview), *Le Monde*, 23 Nov., p. 13.

Battye, Adrian, and Hintze, Marie-Anne (1992), *The French Language Today* (London).

Beijing Review (1989), 'Illiteracy Threatens Modernization' (16 Jan.), 4.

—— (1990*a*), 'The Anti-Illiteracy Campaign Goes On', (10 Sept.), 18.

—— (1990*b*), 'The 1990 Census' (12 Nov.), 17–19.

Bernard, H. Russell (1992), 'Preserving Language Diversity', *Human Organization* (New York), 51/1: 82–9.

Bertranpetit, J., and Cavalli-Sforza, L. L. (1991), 'A Genetic Reconstruction of the History of the Population of the Iberian Peninsula', *Annals of Human Genetics* (London), 55: 51–67.

Bhatt, A., Martin-Jones, M., Barton, D., and Saxena, M. (1993–5), 'Multilingual Practices: Home, Community and School' (project in progress, Lancaster University Department of Linguistics—Economic and Social Science Research Council).

Bhola, H. S. (1984), *Campaigning for Literacy* (Paris).

Bloomfield, Leonard (1933), *Language* (New York).

Bokamba, Eyamba G. (1991), 'French Colonial Language Policies in Africa and their Legacies', in D. F. Marshall (ed.), *Language Planning* (Amsterdam and Philadelphia), 175–213.

Bolton, Kingsley, and Kwok, Helen (1992) (eds.) *Sociolinguistics Today: International Perspectives* (London).

Boos-Nunning, U. (1986), *Towards Intercultural Education* (London).

Boulot, S., and Boyzon-Fradet, D. (1987), 'Un siècle de règlementation des langues à l'école', in Vermès and Boutet (1987), i. 163–88.

Bouquiaux, L., Diki-Kidiri, M., and Kobozo, J. M. (1978), *Dictionnaire Sango-Français* (Paris).

BPP (1911): *British Parliamentary Papers, Colonies, 1911, Education: Imperial Education Conference Proceedings*, Appendix I. *Conference on Bilingualism* (London), 244–66.

Bright, William (1992) (ed.), *International Encyclopaedia of Linguistics* (4 vols.; New York).

Bull, Tove (1985), *Lesing og barns talemal* (Oslo).

—— (1990), 'Teaching School Beginners to Read and Write in their Vernaculars: Some Lessons from one Norwegian Experience', in *Abstracts* (1990), 45–50.

Bullock, Sir Allan (1975), *A Language for Life* (The Bullock Report), report by the Department of Education and Science Committee of Inquiry (London).

Burke, R. C. (1976), *The Use of Radio in Adult Literacy Education* (Literacy in Development, ed. H. S. Bhola; Tehran).

Burnaby, Barbara (1985) (ed.), *Promoting Native Writing Systems in Canada* (Ontario Institute for Studies in Education, Ontario).

Camden, W. G. (1971), 'Dictionary—English to Bislama' (Port Vila) (mimeo).

Carr-Hill, Roy A., *et al.* (1991), *The Functioning and Effects of the Tanzanian Literacy Programme* (International Institute for Educational Planning, Unesco, Research Report No. 90; Paris).

Carrell, P. L., and Eisterhold, J. C. (1988), 'Schema Theory and ESL Reading Pedagogy', in P. L. Carrell, J. Devine, and D. E. Eskey (eds.), *Interactive Approaches to Second Language Reading* (New York), 73–92.

Carrington, Lawrence D. (1988*a*), *Creole Discourse and Social Development* (Ottawa).

—— (1988*b*), 'The Instrumentalization of St Lucian', in *Abstracts* (1988), 30–8.

—— (1990), 'Standardization and Vernacularization: Some Observations from the Study of Antillean', in *Abstracts* (1990), 38–41.

Carron, G., Mwiria, K., and Righa, G. (1989), *The Functioning and Effect of the Kenya Literacy Programme* (Paris).

Cassidy, Frederic G. (1961), *Jamaica Talk* (London).

—— (1978), *A Revised Phonemic Orthography for Anglophone Caribbean Creoles*, Proceedings of the Conference of the Society for Caribbean Linguistics, 17–21 July (no ed.; separately paginated) (Cave Hill (Barbados) University of the West Indies, Unit of Use of English and Linguistics).

—— (1993), 'Short Note on Creole Orthography', *Journal of Pidgin and Crede Languages* (Amsterdam), 8: 135–7.

—— and Le Page, R. B. (1967), *Dictionary of Jamaican English* (Cambridge; 2nd edn., 1980).

Cato, V., and Whetton, C. (1991), *An Enquiry into LEA Evidence on Standards of Reading of Seven-Year Old Children* (National Foundation for Educational Research, London).

Cavalli-Sforza, L. L. (1991), 'Genes, Peoples and Languages', *Scientific American* (New York) (Nov.): 72–8.

Centre for Educational Research and Innovation (1992), *Adult Illiteracy and Economic Performance* (Paris).

Chai Hon Chan (1977), *Education and Nation-Building in Plural Societies: The West Malaysian Experience* (Canberra).

Chall, J. (1967), *Learning to Read: The Great Debate: An Enquiry into the Science, Art, Ideology of Old and New Methods of Teaching Children to Read, 1910–1965* (New York).

Chambers, J., and Trudgill, P. (1980), *Dialectology* (Cambridge).

Chana, U., and Romaine, S. (1984), 'Evaluative Reactions to Panjabi–English Code-switching', *Journal of Multicultural and Multilingual Development* (Clevedon), 6: 447–73.

Chander, R. (1972), *Population and Housing Census of Malaysia, 1970: Community Groups* (Kuala Lumpur).

Chang, Jung (1991), *Wild Swans: Three Daughters of China* (London).

Charpentier, Jean-Michel (1979), *Le Pidgin Bislama(n) et le multilinguisme aux Nouvelles-Hébrides* (Paris).

—— (1992), 'Interaction between Spoken and Written Language' (mimeo).

Chimhundu, Herbert (1992), 'Zimbabwe. Standard Shona: Myth and Reality', in Nigel T. Crawhall (ed.), *Democratically Speaking: International Perspectives on Language Planning* (Salt River, South Africa), 77–88.

Chomsky, Noam, and Halle, Morris (1968), *The Sound Pattern of English* (New York).

Christaller, J. G. (1881), *Dictionary of the Asante and Fante language called Tshi* (Evangelical Missionary Society, Basle).

Christie, Pauline (1990), 'Why Vernacular Literacy?', in *Abstracts* (1990), 125–28.

Clammer, J. R. (1976), *Literacy and Social Change* (Leiden).

Comrie, Bernard (1981), *The Languages of the Soviet Union* (Cambridge).

Congreso (1988): Congreso de la Lengua Vasca, *Il Congreso Mundial Vasco* (3 vols.; Vitoria Gasteiz).

Cook, B. L. (1981), *Understanding Pictures in Papua New Guinea* (Elgin, Ill.).

Cooper, C., and Devonish, H. (1992), 'A Tale of Two States: Language, Literature and the Two Jamaicas', paper prepared for the Creativity in Language subsection of the IGLSVL workshop, Sèvres, France, 10–13 Apr.

Costa-Lascoux, Jacqueline (1993), 'Continuité ou rupture dans la politique française de l'immigration: Les Lois de 1993', *Revue Européenne des Migrations Internationales* (Montrouge), 9/3: 233–61.

Coulmas, Florian (1993–4), 'Language Policy and Planning: Political Perspectives', *Annual Review of Applied Linguistics* (Cambridge), 14: 34–52.

Cowan, J. R. (1984), 'Literacy in the Southern Sudan: A Case Study of Variables Affecting Literacy Programs', in Kaplan (1984), 75–92.

Cressy, David (1980), *Literacy and the Social Order: Reading and Writing in Tudor England* (Cambridge).

—— (1983), 'The Environment for Literacy: Accomplishment and Context in Seventeenth-Century England and New England', in Resnick (1983), 23–42.

Crowley, T. (1990), *Beach-la-mar to Bislama, the Emergence of a National Language in Vanuatu* (Oxford).

Crowther, Samuel Ajayi (1852), *A Vocabulary and Grammar of the Yoruba Language* (London).

Crystal, David (1987), *The Cambridge Encyclopedia of Language* (Cambridge).

Cummins, J. (1979), 'Linguistic Interdependence and the Educational Development of Bilingual Children', *Review of Educational Research* (Washington, DC), 49: 222–51.

—— (1981), 'Age on Arrival and Immigrant Second Language Learning in Canada: A Reassessment', *Applied Linguistics* (Oxford), 2: 132–49.

—— (1991), 'Interdependence of First and Second Language Proficiency in Bilingual Children', in E. Bialystok (ed.), *Language Processing in Bilingual Children* (Cambridge), 70–89.

Dabène, L., and Billiez, J. (1987), 'Le Parler des jeunes issus de l'immigration', in Vermès and Boutet (1987), ii. 62–77.

Daiches, David (1975), *Was: A Pastime from Time Past* (London).

Dalby, David (1967), 'A Survey of the Indigenous Scripts of Liberia and Sierra Leone: Vai, Mende, Loma, Kpelle and Bassa', *African Language Studies* (London), 8: 1–31.

—— (1968), 'The Indigenous Scripts of West Africa and Surinam: Their Inspiration and Design', *African Language Studies* (London), 9: 156–97.

—— (1969), 'Further Indigenous Scripts of West Africa: Manding, Wolof and Fula Alphabets and Yoruba "holy" writing', *African Language Studies* (London), 10: 161–81.

Dante Alighiere (c. 1300), *De vulgari eloquentia* (Florence).

DeFrancis, John (1950), *Nationalism and Language Reform in China* (Princeton, NJ).

—— (1977a), *Colonialism and Language Policy in Viet Nam* (The Hague).

—— (1977b), 'Language and Script Reform in China', in Fishman (1977), 121–48.

—— (1984), *The Chinese Language: Fact and Fantasy* (Honolulu).

Denison, N. (1982), 'A Linguistic Ecology for Europe', *Folia Linguistica: Acta Societatis Linguisticae Europeae* (Berlin), 16/1–4: 65–75.

—— (1987), 'Sauris, a Typical "Linguistic Island" in the Carnian Alps', in *Isole linguistiche e culturali* (Proceedings of the Twenty-Fourth AIMAV Colloquy, University of Udine, 13–16 May), 65–75.

—— et al. (1986) (eds.), *Muttersprache(n)* (Grazer Linguistiche Studien, 27; Graz).

Department of Statistics (1991*a*), *Census of Population 1990: Advanced Data Release* (Singapore).

—— (1991*b*), *Government of Singapore Report on the Singapore Census* (Singapore).

Deprez, Christine de (1994), *Les Enfants bilingues: Langues et familles* (Paris).

Derycke, Marc (1989), 'Variations et limites dans l'insertion de la parole batelière', *Langage et société* (Paris), 47: 29–53.

—— (1994), 'L'Alternance des formes "relatives" chez des bateliers faiblements scolarisés', *Langage et société* (Paris), 69: 5–36.

DES (1975), see Bullock (1975).

—— (1985), see Swann (1985).

Devonish, Hubert (1990), 'On the Ideological Barriers to the Use of Vernacular Languages in Education', in *Abstracts* (1990), 96–8.

—— (1992), 'Vernacular Languages and Writing Technology Transfer: The Jamaica Case' (mimeo), 13 pp.

—— and Seiler, Walter (1991), *A Reanalysis of the Phonological System of Jamaican Creole* (Society for Caribbean Linguistics Occasional Paper 24; Trinidad).

Diki-Kidiri, M. (1988), 'Elicitation of Orthography Choices in Writing Sango Language', in *Abstracts* (1988), 62–9.

Dinh-Hoa Nguyen (1992), 'Vietnamese', in Bright (1992), iv. 223–31.

Diringer, D. (1953), *The Alphabet* (London).

Dittmar, N. (1988), 'Literacy in Germany', in *Abstracts* (1988), 86–8.

Djaffri, Y. (1983), 'Enseigner le berbère aux immigrés', *Langage et Société* (Paris), 23: 77–85.

Dorian, N. (1988), *Investigating Obsolescence: Studies in Language Contraction and Death* (Cambridge).

Dubin, F. (1989), 'Situating Literacy within Traditions of Communicative Competence', *Applied Linguistics* (Oxford), 10/2: 171–81.

Duke, Antera (1968), diary, ed. and trans. in D. Forde, *Efik Traders of Old Calabar* (London).

Dwyer, David (1968), '*An Introduction to West African Pidgin English*' (Michigan State University African Studies Center, for US Peace Corps) (mimeo).

Eberhard, Wolfram (1982), *China's Minorities: Yesterday and Today* (Delmonts, Calif.).

The Economist Atlas (1991) (London).

Edwards, V. (1984), 'Language Policy in Multicultural Britain', in J. Edwards (ed.), *Linguistic Minorities, Policies and Pluralism* (London), 49–80.

EEC (1977*a*): European Economic Community, *European Charter for Minority and Regional Languages. The Children of Migrant Workers* (Brussels).

—— (1977*b*), *Council Directive of 25 July 1977 on the Education of Migrant Workers* (77/486/EEC) (Brussels).

—— (1985) *Accession to the European Community EEC Treaty: Portugal and Spain* (OJL1/302/9) (Brussels).

—— (1992), *European Charter for Minority and Regional Languages of Maastricht* (Brussels).

Ekwensi, C. (1961), *Jagua Nana* (New York).

England, Nora C. (1983), *A Grammar of Mam, a Mayan Language* (Austin, Tex.).

ESF (1993): European Science Foundation Network on Written Language and Literacy, *Proceedings of the Workshop on ORALITY versus LITERACY: Concepts, Methods,*

Data, Siena, Italy, 24–26 September 1992, ed. Clotilde Pontecorvo and Claire Blanche-Benveniste (Strasbourg).

Etim, J. S. (1985), 'The Attitude of Primary School Teachers and Headmasters towards the Use of some Mother Tongues as the Medium of Instruction in Primary Schools in Plateau State, Nigeria', in Williamson (1985), 39–54.

Etxebarria, M. (1985), *Sociolingüística Urbana* (Salamanca).

—— (1988), 'Vigencia y Uso del Léxico Vasco en al Castellano hablado en el Pais vasco', in Congreso (1988), ii. 359–65.

European Parliament (1982), *Rapport sur la lutte contre l'analphabétisme* (Strasbourg).

Experimental World Literacy Project (1976), *Experimental World Literacy Programme: A Critical Assessment* (Unesco, Paris).

Eze, S. (1980), *Nigerian Pidgin English Sentence Complexity* (Vienna).

Falla, Jonathan (1991), *True Love and Bartholomew: Rebels on the Burmese Border* (Cambridge).

Fasold, Ralph W. (1984), *The Sociolinguistics of Society* (Oxford).

—— (1990), 'Sustainable Vernacular Language Literacy Illustrated by US Vernacular Black English', in *Abstracts* (1990), 34–7.

Féral, C. de. (1979), 'Ce que pidgin veut dire. Essai de définition linguistique et socio-linguistique du *Pidgin English* camerounais', in P. Wald and G. Manessy (eds.), *Plurilinguisme, normes, situations et stratégies* (Paris), 103–27.

—— (1989), *Pidgin English du Cameroun* (Paris).

Ferguson, Charles A. (1959), 'Diglossia', in André Martinet *et al.* (eds.), *Word* (New York), xv. 325–40.

Février, James G. (1948), *Histoire de l'écriture* (Paris).

Fishman, Joshua A. (1968), 'Sociolinguistics and the Language Problems of Developing Nations' in Fishman *et al.* (1968), 8–16.

—— (1971), *Sociolinguistics* (Rowley, Mass).

—— (1977) (ed.), *Advances in the Creation and Revision of Writing Systems* (The Hague).

—— *et al.* (1968) (eds.), *Language Problems of Developing Nations* (New York).

—— *et al.* (1982), 'Maintien des langues, "renouveau ethnique" et diglossie aux États-Unis', *La Linguistique* (Evry, France), 18: 45–64.

Forbes, Duncan (1859), *A Dictionary, Hindustani and English: Accompanied by a Reversed Dictionary, English and Hindustani* (London).

Foster, P. J. (1971), 'Problems of Literacy in Sub-Saharan Africa', in Sebeok (1971), 587–617.

Fraenkel, B., Fregosi, D., Girodet, M.-A., and Vasseur, M.-T. (1989), 'L'Écrit et les illettrés. Pratiques langagières, scripturales et mathématiques' (Université René Descartes, Centre d'Education Permanente Internationale, Paris) (mimeo).

Franke, Wolfgang (1960), *The Reform and Abolition of the Traditional Chinese Examination System* (Harvard University, Center for East Asian Studies).

Freire, P. (1970), *Pedagogy of the Oppressed* (New York).

—— (1972), *Cultural Action for Freedom* (London).

—— (1976), *Education as the Practice of Freedom* (London).

Fyle, C. N., and Jones, E. D. (1980), *A Krio-English Dictionary* (Oxford).

Gal, S. (1979), *Language Shift: Social Determinants of Linguistic Change in Bilingual Austria* (New York).

Gardner, P. and J. P. (1986), 'The Legal Protection of Linguistic Rights and of the Mother-Tongue by the European Institutions', in Denison *et al.* (1986), 45–56.

Gardner-Chloros, P. (1991), *Language Selection and Switching in Strasbourg* (Oxford).

—— (1992), 'The Sociolinguistics of the Greek-Cypriot Community of London', *Plurilinguismes*, 4 (Université Louis Descartes, Paris), 112–36.

Garmendia Lasa, M. Carmen (1991, 1992, 1994), *Submissions by the Secretary-General for Language Policy made to the Institutions and Home Affairs Commissions of the Basque Parliament* (Vitoria-Gasteiz).

—— (n.d.), 'A few Comments about the Path which has been followed and the situation at the Present Time' (mimeo).

Gaudart, Hyacinth Marie (1985), 'A Descriptive Study of Bilingual Education in Malaysia' (Ph.D. diss., University of Hawaii).

Gelb, Ignace J. (1952), *A Study of Writing* (Chicago).

Gerbault, Jeannine (1987), 'Utilisation des langues et attitudes: la montée du sango', *Bulletin de l'Observatoire du Français Contemporain en Afrique Noire* (Paris), 8: 25–68.

—— (1988), 'Attitudes and Problems Regarding the Development of Literacy in Sango', in *Abstracts* (1988), 70–8.

—— (1989), 'Modes d'appropriation langagière en République Centrafricaine', *Bulletin du Centre d'Études des Plurilinguismes* (IDERIC, Université de Nice), 11: 10.

—— (1990), 'Conflicting Forces in the Standardization of Sango and the Development of Vernacular Literacy in the Central African Republic', in *Abstracts* (1990), 8–11.

—— (1992), 'Political and economic aspects of vernacular literacy developments in Cameroon' (mimeo).

—— and Wenezoui, M. (1988), 'Attitudes vis à vis du français, du sango, et du fransango: une expérience de "matched-guise"', communication présentée au Symposium International 'Contact + Confli(c)t '88', Brussels, June.

Girodet, M. A. (1983), *Calculs écrits, données culturelles et alphabétisation* (Paris).

Gleason, H. A. (1961) *An Introduction to Descriptive Linguistics* (2nd edn., New York).

Gleitman, Lila R., and Rozin, Paul (1977), 'The Structure and Acquisition of Reading 1: Relations between Orthographies and the Structure of Language', in Reber and Scarborough (1977), 1–53.

Gordon, D. C. (1978), *The French Language and National Identity* (The Hague).

Gorman, T. P. (1968), 'Bilingualism in the Educational System of Kenya', in Edmund King (ed.), *Comparative Education* (Oxford), iv. 213–21.

—— (1971), 'Sociolinguistic Implications of a Choice of Media of Instruction', in W. H. Whiteley (ed.), *Language Use and Social Change* (Oxford), 198–220.

—— (1977), 'Literacy in the Mother Tongue: A Reappraisal of Research and Practice', in T. P. Gorman (ed.), *Language and Literacy: Current Issues and Research* (Tehran), 271–90.

Gott, Richard (1995), 'The Latin Conversion', *Guardian Weekend Magazine* (London), 10 June, pp. 14–27.

—— (1995), *Land without Evil: Utopian Journeys across the South American Watershed* (London).

Gough, Kathleen (1968), 'Literacy in Kerala', in J. Goody (ed.), *Literacy in Traditional Societies* (Cambridge), 132–60.

Government of France (1982), Circular No. 82–261 of 21 June 1982, *Bulletin Officiel*, No. 26 (1 July).

Grace, George W. (1992), *Ethnolinguistic Notes*, Series 3, 43 (University of Hawaii).

Graff, Harvey J. (1981) (ed.), *Literacy and Social Development in the West* (Cambridge).

Greenfield, Patricia M. (1972), 'Oral or Written Language: The Consequences for Cognitive Development in Africa, the United States, and England', in D. B. Fry (ed.) *Language and Speech* (Teddington, Middlesex), xv. 169–78.

Grin, François (1994), 'L'Identification des bénéfices de l'aménagement linguistique: La langue comme actif naturel', in C. Philipponeau (ed.), *Sociolinguistic Studies and Language Planning* (CRLA, University of Moncton), 67–101.

Gudschinsky, S. C. (1962), *Handbook of Literacy* (Dallas).

—— (1968), 'The Relationship of Language and Linguistics to Reading', *Kivung* (Boroko, Papua New Guinea), i. 146–152.

—— (1973), *Manual of Literacy for Preliterate Peoples* (Karumpa, New Guinea).

Gupta, Anthea Fraser (1994*a*), 'The Truth about Singapore English,' in Tom McArthur (ed.), *English Today*, 38, IV (ii): 15–17.

—— (1994*b*), *The Step-Tongue: Children's English in Singapore* (Clevedon).

Gustaffson, U. (forthcoming), *The Adivasi-Oriya-Telugu Adult Literacy and Education Programme*.

Guy, Jacques (1992), 'A criticism of Cavalli-Sforza' (E-Mail message, 27 Jan., from j.guy@.oz.au, and subsequent interchanges).

Hagège, C. (1990), *The Dialogic Species* (New York).

Hall, Robert A., Jr. (1943), *Melanesian Pidgin English* (Baltimore).

—— (1953), *Haitian Creole: Grammar, Texts, Vocabulary* (Washington, DC).

—— (1955), 'A Standard Orthography and List of Suggested Spellings for Neo-Melanesian' (Department of Education, Port Moresby) (mimeo).

—— (1966), *Pidgin and Creole Languages* (Ithaca, NY).

—— (1972), 'Pidgins and Creoles as Standard Languages', in J. Pride and J. Holmes (eds.), *Sociolinguistics* (Harmondsworth), 142–54.

Hamadache, A., and Martin, D. (1986), *Theory and Practice of Literacy Work: Policies, Strategies, and Examples* (Paris).

Hamers, J., and Blanc, M. (1989), *Bilinguality and Bilingualism* (Cambridge).

Hartley, T. (1993), 'Generations of Literacy among Women in a Bilingual Community', in M. Hamilton, D. Barton, and R. Ivanic (eds.), *Worlds of Literacy* (Clevedon), 29–40.

Hawkins, Eric (1992), 'La Réflexion sur le langage comme "matière-pont" dans le programme scolaire', in G. Ducanel (ed.), *Langues vivantes et français à l'école* (Institut National Recherche Pédagogique, Reperes No. 6; Paris), 41–56.

Hayhoe, Ruth (1992) (ed.), *Education and Modernization: The Chinese Experience* (Oxford).

Hazaël-Massieux, Marie-Christine (1994), *Écrire en Créole* (Paris).

Heberer, Thomas (1989), *China and its National Minorities: Autonomy or Assimilation* (Armonk NY).

Hébert, Yvonne M., and Lindley, Sharon (1985), 'Evaluating an Orthography', in Burnaby (1985), 185–200.

Henze, Paul B. (1977), 'Politics and Alphabets in Inner Asia', in Fishman (1977), 371–420.

Heredia-Deprez, C. de. (1989), 'Le Plurilinguisme des enfants à Paris', *Revue Européenne des Migrations Internationales* (Montrouge), 5/2: 71–87.

Highton, D. (1986), 'Television and Basic Skills: Getting Beyond the Screen', in A. K. Pugh and C. Volkmar (eds.), *Aspects of Adult Literacy* (Munich), 124–31.

HMI (1990): Her Majesty's Inspectorate of Schools, Great Britain, *The Teaching of Learning and Reading in Primary Schools* (HMSO, London).

Hobsbawm, Eric (1990), *Nations and Nationalism since 1780* (Cambridge).

—— (1994), *Age of Extremes: The Short Twentieth Century 1914–1991* (London).

Holm, John (1978) 'The Creole English of Nicaragua's Miskito Coast: Its Sociolinguistic History and a Comparative Study of its Lexicon and Syntax' (doctoral diss, University College, University of London).

—— (1989), *Pidgins and Creoles*, ii. *Reference Survey* (Cambridge).

—— (1981) (ed.), *Central American English: Creole Texts from the Western Caribbean* (Heidelberg).

Holme, Randal (1994) (ed.), *Dunford Seminar Report 1994: Functional Literacy for Development: Issues of Language and Method* (Manchester).

Hong Kong Census and Statistics Department (1992), *Population Census: Summary Results* (Hong Kong).

Hosking, R. F., and Meredith-Owens, G. M. (1966), *A Handbook of Asian Scripts* (London).

Houston, R. A. (1985), *Scottish Literacy and the Scottish Identity* (Cambridge).

—— (1987), 'The Literacy Campaign in Scotland, 1560–1803', in Arnove and Graff (1987), 49–64.

Howes, Stephen (1992), *Purchasing Power, Infant Mortality and Literacy in China and India: An Inter-Provincial Analysis* (London).

Hu Shi Ming and Seifman, Eli. (1976) (eds.), *Towards a New World Outlook: A Documentary History of Education in the People's Republic of China, 1949–1976* (New York).

—— (1987), *Education and Socialist Modernization: A Documentary History of Education in the People's Republic of China, 1977–1986* (New York).

Huffines, Marion Luks (1980), 'Pennsylvania German: Maintenance and Shift', in Robert C. Williamson (ed.), *International Journal of the Sociology of Language* (The Hague), 43–58.

Hyman, Larry M. (1975), *Phonology: Theory and Analysis* (New York).

INSEE (1994): Institut National de la Statistique et des Études Économiques, *Les Etrangers en France: Portrait social* (Collection 'Contours et caractères'; Paris).

Intercultural Education for Migrant Children (1992), 'National Report to the Commission of the European Communities, established by J. Prunet, Inspecteur d'Académie (July)' (Paris: Ministère de L'Éducation Nationale) (mimeo).

International Institute for African Languages and Cultures (1930), *Practical Orthography of African Languages* (London).

Inter-Territorial Language Committee for the East African Dependencies (1939), *A Standard Swahili–English Dictionary* (2 vols.; London).

Ismail, Abdul Razak, and Omar, Asmah Haji (1973), *The Sociolinguistic Situation in Malaysia. Report of a Regional Workshop on the Feasibility of a Sociolinguistic Survey of Southeast Asia* (Regional English Language Centre, Singapore).

Itebete, P. A. N. (1974), 'Language Standardization in Western Luyia', in Whiteley (1974), 87–114.

Izquierdo, D. M. (1985), 'Fortores determinantes y consecuenciase educativas de la perseverancia de los adultos en los circulos de alfabetizacion', in E. P. Roldan (ed.), *Revista Latinoamericano de Estudios Educativos* (Mexico), xv. 3.

Jeffries, Sir Charles Joseph (1967), *Illiteracy: A World Problem* (New York).

Jensen, Hans (1970), *Sign, Symbol and Script* (London).

Jerab, N. (1988), 'L'Arabe des Maghrébins: Une langue, des langues', in Vermès (1988), ii. 31–59.

Jernudd, B. H. (1986) (ed.), *Chinese Language Planning: Perspectives from China and abroad*, special issue of the *International Journal of the Sociology of Language* (Berlin), 59.

Johnson, Eric (1992), 'Problems Relating to the Publication of Krio Materials', in Jones *et al.* (1992), 55–60.

Jones, Daniel (1966), *The Pronunciation of English* (Cambridge) (1st edn., 1909).

—— and Plaatje, Solomon Tshekisho (1916), *A Sechuana Reader in International Phonetic Orthography* (London).

Jones, Eldred D., Sandred, Karl I., and Shrimpton, Neville (1992) (eds.), *Reading and Writing Krio* (Uppsala).

Jordan, A. C. (1960), *A Practical Course in Xhosa* (Cape Town).

Juillard, Caroline (1988), 'Senegal: The Situation Today Regarding Literacy in the National Languages', in *Abstracts* (1988), 99–105.

—— (1990), 'A Case Study of Literacy in Vernacular Languages in Ziguinchor, Southern Senegal', in *Abstracts* (1990), 12–14.

Kalu, Ukoha (1990), 'Murdering Mother Tongues', *Daily Champion*, 17 Mar.

Kamwella, A. J. (1985), *Impact of Adult Education in Tanzania* (Department of Adult Education, Ministry of Education, Dar es Salaam).

Kaplan, Robert B. (1984) (ed.), *Annual Review of Applied Linguistics* (Cambridge), iv.

Karim, Nik Safiah (1981), 'Bahasa Malaysia as a Medium of Instruction in a Modern Plural Society', in Asmah Haji Omar (ed.), *National Language as Medium of Instruction* (Kuala Lumpur), 44–57.

Kavanagh, J. F., and Mattingley, I. G. (1972), *Language by Ear and Eye* (Cambridge, Mass.).

Khan, V. S. (1984), 'The Mother-Tongue Teaching Directory Survey of the Linguistic Minorities Project', unpublished report to the National Council for Mother-Tongue Teaching and the Institute of Education, University of London.

—— Reid, E., and Couilland, X. (1984), *The Mother-Tongue Teaching Directory Survey of the Linguistic Minorities Project* (LMP/CLE Working Paper No. 6; University of London: Institute of Education).

Khanna, A. L., and Agnihotri, R. K. (1992), 'A Plea for Bilingual Literacy', paper presented at the fourth IGLSVL workshop, Sèvres, France, 10–13 Apr.

Khubchandani, Lachman M. (1969), 'Sindhi', in Thomas A. Sebeok (ed.), *Current Trends in Linguistics*, v. *Linguistics in South Asia* (The Hague), 201–34.

Kindell, G. (1984), 'Linguistics and Literacy', in Kaplan (1984), 8–22.

Klassen, C. (1991), 'Bilingual Written Language Use by Low-Education Latin-American Newcomers', in D. Barton and R. Ivanic (eds.), *Writing in the Community: Written Communication Annual* (London), 38–58.

Krieger, M. (1991), 'Language in Cameroon, 1960–1990: Bilingual Policy, Multilingual Practice', *Issues in Language Education* (Boston, Mass.), 4.

Kuo, Eddie C. Y. (1980), 'The Sociolinguistic Situation in Singapore', in Evangelos A. Afendras and Eddie C. Y. Kuo (eds.), *Language and Society in Singapore* (Singapore), 39–62.

Kwan-Terry, Anna (1989), 'Education and the Pattern of Language Use among Ethnic Chinese School Children in Singapore', *International Journal of the Sociology of Language* (Berlin), 80: 5–31.

—— (1993), 'Cross Currents in the Use of English in Singapore', in Braj Kachra (ed.), *World Englishes* (Oxford), 12/1: 75–84.

—— and Kwan-Terry, John. (1993), 'Literacy and the Dynamics of Language Planning: The Case of Singapore', in Peter Freebody and Anthony R. Welch (eds.), *Knowledge, Culture and Power* (London), 142–61.

Laitin, David D. (1992), *Language Repertoires and State Construction in Africa* (Cambridge).

Lamb, P., and Arnold, R. (1980), *Teaching Reading: Foundations and Strategies* (2nd edn., New York).

Lambert, W. E. (1972), *Language, Psychology and Culture: Essays by Wallace E. Lambert*, ed. A. S. Dil (Stanford, Calif.).

—— (1977), 'Effects of Bilingualism on the Individual', in P. A. Hornby (ed.), *Bilingualism: Psychological, Social and Educational Implications* (New York), 15–28.

Lau Kak Eng (1993), *Singapore Census of Population 1990* (Singapore).

Laqueur, Thomas W. (1983), 'Toward a Cultural Ecology of Literacy in England, 1600–1850', in Resnick (1983), 43–58.

Laubach, F. C., and Laubach, R. S. (1960), *Towards World Literacy: The Each One Teach One Way* (Syracuse, NY).

Laycock, D. (1982), 'Melanesian Linguistic Diversity: A Linguistic Choice?', in R. J. May and H. Nelson (eds.), *Melanesia: Beyond Diversity* (Canberra), i. 33–8.

Lee, E. W. (1982), *Literacy Primers: The Gudschinsky Method* (Dallas).

Lefebvre, Claire, and Muysken, Pieter (1988), *Mixed Categories: Nominalizations in Quechua* (Dordrecht).

Le Monde de l'éducation (1989), 'Familles immigrées: Un pied dans l'école' (Paris) (May), 35.

—— (1990), 'L'Arabe, rue de Tanger' (Paris) (Jan.).

Le Page, R. B. (1952), 'A Survey of Dialects in the British Caribbean', *Caribbean Quarterly* (University College of the West Indies, Jamaica), 2/2: 4–11.

—— (1960), 'An Historical Introduction to Jamaican Creole', in R. B. Le Page (ed.), *Jamaican Creole* (London), 3–124.

—— (1964a), *The National Language Question* (Oxford).

—— (1964b), 'Multilingualism in Malaya', in *Inter-African Committee on Linguistics, Symposium on Multilingualism . . . Brazzaville . . . 1962* (Scientific Council for Africa, 89; London), 133–46.

—— (1968a), 'Problems to be Faced in the Use of English as the Medium of Education in Four West Indian Territories', in Fishman *et al.* (1968), 431–41.

—— (1968b), 'Problems of Description in Multilingual Communities', *Transactions of the Philological Society* (Oxford), 189–212.

—— (1978), '"Projection, Focussing, Diffusion", or, Steps towards a Sociolinguistic Theory of Language etc.' (Society for Caribbean Linguistics, Occasional Paper, 9; St Augustine, Trinidad).

—— (1985), 'The Standardization of Languages and the Vernacularization of Literacy', in Peter S. Green (ed.), *York Papers in Language Teaching: Festschrift for Eric Hawkins on his 70th birthday* (University of York, Language Teaching Centre), 129–137.

Le Page, R. B. (1989), 'What is a Language?' in Paul Livesey and Mahendra Verma (eds.), *York Papers in Linguistics* (Department of Language and Linguistic Science, University of York), 13: 9–24.

—— (1960) (ed.), *Jamaican Creole: Creole Language Studies I* (London).

—— and Tabouret-Keller, Andrée (1985), *Acts of Identity* (Cambridge).

Lepsius, R. (1855), *Standard Alphabet for Reducing Unwritten Languages and Foreign Graphic Systems to Uniform Orthography in European Letters* (London).

Lê Thành Khôi (1976), 'Literacy Training and Revolution: The Vietnamese Experience', in Leon Bataille (ed.), *A Turning Point for Literacy* (Oxford), 125–6.

Lewis, E. G. (1981), *Bilingualism and Bilingual Education* (Oxford).

Lieten, G. K. (1982), *The First Communist Ministry in Kerala, 1957–59* (Calcutta).

—— (1992), 'Literacy in a Post-Land Reform Village', *Economic and Political Weekly* (Bombay), 27: 3.

Ligo, G. (1987), 'Lanwis blong Nyus', in T. Crowley (ed.) *Introdaksen lon Stadi blong Bislama: Buk blong Ridim* (Suva, University of the South Pacific), 81–4.

Li Haibo (1989), 'Illiteracy Threatens Modernization', *Beijing Review* (16–22 Jan.), 4–5.

Limage, L. J. (1987), 'Adult Literacy Policy in Industrialised Countries', in Arnove and Graff (1987), 293–315.

Lind, A., and Johnston, A. (1990), *Adult Literacy in the Third World: A Review of Objectives and Strategies* (Stockholm).

Livesey, Paul (1986), 'Language Reform in China', in *Abstracts* (1986), 59–61.

Llamzon, Teodor A. (1977), 'Emerging Patterns in the English Language Situation in Singapore Today', in William Crewe (ed.), *The English language in Singapore* (Singapore), 34–45.

Long, Edward (1774), *History of Jamaica* (3 vols., London).

Lord, R., and Cheng, H. N. L. (1987) (eds.), *Language Education in Hong Kong* (Hong Kong).

Lowenberg, P. H. (1984), 'Literacy in Indonesia', in Kaplan (1984), 124–40.

Lüdi, G. (1988), 'Polyglossia and Literacy', in *Abstracts* (1988), 101–6.

Luke, K. K. (1992) (ed.), *Into the Twenty First Century: Issues of Language in Education in Hong Kong* (Linguistic Society of Hong Kong).

McCarvell, P. (1991), 'Understanding Language Shift', in S. Romaine (ed.), *Language in Australia* (Cambridge), 142–55.

Mahadevan, I. (1971), *The Indus Script: Texts, Concordance and Tables* (New Delhi).

Mahapatra, B. P. (1990), 'A Demographic Appraisal of Multilingualism in India', in D. P. Pattanayak (ed.), *Multilingualism in India* (Clevedon), 1–14.

Mallon, S. T. (1985), 'Six Years Later: The ICI Dual Orthography for Inuktitut, 1976–1982', in Burnaby (1985), 137–57.

Manessy, G. (1991), *Norme endogène et normes pédagogiques en Afrique noire francophone*, (Rapport scientifique, Centre d'Étude des Plurilinguismes, Institut d'Études et de Recherches Interethniques et Interculturelles, Nice).

Mann, Michael. (1969), 'Tone-Marking an African Language, with Application to Bemba', in David Dalby (ed.) *African Language Review* (London), 8: 98–107.

—— Dalby, David, *et al.* (1987), *A Thesaurus of African Languages* (London).

Martin-Jones, M., and Romaine, S. (1985), 'Semilingualism: A Half-baked Theory of Communicative Competence', *Applied Linguistics*, 6/2: 105–17.

Meier, Paul, Meier, Inge, and Bendor-Samuel, John (1975), *A Grammar of Izi* (Norman, Okla.).

Mendikoetxea, A. (1987), 'Discuss and Exemplify the Possible Relationship between Language and Ethnicity' (MA Set Essay, University of York).

Meyer, Bernard F., and Wempe, Theodore F. (1947), *The Student's Cantonese–English Dictionary* (New York).

Mezei, R. (1989), 'Somali Language and Literacy', in H. Tonkin (ed.), *Language Problems and Language Planning* (Austin, Tex.), 13/3: 211–23.

Mihalic, F. (1957), *Grammar and Dictionary of Neo-Melanesian* (Westmead, New South Wales).

Mishra, Lakshmidar (1990), 'Literacy-Now or Never', *Yojana*, 1–15 Nov.

Mitter, W., and Schäfer U. (1994), *Erwachsenen Analphabetismus und wirtschaftliche Leistungsfähigkeit. Ein OECD/CERI Bericht* (Frankfurt/Main).

Mitton, R. (1976), *Understanding Print* (Maseru, Lesotho).

Miyazaki, Ichisada (1976), *China's Examination Hell: The Civil Service Examinations of Imperial China*, trans. from the Japanese by Conrad Schirokauer (New York).

Mkanganwi, K. G. (1990), 'Orthographic Problems and Decisions: The Zimbabwean Experience', in *Abstracts* (1990), 71–4.

Molisa, Sela G. (1979), *Black Stones* (Port-Vila).

Moore, G. A. (1976), 'Alternative Attempts at Instruction in Atchalan', in J. I. Roberts and S. K. Akinsanya (eds.), *Schooling in the Cultural Context* (New York), 65–84.

Moorhouse, A. C. (1946), *Writing and the Alphabet* (London).

Morris, Jan. (1993), *A Machynlleth Triad* (Gwasg Gregynog); extract in *Independent* magazine, 1 Aug. 1992, pp. 30–5.

Moser, Leo J. (1985), *The Chinese Mosaic: The Peoples and Provinces of China* (Boulder, Colo.).

Mourant, A. E. (1947), 'The Blood Groups of the Basques', *Nature* (London), 160: 505.

Mpogolo, Z. J. (1985), *Methods of Functional Literacy* (Dar es Salaam).

Mühlhäusler, Peter (1986a), 'The Standardization of Tok Pisin', in *Abstracts* (1986), 105–7.

—— (1986b). *Pidgin and Creole Linguistics* (Oxford).

—— (1988), 'The Written Communication of P. Mühlhäusler', *Abstracts* (1988), 53–4.

—— (1990), ' "Reducing" Pacific Languages to Writing', in T. J. Taylor (ed.), *Ideologies of Language* (London), 189–205.

—— (1992), 'Non-Published Working Paper Circulated at the Sèvres Workshop, 1992', 12pp.

—— and Charpentier, J.-M. (1993), 'Literacy for Small Languages with Special Reference to Melanesian and its Pidgin Languages' (mimeo).

Muñoz, M.-C. (1991), 'La Langue "précieuse mais précaire" ', in Kees De Bot and Willem Fase (eds.), *Migrant Languages in Western Europe. International Journal of the Sociology of Language* (Berlin), 90: 57–76.

Mwansoko, Hermas (1990), 'The Modernization of Swahili Technical Terminologies; An Investigation of the Linguistics and Literature Terminologies' (D.Phil. diss, University of York).

Myers, D. (1992) (ed.), *The Great Literacy Debate* (Melbourne).

National Language Project (1991), Conference Report (University of Cape Town).

—— (1992), Conference Report. International Conference of Democratic Approaches to Language Planning and Standardization, 12–14 September 1991 (Salt River, RSA).

NCNA (1951): New China News Agency, 'Minister of Education Reports on Educational

352 *References*

Accomplishments during the Past Year', (21 July, Beijing). Translation in Hu and Seifman (1976), 23–9.
Ndukwe, Pat (1984), 'Planning for Standard Varieties in two Nigerian Languages' (D.Phil. diss., University of York).
—— (1990), 'Vernacular Literacy in Nigeria: An Evaluation', in *Abstracts* (1990), 129–33.
Newnham, Richard (1971), *About Chinese* (Harmondsworth).
Ng Chye Len (1986), *Newspaper: A Case Study in Language Policy and Mass Media in Singapore* (Academic Exercise, National University of Singapore).
Ng Lun Ngai-ha (1984), *Interactions of East and West: Development of Public Education in Early Hong Kong* (Hong Kong).
Nida, Eugene A. (1946), *Morphology: The Descriptive Analysis of Words* (Ann Arbor).
Norman, Jerry (1988), *Chinese* (Cambridge).
Nyerere, J. K. (1969/70), 'Education never ends', Tanzanian radio broadcast for Adult Education Year; printed by National Association of Adult Education Teachers (Dar es Salaam, 1975).
Odumuh, Adama E. (1986), 'Standardization of Nigerian English', in *Abstracts* (1986), 79–85.
—— (1992), 'Literacy by the Year 2000: An Evaluation of Literacy Campaigns in Nigeria (1950–1990)' (mimeo).
Oke, D. O. (1972), 'Language Choice in the Yoruba-Edo Border Area', *ODU* (Ile-Ife, Nigeria), 7 (Apr.): 49–67.
Omar, Asmah Haji (1979), *Language Planning for Unity and Efficiency* (Kuala Lumpur).
—— (1982), *Language and Society in Malaysia* (Kuala Lumpur).
—— (1983), *The Malay Peoples of Malaysia and their Languages* (Kuala Lumpur).
Ornstein-Galicia, J. (1988), 'Approaches to Contact Study: Implications for Euskera', in *Congreso* (1988), ii. 435–55.
Oxfam (1993), *Africa: Make or Break.* (Oxford).
Parker, E. M., and Hayward, R. J. (1985), *An Afar–English–French Dictionary* (London).
Patel, P. G. (1991), 'Literacy in Ancient India' (project proposal) (mimeo).
Pattanayak, D. P. (1990) (ed.), *Multilingualism in India* (Clevedon).
Pavier, B. (1986), *The Telengana Movement, 1944–51* (New Delhi).
The Peterborough Chronicle, ed. from Bodleian MS Laud Misc. 636, in B. Thorpe (ed.), (1861), *The Anglo-Saxon Chronicle* (2 vols.; London).
Petrick, D. (1986), 'Distance Learning Materials in Adult Literacy Programmes', in Pugh and Volkmar (1986), 132–5.
Pike, Kenneth L. (1947), *Phonemics: A Technique for Reducing Languages to Writing* (Ann Arbor).
Platiel, S. (1988), 'Les Langues d'Afrique Noire en France: Des langues de culture face à une langue de communication', in Vermès (1988), ii. 9–30.
Plissoneau, J. (1926), *Catéchisme* (Metz).
Poplack, S. (1980), 'Sometimes I'll start a sentence in English *y termino en espanol*: Toward a typology of code-switching', in W. Klein (ed.) *Linguistics* (Berlin), 18: 581–618.
Populi (1992 *et seq.*), magazine of the United Nations Population fund, monthly from vol. 1, no. 1 (June 1992) (New York).
—— (1994), report on the *International Conference on Population and Development, Cairo*, 21/9 (October), 4–13.
Postiglione, Gerard A. (1992), 'The Implications of Modernization for the Education of China's National Minorities', in Hayhoe (1992), 307–36.

Price, R. F. (1970), *Education in Communist China* (London).

Prunet, J. (1992) (ed.), *L'education interculturelle des enfants de migrants*. Rapport national à la Commission des Communantés Européennes, établi sous la direction de J. Prunet, Inspecteur d'académie (Paris).

Pugh, A. K., and Volkmar, C. (1986) (eds.), *Aspects of Adult Literacy* (Munich).

Purcell, Victor (1936), *Problems of Chinese Education* (London).

Pyle, A. (1995), 'Classes à part pour les Hispaniques et les Asiatiques', *Courrier International*, 255: pp. xxi–xxii (from *Los Angeles Times*).

Ramiah, K. (1991), 'The Pattern of Tamil Language Use among Primary School Pupils in Singapore', in S. Gopinathan (ed.), *Singapore Journal of Education* (Singapore), 2/2: 45–53.

Ramsey, S. Robert (1987), *The Languages of China* (Princeton).

Rauch, S. (1969) (ed.), *Handbooks for the Volunteer Tutor* (Newark, Del.).

Reber, Arthur S., and Scarborough, Don L. (1977) (eds.), *Toward a Psychology of Reading* (Hillsdale, NJ).

Redcam, Tom (1903), *Becka's Buckra Baby* (Kingston, Jamaica).

Redfern, A., and Edwards, V. (1992), *How Schools Teach Reading* (Reading and Language Information Centre, University of Reading).

Reid, E., and Reich, H. H. (1992), *Breaking the Boundaries: Migrant Workers' Children in the EEC* (Clevedon).

Reid, V. S. (1950), *New Day* (London).

Reinecke, J. E., and Tsuzaki, S. M., *et al.* (1975) (eds.), *A Bibliography of Pidgin and Creole Languages* (Honolulu).

Report of the All-Party Committee, see Singapore Legislative Assembly (1956).

Resnick, Daniel P. (1983) (ed.), *Literacy in Historical Perspective* (Washington).

Rhodes, Alexandre de (1651), *Dictionarium annamiticium, lusitanum et latinum* (Rome).

Rigsby, B. (1987), 'Indigenous Language Shift and Maintenance in Fourth World Settings', in R. J. Watts (ed.), *Multilingua* (Berlin), 6/4: 359–78.

Robinson, W. P. (n.d.) (ed.), *The Complete Works of Geoffrey Chaucer* (Oxford).

Romaine, S. (1976), 'The Syntax and Semantics of the Code-Mixed Compound Verb in Panjabi–English Bilingual Discourse', in D. Tannen and J. Alatis (eds.), *Language and Linguistics: The Interdependence of Theory, Data and Application* (Washington: Georgetown University Press), 35–49.

—— (1984), *The Language of Children and Adolescents* (Oxford).

—— (1988), *Pidgin and Creole Languages* (London).

—— (1992), *Language, Education and Development: Urban and Rural Tok Pisin in Papua New Guinea* (Oxford).

—— (1993), 'Standardization, Literacy and the Origins of Linguistic Inequality in Papua New Guinea' (mimeo).

Rotimi, Ole (1977), *Nigerian Pidgin English Dictionary* (Ile-Ife).

Russell, Joan (1981), *Communicative Competence in a Minority Group: A Sociolinguistic Study of a Swahili-Speaking Community in Mombasa* (Leiden).

—— (1986), 'Standardization of Swahili', in *Abstracts* (1986), 74–8.

—— (1990), 'The Concept of "Development" and the Vernacularization of Literacy', in *Abstracts* (1990), 111–15.

Saladin, J., Boyzon-Fradet, D., Monserie, M.-C., and Seksig, A. (1993), *Scolarisation des enfants et adolescents nouvellement arrivés en France. Recueil de Textes Officiels* (2 vols.; Paris).

354 *References*

Samarin, W. J. (1963), *A Grammar of Sango* (Hartford, Conn.).
—— (1986), 'Sango of the Centralafrican Republic', in *Abstracts* (1986), 67–73.
—— (1988), 'Literacy in the Centralafrican Republic', in *Abstracts* (1988), 57–61.
—— (1992), 'The Orthography of Sango', unpub. paper, 3 Nov.
Sampson, Geoffrey (1985), *Writing Systems* (London).
Sankoff, G. (1980), *The Social Life of a Language* (Baltimore).
Savard, J. G., and Vigneault, R. (1975), *Les États multilingues: Problèmes et solutions* (Quebec).
Saxena, M. (1993), 'Literacies among the Panjabis in Southall', in M. Hamilton, D. Barton, and R. Ivanic (eds.) *Worlds of Literacy* (Clevedon), 195–214.
Saxena, S. (1990), 'A Note on Documentary Evidence Regarding the Place of Literacy and Adult Education in Telengana and Jharkhand movements' (mimeo for private circulation).
—— (1992), '"Total Literacy in Narsinghpur", a Report on a Brief Visit', *Economic and Political Weekly* (Bombay), 27/45 (7 Nov.), 2406–8 (the quotations here are from the typescript, p.c.).
Schneider, Gilbert D. (1960), 'Cameroon Creole Dictionary' first draft (Bamenda) (mimeo).
—— (1966), *West-African Pidgin-English, a Descriptive Linguistic Analysis with Texts and Glossary for the Cameroon Area* (Athens, Oh.).
—— et al. (1974), *Masa Troki Tok Sey: A Compilation of West-African Pidgin-English Materials for Student Use Only* (Athens, Oh.) (mimeo).
Schools Language Survey Manual of Use (1985), *Community Languages and Education Project* (University of London: Institute of Education).
Schuchardt, H. (1882), *Kreolische Studien I* (Vienna).
Scott, M. (1829/1833), *Tom Cringle's Log* (Edinburgh).
Sebba, M. (1994), *London Jamaican* (Harlow, Essex).
Sebeok, Th. A. (1971) (ed.), *Linguistics in Sub-Saharan Africa* (Current Trends in Linguistics, 7; The Hague).
Sey, K. A. (1973), *Ghanaian English: An Exploratory Survey* (London).
Seybolt, Peter J., and Kuei-ke Chiang, Gregory (1978) (eds.), *Language Reform in China* (White Plains, NY).
Shannon, P. (1989), *Broken Promises: Reading Instruction in Twentieth Century America* (Cranby, Mass.).
Shepherd, Alan I. (1980),'The Origins and Development of Literacy in English in Old Calabar to c.1860' (M.Litt diss, University of Aberdeen).
SIL (1990): Summer Institute of Linguistics, *Annual Report for 1990* (Dallas, Tex.).
Simpson, J. M. Y. (1994), 'Writing Systems: Principles and Typology', in Asher (1994), 5052–61.
Singapore Legislative Assembly (1956), *Report of the All-Party Committee on Chinese Education, 1956* (Singapore).
Singler, John Victor (1990), 'The Impact of Decreolization upon T-M-A: Tenselessness, Mood and Aspect in Kru Pidgin English', in J. V. Singler (ed.), *Pidgin and Creole Tense–Mood–Aspect Systems* (Amsterdam), 203–30.
Skutnabb-Kangas, T. (1984), 'Children of Guest Workers and Immigrants: Linguistic and Educational Issues', in J. Edwards (ed.), *Linguistic Minorities, Policies and Pluralism* (London), 17–48.

—— (1988), 'Multilingualism and the Education of Minority Children', in T. Skutnabb-Kangas and J. Cummins (eds.), *Minority Education: From Shame to Struggle* (Clevedon), 9–45.

—— and Toukomaa, P. (1976), 'Teaching Migrant Children their Mother Tongue and Learning the Language of the Host Country in the Context of the Socio-Cultural Situation of the Migrant Family', *Tutkimuksia Research Report* (Tampere, Finland).

Smalley, William A. (1964), 'Writing systems and their characteristics', in Smalley *et al.* (1964), 1–17.

—— *et al.* (1964) (eds.), *Orthography Studies: Articles on New Writing Systems* (London).

Smolicz, J. J. (1985), 'Greek-Australians: A Question of Survival in Multicultural Australia', *Journal of Multilingual and Multicultural Development* (Clevedon), 6/1: 17–29.

Smollett, Tobias (1748), *The Adventures of Roderick Random* (London).

Sneddon, R. (1993*a*), 'The Education of Children from New Minority Communities in EC Countries', (MA diss. Birkbeck College, University of London).

—— (1993*b*), 'Children Developing Biliteracy at Home and at School' (MA project, Birkbeck College, University of London).

Solntsev, V. M., and Mikhalshenko, V. Yu. (1992), 'National Language Relations in Present-Day Russia', in Solntsev *et al.* (1992), 135–52.

—— —— Bakhyan, K. V., Isayev, M. I., and Kryuchkova, T. B. (1992), *The Language Situation in the Russian Federation: 1992* (Académie russe des sciences, Institut de linguistique, Moscow).

South Africa (1962): South Africa, Department of Education, *Venda. Terminology and spelling*, no. 2 (Pretoria).

Soyinka, W. (1964), *The Trials of Brother Jero* (London).

Spence, Jonathan D. (1990), *The Search for Modern China* (London).

Spiik, Nils Eric (1989), *Lulesamisk grammatik* (Umeå, Sweden).

Srivastava, A. K. (1990), 'Multilingualism and School Education in India: Special Features, Problems and Prospects', in D. P. Pattanayak (ed.), *Multilingualism in India* (Clevedon) 37–53.

Srivastava, R. N. (1984), 'Literacy in South Asia', in Kaplan (1984), 93–110.

—— and Gupta, R. S. (1990), 'Literacy in a Multilingual Context', in Pattanayak (1990), 67–78.

Street, Brian V. (1984), *Literacy in Theory and Practice* (Cambridge).

—— (1993) (ed.), *Cross Cultural Approaches to Literacy* (New York).

—— (1994), 'What is Meant by Local Literacy?', in Barton (1994), 9–18.

Stubbs, M. (1985) (ed.), *The Other Languages of England: The Linguistic Minorities* (London).

Sundarayya, P. (1972), *Telengana People's Struggle and its lessons* (Calcutta).

Sun Shuyun (1992), 'Real Life: Teach Women and Everyone will Learn', *Independent on Sunday* (London), magazine (7 June), 22.

Swann, Michael Meredith (1985), *Education for All* (The Swann Report), report by the Department of Education and Science Committee of Inquiry into the Education of Children from the Ethnic Minority Groups (London).

Sweeting, Anthony (1990), *Education in Hong Kong Pre-1841 to 1941: Fact and Opinion* (Hong Kong).

Swift, Lloyd B. (1961), *A Reference Grammar of Modern Turkish* (Bloomington, Ind.).

Taber, Charles R. (1965), *A Dictionary of Sango* (Hartford, Conn.).

Tabouret-Keller, Andrée (1968), 'Sociological Factors of Language Maintenance and Language Shift', in Fishman *et al.* (1968), 107–18.

—— (1988a), 'French Literacy: Some Aspects in Korhogo', in *Abstracts* (1988), 106–11.

Tabouret-Keller, Andrée (1988b), 'Les Effets nocifs du bilinguisme, cent ans d'errance', in Congreso (1988), iii. 157–69.

—— (1990a), 'Le Bilinguisme: Pourquoi la mauvaise réputation?', in *Un bilinguisme particulier: Migrants-Formation*, 83 (Dec.): 18–23.

—— (1990b), 'Are vernaculars a Hopeless Cause?', in *Abstracts* (1990), 117–22.

—— and Le Page, R. B. (1986), 'The Mother-Tongue Metaphor', in Denison *et al.* (1986), 249–59.

Tadadjeu, M. (1975), 'Language Planning in Cameroon: Toward a Trilingual Educational System', in R. K. Herbert (ed.), *Patterns in Language, Culture, and Society: Sub-Saharan Africa* (Columbus, Oh.), 53–75.

—— (1977a), 'Cost-Benefit Analysis and Language Education in Sub-Saharan Africa', in P. Kotey and H. D. Houssikian (eds.), *Language and Linguistic Problems in Africa* (Columbus, Oh.), 3–35.

—— (1977b), 'A Model for Functional Trilingual Education Planning in Africa' (Ph.D. thesis, University of Southern California).

—— (1990), *Le Défi de Babel au Cameroun* (Collection PROPELCA, 53; Université de Yaoundé).

—— and Gfeller, E., Mba, G. (1986), 'Introducing an Official Language into an Initial Mother Tongue Education Program: The Case of Cameroon', in *Annales de la Faculté des Lettres et Sciences Humaines. Série Sciences Humaines*, 2/2 (July).

Tansley, P. (1986), *Community Languages in Primary Education* (National Foundation for Education Research, Windsor).

Tay, Mary W. J. (1984), 'Constructing a Sociolinguistic Profile of the Multilingual Individual', in P. H. Nelde (ed.), *Theory, Methods and Models of Contact Linguistics* (Bonn), 175–89.

Thomas, Ned. (1971), *The Welsh Extremist: A Culture in Crisis* (London).

Todd, Loreto (1974a), *West African Pidgin Folktales* (London).

—— (1974b), *Pidgins and Creoles* (London).

—— (1984a), *Modern Englishes: Pidgins and Creoles* (Oxford).

—— (1984b), '"E Pluribus Unum?" The Language for a National Literature in a Multilingual Society', in *ARIEL* (Calgary, Alberta), 15/4: 69–82.

—— (1990), *Pidgins and Creoles* (2nd edn., London).

—— (1991), *Talk Pidgin: A Structured Course in West African Pidgin English* (Leeds).

—— (1995), 'Tracking the Homing Pidgin: A Millennium Report', in Tom McArthur (ed.) *English Today* (Cambridge), 11/1: 33–41.

Tonkin, Elizabeth (1990), 'Liberia and its Literacies: A Historical Perspective', in *Abstracts* (1990), 15–18.

Tosi, A. (1984), *Immigration and Bilingual Education* (Oxford).

Trevelyan, C. E., *et al.* (1854), *Papers Originally Published at Calcutta in 1834 and 1836 on the Application of the Roman Letters to the Languages of Asia* (London).

Troike, R. C. (1984), 'SCALP: Social and Cultural Aspects of Language Proficiency', in C. Rivera (ed.), *Language Proficiency and Academic Achievement* (Clevedon), 44–54.

Tryon, D. T. (n.d.), *Evri samting yu wantem save long Bislama be yu Fraet tumas blong askem: A traveller's guide to Vanuatu Pidgin English* (Media Masters; place of publication unknown).

Tse, Kwock-ping J. (1986), 'Standardization of Chinese in Taiwan', in Jernudd (1986), 25–32.

Tucker, A. N. (1964), 'Systems of Tone-Marking African Languages', *Bulletin of the School of Oriental and African Studies* (London), 27: 594–611.

—— (1971), 'Orthographic Systems and Conventions in Sub-Saharan Africa', in Sebeok (1971), vii. 618–53.

Turcotte, D. (1981), *La Politique linguistique en Afrique francophone: Une étude comparative de la Côte d'Ivoire et de Madagascar* (Quebec).

Unesco (1953): United Nations Educational, Scientific, and Cultural Organization, *The Use of Vernacular Languages in Education* (Monograph on Fundamental Education VIII; Paris).

—— (1972), *Literacy, 1969–71: Progress Achieved in Literacy throughout the World* (Paris).

—— (1975), *Final Report for International Symposium for Literacy, Persepolis* (Paris).

—— (1976), *The Experimental World Literacy Programme* (Paris).

—— (1981), *Literacy Curriculum and Materials Development* (Bangkok).

—— (1983), *Introduction to Intercultural Studies: Outline of a Project for Elucidating and Promoting Communication between Cultures (1976–1980)* (Paris).

—— (1985), *Fourth International Conference on Adult Education: Draft Final Report* (Paris).

—— (1990), *World Conference on Education for all, Jomtien, Thailand, and World Summit for Children* (Paris).

Unesco Institute for Education (1987), 'Internal Report of the Proceedings of the Orientation Seminar on Post-Literacy and Continuing Education' (Hamburg: International Institute for Education) (mimeo).

Unfpa (1990 *et seq.*), *United Nation Population Fund: Annual Reports* (New York).

Unfpa, see also *Populi*.

UNICEF/WHO/Unesco/UNFPA (1993): United Nations Children's Fund/World Health Organization/United Nations Educational, Scientific, and Cultural Organization/United Nations Population Fund, *Facts for Life: A Communication Challenge* (rev. edn.; P & LA, Oxfordshire OX10 6NU, UK).

Unsicker, J. (1987), 'Tanzania's Literacy Campaign in Historical-Structural Perspective', in Arnove and Graff (1987), 219–44.

Urla, J. (1987a), *Being Basque, Speaking Basque: The Politics of Language and Identity in the Basque Country* (Ann Arbor, Mich.).

—— (1987b), 'Language Planning: Inventing New Realities', in Congreso (1988), ii. 141–4.

Valdman, Albert (1978), *Le Créole: Structure, statut et origine* (Paris).

—— (1988), 'Introduction' in Vermès (1988), ii. 7–28.

—— (1977) (ed.), *Pidgin and Creole Linguistics* (Bloomington, Ind.).

—— et al. (1981), *Haitian Creole–English–French Dictionary* (Bloomington, Ind.).

Van Warmelo, N. J. (1989), *Venda dictionary. Tshivenda–English* (Pretoria).

Varro, Gabrielle (1990), 'Les Représentations autour du bilinguisme des primo-arrivants', *Un Bilinguisme particulier, Migrants-Formation*, 83 (Dec.): 24–39.

—— (1992), 'Les «Langues immigrées» face à l'école française', in H. Tonkin (ed.), *Language Problems and Language Planning* (Austin, Tex.), 16/2: 137–62.

—— (forthcoming), 'Des bilingues sacrifiés, ou: à quoi pourraient servir les langues d'origine?', in *Bulletin de l'Institut de Linguistique de Louvain*.

Verhoeven, L. (1987), *Ethnic Minority Children Acquiring Literacy* (Dordrecht).

Verma, Mahendra (1988), 'Diglossia, literacy and the minorities in India', in *Abstracts* (1988), 129–35.

Vermès, Geneviève (1988) (ed.), *Vingt-cinq communautés linguistiques de la France* (2 vols.; Paris).

—— and Bazin, C. (1991), 'L'Enseignement du portugais et de l'arabe dans le secteur associatif: Premiers résultats d'une recherche-action', *Migrants-Formation*, 83: 76–89.

—— and Boutet, J. (1987) (eds.), *France, pays multilingue* (2 vols.; Paris).

Vikör, L. S. (1993), *The Nordic Languages: Their Status and Interrelations* (Oslo).

Villanova, R. de. (1988), 'Identité et performance académique chez les étudiants bilingues', in M. Oriol (ed.), *Les Identités collectives en question. Revue des Sciences Sociales* (Jan.–Dec.), 203–20.

Vincent, David (1989), *Literacy and Popular Culture* (Cambridge).

Von Freyhold, M. (1979), *Ujamaa Villages in Tanzania: Analysis of a Social Experiment* (London).

Walcott, Derek (1950a), *Poems* (Kingston, Jamaica).

—— (1950b), *Henri Christophe* (a play) (Barbados).

—— (1958), *The Sea at Dauphin* (a play in one act) (University College of the West Indies, Jamaica).

—— (1970), *Dream on Monkey Mountain, and other plays* (New York).

—— (1980), *The Star-Apple Kingdom, Poems 1977, 1978, 1979* (London).

—— (1987), *Collected Poems 1948–1984* (London).

—— (1987), *The Arkansas Testament* (New York).

—— (1990), *Omeros* (New York, Toronto, and London).

—— (n.d.), *Harry Dernier* (a play for radio production) (Barbados).

Wall Street Journal (1989), 'Filipino by Turtle', 27 Oct.

Wee Hock Ann (1990), 'Language and Identity among First Year Chinese Undergraduates in Singapore' (MA thesis, Department of English Language and Literature, National University of Singapore).

Wen Hua (1973), 'On Reforming Written Chinese', *Peking Review* (10 Aug.), 11–13. Translation in Hu and Seifman (1976), 291–4.

Weinstein, B. (1987), 'Language Planning and Interests', in Lorne Laforge (ed.), *Proceedings of the International Colloquium on Language Planning, 25–9 May 1986* (Quebec).

Whiteley, W. H. (1974) (ed.), *Language in Kenya* (Oxford).

Williamson, K. (1976), 'The Rivers Readers Project in Nigeria', in Bamgbose (1976), 135–53.

—— (1985) (ed.), *West African Languages in Education, Beiträge zur Afrikanistik* (Vienna), 27.

Woodside, Alexander (1992), 'Real and Imagined Continuities in the Chinese Struggle for Literacy', in Hayhoe (1992), 23–46.

World Bank (1992), *World Development Report, 1992* (Washington).

Zuanelli Sonino, Elizabeth (1986), 'Standardization and Vernacularization of Italian', in *Abstracts* (1986), 29–31.

Full use has been made in this book of the publications of Unesco and the United Nations Population Fund (Unfpa), and we acknowledge in particular the help of Unfpa, its magazine *Populi*, and its special reports. These are available from the offices of United Nations agencies.

Index

Sahara 25
Sakwatanci (Sokoto Hausa) 269
Saladin, J., Boyzon-Fradet, D. Monserie,
  M. -C. and Seksig, A. 196 n., 213
Samarin, W. 23, 60, 126, 127
Sandinistas 28 (*see also* Nicaragua)
Sango 60, 126, 225, 256–61, 267, 269
Sanskrit 125
Santhal 111
Savard, J. G. 257
Saxena, S. 23, 49, 178
Saxena, M. 212
Scandinavia 207
SCE *see* Singapore
Schneider, G. D. 63
Schuchardt, H. 243
Scotland 24, 29, 31–3
Scottish Calvinists 31
scripts
  Devanagari 45
  harmonization 138–9
  language specific 139
  linear 122
  semi-syllabic 95, 96, 97, 109–10, 122–3,
    129
  syllabic 130
  see also logographs, logographic systems,
    orthographies
Sebba, M. 215
second generation immigrants 214–17
Senegal 57, 117, 138, 324
  see also Ziguinchor
Seoh, J. L. K. 271
Serbo-Croatian 11
Seybolt, P. and Kuei-ke Chiang, G. 111
Shail Jha 23
Shrimpton, N. 23
SIL, Summer Institute of Linguistics 16, 61,
    163, (1900) 263
Singapore 19, 293–304
  alternative education policies 302–4
  economic and cultural motivation 303–4
  ethnic composition 293–4
  home languages 294–5
  language examinations 301–2
  mother tongue in education 298; redefined
    297–8
  SCE, Singapore Colloquial English 229
  shift to English 294–5; to Mandarin
    294–5
  Tamil and Indian languages 293–6
  use of Malay 293–6
  varieties of English 298–9
Singler, J. V. 63
Singlish 299
Skutnabb-Kangas, T. 195, 207, 208, 209
Smalley, W. A. 123, 131

Smolicz, J. J. 211
Smollett, T. 32
Sneddon, R. 194, 203, 204
social contexts for vernacular literacy 82–92
sociolinguistic survey, Basque 41, variables
    40
Sokoto 265
Solntsev, V. M., Mikhalshenko, V. Y., 326
Summer Institute of Linguistics, *see* SIL
Solomon Islands 231
Somalia 117
South Africa (Republic of) 117, 169
Soyinka, W. 243, 244
Spain 24, 25, 26
Spanish 25, 37, 72, 73, 74, 78
Srivastava, R. N. 145
Srivastava, R. N. and Gupta, R. S. 148
standard varieties and standardization 165–6
    standards of evaluation 185
    varieties, Nigeria 265
status of a language, legal/official 88, 89
Street, B. V. 145, 152, 154–5, 167, 322, 326
structuralism 12
Sub-Saharan Africa 8, 28, 330
Sumerian 95
summary of the chapters in this book 16–19
Sun Shuyun 50
Sundarayya, P. 51
Swahili 69–71, 88, 107, 126, 318
Swann Report 205
Sweeting, A. 291
Swiss German 23
syllabaries 95, 97
  Japanese hiragana 95; kangi 95; katakana 95
  Loma 112–13
  Ol Chiki 111
symbolic status of linguistic legislation 88
SYYP, Six Year Yoruba Project 262–9

Taber, C. R. 60
Tabouret-Keller, A. 35, 58, 73, 78, 79, 142,
    156, 159, 207
Tadadjeu, M. 160, 162, 168, 180, 183, 260
Taiwan 111, 276
Tamil 54, 304
  script 129
Tanzania 29, 69–72, 88, 177–8, 247–56
Tasker, I. 142, 152
Tay, M. 297
teachers and teacher training 39, 68, 147,
    151–5
technology 83
  advances in 132–3, 140
television 25, 39, 77, 83, 173–5
Teo, S. C. 271
terminology 190–2
test, national (Tanzania) 248